WHO'S 50

THE 50 *DOCTOR WHO* STORIES TO WATCH BEFORE YOU DIE

AN UNOFFICIAL COMPANION

· ·

GRAEME BURK & ROBERT SMITH?

ECW PRESS

Published by ECW Press
2120 Queen Street East, Suite 200,
Toronto, Ontario, Canada M4E 1E2
416-694-3348 | info@ecwpress.com

Printing: Webcom 5 4 3 2 1
PRINTED AND BOUND IN CANADA

LIBRARY AND ARCHIVES CANADA CATALOGUING IN PUBLICATION

Burk, Graeme, 1969–, author
Who's 50 : the 50 Doctor Who stories
to watch before you die : an unofficial
companion / Graeme Burk, Robert Smith?

ISBN 978-1-77041-166-1 (pbk.)
Also issued as: 978-1-77090-474-3 (PDF);
978-1-77090-475-0 (ePub)

1. Doctor Who (Television program).
I. Smith?, Robert J.
(Robert Joseph), 1972–, author II. Title.
III. Title: 50 Doctor
Who stories to watch before you die.
IV. Title: Fifty Doctor
Who stories to watch before you die.

PN1992.77.D63B868 2013
791.45'72   C2013-902479-4

Editor for the press: Jennifer Hale
Cover design and Doctor illustrations:
Carolyn McNeillie
Text design: Tania Craan
Typesetting: Kendra Martin
Author photo: Cadence Gillard

We acknowledge the financial support of the Government of Canada through the Canada Book
Fund for our publishing activities, and the contribution of the Government of Ontario through
the Ontario Book Publishing Tax Credit and the Ontario Media Development Corporation.

Ontario
Ontario Media Development
Corporation

Canada

· ·

For Dennis and Christine Turner. The best of nerds.
And the best of friends.
— GB

For Jaymie Maley. Not a nerd, but the best of friends nonetheless.
— RS?

Contents

....

Introduction

"So what Classic Series Doctor Who *should I watch if I've never seen it before?"*

"What stories would you recommend to people who have never seen Doctor Who?*"*

"What Doctor Who *stories would you suggest I get on DVD?"*

These three questions dominated the discussions during launch events, convention panels and in general conversation around the release of our last book, *Who Is The Doctor: The Unofficial Guide to Doctor Who — The New Series.*

There's good reason for that. With the 50th anniversary of *Doctor Who* in November 2013, there is interest from *Doctor Who* fans and a broader group of TV fans in the entirety of the series, not just the very popular post-2005 version.

And why not? *Doctor Who*'s versatile format encompasses horror, science fiction, comedy, action and historical adventure, and the series is loved by millions worldwide for its British wit and clever scripting. With 50 years' worth of stories, some of them penned by legendary writers such as Douglas Adams and Neil Gaiman, *Doctor Who* has a rich heritage worth celebrating.

This book is designed to give an enthusiastic guided tour through the wonderful, incredible, bizarre and radical television experience that is *Doctor Who*. It's a tour we're really excited to give you. As we said in our last book, we're here because *Doctor Who* is the greatest show on television.

We still mean this, by the way. We're still not exaggerating.

Who We Are

This book is a co-authored affair, written by two people with very different experiences. We thought we'd give you a quick introduction to each author.

Graeme Burk (GB)

- **What do you do?** I'm a freelance writer and a communications professional. I have a screenplay in development. I love *Doctor Who*.
- **When did you first watch *Doctor Who*?** I remember seeing episode two of "The Three Doctors" when it first aired in Canada in 1976. I was six. I thought it was strange and the title sequence was super-spooky. But I didn't become a fan until I saw episode two of "Pyramids of Mars" in 1984 on PBS. A month later, I was trying to watch every episode; three months later, I knew the title, writer and director of every episode. And that was the beginning of the rest of my life . . .
- **Who is your favourite Doctor?** Tom Baker. On the days Baker's busy, David Tennant. When Tennant's away, Peter Davison. Really, all of them.
- **What object of the Doctor's would you most like to have?** The TARDIS, not just because I could travel anywhere in time and space, but because the police box is awfully cool-looking.
- **Tell us something about your co-author.** It's more than a question mark at the end of his name. It's a manifesto.
- **Describe *Doctor Who* in five words.** Fun. Imaginative. Bold. Adventurous. Secular.

Robert Smith? (RS?)

- **What do you do?** I'm a professor of disease modelling at the University of Ottawa. I'm also the world's leading academic expert on the spread of Bieber Fever. Okay, so I'm the *only* academic expert on the spread of Bieber Fever. I also inadvertently created the academic subdiscipline that is mathematical modelling of zombies. One day, I really should get around to modelling a Dalek invasion . . .
- **When did you first watch *Doctor Who*?** I was five years old and I got hooked by the final episode of "The Green Death." I never looked back.
- **Who is your favourite Doctor?** To paraphrase Boromir from *Lord of the Rings*: "One does not simply *have* a favourite Doctor." It's like picking a favourite sibling. Really, don't make me choose!
- **What object of the Doctor's would you most like to have?** His sonic screwdriver. Nothing impresses the ladies like being able to repair

pretty much anything. No wonder they leap into a tiny cupboard with him at the first opportunity.

- **Tell us something about your co-author.** He once described himself as the John Lennon to my Paul McCartney. At the time, I thought this was a metaphor. I was wrong.
- **Describe _Doctor Who_ in five words.** Woo. Eee. Woo. Diddly Dum.

About the Book

In this book, we've picked 50 stories from the 50-year history of _Doctor Who_ that we feel you should watch before you die. All of these stories are readily available on DVD.

Note we said these are stories _you should watch_. These aren't necessarily the best _Doctor Who_ stories of all time, though many we've selected are just that. But other choices are much more idiosyncratic: they're stories you should watch because they have some curiosity value, or they show something unique about _Doctor Who_. There are some stories in here that one or the other of us disagrees about their very inclusion. But we think you should watch them, nonetheless.

Why did we take this approach? Because we think the best kind of tour is not one where you're shown only the best and most beautiful things, but one where you wander into odd places and see things that are eclectic and strange and beautiful in their own right. In its 50 years of televised adventures in time and space, _Doctor Who_ has always been an unconventional show; we thought we'd do a book that reflected on its history and was just as eccentric as its titular character.

While presenting these 50 stories, we also give you a sense of the history of _Doctor Who_ behind the scenes and the history of British television. _Doctor Who_'s enduring popularity is the result of a lot of talented people, and their stories are often as interesting and intriguing as what's shown on television.

Like _Who Is The Doctor_, this book is designed both for the newbie who has never seen a pre-2005 story (or indeed any _Doctor Who_) and for the long-time fan. We hope this book will give the newbie the interest to Netflix a story from an era long ago, and we hope it will give the long-time fan insight into a story they haven't thought about for decades.

The Guide

We picked 50 stories (of the nearly 250 that have aired from 1963 to 2013). Like *Who Is The Doctor*, each of these has a guide entry, which includes the following categories:

The Big Idea A short plot synopsis.

Roots and References These are the sources that either influenced a story or are directly cited in a particular episode, whether literary, film, TV, music or pop-culture references. We track them here.

Time And Relative Dimensions In Space We set the stage, explaining the context for how this particular story came to be made.

Adventures in Time and Space Connections to past episodes of *Doctor Who*.

Who is the Doctor? New information about the Doctor, including insight into his character.

Companion Chronicles Information about the different companions who appear in these stories.

Monster of the Week Time to wave a tentacle out to the crowd.

Stand Up and Cheer The great moment in this story . . .

Roll Your Eyes . . . and the one that made you cringe.

You're Not Making Any Sense The most gaping plot hole.

Interesting Trivia Intriguing facts about the story, the *Doctor Who* universe and what was going on behind the scenes.

The TARDIS Chronometer Where and when the story takes place.

Hmm?/Oh My Giddy Aunt?/Hai?/What?/Brave Heart?/Unstable? Unstable?! UNSTABLE?!?/Wicked?/Yes Yes Yes?/Fantastic?/Brilliant?/Cool? The bottom-line critique by one of the authors.

Second Opinion The co-author also gets his say. Sometimes the two authors agree. Sometimes we don't. Sometimes we *really* don't. And then the fun begins . . .

The Psychic Papers

Also included in the book are chronicles of the history of various elements of the series' mythos and production. These entries give complete histories, and therefore contain spoilers of the Classic Series and New Series in some instances.

Tips for Newbies

It can be daunting watching television from 20, 30, 40 and even 50 years ago. In this section, we give you some hints and tips to aid your viewing experience.

The Unbelievably Geeky Part

If you're not a hardcore fan, you can skip to the end of this introduction. If you are, stick around, as we need to talk about the stuff we know you're dying to argue over.

First of all, our criteria and methodology for selection: each of the authors picked 50 stories. The stories that were chosen by both of us immediately made the list of 50. From the remainder, each author decided on an equal number of must-have stories to include. It's no more scientific than that.

We only chose complete stories that were available on DVD. So we don't include any of the stories that are missing from the BBC Archives and only available on audio.

We use the episode titles on the DVD releases, so "An Unearthly Child," not "100,000 BC." For a similar reason, we consider the New Series that began in 2005 to be effectively a new TV series, albeit one linked by continuity and heritage with the original, or what we call the Classic Series of *Doctor Who*. As a result, we talk about Series One of the New Series, not Season 27.

Lastly . . .

Still with us? Brilliant!

Like we said in our introduction to *Who Is The Doctor*, if there's one thing we want this book to be, it's fun. At the end of the day, *Doctor Who* should always be that. And if there's anything that *Doctor Who* has tried to be since 1963, it's fun.

We think delving back through 50 years of *Doctor Who* should be nothing to be scared of. Quite the contrary: we think it will be the most exciting, thrill-capped, funny, scary, bizarre, suspenseful, dramatic and romantic experience you'll go on.

Quite simply, it's the trip of a lifetime.

Are you ready then?

Geronimo!

The Genesis of *Doctor Who*

"The past is a foreign country, they do things differently there," said the British author L.P. Hartley. (If this sounds familiar, it was misquoted by the ninth Doctor in "Father's Day.") If that's true, the early 1960s is another planet. Especially the world of British television.

The British Broadcasting Corporation began its television service in 1934 as an experimental service watched by a handful of people who could afford a novelty like a television set. After World War II, the BBC's television service grew in earnest, particularly after the televised coronation of Queen Elizabeth II in 1953 prompted a sharp increase in the purchase of TV sets.

By the mid-to-late 1950s, television in Britain had become much more sophisticated. Although often still tiny, studios were more plentiful. The technology was rapidly changing. The advent of videotape meant that live broadcast was no longer necessary, allowing for greater flexibility. The standard picture size was 405 lines (significantly worse than the 625 lines that would replace it, much less the HD format that eventually followed), but there was more and more content being broadcast. In 1955, the British government allowed for a second, independent, private broadcast network: a federation of small television companies that would be collectively known as ITV. Moreover, the BBC went from an experimental service to a major broadcaster watched by 10 million viewers. It had a full schedule from midday (with occasional close-downs) to 11 p.m. seven days a week.

In 1963, however, the problem was Saturday.

Doctor Who owes its very existence to a problem with scheduling the early evening timeslot on Saturdays. In the early 1960s, Saturday afternoon programming featured the sports highlights show, *Grandstand*, which broadcast from 12:15 p.m. until just after 5 p.m.; later in the evening, the pop music show, *Juke Box Jury*, attracted teenage viewers. After that, it was family shows and movies.

Bridging *Grandstand* to *Juke Box Jury* was the problem. The network wanted a show that skewed younger, towards children, given its tea-time placement. But dramatizations of Dickens and other classics died a quick death in that slot. American cartoons didn't fare much better. What to do?

It was a Canadian who was asked to solve that dilemma. Sydney Newman had had been poached from the Canadian Broadcasting Corporation to become head of drama at one of ITV's networks. Newman had great success: he created *The Avengers* and made the weekly play series *Armchair Theatre* one of the most watched series in Britain. With a competitor to the BBC after 1955, ratings became important. The BBC hired the maverick producer in 1963 in the hopes that he could work the same magic for them.

Newman turned to his colleague Donald Wilson, a producer and writer who became head of serials after Newman reorganized the BBC drama department. A year before, in 1962, Wilson had launched a study on science fiction in television that produced two reports. The reports were all but dismissive of literary science fiction, but suggested there was potential around telepathy or time travel.

Wilson regrouped his brain trust of researchers to come up with something more concrete and added to them writer C.E. Webber (who, for reasons lost to the mists of time, was nicknamed "Bunny"). What came back was a proposal for a series called *The Troubleshooters* about a team of professionals solving scientific problems. (It bears a small resemblance to later series such as *Doomwatch* and *Torchwood*.) Newman didn't like it. However, Wilson also passed on a memo by the same group outlining the viable concepts for a science-fiction series; Newman liked the time-travel idea. Many of the children's dramas that had come out under his auspices in Canada at the CBC in the 1950s were entertaining and dramatic, but also designed to "painlessly" educate children. The conceit of time travel, with its ability to move the central characters anywhere in history or the imagined future, allowed for his tea-time serial project to become this sort of drama.

Everything began to come together. Bunny Webber wrote a proposal. An in-house director, Rex Tucker, was brought in to produce. And someone — reports vary whether it was Newman or Tucker — came up with the name for this series: *Doctor Who*.

Webber's initial proposal, about a handsome young male lead, a female lead and a teenaged girl, along with an irascible scientist, the Doctor, would appeal to Newman's prescribed demographic group.

Webber imagined the Doctor as a revolutionary who travelled through time to find an "ideal" society, and then destroy it and any form of science. Newman rejected this outright (the handwritten exclamation "Nuts!" can be seen in Newman's marginalia on the proposal). Newman wanted the character to be a grandfather figure, not a time-travelling anarchist.

During this stage of development, Newman appointed a permanent producer. Verity Lambert was 24 and had been Newman's assistant at ITV. To hire a young woman for this job was quite radical in the men's club that was the British Broadcasting Corporation in 1963. She was capable of standing up for herself; Rex Tucker soon learned that Lambert couldn't be steamrolled into decisions and he left the show. Lambert's cool head saved the series while it was still in its infancy when BBC upper management decided the show was too expensive and should be killed after the initial four episodes were broadcast. Lambert held firm with her facts and figures on the costs of making the series, and she convinced the powers-that-be in the upper echelons to let it survive.

Lambert soon had a script editor, David Whitaker, who developed the series and its format further; her first story had a director, Waris Hussein. (Hiring Hussein, an Anglo-Indian, was also against the status quo.) Hussein and Lambert immediately worked on casting. Their first choices for the role of the Doctor were Leslie French and Cyril Cusack. Neither were interested. Lambert turned to an actor she had been considering since she saw the 1963 film *This Sporting Life*. William Hartnell wasn't sure if he wanted to commit himself to this children's series, but he was persuaded by Lambert and by how different the Doctor was from the army sergeants and villains he usually played.

A first episode based on Webber's story idea but written by Anthony Coburn was shot in September 1963. In that episode, two schoolteachers, Barbara Wright and Ian Chesterton, are puzzled by a new student of theirs, Susan Foreman. They follow her to a junkyard where they find a police telephone box and an old man. They stumble inside the police box and discover it's a spaceship called the TARDIS (an acronym standing for Time And Relative Dimension In Space). Fearing the teachers will alert others, the old man, who is Susan's grandfather (later to be known as the Doctor), sends the time machine back to the Stone Age.

Sydney Newman hated that first episode. He felt the Doctor was too anti-heroic and other elements weren't right. However, instead of scrapping it and firing either Verity Lambert or Waris Hussein, he had them re-do it. The final result was broadcast on November 23, 1963, at 5:16 p.m.

During the 1960s, *Doctor Who* evolved rapidly, moving from an educational series to something bolder and more adventurous. And yet, this change had been prophesied right from the start. Bunny Webber's original proposal for *Doctor Who* bears this interesting passage:

> We are not writing Science Fiction. We shall provide scientific explanations too, sometimes, but we shall not bend over backwards to do so, if we decide to achieve credibility by other means. Neither are we writing fantasy: the events have got to be credible to the three ordinary people who are our main characters, and they are sharp-witted enough to spot a phoney. I think the writer's safeguard here will be, if he remembers that he is writing for an audience aged fourteen . . . the most difficult, critical, even sophisticated, audience there is, for TV. In brief, avoid the limitations of any label and use the best in any style or category, as it suits us, so long as it works in our medium.

Newman was skeptical of this comment (writing "not clear" in his notes), but we think this is the closest thing to a mission statement *Doctor Who* has ever been given.

The 1960s

Starring
William Hartnell (1963–1966)
Patrick Troughton (1966–1969)
as the Doctor

Tips for Newbies

- **A "story" is made up of several episodes.** *Doctor Who* in its first 26 years was a serial. Stories were made up of four, six or even more episodes. During the first three years of the show, each individual episode had a title; later on, they were simply numbered. Bear in mind that most *Doctor Who* stories in the Classic Series range from 90 to 120 minutes (sometimes more).

- **Don't watch more than one episode at a time!** We know what you're thinking. "But I watch TV on DVD all the time, and hours at a time. And *Doctor Who* is only a half hour per episode! Pfft. I can totally watch an entire story in one sitting." Take it from us, the hour-long TV shows of the 21st century were meant to be marathoned; *Doctor Who* was not. The experience of watching television was vastly different in the 1960s. Scenes were languorous. Episodes were meant to be watched one at a time, with the cliffhangers holding you over, leaving you pondering what you'd seen over the following week. Such episodes will start to feel interminable if you watch several in a row. Trust us.

- **Watch it like you're at the theatre.** That's what British television was in the early 1960s: a televised theatrical play. Everything happens continuously, in real time, with a minimum of editing. It's all about the acting and the performances.

- **Don't worry about the effects.** Because it was made on a tiny budget, filmed as though it were live and for a tiny screen resolution, the special effects aren't always so convincing. Some are even laughable. But try not to let that bother you. Instead, marvel at the fact that they gamely try to convince you that some plastic bottles, a black backdrop and three character actors giving it their all constitute an alien planet with its own intricate society. And guess what? They do!

- **If all else fails, watch what William Hartnell or Patrick Troughton is doing.** If you're at the end of your tether with the languid pacing and low budget, pay attention to the Doctor. William Hartnell and Patrick Troughton are canny and instinctive actors who add interesting nuances to every scene they're in. Watch the Doctor and you'll never be bored.

> **DVD Note** Do not press "play all" on "An Unearthly Child"! Trust
> us on this. Before you start watching the very first *Doctor Who*
> story, note that if you use the "play all" feature on the DVD for "An
> Unearthly Child," it begins with an edited version of the rejected first
> episode before showing the broadcast version of the first episode
> (and the rest of the serial). We humbly suggest that you instead go
> to the "view episodes" menu and watch the transmitted first epi-
> sode. There are two reasons for this: the transmitted version is (much)
> better, and the rejected episode has been edited together (using
> methods impossible in 1963) from incomplete rushes, resulting in a
> new and inauthentic version.

An Unearthly Child (1963)

Written by Anthony Coburn (with C.E. Webber, uncredited, on episode one)

Directed by Waris Hussein

Featuring William Hartnell (Doctor Who), William Russell (Ian Chesterton),
Jacqueline Hill (Barbara Wright), Carole Ann Ford (Susan)

Supporting cast Derek Newark (Za), Alethea Charlton (Hur), Eileen Way (Old
Mother), Jeremy Young (Kal), Howard Lang (Horg)

Episodes "An Unearthly Child," "The Cave of Skulls," "The Forest of Fear,"
"The Firemaker"

Original airdates November 23, 30, December 7, 14, 1963

The Big Idea London school teachers Ian Chesterton and Barbara
Wright decide to follow a strange student, Susan Foreman, home to
a junkyard. There, they meet Susan's difficult grandfather, the Doctor,
discover his secret, which is kept inside a police box — and wind up in
the Stone Age.

Roots and References H.G. Wells's *The Time Machine* (the TARDIS);
Sir Arthur Conan Doyle's *The Lost World* and Edgar Rice Burroughs's
The Land That Time Forgot (modern-day people encountering primitive cavemen); the BBC TV series *Dixon of Dock Green* (the opening
sequence in the fog with the bobby walking the beat); C.S. Lewis's *Out
of the Silent Planet* (the kidnapping of Ian and Barbara through time
and space) and *The Lion, the Witch and the Wardrobe* (the magic door
into another world; curiously, Lewis died the day before this story was
first broadcast).

Time And Relative Dimensions In Space By early 1963, the *Doctor Who* production team had pretty much established the format of their new science-fiction series, with an elder scientist taking a schoolgirl and her two schoolteachers away from the present era in his time machine. However, where they would wind up in this first story was still to be determined. For a long time, the intent was to go with Sydney Newman's idea: the central characters would be shrunk to an inch tall and then face ordinary menaces. However, the script for this scenario by writer C.E. Webber never gelled. (It was later rewritten by someone else and made in 1964 as "Planet of Giants.")

Australian writer Anthony Coburn was brought in to overhaul Webber's first episode; he combined it with a story he'd written set in the Stone Age, and in so doing made several innovations that stayed in the ensuing years. It was Coburn who chose a metropolitan police box as the time machine's camouflage and who gave it the acronym TARDIS. Coburn also felt it was improper that the teenager (now named Susan) would travel alone with the Doctor and so he made her the Doctor's granddaughter.

The first episode was taped in September 1963 and then reshot at Newman's command. (While this unaired original version is generally referred to as a pilot, in fan lore and on the DVD, it really isn't one. Pilots are made to secure funding for a full series and there was already an initial commitment to a run of 13 episodes when this was filmed.)

Adventures in Time and Space While this is the very first *Doctor Who* story and the starting point for all continuity, there are already hints of backstory: the Doctor's ship (which Susan named TARDIS as an acronym for Time And Relative Dimension In Space) can usually change its shape (it's been an Ionic column and a sedan chair), but it's now stuck in the shape of the police box.

Who is the Doctor? Interestingly, while Ian says of Susan's grandfather, "He's a doctor, isn't he?" the character isn't called "Doctor" until the second episode of this story. (When Ian calls him "Dr. Foreman," the Doctor responds, "Eh? Doctor who? What's he talking about?") The character in his first appearance is selfish and imperious; Barbara says, "You treat everyone and everything as something less important than yourself." He is pragmatic to the point of lacking the compassion of his fellow travellers: he considers killing the wounded Za in order to escape. However, we also see many admirable traits in the

Doctor: we see his brilliance in how he gets Kal to prove he killed the old woman; his resourcefulness in capitalizing on this to drive out Kal; and a nascent understanding of justice, when he tries to do it in a way that will ultimately democratize the tribe.

In episode two, the Doctor also smokes for the first and only time in 50 years when he puffs from what must be one of the most ostentatious-looking pipes in the known universe.

Companion Chronicles When we meet him, the Doctor is travelling with his granddaughter Susan, the "unearthly child" of the title; she's exceptionally bright and curious, but in many ways a typical teenager. The Doctor is fiercely protective of Susan, to the point where he kidnaps Susan's schoolteachers Ian and Barbara. Ian, a science teacher, knows his subject well and at first assumes a leadership role when the time travellers are held prisoner by a Stone Age tribe. Gradually, he defers more and more to the Doctor (and the Doctor in turn grows to trust him). Barbara, a history teacher, is profoundly compassionate and more than prepared to tell the Doctor what she thinks of him.

Monster of the Week There are no monsters . . . yet. (Stay tuned for the next story!)

Stand Up and Cheer The final half of the first episode pretty much changes everything. For the first 14 and a half minutes, it's a contemporary drama about a slightly odd teenager. Once we're inside a police box that's really a spaceship that's bigger on the inside, we're playing a different game. Ian and Barbara struggle to understand what's happening, the Doctor and Susan rebuff them — and the result is glorious drama.

Roll Your Eyes The Doctor talks about the "red Indians" and their savage minds. Thank you for the reminder that we're watching a drama from 1963.

You're Not Making Any Sense The first episode ends with Ian and Barbara collapsing as the TARDIS dematerializes, with Ian being disoriented afterwards. Why is this? No explanation is ever given; furthermore, on their next journey (at the end of the story), they travel with no ill effects. (And no other companion will ever experience the same initial discombobulation.)

Interesting Trivia Okay, let's get this out of the way for the New Series fans right away: at the start of *Doctor Who*, the Doctor travels with his granddaughter, Susan. Yes, his *granddaughter*. No, we don't know who Susan is, if she's his biological granddaughter or if she just calls him that. We don't know who her parents are (or if they're the children the Doctor referred to in New Series stories like 2006's "Fear Her" or 2008's "The Doctor's Daughter"). We do know she's an alien, born in "another time, another world" (and we later see in "The Name of the Doctor" that she left Gallifrey with the Doctor). But we don't know anything more than that. So now you know everything we know.

The original first episode (the "pilot") only exists as unedited rushes. Its first 12 minutes are continuous footage, and the remaining sequence was shot twice, with the first take aborted a few minutes in due to the TARDIS doors not closing properly. The unedited version is included as a special feature on the DVD and it's worth watching if you want to see how *Doctor Who* was made during its first years. Many of the differences between the rejected and transmitted first episodes are cosmetic in nature, ranging from thunderclaps in the theme song to fluffed lines, costume changes and unintentional camera bounces.

The more substantial changes are to Susan and the Doctor. Originally, Susan was much more alien. When Ian and Barbara encounter her in the TARDIS, she is haughty, superior and mature — as though she was only acting like a teenager at school. In the broadcast version, Susan is a more ordinary teenager the audience could identify with. The changes to the Doctor are more radical: his severe and anti-heroical qualities in the original version are softened to create a less angry, more absent-minded and impish Doctor. Even so, the Doctor is still somewhat menacing; William Hartnell tones this down over the next few episodes.

There's also one key change to the Doctor and Susan's backstory. In the original, Susan states that she was born in the 49th century; in the broadcast first episode, she says she's "from another time, another world," which changes the motivation for kidnapping Ian and Barbara. In the original, as the Doctor and Susan were explicitly time travellers from the future, the Doctor has to take the schoolteachers with them because he can't let their knowledge of future technology adversely affect the timeline. By changing that detail, the Doctor's motivation for resorting to kidnapping becomes less clear and the characters more mysterious.

When did the time travellers wind up? The story was called "100,000 BC" in publicity documents, which broadly lines up with the fossil record of anatomically modern humans. The nomadic tribe seen here are clearly *Homo sapiens*, though their knowledge of fire is scant (which would still place the story within the 50,000–100,000 year window for the human discovery of fire) and they haven't invented basic tools beyond axes and knives.

Barbara's frustration that Susan didn't know how many shillings were in a pound is itself now a quaint archaism: in 1963, British currency still utilized a system that dated back to 1066 whereby 20 shillings were in a pound, 12 pennies were in a shilling and two halfpennies were in a penny. (And we haven't even discussed florins, crowns and thruppence.) Susan's "futuristic" assumption that Britain used decimalized currency was a prescient reference: an inquiry into decimalization had occurred in 1963, though the British economy didn't fully switch until 1971.

Real-world events impinged on "An Unearthly Child" in one concrete way: the first episode was broadcast the day after the assassination of U.S. president John F. Kennedy, leaving the show to debut in less than optimal conditions. The BBC elected to repeat the first episode before the broadcast of the second episode on November 30 in the hopes the show would gain greater exposure.

The TARDIS Chronometer Initially the Coal Hill School and at I.M. Foreman's junkyard at 76 Totter's Lane in London, sometime in 1963. Presumably, they travel back to Earth's past, though it's never established where or indeed when (the TARDIS yearometer reads zero).

Hmm? (GB) In the beginning, there was a junkyard somewhere in the dark foggy streets of London. And in the junkyard was a police box. It's hard to believe from that humble opening shot that we would still have a program 50 years later. But here we are.

One of the reasons for *Doctor Who*'s endurance is that the very first episode of "An Unearthly Child" may be one of the best first episodes of a TV show ever. It is itself a microcosm of everything *Doctor Who* does best, even after five decades: establish a setting and characters that are totally believable and then pivot that in an unthinkable direction. The first half of the episode establishes the comfortable relationship Ian and Barbara have with each other (William Russell and Jacqueline Hill have wonderful chemistry), introduces the slightly odd teenager Susan and explores why she doesn't quite fit in. And then we arrive at the junkyard and meet a difficult old man who is about to open a police box.

The performances vividly establish the characters. William Hartnell is wonderfully enigmatic. The first encounter between the old man and the schoolteachers has him never raising his voice, but taking authority nonetheless — and all the while he's demonstrably hiding something. It's a masterful job by Hartnell.

And then things go quite mad.

It's incredible to see how television drama has changed since. The first scene in the TARDIS — arguably, the scene that establishes what *Doctor Who* is and what it will be capable of doing — takes up the entire second half of the episode. Having a scene of that duration is unthinkable in TV nowadays. And yet, that scene is palpably brilliant drama, as two characters try to cope with the impossible, while the other two treat it as commonplace. Then the Doctor refuses to let Ian and Barbara go, which adds a sinister note to everything (including his character, in a moment that is almost never bettered). But this isn't just a nifty mini-play; the episode establishes almost everything you need to know about *Doctor Who* in its first year: the relationships, the characters, the possibilities.

The adventure is brought down to Earth with episodes two through four, which constitute a separate story of their own. The three episodes set in the Stone Age — where the Doctor and his party's perceived ability to make fire becomes part of a power struggle between two alpha males — do drag a little, particularly for people not used to television from 50 years ago. There's a very stagey, literary quality to writer Anthony Coburn's cavemen as they argue in faux-early language as though they're in a Google-translated version of *The Crucible*. But when it works — as it does in the scene where the Doctor talks with Kal about Za's "good knife" — it's really breathtaking.

Really, the only episode that truly drags is the second one, which features a lot of the Stone Age equivalent of parliamentary debate. Episode three picks up the pace with the first (but not the last) abortive escape attempt in *Doctor Who* (with a wild boar goring Za for added drama, which is heightened when the Doctor ponders braining Za with a rock). And episode four neatly resolves the conflict between Za and Kal, makes the invention of fire tense and provides a great escape sequence.

It all hangs together thanks to Waris Hussein, who directs the story with a naturalism not seen in *Doctor Who* since. The TARDIS crew's situation is played realistically (even their clothes are soiled and tattered by the end), with white-knuckle terror at every turn. (Hussein's use of extreme closeups works really well here, mitigating the limitations of the tiny studio space he's shooting in.) Future stories downplay this aspect, as a spirit of jolly adventure takes the series in a completely different direction, but it's interesting to see the show as it was originally conceived: ordinary people are set down in an historical epoch and we watch them cope with the sheer terror of it.

In the beginning, there was mystery, strangeness, fear, vivid character moments and even a little humour. Fortunately, that turned out to be exactly the template for the next 50 years.

Second opinion (RS?) My girlfriend really doesn't like *Doctor Who*. It's not for want of trying. Over the years, I've shown her all sorts of stories: populist classics, the New Series in order, you name it. Sometimes she'll say, "That one wasn't too bad," or, more often, "Meh." (And yes, I can confirm it is possible to survive this massive obstacle in one's relationship, though I wouldn't recommend it to the unwary.) When I was starting this book, I asked her to watch the first episode with me, warning her that it was almost 50 years old, in black and white, and so forth.

"An Unearthly Child" blew her away. She not only adored it, she even told other people about it. I really cannot tell you how happy this makes me and how, later that night, we —

But I digress.

As my experiment illustrates, this episode was put on this Earth to attract new viewers. And boy does it go all out! From the ordinariness of the school setting with an intriguing mystery to the sheer wonder that is the TARDIS's interior, this is a master class in how to intrigue new viewers. In just 25 minutes, the four characters are incredibly well developed, so that you feel deeply for Ian and Barbara, while nevertheless understanding just how out of their depth they are.

What's especially brilliant is the direction: Ian and Barbara are shot straight on, the camera looks down on Susan, and up at the Doctor. It's a subtle trick, but it does so much to indicate the roles that each of them play. All four actors are acting their socks off, but particular mention must go to Hartnell, who gives a tour de force performance.

Even if you're familiar with what the show eventually became, there are still surprises. The interior of the TARDIS is enormous, especially compared to the cramped junkyard outside it, and has lost none of its original wonder even today. And the Doctor's irascibility isn't something later viewers will be familiar with — my girlfriend didn't actually realize the old man was the Doctor at first — but it works a treat in this context.

In "An Unearthly Child," we see *Doctor Who* hit the ground running. Thanks to the reshoot, this is an incredibly polished production, even 50 years on. Before anyone involved even knew what type of show they wanted to make, they created something magical that still stands up today. A masterpiece . . .

. . . wait, what do you mean there are three more episodes?

Making *Doctor Who* in the 1960s

For much of its early days, *Doctor Who* was made in the tiny, narrow confines of Lime Grove Studio D, a place so small the actors had to run in place and let scenery hands hit them with tree branches to give the illusion of movement during the first two stories. Lime Grove Studio, built in the silent movie days, was unbearably hot under the lights necessary for making TV and was ill-suited for filming a program with a variety of sets and special effects.

Doctor Who wasn't broadcast live, but practically every episode in the 1960s was shot as though it were, with two (sometimes three) continuous takes lasting 10 or so minutes. (These two sequences were joined by a fade in and out that enabled foreign broadcasters to add in commercials.) Videotape was expensive, so the number of splices was minimized (the tape was later reused for other programs, and complex editing often required that the footage be transferred to film). Every scene was therefore performed in order, with actors waiting on other sets while scenes without them were shot.

The video cameras were gigantic and unsophisticated — there were three lenses on them that had to be adjusted manually — and a zoom was achieved by physically moving the camera towards the subject. Effects shots were often played live in studio, though others were made separately on film. Footage filmed on location didn't appear until the end of the series' first year, while larger, more complicated sequences were filmed on the soundstage at the BBC film studios in Ealing.

With the BBC's in-house special effects department unable (and unwilling) to make a commitment to the series, many of *Doctor Who*'s special effects in its early years were outsourced to model building and effects firms. (The designer on a particular story was not only responsible for the sets, but also the props and special effects, and had the authority to outsource the build.) Shawcraft — a Middlesex firm that specialized in model-making for trade shows, and had started to pick up work from the film and television industry — created the Daleks from Raymond Cusick's designs. Shawcraft and other firms built many of the other props and models used throughout the 1960s.

As time went on, the BBC gave *Doctor Who* better resources. Many of its later episodes were filmed at the bigger Riverside Studios and the new facilities at the BBC Television Centre, though *Doctor Who* was still mostly being made in Lime Grove Studio D as late as 1969.

• •

The Daleks (1963)

Written by Terry Nation **Directed by** Christopher Barry, Richard Martin
Featuring William Hartnell (Doctor Who), Jacqueline Hill (Barbara Wright), William Russell (Ian Chesterton), Carole Ann Ford (Susan Foreman)
Supporting cast Alan Wheatley (Temmosus); John Lee (Alydon); Virginia Wetherall (Dyoni); Philip Bond (Ganatus); Marcus Hammond (Antodus); Gerald Curtis (Elydon); Jonathan Crane (Kristas); Peter Hawkins, David Graham (Dalek voices); Robert Jewell, Kevin Manser, Michael Summerton, Gerald Taylor, Peter Murphy (Dalek operators)
Episodes "The Dead Planet," "The Survivors," "The Escape," "The Ambush," "The Expedition," "The Ordeal," "The Rescue"
Original airdates December 21, 28, 1963; January 4, 11, 18, 25, February 1, 1964

The Big Idea In the aftermath of a neutron war, the TARDIS crew finds two sets of survivors on the planet Skaro: the beautiful Thals and the terrifying machine creatures called the Daleks.

Roots and References World War II (the Daleks as single-minded fascists, genocide, inaction against a mighty aggressor being shown to be wrong); the 1959 film *On the Beach* (the aftermath of a nuclear bomb); *Lord of the Rings* (the Lake of Mutations); *The Time Machine* (two races in the far future, one hideous underground dwellers, the other ineffectual and beautiful); the 1930s *Flash Gordon* serials (the expedition).

Time And Relative Dimensions In Space The man who created *Doctor Who* didn't want this story to air. When Sydney Newman developed the brief for *Doctor Who*, he explicitly specified "no bug-eyed monsters," envisioning this new series as educational and for a family audience. Newman objected to the scripts for "The Daleks," despite producer Verity Lambert's explanation that they were mutants inside casings, with a very structured society. However, the lack of viable alternative scripts forced Newman's hand and the serial proceeded to be filmed and broadcast. When the ratings declared the Daleks a success, Newman apologized and subsequently reduced his involvement in *Doctor Who*, claiming Lambert clearly knew this show better than he did.

Writer Terry Nation had initially refused the invitation to pen a script for a children's show. But after he found himself out of work, he wrote the episodes relatively quickly and thought little of them . . . until the first episode aired, ending with the shot of the Dalek plunger and people desperately asking, "What *is* it?" Dalekmania was born.

However, the Daleks as scripted were fairly generic, though Nation did come up with the innovation of them gliding, inspired by the Georgian State Dancers and their floor-length hooped skirts. The aim was to create a monster that in no way resembled a human being. (Indeed, for some time, the fact that there were humans inside the casings was kept from the public, leading to the onscreen credit "Dalek operator.") Designer Raymond Cusick was largely responsible for their look. (Cusick was a last-minute replacement for another BBC designer who couldn't work on this story due to a scheduling conflict: future film director Ridley Scott!) As a BBC employee, Cusick received no royalties for the design that made the Daleks famous, except for a one-off *ex gratia* payment. Terry Nation, on the other hand, had a canny agent — future British TV industry legend, and future mother-in-law to Steven Moffat, Beryl Vertue — who negotiated that he keep a portion of the rights to his creation; as a result, he became a millionaire on the back of the Daleks' success.

Indeed, the issue of copyright was and is complex: Nation owned the right to the concept, but the BBC owned the right to the design. This led to a complicated situation. Even after Nation's death in 1997, the BBC's occasionally cavalier attitude to their arrangement compelled Nation's estate to be very protective of their share of the rights, which almost derailed the Daleks' reintroduction to the series in 2005.

Episode one had to be reshot when the "talkback" (the director's messages, from the production gallery, that were transmitted to the camera personnel's headphones) was audible on the soundtrack. Fortunately, the episode only features the four regulars, so the remount wasn't too expensive. However, this meant that the *Doctor Who* production team had re-filmed an episode in both of its first two stories, creating a budget nightmare and playing havoc with the actors' contracts.

The cliffhanger reprise at the beginning of episode two is slightly different from the cliffhanger in the previous episode. The reprise is taken from the original footage of episode one, the only piece of footage from it known to survive.

Adventures in Time and Space Ian mentions being violently uprooted from their own time, referring to the previous story; the Doctor counters that they pushed their way into the TARDIS.

Who is the Doctor? The Doctor still shows a ruthless streak: he lies about the fluid link being damaged so he can explore the Dalek city. He later wants to abandon the Thals to their ambush, a far cry from the Doctor we'll come to know, and is keen to leave in the TARDIS at the first opportunity. Once he commits to helping the Thals, he effortlessly becomes the brains behind the assault on the city and overcomes the Dalek surveillance using "only a few simple tools and a superior mind" . . . only to be immediately captured by Daleks. He says he was once a pioneer among his own people.

Companion Chronicles Susan is consistently childlike in her initial exploration of the jungle, in contrast to Ian and Barbara's fear and caution. Ian grows into the role of action hero, making hard choices and leading a party of Thals. When they express their fear that the Doctor won't ever be able to return them home, Ian insists to Barbara that she'll always have him, indicating a budding romance. However, in the later episodes of "The Daleks," Barbara and the Thal Ganatus have a flirtation, which culminates in her kissing him at the story's conclusion, so perhaps not.

Monster of the Week On *Doctor Who*'s first alien planet, Skaro, we meet the first monster: the Daleks. They're unknown to the Doctor, cannot leave their city and are powered by static electricity. They have a gun that can paralyze or kill, a flexible eye and a sink-plunger arm, with which they can hand each other objects (such as a piece of paper, in a neat move). They've become dependent on radiation (a plot point that's abandoned in later stories) and plan to bombard Skaro with it so they can leave the confines of their city. As for the creature inside, we see just a hint of a claw under a cloak. The casing without the mutant is just big enough for Ian to fit into.

Stand Up and Cheer The moral debate about whether the TARDIS crew has the right to ask for the Thals' help is really great. Ian knows that they're only asking the Thals for help so that they can recover the fluid link and he refuses to send innocents to war for such a selfish motive. William Russell is particularly good here, and the scene leads into the pacifism debate very nicely.

Roll Your Eyes The Thal costumes are ridiculous. The bare-chested men wear vests that keep slipping off their shoulders and pants with evenly cut holes in them. The women wear a leotard and what looks like an upside-down sandwich board. It's especially odd when Barbara changes into Thal pants for the expedition to the swamp.

You're Not Making Any Sense Why would the Doctor only have one fluid link, given how vital a component it is? It's implied later that he only really needs the mercury, so why wouldn't he have extra supplies?

Interesting Trivia The Daleks converse in a reasonably chatty manner, saying things like "A few questions will reduce the mystery" and "The truth is, your supply of drugs has failed and you came into the city to see if you could find more." To anyone familiar with the creatures the Daleks became, this must come as something of a surprise. The reason is because the Daleks were first written as a more generic villain; the mechanical treatment of their voices (using a device called a ring modulator) and the robotic method of speech were later additions. Future scripts adapted the dialogue to the voices heard on television, making it terser. Nonetheless, it should be noted that it actually works quite well, so it's a shame the more conversational style wasn't continued.

We learn all manner of things about the TARDIS in this story. There's a fault locator, consisting of a bank of lights on the wall, with a printout much like an earthquake measurement. The food machine, which can be programmed for a variety of flavours, produces bars wrapped in foil. The scanner rotates 360 degrees. And finally, the whole lock comes away from the TARDIS door (there are 21 places inside the lock, 20 of which are wrong; if you make a mistake, the inside of the lock will melt). What these details demonstrate is the idea of the TARDIS as a place to live in, rather than just a travel machine.

The people behind the scenes gave significant thought to what life in a spaceship, with all its day-to-day minutiae, involves.

Who were the Daleks originally? The Doctor looks through the Thals' records and says the Daleks — who've borne that name for 50 years — used to be called Dals. They were once teachers and philosophers, just as the Thals were once warriors; both groups have changed drastically. This is a reasonable idea: the Thals and the Dals as two similar races on the planet Skaro who went to war, one of whom mutated drastically, is a perfectly serviceable backstory. However, this will change somewhat. Stick around for "Genesis of the Daleks" to find out why.

Did the Doctor accidentally inspire the Dalek empire? It's an enduring mystery as to why the Doctor doesn't know the Daleks in this story. They're a time-travelling, galactic empire of evil who are later revealed to be a threat even to the Time Lords. So why wouldn't he know them? Near the end of the story, when trying to save the situation, the Doctor tells the Daleks about his TARDIS and its capability of time travel. The Daleks are interested and believe they can learn its secrets. The Doctor insists they couldn't without him, but they're confident they could master time travel on their own. Assuming some Daleks survive the story, they have knowledge that time travel is possible and the technical skills to at least understand such a machine, if not build one themselves. It's possible that this conversation inadvertently inspired the Daleks to develop time travel, thus changing the course of history.

The explosion at the end of the story was a cliffhanger that led into the next story, 1964's "The Edge of Destruction" (where the TARDIS was on a collision course with the beginning of time). Most stories in the Hartnell era ended on cliffhangers, giving the feel of a mostly continuous narrative.

The TARDIS Chronometer The planet Skaro. The date is unclear, although the default assumption is the far future, because the original format tended to alternate between past and future, with occasional forays "sideways." This story's sequel, 1964's "The Dalek Invasion of Earth," suggests that these events are many millennia in the future, but later stories imply that it was the past. And thus begins the fan challenge of establishing a Dalek timeline.

Hmm? (RS?) This was the story that launched *Doctor Who*. And you can tell.

Where the first story was all about character, this story does something entirely different: it creates the format. Given just how slippery a concept *Doctor Who* is, that's a big ask. How do you create something as complex and multi-faceted as *Doctor Who* in just seven episodes?

Simple: you do it by world-building. With monsters.

"The Daleks" features the first alien planet in *Doctor Who*. This isn't a fact to be taken lightly. When the New Series showed up in 2005, complete with a big budget and glossy special effects, it avoided alien planets like the plague. Even when it did start to branch out, the planets always looked like somewhere on Earth. "The Daleks" is different. Made on a budget of thruppence ha'penny and a piece of string, it creates an entire world from scratch, complete with history, aliens, the aftermath of a tragedy and a moment of sheer wonder in the city itself. This is a template for Classic Series *Who* from this moment on: it's a show that's completely unafraid to try anything.

Where this story really shines — and where you can see why Dalekmania took off in force as a result — is with the Daleks themselves. They're magnificent, right from the get-go. There are multiple levels of genius in their conception, design and realization: they're so perfectly suited to their environment, it's surprising that anyone dared take them out of it for the sequel; they're so shockingly inhuman that the plunger and egg whisk don't matter in the slightest; and they're ruthlessly evil and cunning psychologists.

The city is quite magnificent. Like the Daleks within it, it's a triumph of design. Walls are at unusual angles, doorways are rounded and too low for a human, while the floors are all metal. It's also full of lifts and almost the entire structure is miles underground. This effectively conveys the alien nature of the planet they've landed on, especially in the first episode when it's apparently deserted. The subsequent escape from the Dalek city, with the lift as the "ticking bomb," is exciting stuff.

On the downside, the *Doctor Who* format created here even includes the dodgy bits. There are two alien factions at war, one of which looks ridiculous. After several episodes of intrigue and tension with our heroes being captured and escaping from the Daleks, the first scene with the drippy Thals sucks all the drama from the story. There are some valiant attempts to re-inject tension in the latter episodes, but everything to do with the Thals, from the overblown speech by their leader to the way the Thal Smurfette isn't allowed to do anything other than be the angel in the jungle, works against the rest of the story. They're the most effete alien race ever devised.

Imagine a story that's split in two, featuring a reaction to the then-imminent threat of nuclear war, which consists of only the regular cast in the opening episode, sees Susan desperately run through a forest and has a wacky swirl effect at the end of an episode. But anyway, enough about "An Unearthly Child."

What's surprising is just how similar — and how different — the first two stories are. Both are concerned with the issues of the day, twisted through a metaphorical prism. Both put an enormous amount of effort into character development in their first episode. And after all their hard work at establishing who these people are, both stories then let them loose on a society that's so different from their own that it tests them to the very limit.

However, it's in the differences that the success of "The Daleks" is evident, thanks to its sheer chutzpah. We don't just have two mildly different races at war, we have two whole societies. (Well, one entirely alien society and some rejects from a bad gay pride parade.) The environment itself is a character in several episodes, not just in the lengthy exploration of the jungle at the beginning, but in the way the entirety of episode six is spent trying to conquer a ravine. Contrary to popular opinion, this is really exciting stuff. It might be *Boys' Own* adventuring, but the fact that this sequence takes so much time actually makes the success feel earned. A comparable story in later *Doctor Who* would compress the entire ravine sequence into just one scene, but by having it so drawn out, you feel both the pain and the triumph of the mission.

In fact, the whole story has this verisimilitude. The first few episodes involve our heroes dying from radiation poisoning because they've blundered into an environment they don't understand. (And it's sheer happenstance that the Thals help them out; otherwise, it would have been a very short series.) This twists our expectations and forces our four regulars to step out of their comfort zone. The three adults are almost instantly rendered useless (the radiation affects the Doctor more than anyone, Ian is paralyzed from the Dalek shot and Barbara is also incapacitated), leaving Susan as the only one physically able to go into the jungle, upping the tension even more. These are excellent storytelling choices, because they allow the regulars to shine, as well as function as a team.

Terry Nation wrote this story in just seven days, cranking out one episode a day and then going on to work that interested him more, little realizing that the Daleks were going to make him a millionaire. But it's this very speed of creation that likely made "The Daleks" work so well, because he was clearly writing from a place of sheer instinct. So the Daleks become Nazis — they even do a Nazi salute at one point! — because that's not only what he's interested in, it's what resonates emotionally for him. What we get in "The Daleks" is a kind of snapshot of an entire world suffering the aftermath of an intense trauma, exactly the post-war world that Nation was living in at the time.

"The Daleks" is often dismissed as a four-part story that introduces the eponymous monsters, followed by three boring episodes tacked onto the end. But it's more than that. It's groundbreaking in many ways that we don't even notice today, because it set the template for so much that followed. Where the opening story achieved some of the key elements that *Doctor Who* was initially imagined to have, this story flips the intended format on its head — in the second-ever story, note — and creates something magical. Something amazing. Something unlike anything ever seen before. It creates *Doctor Who*.

Second Opinion (GB) I must disagree with my co-author. The reason why "The Daleks" is often dismissed as a four-part story that introduces the eponymous monsters followed by three boring episodes tacked on to the end is because that's exactly what it is.

I watched "The Daleks" exactly as we recommend to new viewers, an episode a day. I loved the first half of the story, but the second half bored me to tears. The great thing about Terry Nation's script is that there's a dramatic set piece for every episode. When the Daleks are the central characters of that set piece, it's amazing television. The more we hang out with the Thals, the more the ennui sets in. Episode six is titled "The Ordeal" and it is: it's a slow-moving, tedious experience where the most that's accomplished is using a rope to jump over a chasm. For ten excruciating minutes. There's realism and there's watching paint dry.

Fortunately, there are Daleks, and every time they show up onscreen the viewer's attention immediately perks up. And the last episode finds its groove again with the final conflict between Daleks and Thals. It's a shame the pasty paragons of virtue had to win.

The other problem is that the first four episodes are not just excellent: they're iconic, which throws the draggy second half into sharp relief. For the second story in a row, the entirety of the first episode is bound up in the drama between the four leads and it's riveting to watch. Terry Nation adds just the right notes of a broader mystery (the petrified trees and animal, the city, the person who taps Susan's shoulder) to make it all the more intriguing. And then when the Daleks show up, all bets are off.

The Daleks are stunning in their debut. The atypically glib remarks they make really suit them well. They're an imposing menace from the start (the interrogation of the Doctor is incredible), which only ratchets up the tension of the time travellers' escape from the Dalek city and their attempt to avert the Dalek ambush of the Thals.

Something that is hardly ever mentioned is that the music by Tristam Cary is breathtakingly good. It anticipates ambient music (without synthesizers!) by a good four decades and creates a moody, atmospheric soundscape. Few *Doctor Who* soundtracks have bettered it. It's a masterpiece. Just like "The Daleks." Or at least the first four episodes.

Story Titles in the Hartnell Era

Over the years, a question for *Doctor Who* fans and reference writers has been what to call the early stories. For the producers of *Doctor Who*, this wasn't a problem. The stories were generally known by their internal serial production code. So the very first story was "Serial A" and the following stories were given a sequential alphabetic designation.

For everyone else though, it's a bit more complicated. The early reference books about the series — culminating in *The Programme Guide* (1981) — used what would best be called "notional" titles derived from the title of the first episode, or titles based on other sources. So Serial A became known as "An Unearthly Child"; Serial B was first known as "The Dead Planet" (the title of the first episode) and then "The Daleks" (based on the title of the 1965 film version and the 1964 novelization). Because of the popularity of *The Programme Guide*, these titles came into common use during the 1980s and were used on the BBC's video releases, and for subsequent television broadcast listings.

In the 1990s, fan researchers began to go through the BBC's archives and discovered that there were, in fact, collective titles for many of these stories. Serial A, the first story, was called "100,000 BC." The second story, Serial B, was called "The Mutants." (Which creates further confusion as there is a 1972 Jon Pertwee story with the same title.) Other stories with different titles included 1963's "The Edge of Destruction" (actually "Inside the Spaceship") and 1966's "The Massacre" (actually "The Massacre of St. Bartholomew's Eve").

This led to a controversy among fans: do we call the story by the title now in common usage, or by the more historically accurate title? Many have elected to go by the more historically accurate title, including *Doctor Who Magazine*. We have chosen in this book to go with what is commonly accepted, as it is how the BBC itself has chosen to title the DVD releases.

In the New Series, multi-part stories are usually given separate titles (e.g., "Aliens of London" and "World War Three"). Curiously, the common practice with these stories is to refer to both titles rather than use a collective story title for both episodes. Thank goodness.

The Psychic Papers: Dalekmania

In late 1963, "Beatlemania" gripped the U.K. and quickly spread throughout the world within months. Shortly afterwards, another kind of fanaticism gripped the U.K.: Dalekmania.

It started with *Doctor Who*'s second story, "The Daleks," which was broadcast around the same time that Beatlemania was at its height. Like the mop-topped Liverpudlians before them, the Daleks suddenly became the hottest thing around — and that took everybody by surprise.

Nowadays, tie-in merchandise associated with a TV show is nothing out of the ordinary, and it was common in America even in the '50s and '60s. However, in 1964 in Britain, TV-related merchandise was limited. That changed with Dalekmania. It helped that Terry Nation owned part of the rights to the Daleks; he was quite happy to say yes to financial opportunities the high-minded BBC might have otherwise turned down.

Initially, demand was high, but supply was a little slower to kick in. However, by Christmas 1964, Dalekmania hit fever pitch: "The Dalek Invasion of Earth," the sequel to "The Daleks," aired throughout December. Terry Nation's *The Dalek Book* (co-written by David Whitaker, *Doctor Who*'s script editor) had been published in June; it purported to be based on Dalek chronicles discovered and translated by Terry Nation. Canny merchandisers were marketing a range of Dalek-themed products for the Christmas sales. The very first novelization, *Doctor Who in an Exciting Adventure with the*

Daleks (again by Whitaker), came out in November and was a runaway hit, selling out its original 20,000-copy print run within one month. There was even that most British of institutions, a Christmas novelty single, "I'm Going to Spend My Christmas with a Dalek" by the Newcastle band The Go-Go's.

The Daleks were everywhere. There were Dalek badges, Dalek soap, toy Rolykins Daleks (which could move about on a ball bearing in the base), Give-A-Show projectors and candy cigarettes with picture cards. The phenomenon even had a Beatlemania crossover moment with the famous photo of John Lennon meeting a Dalek at the Cannes Film Festival. (A clip of the Beatles performing "Ticket to Ride" featured in 1965's "The Chase.")

The Christmas madness convinced filmmaker Milton Subotsky that the Daleks needed to be on the big screen and in colour. Made by the British film company Amicus (best known for their '60s horror films) under its AARU production company, *Dr. Who and the Daleks* was released in August 1965.

Written by Subotsky and an uncredited David Whitaker, based on Terry Nation's TV scripts and directed by Gordon Flemyng, *Dr. Who and the Daleks* featured British horror stalwart Peter Cushing as Dr. Who, a human scientist whose surname was indeed Who (the film dispensed with the backstory of the TV series). In the film's opening scene, Dr. Who is showing his time machine *Tardis* to his granddaughters Suzie and Barbara (Roberta Tovey and Jennie Linden), and Barbara's new boyfriend Ian (British comedy actor Roy Castle) before an accident whisks them to the planet Skaro.

Cushing portrayed Dr. Who as a dotty old coot (in stark contrast not only to William Hartnell's TV portrayal but also the villainous figures Cushing played in Hammer and Amicus films) and Ian was the comic relief. Otherwise, the film follows the same beats as the television serial, although the scope and sets were vastly bigger and more colourful. It was critically derided, but went on to become one of the top ten films of that year in Britain, and made it to North America on the B-movie circuit.

A sequel, *Daleks — Invasion Earth: 2150 A.D.*, was immediately commissioned, based on "The Dalek Invasion of Earth" (with Subotsky and Whitaker writing, and Flemyng directing again). Peter Cushing and Roberta Tovey stayed on, but Jennie Linden and Roy Castle were replaced by Jill Curzon (playing Dr. Who's niece, Louise) and Bernard Cribbins (best known to fans of the New Series as Donna's grandfather Wilfred Mott) as police officer Tom Campbell. Campbell stumbles into *Tardis* while trying to stop a robbery, and he travels along with the rest of the crew to a future where the Daleks have invaded. While the film was less successful than its predecessor, it is notable as one of the first movies to include product placement within its narrative, as posters for Sugar Puffs cereal appear throughout the film (and there was a Dalek-themed promotion on cereal boxes when the movie was released).

The Daleks also made their comic book debut (a medium they adapted to perfectly) in *TV Century 21*, starting in January 1965. There the Daleks were the creations of a scientist named Yarvelling; innovations included Daleks flying about on hovering platforms, as well as a "budget" for Dalek armies that the TV show could only dream of. There was also *The Dalek World* (1965), a follow-up to *The Dalek Book*.

Meanwhile, on TV, the immense popularity of the Daleks convinced BBC director Huw Wheldon to commission a 12-part epic (plus a prequel episode), 1965's "The Daleks' Master Plan," which remains the second-longest *Doctor Who* story ever televised. This was the fourth Dalek story in three years ("The Chase" had been broadcast earlier that year); it seemed as though the Daleks were unstoppable. In 1966, when the risky concept of regeneration was used to replace William Hartnell with Patrick Troughton, the Daleks were brought in for Troughton's first story, "The Power of the Daleks," so that viewers would feel more comfortable with the change in lead actor.

Fads eventually fade, of course, and Dalekmania was no exception. Throughout 1966 and early 1967, Terry Nation tried to launch an American series featuring the Daleks, but nothing came of it. This had the side effect of putting Dalek stories on hold in *Doctor Who* itself; 1967's "The Evil of the Daleks," which attempted to write them out of *Doctor Who* forever, was the last Dalek story for several years. However, as we all know, every time the Daleks appear to be dead, they have a way of coming back . . .

· ·

The Aztecs (1964)

Written by John Lucarotti **Directed by** John Crockett

Featuring William Hartnell (Doctor Who), Jacqueline Hill (Barbara Wright), William Russell (Ian Chesterton), Carole Ann Ford (Susan Foreman)

Supporting cast Keith Pyott (Autloc), John Ringham (Tlotoxl), Ian Cullen (Ixta), Margot Van der Burgh (Cameca), Walter Randall (Tonila), André Boulay (Perfect Victim)

Episodes "The Temple of Evil," "The Warriors of Death," "The Bride of Sacrifice," The Day of Darkness"

Original airdates May 23, 30, June 6, 13, 1964

The Big Idea When Barbara is mistaken for a reincarnated Aztec ｟ she decides to seize the opportunity to make the Aztecs abandon human sacrifice and become a more civilized people. But can history be changed so easily?

Roots and References The 1947 film *Captain From Castille* (Cortés and the Aztecs); the works of Shakespeare, particularly *Hamlet* (Ixta's poisoned nettle echoes Laertes's poisoned sword).

Time And Relative Dimensions In Space *Doctor Who* was originally designed to educate viewers about history and science; the positioning of two of its leads as history and science teachers was intended to further this purpose. While Ian's knowledge of science was used far less on the whole, this story capitalizes on Barbara's knowledge of history. At this point in the young series, the go-to writer for historical stories was veteran John Lucarotti, who had already scripted the successful journey into 12th-century China, 1964's "Marco Polo." This time, Lucarotti drew on his own travels to Mexico and his fascination with the Aztec people, with their interests in science, engineering and the arts contrasting with their need for human sacrifice.

Who is the Doctor? The Doctor says, "They call me the Doctor," an acknowledgement of the title he's adopted, and describes himself as a scientist and engineer. It's strongly implied that he once tried to change history just as Barbara is attempting — and likewise failed, just as badly. His close friendship and ultimate engagement to the widow Cameca is played for laughs, but it's clear that she means more to him than he lets on.

Companion Chronicles The Doctor is furious with Barbara's attempt to change history, but decides to goes along with Barbara's plan, even comforting her when she realizes the ultimate futility of her efforts. Barbara proves herself resourceful when posing as the reincarnated High Priest Yetaxa, while Ian demonstrates his skill at fighting the warrior Ixta. Ian also can see the flaw in Barbara's belief that the Aztec culture can reform itself.

Monster of the Week As it's a historical episode, there is no alien monster, though Tlotoxl, the High Priest of Sacrifice — whom the Doctor calls "the local butcher" — certainly could qualify, looking like the bastard offspring of Richard III and Ronald McDonald.

Stand Up and Cheer Tlotoxl demands to see Barbara-as-Yetaxa take action and divinely intervene to prevent Ixta from killing Ian. And she does . . . by putting a knife to Tlotoxl's throat. It's the combination of a cunning move, the threat of hardcore violence and a riveting performance by Jacqueline Hill that makes this moment so powerful and so satisfying.

Roll Your Eyes The stone block in front of the tomb is obviously polystyrene, and no amount of acting on William Russell's and Ian Cullen's parts can disguise that at all.

You're Not Making Any Sense Having foiled Tlotoxl's plot to poison her, and having demonstrated considerable aplomb in deflecting Tlotoxl's attempt to prove her a fraud, Barbara's sudden admission to Tlotoxl that she's not Yetaxa comes out of nowhere and seems to be on a whim.

Interesting Trivia Here we have a story set in the days of the height of Mesoamerican culture that's surprisingly well researched and realized for 1960s television. (Even the costumes, which at first glance seem wrong for the climate given how much flesh they cover, are actually accurate.) However, it's doubtful that the Nahuatl-speaking tribes within that part of Central Mexico would have called themselves "Aztecs" as the characters do throughout. (The word derives from the collective noun for disparate people with a common heritage of belonging to a mythical place of origin called Aztlan.) The Aztec tradition of human sacrifice was indeed horrific — and usually involved cutting out the victim's still-beating heart — though the narrative in "The Aztecs" ignores the fact that many of those sacrificed were not willing "perfect victims" but prisoners of war, kept alive for this purpose.

The Doctor asserts, "You cannot change history. Not one line." This was the cosmology of *Doctor Who* at the time; a story at the end of *Doctor Who*'s first season in 1964, "The Reign of Terror," asserts outright that it is impossible for the time travellers to alter historical events. This view changed within a couple of years, starting with "The Time Meddler" (1965) to the point where, 50 years later, it's widely established that history can indeed be rewritten in *Doctor Who*. So how does "The Aztecs" fit into this? The best theory is that this part of the timeline was a "fixed" point in time (as later explained in 2008's "The Fires of Pompeii"). On the other hand, Barbara does change a single line in this story — Autloc chooses a new destiny as the result of her interference — so it's clear that the assertion isn't meant to be taken literally.

Doctor Who was in production for 48 weeks during 1963–1964 (and that doesn't count the reshoots of the first episodes of "An Unearthly

Child" and "The Daleks"), and provision had to be made so the cast could take a vacation. Thus Susan is only in a couple of brief scenes in episodes two and three, which were filmed at the BBC's film studios in Ealing, enabling Carole Ann Ford to take two weeks off. In the previous story, "The Keys of Marinus," William Hartnell had two weeks' holiday and wasn't onscreen at all (though his contract required he still be credited). Jacqueline Hill and William Russell took their annual leave during the next two stories, "The Sensorites" and "The Reign of Terror."

The TARDIS Chronometer Mexico, sometime before the arrival of Cortés in 1519.

Hmm? (GB) Before Amy Pond, before Rose Tyler and before Donna Noble, there was Barbara Wright. You know, the schoolteacher with the bouffant hairdo, who, even in an era that skewed mature and matronly in their tastes for sexy women (this was the age when Honor Blackman played Pussy Galore in *Goldfinger*), looked and behaved like someone's mother.

But that assessment grandly misses the point about Barbara. I think she's the most influential *Doctor Who* companion ever. Watch "An Unearthly Child." Who gets in the Doctor's face when he doesn't want to care for the wounded Za? It's Barbara. In the next story, "The Daleks," the Doctor wants nothing to do with the Thals and the Daleks, and who is it that pleads for the Thals' lives? Barbara again.

In the following story, "The Edge of Destruction," Barbara finally loses all patience and tells the Doctor exactly what she thinks of him, no holds barred. And, at the end of that story, the Doctor suddenly softens and becomes friendlier towards the human companions, admitting to Barbara, "As we learn about each other, so we learn about ourselves."

I think the Doctor's absolutely right. As he learns about Barbara, so he learns about himself. Barbara is the one who humanizes the Doctor. Forty-two years before Rose Tyler and the ninth Doctor did the same thing in the first season of the New Series, Barbara Wright taught the Doctor empathy and made him better as a result.

We see this dynamic at its apogee in "The Aztecs." It's the Classic Series' equivalent of "Father's Day": Barbara gets the opportunity to change history and, because she's human and fallible, the plan fails. Both "The Aztecs" and "Father's Day" have scenes where the Doctor is disappointed but also understands why the companion does what she does. However, what's distinctive about "The Aztecs" is the moment where the Doctor generously points out to Barbara that, while she couldn't save the Aztecs, she did save Autloc — even if she betrayed him.

Frankly, it's generous of the Doctor. Because, really, as Barbara's grandchildren would no doubt say, her plan has "epic fail" written all over it.

Where "The Aztecs" really departs from reality is with Barbara's belief that Cortés would look kindly on Aztecs who no longer engaged in human sacrifice. For someone seemingly so well-versed in history, Barbara is profoundly naïve. While Cortés wrote about the sacrifices and was disgusted by the practice, there were plenty of other political and personal reasons motivating Cortés's conquest of the Aztec empire.

But then, Barbara's whole outlook is somewhat faulty. Her view of the Aztecs is that they are, effectively, "noble savages." Barbara repeatedly repudiates the Aztecs' practices as "evil" but never tries to go beyond that to examine the root causes, thinking she can "civilize" a whole race just by ending one solitary monstrous practice. Is it any wonder that Barbara is doomed to failure? Historical stories often say as much about the period they were made in as the period in which they're set: the view of the late fifteenth century Aztecs is very much a product of 1964 England. (Hence a story set in Mexico performed by white British actors.)

The fashion in these early *Doctor Who* historical stories are to "Shakespeare" them up a bit, both in terms of the language (Tlotoxl speaks on several occasions in blank verse, and even throws in some iambics for good measure!) and the theatricality of the piece, which pleasingly draws the viewer into the stunning performances. William Hartnell may have to recover from the odd fluffed line, but he puts an incredible amount of intensity into his performance. From his disgust at Tlotoxl and his whimsical scheming to get the plans to the tomb to his tender moments with Cameca, you always get the sense that Hartnell, in the best theatrical tradition, is trying to get the most out of every scene he's in.

The same is true of the rest of this talented cast. John Ringham's Tlotoxl might well be *Doctor Who*'s first larger-than-life villain, but he keeps it all rooted in an overall vision of a man who is fundamentally afraid of change. Keith Pyott underplays Autloc as if to deliberately contrast with Ringham's performance. And Margot Van der Burgh as

Cameca is sublime. She has fantastic chemistry with William Hartnell, and you genuinely feel for her when the Doctor inevitably dumps her.

Jacqueline Hill, though, is the true star of "The Aztecs." Her Barbara is smart and cunning and, thanks to her doomed quest, very human. Seeing her stare down Tlotoxl is breathtaking to watch. Barbara is central to the actions of several of the stories she's in, and "The Aztecs" is a shining example of that. You take Barbara out of "The Aztecs" and the whole story collapses: the plot is motivated by Barbara's hubris and her desire to challenge the Doctor. There is no other story in the Classic Series that does this. After Barbara, the female lead falls into the assistant role.

I don't think Jacqueline Hill, or Barbara as a character, receives nearly the credit she deserves. Barbara and the Doctor didn't just love each other, they respected each other. I don't think you can say that of other companions. The Doctor might have had affection for them and the companion might have had awe for the Doctor, but the Doctor and Barbara had unwavering, hard-earned respect. Watch "The Aztecs" and you can see why. Without Barbara, the Doctor would still be an anti-heroical bastard.

Second Opinion (RS?) "The Aztecs" is often noted for its historical accuracy and flavour (including by my co-author above), especially as it's the earliest surviving "pure" historical. It looks gorgeous, because it's the BBC doing what it does best: costume drama, researched to the nth degree and brought to life by actors determined to give it their all so that you don't notice the painted backdrops.

However, "The Aztecs" isn't really a historical story at all. The previous historical, also by Lucarotti, was a travelogue with Marco Polo. This is something quite different: a genuine science-fiction dilemma. And, like all good science fiction, it has something profound to say about our own society. Namely, can one person — no matter how powerful — make a difference? The answer is no, because power isn't held in political office or even godhood; power is instead held within institutional structures and that's a much harder thing to alter on one's own.

The entire story is predicated on people from the future grappling with the ethical dilemmas about whether to change the past. Almost every major arc, from Ian's physical superiority over Ixta to the Doctor solving the problem of the tomb with a pulley to Susan's unwilling engagement, stems from the fact that the TARDIS regulars have access to information or technology that the Aztecs lack. It's not possible to do this kind of story in any genre except science fiction.

And yet, despite their obvious superiority, our heroes lose — and they lose badly. Barbara ruins the life of the one man she trusted; she can't stop the sacrifices; Ian is forced to kill Ixta; and Tlotoxl ends the story with more power than he started with, remaining the only villain in the entirety of *Doctor Who* to be undefeated. And as for the Doctor . . . he loses most of all. By duping Cameca into helping him, he opens himself up emotionally — and the loss of their relationship turns out to be more painful for him than Barbara's dilemma is for her. Barbara is the pivot around which this story is structured, but ultimately this is just as much the Doctor's story. It's no coincidence that the final shot isn't Yetaxa's bracelet being replaced on the corpse, but rather the Doctor deciding to keep Cameca's brooch after all.

The romance between the Doctor and Cameca is often dismissed as the show in its infancy, not having realized it wanted an asexual Doctor. But time has been kind to "The Aztecs": its plotline would be right at home in the New Series. By giving the Doctor something to lose, the story makes us care, both about the grand sweep of history and the bittersweet losses that come from travelling in time. It's a shame they don't revisit this again. At least not for another four decades or so.

The Psychic Papers: The Historical Stories

As script editor David Whitaker wrote in the original format document for the series, *Doctor Who* was meant to show stories on three planes: "backwards in time," "forwards in time" and the occasional story set "sideways in time": odd situations such as alternative versions of Earth or the time travellers being miniaturized.

The "sideways in time" concept fell by the wayside fairly quickly. And, while they were very popular in *Doctor Who*'s first two seasons, the "backwards in time" historical stories soon became an endangered species.

The success of the Daleks, with their more populist bent, changed the direction for the "forwards" stories, originally conceived to be Orwellian or Wellsian parables for our world. Writer Terry Nation had been commissioned to write a historical story set in the British Raj in India, called "The

Red Fort," but, after the success of his Daleks story, he was quickly taken off that project to write another futuristic science-fiction story, "The Keys of Marinus" (1964), full of monsters and exciting, fast-paced set pieces.

As the series made its most important evolutionary leap forward with its science-fiction serials, the historical stories, though initially popular, struggled to make a similar impact. Part of the problem, viewed with hindsight, was that it was explicitly established that history could not be changed in the *Doctor Who* universe, which meant that the Doctor and his companions interacted with history in incidental ways, like the Doctor's quest to regain the TARDIS from Marco Polo, or Barbara's attempt to civilize the Aztecs.

In 1965, a new script editor, Dennis Spooner, took over *Doctor Who* (the script editor in the Classic Series in many ways functioned as the writer/executive producer does on the New Series). Spooner attempted to overhaul the historical to fulfill the same populist vision of the science-fiction serials. He wrote the 1965 story "The Romans" as a full-on comedy, with Nero lustfully chasing Barbara, and the Doctor giving Nero the idea to burn Rome by accidentally setting a map of the city on fire with his spectacles!

Dennis Spooner also gave us 1965's "The Time Meddler," which featured the first appearance of another member of the Doctor's race (other than his granddaughter Susan). This story, with a mischievous time traveller using his TARDIS and futuristic technology to try to prevent William the Conqueror's arrival, challenged the notion that history could not be changed. It also introduced a new genre to *Doctor Who*: the "pseudo-historical," stories set in history with a science-fiction element (beyond the TARDIS).

Subsequent production teams followed the lead taken in the second season. New producers John Wiles and Donald Tosh brought in writer Donald Cotton to make the historicals even more farcical and satirical, resulting in 1965's "The Myth Makers" and "The Gunfighters." (At the same time, Donald Tosh rewrote John Lucarotti's script about the 1572 Huguenot massacre — made in 1966 as "The Massacre" — as a dark treatise on what it would be like for a companion to be trapped in history without the Doctor. It received the worst ratings for any historical story in the entire series.) Wiles and Tosh's successors, Innes Lloyd and Gerry Davis, opted for Robert Louis Stevenson–style swashbuckling with "The Smugglers" and "The Highlanders" (both 1966).

By this point, the historicals had drifted far outside their original remit of educating viewers about history; they were a relic of an idea of what *Doctor Who* should be that was effectively stillborn as soon as the Daleks appeared.

As third season producer Innes Lloyd noted afterwards, by this point they were effectively the same sort of costume dramas the BBC excelled at in its other programming. Also, new sub-genres were emerging in *Doctor Who*: stories set in contemporary times and occasional fantasy-based stories that were, in many ways, the successor to the "sideways" story.

The pure historical stories ended with "The Highlanders" in 1966. The pseudo-historicals also started to peter out so *Doctor Who* became, for all intents and purposes, a show about the present day, the near future or outer space.

"The Time Warrior" (1973) was, in fact, the third Doctor's only outing to Earth's history (unless you count a completely fanciful jaunt to Atlantis in 1972's "The Time Monster"), as he battled a Sontaran in the Middle Ages. That story heralded a mini-renaissance of pseudo-historical stories in the early fourth Doctor era. These stories fit nicely with new producer Philip Hinchcliffe and script editor Robert Holmes's vision of *Doctor Who*, which filched from various pulp and horror genres. But the revival came to a halt with Hinchcliffe's and Holmes's departures; "Horror of Fang Rock," set in a lighthouse in the Edwardian era, was the last pseudo-historical for many years.

The historical story came back for two nights only in 1982's "Black Orchid," an Agatha Christie–style murder mystery set in the 1920s, but — in an utter surprise at the time — it featured no monsters and no future technology, just upper-class Brits.

The New Series has had at least one historical story per season, and it has introduced a new sub-genre, the "celebrity historical": pseudo-historical stories that focus on an important historic figure, starting with Charles Dickens (2005's "The Unquiet Dead") and continuing through to Richard Nixon (2011's "The Impossible Astronaut"/"The Day of the Moon"). All of these, however, feature monsters and futuristic technology.

It's odd that the New Series, which has demonstrated a mastery of genres and storytelling methods, has yet to essay the pure historical story. As *Doctor Who* passes into its sixth decade, perhaps its next challenge is to go back to its own past . . . by returning to the past.

. . . .

The Gunfighters (1966)

Written by Donald Cotton **Directed by** Rex Tucker

Featuring William Hartnell (Doctor Who), Peter Purves (Steven), Jackie Lane (Dodo)

Supporting cast John Alderson (Marshal Wyatt Earp), Anthony Jacobs (Doc Holliday), Richard Beale (Bat Masterson), Laurence Payne (Johnny Ringo), Shane Rimmer (Seth Harper), Martyn Huntley (Warren Earp), Victor Carin (Virgil Earp), Reed De Rouen (Pa Clanton), William Hurndell (Ike Clanton), Maurice Good (Phineas Clanton), David Cole (Billy Clanton), Sheena Marshe (Kate), David Graham (Charlie)

Episodes "A Holiday for the Doctor," "Don't Shoot the Pianist," "Johnny Ringo," "The OK Corral"

Original airdates April 30, May 7, 14, 21, 1966

The Big Idea The Doctor has a toothache, so he goes to the local dentist. Only the TARDIS has touched down in Tombstone in 1881 just before the gunfight at the O.K. Corral — and the local dentist is gunfighter Doc Holliday.

Roots and References The 1965 film *Cat Ballou* (the comedy-western, the song as framing device); the Lorne Greene 1964 spoken word song "Ringo" (Johnny Ringo); the 1958–61 U.S. TV series *Bat Masterson* (Masterson's anachronistic presence in the story). Most of the story is a spoof of the 1957 film *Gunfight at the O.K. Corral*, with other tropes from Westerns thrown in for good measure; the Doctor mentions Tom Mix (and Steven's get-up is designed to look like a "singing cowboy"); the Doctor claims the pseudonym "Dr. Caligari" (after the 1920 F.W. Murnau film *The Cabinet of Dr. Caligari*); and the second episode is titled "Don't Shoot the Pianist," presumably a play on the title of the 1960 François Truffaut film *Shoot the Piano Player*.

Time And Relative Dimensions In Space Legend has it William Hartnell himself wanted a Western. Producer John Wiles and script editor Donald Tosh were happy to facilitate this and commissioned Donald Cotton (who in 1965 had written *Doctor Who*'s sophisticated farce about the fall of Troy, "The Myth Makers") in the hopes that he could give the American West a similar treatment. Unfortunately, Wiles and Tosh left *Doctor Who* in early 1966, and the new production team, producer Innes Lloyd and script editor Gerry Davis, didn't quite know what to make of the story they had inherited.

The 1960s

31

Adventures in Time and Space At the end of the previous serial, 1966's "The Celestial Toymaker," it seemed like the Doctor had been poisoned by a sweet given to the travellers by the evil Toymaker's creation, Cyril. It turned out the sweet had simply hurt the Doctor's tooth.

Who is the Doctor? The Doctor can stare down Daleks but he's afraid of going to the dentist! (Given the era he's in and the dentist he has, perhaps that's understandable.) He insists that he never touches alcohol and he explicitly states that he doesn't approve of violence. His longstanding abhorrence of guns makes its first appearance here.

Companion Chronicles Space pilot Steven Taylor was rescued by the Doctor from the planet of the Mechanoids. The Doctor and Steven later met Dodo Chaplet, a girl who wandered into the TARDIS when it briefly landed on Wimbledon Common in 1966.

Monster of the Week There isn't one, but the attempt to film a Western in a cramped television studio in London is fairly monstrous.

Stand Up and Cheer Dodo threatening Holliday with a gun is a beautifully played farcical scene. Dodo politely suggests that she will merely wound Holliday, to which Holliday gently points out she's actually pointing the gun between his eyes. She moves it and asks, "Is that any better?" The whole scene has a brilliant punchline with darker undertones, when it's revealed Holliday had his Derringer all along.

Roll Your Eyes As we will see, hoping for credible American accents on *Doctor Who* is something of a fool's errand. While we have a few decent accents in this serial (and even a Canadian, Shane Rimmer, to provide some authenticity), in the opening scene, the Clanton brothers give us the first and only instance of a Cockney-American accent in the history of British television. While the real American West was full of Scottish and Irish accents, this strains credulity a mite too far.

You're Not Making Any Sense Having established how completely young and inexperienced Warren Earp is, everyone else leaves the jail, with one of the Clanton brothers in it, under Warren's tender care. What's wrong with this picture?

Interesting Trivia British television programs are evaluated by two means: ratings (a measure of how many people watched a particular program) and Audience Appreciation scores (now called an Appreciation Index), gathered with a survey that asks a sampling of viewers how much they enjoyed an episode. While ratings for "The Gunfighters" were far from the worst for the Hartnell era (though they did start a downward slide for the next year or so), the Audience Appreciation figures for episode four were the worst in *Doctor Who* history, with only 30% of viewers thinking the program was worthwhile viewing. However — appropriately for the Western genre, where the legend is often more interesting than the facts — it wasn't as if *Doctor Who* was otherwise triumphing in these surveys: most stories of the era hovered around a 50% appreciation figure. The story broadcast immediately before "The Gunfighters" was already slipping into the 40s, and subsequent stories didn't rate above 50% until mid-1967. Nonetheless, the damage was done; producer Innes Lloyd began phasing out the historical story, and "The Gunfighters" carried with it the stink of being "the worst *Doctor Who* story ever" in fan lore.

Here's a tip about looking for historical accuracy in "The Gunfighters": don't bother. Donald Cotton explicitly wrote a story based on the legend of the gunfight at the O.K. Corral, rather than the actual events. Much of the tale is a parody of the 1957 film, which accounts for Wyatt Earp being the marshal (in real life, Virgil Earp was the lawman; Wyatt Earp was an inveterate gambler, much like Holliday), the addition of Johnny Ringo to events (unlike in the film, Ringo is killed off here) and the gunfight being a protracted affair (the actual events lasted about 30 seconds and took place at close range). Cotton added inventions of his own, like the Earps' younger brother, Warren, and historical figures, like Bat Masterson, who was nowhere near Tombstone at the time.

Two people involved with "The Gunfighters" have important connections to *Doctor Who*'s past and future. Director Rex Tucker was briefly producer of *Doctor Who* while the series was still in development, while actor Anthony Jacobs's son, Matthew Jacobs — who visited the set of "The Gunfighters" — grew up to become the writer of the 1996 *Doctor Who* TV Movie, starring Paul McGann.

The song "The Ballad of the Last Chance Saloon" (written by Donald Cotton with music by Tristram Cary and performed by Lynda Baron) was originally limited to the verses we hear in episodes one and two. But Rex Tucker, who was encouraged by the incoming production team to enhance the farcical elements, took to writing new verses. Tucker's verses are the ones that directly comment on the actions onscreen ("And it's curtains for Charlie . . ."), a departure from the indirect, scene-setting verses Cotton wrote. Regardless of who wrote what, we apologize in advance: that song stays in your head for days. It's best not to fight it. All together now: "With rings on her fingers . . ."

The TARDIS Chronometer Tombstone, Arizona, 1882 (the gunfight took place October 26, and the Doctor, Steven and Dodo arrive two days earlier).

Hmm? (GB) I'm going to hang my banner high here. This is a *Doctor Who* story that everyone should watch. That's why it's here. I think "The Gunfighters" is one of the best and smartest *Doctor Who* stories ever made.

You heard me.

Among the greatest of my very minor achievements in life was convincing Peter Purves, who plays Steven, that "The Gunfighters" was not only a comedy, but a brilliant one. I remember how shocked he was when I told him that I loved this story during an interview with him in 2004.

It's easy to understand why he might have found that surprising. Received wisdom for decades was that "The Gunfighters" was a failed historical at best, and a failed *Doctor Who* story generally. And yet, I'm here today to tell you it's as far from that as possible.

What it is instead is an incredibly smart and funny parody of the Western genre. The Doctor, Steven and Dodo wind up in 1882 Tombstone and become part of the events that lead up to the gunfight at the O.K. Corral. Along the way, everyone tries to give the Doctor a gun, Steven and Dodo are forced to sing at gunpoint, Dodo is embroiled in the world's most cordial kidnapping and the body count in Tombstone keeps increasing. All the while, the action is sung about in an increasingly dippy ballad.

Doctor Who had attempted to parody movies before, but with "The Gunfighters" it goes after the very iconography of a Western, and does it with wit, panache and intelligence. (I understand why some would hate "The Ballad of the Last Chance Saloon," but they're wrong to dismiss it: it's a brilliant example of an experiment in storytelling that *Doctor Who* rarely does, using a song as a framing device, and one that giddily skewers every Western convention to boot.) A character in John Ford's *The Man Who Shot Liberty Valance* (made only a few years before) says of frontier mythmaking, "print the legend." "The Gunfighters" points out how ridiculous the legend is, courtesy of the writer of "The Myth Makers." It's a glorious commentary on the gun-obsessed, grudge-holding, law-and-order-in-lawlessness world of the Western. My favourite scene is when Doc Holliday goes off to rustle up some food. Pause. Gunshots. (Kate groans in annoyance.) Holliday comes back with a tray of food, saying, "Now ladies, it's all right. I just ran into an old friend and he . . . he kind of lost his appetite." It's comic genius.

We get scene after scene with brilliant dialogue like this. "Ringo was here." "And?" "He is no more." Or, "You kill a guy out of sheer professional ethics . . ." Or, the Doctor indicating he's quite happy to go along with the sheer absurdity of the situation: "Doc Holliday is a great friend of mine. He gave me a gun, he extracted my tooth — good gracious me, what more do you want?"

The entire saloon scene with the Doctor in episode two is a triumph of farce. William Hartnell is never better than when he does comedy and he's exultant with deadpan lines like, "After a bereavement, it's hard to find the right words." This is so perfectly delivered that I had to pause the DVD to laugh for a solid two minutes.

But hyping "The Gunfighters" as a comedy makes it sound like *Carry On Cowboy*. It's not. The farce works because the characters are all deadly earnest, particularly Anthony Jacobs's Doc Holliday, who is stellar as he skates the knife-edge of civility and sociopathy; it's worth watching for his performance alone. I adore John Alderson, who plays Wyatt Earp as though he's a pissed-off Sunday-school teacher. Even Laurence Payne, who seems to be playing Johnny Ringo as though he were Lee Marvin by way of Manchester (with an accent about as ridiculous), has real intensity in the role. The story has dramatic weight (let's not forget the set piece where the Doctor and Earp have to stop a lynching), which makes the comedy even more effective.

Director Rex Tucker gives his all to emulate the dramatic heft of a Western . . . from a television studio in London. The end result of dramatizing Donald Cotton's script is something that might have been too smart for the room in 1966 (this is a story that uses a French New Wave film for the title of its second episode), but is vibrant and funny today.

If there is a *Doctor Who* story that urgently deserves reappraisal, it's "The Gunfighters." Peter Purves watched it after the interview and decided I was right. You will too.

Second Opinion (RS?)

Dear Graeme,

Thank you for the kind offer to write another book with you, which I've been very much enjoying. As you know, I share your love of *Doctor Who*, in all its formats. And I've recently drunk the Kool-Aid on the '60s stories, which, I have to say, are thoroughly magnificent. Every time I think about the fact that so many episodes are no longer in existence, I get visibly upset. And I was claiming William Hartnell as my favourite Doctor long before it was cool to do so. (A fact you may or may not remember, given how drunk you were when you accused me of lying about this, back in 2000. Good times.)

I mention all this because I want to ask you a question: Why on earth are we including this story in this book?

Okay, okay, I know part of the answer. The Hartnell era doesn't just succeed on its monster classics or its oddball stories. There's also the genre of historical comedy. It's not to everyone's taste, but I will agree that it's a very refreshing angle to the series. And one of the things I've always admired about the Hartnell era is just how experimental it was: its tone shifts from pop sci-fi stories to desperately serious historicals to experimental one-off stories with no regulars to 12-part Dalek epics. So it's natural that such wild experimentation will produce the odd dud.

But seriously, "The Gunfighters"?! I know our selections are the 50 *Doctor Who* stories people *should* watch, as opposed to the best. I know that we chose stories in a way that allowed individual selections by each author. And I know there are stories coming up that might not be your favourites. But really? "The Gunfighters"?

It's not that I don't see the story's good points. The Doctor's dislike of guns is solidified here. That's great. And the comedy is as fun as you say. But the song is death on a platter and it just goes on and on and on and on. You can argue all you like about its use as a framing device, but that doesn't change its repetitive and distasteful nature. And, although I'm not a "Gunfighters" hater, I still wonder about the wisdom of including it in a list of *Doctor Who* stories that everyone should watch.

If you wanted a fun Hartnell historical, why not "The Romans"? That's a great story! And, crucially, far more accessible, with funnier jokes, a better production and — thankfully — no song. I wish I'd thought of it first time around, actually, but there were so many great

Doctor Who stories to choose from that I overlooked it. And now I'm really regretting that.

So, um, great job for picking a story that people won't expect to be in a book about 50 great *Doctor Who* stories. I appreciate that. But couldn't you have found a better one?

Your co-author,

Robert Smith?

- -

William Hartnell

William Hartnell was born in 1908; he grew up never knowing who his father was and was raised for a time by a foster mother. He dabbled in boxing, but aspired to be a jockey. In his youth, he became friends with an art collector, Hugh Blaker (the man who discovered the Isleworth Mona Lisa), who became his unofficial guardian and helped him enrol at the Italian Conti Academy in the early 1920s. Hartnell began a stage career in the late 1920s and was a character actor in British cinema throughout the 1930s and 1940s. During World War II, Hartnell served in the army tank corps before being invalided out in 1943 when he suffered a nervous breakdown.

Hartnell's big break in film was 1944's film *The Way Ahead*, in which he played a blustering army sergeant. From that point forward, Hartnell's career was defined by playing bullying heavies. He had a notable role in the 1949 film version of Graham Greene's *Brighton Rock*, but was mostly typecast as a sergeant figure, including in the first *Carry On* film, *Carry On Sergeant* (1958), and the television comedy *The Army Game* (1957–1961). A breakout performance in the 1963 Lindsay Anderson film, *This Sporting Life* — Hartnell played an ageing, devoted rugby manager — was noticed by *Doctor Who* producer Verity Lambert and led to his being cast in the role of the Doctor.

Hartnell suffered from arteriosclerosis, a condition that began to make him infirm in his 50s. It affected his ability to remember lines and he became increasingly disagreeable on set. Successive producers on *Doctor Who* pondered ways to replace Hartnell, and eventually Hartnell and producer Innes Lloyd agreed to part ways in 1966.

Hartnell largely retired after *Doctor Who*. He returned to the role of the Doctor in the tenth anniversary story "The Three Doctors" (1972), but by this point his failing memory meant he could only make a cameo, reading his lines off cue cards. He died in 1975, at the age of 67.

- -

The 1960s

The War Machines (1966)

Written by Ian Stuart Black, from an idea by Kit Pedler **Directed by** Michael Ferguson

Featuring William Hartnell (Doctor Who), Jackie Lane (Dodo), Michael Craze (Ben), Anneke Wills (Polly)

Supporting cast John Harvey (Professor Brett); John Cater (Professor Krimpton); William Mervyn (Sir Charles Summer); Alan Curtis (Major Green); Gerald Taylor (voice of WOTAN and War Machine operator); Sandra Bryant (Kitty); George Cross (The Minister); Kenneth Kendall (himself); Ric Felgate, Carl Conway (American journalists); Roy Godfrey (tramp)

Original airdates June 25, July 2, 9, 16, 1966

The Big Idea A computer in the new Post Office Tower attempts to take over the world by brainwashing scientists and building robotic weapons of destruction.

Roots and References *The Manchurian Candidate* (WOTAN's brainwashing), *A for Andromeda* (the Machine as inspiration for WOTAN). Kitty remarks that the Doctor "looks like that DJ," referring to BBC disc jockey Jimmy Savile, who had long hair and dressed in an Edwardian mode similar to the Doctor.

Time And Relative Dimensions In Space Script editor Gerry Davis believed that the show needed a scientific advisor to help with the accuracy of stories and to bounce ideas off where possible. He approached a number of respected scientists, including Patrick Moore and Alex Comfort, before meeting with Kit Pedler, a physician and scientist who worked at the University of London. Davis asked Pedler a question all the other candidates baulked at: how could aliens take over the planet from the recently built Post Office Tower? To Davis's delight, Pedler surmised it could be done with a computer operating from the tower and using telephone lines. Davis immediately had writers Pat Dunlop, and then Ian Stuart Black, turn Pedler's idea into a script. Pedler got the job as the series' scientific adviser; soon after, he and Davis created the Cybermen.

This is the first story to be entirely set on contemporary Earth since the very first episode (while 1964's "Planet of Giants" had them in modern times, the series regulars were only three inches tall and had no interaction with any other humans).

Adventures in Time and Space The Doctor feels a prickling sensation emanating from the Post Office Tower, like he feels when he encounters the Daleks. (It turns out that the Daleks actually are nearby, as we find out in 1967's "Evil of the Daleks," set on the same date.)

Who is the Doctor? The Doctor is immediately accepted by Professor Brett's team and Sir Charles as a knowledgeable authority. This story marks an important sea change for the character: previously, companions like Ian and Steven took on the hero role, while the Doctor acted as mentor figure/grandfather/comic relief. In "The War Machines," the Doctor is now central: taking on, and ultimately taking down, the War Machines himself.

Companion Chronicles Dodo is written out in a perfunctory manner during episode two: she's sent to the country to recover after being hypnotized by WOTAN. This story introduces two new companions: Ben, a cockney sailor, and Polly, an upper-class secretary. The clash of classes provokes a frisson of romance between them.

Monster of the Week The War Machines are mobile computers designed by the supercomputer WOTAN. They move on a caterpillar track and come installed with deadly weaponry.

Stand Up and Cheer The end of episode three, when the Doctor alone stands up to the advancing War Machine, is a breathtaking cliffhanger.

Roll Your Eyes The Inferno Club is meant to be a hot joint in the heart of swinging London, only it's kind of lame. Bad stock music, people dressed like they just came from a Young Conservatives meeting . . . Carnaby Street, it ain't.

You're Not Making Any Sense Why does a supercomputer with the ability to brainwash people over phone lines need to create robots — especially ones that go rogue easily and can be reprogrammed even more easily — when it can simply call the Prime Minister, the military high command, the President of the United States and the BBC Head of Drama, and hypnotize them into doing its bidding?

Interesting Trivia Much is made in this story about the brand-new Post Office Tower (now known as the BT Tower) in the Fitzrovia area in London. Opened to the public in May 1966, the tower was built to beam microwave signals for telecommunications. (It was called the Post Office Tower because Britain's telecommunications were then under the remit of the General Post Office.) At the time of its construction, it was the tallest building in London.

It's incredible how forward thinking "The War Machines" was in positing a network of the world's computers. Theories on networking computers had only begun being discussed a few years before this story's broadcast, and the first actual network (what became known as ARPANET, the predecessor to the modern internet) wasn't created until 1969. Admittedly, "The War Machines" suggests computer networking is the whim of a powerful, sentient, evil machine bent on enslaving humanity. But in this age of Google, Apple and Microsoft, we may be getting ever closer to that reality . . .

Sir Charles states that "C" day (the day all the world's systems connect to WOTAN) is Monday, July 16. Throughout Ben and Polly's tenure as companions, it's stated that they come from 1966. However, in 1966, July 16 fell on a Saturday (the airdate of the final episode of this story), not a Monday.

There's an interesting thing going on with names in this episode. First of all, Polly seems to have no last name. Production documents indicate it was intended to be Wright (whether or not Polly is related to Barbara is for fan fiction to decide), but her surname is never stated onscreen. Also, the Doctor is called "Doctor Who" for the first and last time in the series. Finally, we have WOTAN, an acronym for Will Operating Thought ANalogue. You have to wonder about Professor Brett naming a computer after the Teutonic king of the gods — and, make no mistake, the fact that WOTAN is pronounced the German way, with a "v" sound, indicates that the acronym's meaning was figured out after the computer was named. (Curiously, WOTAN is given its own credit in the serial, as though the actual computer was playing the part. One presumes it moved on from *Doctor Who* to audition for the malevolent computer in Stanley Kubrick's upcoming science-fiction epic . . .)

This story comes with a howler of a blooper as William Hartnell forgets his place in the script, realizes his mistake and then corrects himself leading to the Doctor randomly uttering, "I wonder Sir Charles do you suppose . . . eh . . . uh, no I don't suppose you would." What needs to be remembered here is that *Doctor Who* in the 1960s was made as though it were live. If action was stopped, everything, including all the scenes before it, had to be redone. As a result, the actors pressed on after most fluffs, and mistakes were broadcast, save for any uttered obscenities. That said, one of the best bloopers is a result of botched film editing during the first scene: a man getting out of his car vanishes entirely as the TARDIS materializes.

The TARDIS Chronometer July 12–16, 1966, in London.

Hmm? (GB) In 1966, new producers took over *Doctor Who*. Like so many new producers, they were determined to put their own stamp on the show. They got rid of the companions hired by the previous regime and hired young, dynamic actors as their replacements. They made cosmetic changes, like doing away with individual episode titles. They found a scientific adviser who could help them come up with interesting ideas based in science. They made changes to the character of the Doctor — more on this in a moment — that inevitably led to a different actor taking on the role. They concluded that all this malarkey about never having a story set on contemporary Earth was silly and produced one.

Oh, and they decided that the lead character of the show was actually named "Doctor Who."

Ground zero for most of these changes was "The War Machines," the last story of *Doctor Who*'s third season. That makes for a busy four episodes. And yet, "The War Machines" somehow masks all those backstage machinations with a really exciting story set in as swinging a London as the BBC dared allow in family television.

It's the first time that the series does science fiction in contemporary times. The idea they come up with is boringly commonplace now, but barmy then. A supercomputer goes rogue launching deadly robots from a new London landmark. It's the 1966 equivalent of a Russell T Davies New Series contemporary story, like the ATMOS devices in "The Sontaran Strategem" or the Cybermen invasion launched from Canary Wharf in "Army of Ghosts."

And, like those stories, it's grounded in a loose sense of verisimilitude by having it all play out on the news (even using actual BBC newsreader Kenneth Kendall). This being 1966, we're not given a montage of different news channels, but rather we see people in the pub watching it on telly, or hearing it on a car radio or even watching a print newspaperman (that relic of the past) talking about it to his editor.

The result is probably the Classic Series' first real victory of style over substance. The computer, naturally given the acronym WOTAN (why can't they name these things FLUFFY or KITTY?), has a plan that defies logic: there's no need for WOTAN to create mobile tanks vulnerable to being reprogrammed. However, this detail becomes unimportant because — wh-hey, it's the army fighting robots in the streets of London!

Brilliant, fast-paced direction from Michael Ferguson! There's a companion who looks like a young Michael Caine teamed with the sexiest woman from the 1960s as the new *Doctor Who* girl! There's the Post Office Tower and Covent Garden and real London locations! Plot? Who needs plot? (And we don't need to think about how a tramp merits a headshot that could be used in a newspaper story or how WOTAN apparently planned everything down to branding the boxes of parts shipped to build the War Machines, either.) The eye-candy is quite lovely. The War Machines themselves are a bit daft-looking but, set loose in Central London, they look menacing.

While departing companion Dodo is, undeservedly, written out by the end of the second episode (and doesn't even get a departure scene!), Michael Craze is given a great showcase as the new companion Ben, who imbues the part with scrappy charm. Anneke Wills is lovely as the plucky toff Polly, but although the character is beautifully established in episode one, she spends the rest of the story hypnotized by WOTAN, which is a bit of a waste.

It's clear from this story that the production team has different ideas about the character of the Doctor. The end of episode three signals an end to the Doctor as grandfather figure and the beginning of him as the hero of the series. Even if there hadn't been that laughable flub in episode two, the writing was now definitely on the wall: William Hartnell's tenure as the Doctor was about to come to an end. And yet, while Hartnell has two stories left after this one, "The War Machines" is the last complete extant story. As such, it's a wonderful end to the first Doctor's era.

Second Opinion (RS?) I'd like to apologize for my co-author's snarkiness. The plot of "The War Machines" is awesome! The only person who can reprogram the War Machines is the Doctor and it's done twice in two very different ways (the capture of the rogue War Machine in the electromagnetic field being a really exciting sequence). And the mobile tanks have a real sense of unstoppability. They mow down the army with brutal efficiency, jamming electronics and guns. Had the Doctor not been on hand, WOTAN would have easily succeeded.

What's impressive about this story is its sense of scale. Every episode features a large number of extras, none of them noticeably playing multiple roles. There's the gathering of journalists (which includes a black man!), the hypnotized workers, the swollen army ranks and the busy newsroom. However, it's not just the sheer number of people onscreen, it's the story's scope that makes it feel bigger than it is. There's the worldwide hook-up of computers, the news bulletin (initially seen on a TV in a pub), the reports of cabinet meetings, a government minister, public announcements by the army to stay off the streets . . . This is a story that really feels global.

And you have to admire the attention to detail: the meticulous assembly of machines in episode two and the military manoeuvres before the battle in episode three give the following sequences a level of depth that might not be strictly necessary, but adds a degree of realism to sell us on what's happening. Later *Doctor Who* stories will convey worldwide or interplanetary threats using a minimum of actors on a set or two. Here, in the show's third year, with all the restrictions that come with TV made in the 1960s, we see how to do it right.

Man, I love this story.

. . . .

The Doctor's Name

It's one of those things that fans know instinctively, but the media (and hence the general public) always get wrong: the TV show is called *Doctor Who* (never *Dr. Who*) but the character is simply called the Doctor. Part of the alluring mystery of the character is that his name is never revealed, only his title. Indeed, series seven of the New Series includes an arc driven by the fact that nobody knows the Doctor's real name.

In "The War Machines," WOTAN impresses us by knowing about things it couldn't possibly, like the TARDIS. Shortly afterwards, it announces, "Doctor Who is required." Does that mean the Doctor's surname is "Who"?

Many fans have dismissed this as an aberration. WOTAN is simply an advanced computer built by humans in the 1960s, and, over the years, all sorts of fan theories have been advanced, such as the idea that "Who" is just a placeholder, since the Doctor has no surname. Given that the Doctor isn't present when WOTAN calls him "Doctor Who," it's (somewhat) easy for most fans to dismiss this moment. It should also be noted that WOTAN only calls the Doctor "Doctor Who" in scenes where William Hartnell isn't present. This suggests that it was probably Hartnell himself who was largely responsible for keeping the character's name correct from the outset.

And yet, in 1966's "The Highlanders," the Doctor uses the pseudonym "Doctor von Wer," which is German for "Doctor Who." This is harder to rationalize away, because it's the Doctor himself who says it. Although technically he doesn't use "Who" as a surname, it's about as close as you can get. He also signs his name "Dr. W" in 1967's "The Underwater Menace." The broad implication from these examples is that producer Innes Lloyd and script editor Gerry Davis likely decided that "Who" was the Doctor's surname.

What's more, the actor playing the character is credited as "Doctor Who," not just during the '60s, but up until 1981's "Logopolis." In the '60s and '70s, the credit is frequently shortened to "Dr. Who"; the character was often named as such in scripts. It's little wonder the media believe his name is "Doctor Who." In fact, when the New Series was brought back, Christopher Eccleston's ninth Doctor was credited as "Doctor Who"; it was David Tennant, longtime fan that he is, who demanded the credit be changed to "The Doctor."

Later stories are much more playful with the Doctor's name. During the third Doctor's era, he often adopts "John Smith" as an obviously fake name (very few characters believe it's a real name, although it's not as unlikely as you might think; one of the authors of this book was very nearly called that). Scenes often ended with a metatextual joke where someone mentions the Doctor and a new character asks, "Doctor who?"

The New Series keeps the mystery of the Doctor's name intact, even using "John Smith" as his human alter ego in "Human Nature"/"The Family of Blood." The end of 2011's "The Wedding of River Song" suggests that the question "Doctor who?" was the oldest question, hidden in plain sight — although it's really only in plain sight if you happen to be a viewer of the TV program *Doctor Who*; less so if you're a fictional character interacting with the Doctor in any way.

In the end, we don't really know. The only available evidence suggests that "Who" really is his surname, but said evidence is flimsy at best. What's more, the character is most compelling with the level of mystery that surrounds him, and not knowing his name goes a long way to preserving this essence.

The Tomb of the Cybermen (1967)

Written by Kit Pedler and Gerry Davis **Directed by** Morris Barry

Featuring Patrick Troughton (Doctor Who), Frazer Hines (Jamie), Deborah Watling (Victoria)

Supporting cast Shirley Cooklin (Kaftan); Roy Stewart (Toberman); George Pastell (Klieg); Aubrey Richards (Professor Parry); Cyril Shaps (Viner); George Roubicek (Captain Hopper); Clive Merrison (Jim Callum); Peter Hawkins (Cybermen voices); Michael Kilgarriff (Cybercontroller); Hans de Vries, Tony Harwood, John Hogan, Richard Kerley, Ronald Lee, Charles Pemberton, Kenneth Seeger, Reg Whitehead (Cybermen)

Original airdates September 2, 9, 16, 23, 1967

The Big Idea An archaeological expedition searching for the last remains of the Cybermen gets more than it bargained for when it turns out those Cybermen are very much alive.

Roots and References The curse of Tutankhamun and various movies and TV shows inspired by it, such as 1964's *The Curse of the Mummy's Tomb* (the tomb); Alan Turing's wartime code-breaking and Enigma machines (the Boolean logic code that needs to be cracked in order to open the hatch).

Time And Relative Dimensions In Space "The Tomb of the Cybermen" was the third Cybermen story, but it's the one that established them as the go-to *Doctor Who* villains in the Troughton era, with no less than four appearances in three years. The Cybermen were conceived of by scientific adviser Kit Pedler (who co-wrote this story) after he was asked about his greatest fear as a doctor: that organ replacement would result in the gradual loss of humanity. Like the Daleks, the popularity of the Cybermen stemmed partly from the fact that they aren't just robots, but have an organic component, and partly because they reflected a present-day fear.

Adventures In Time And Space The Doctor references Victoria's father and Maxtible's attempts to build a time machine, from 1967's "The Evil of the Daleks," the previous story. The Cybermen recognize the Doctor from "the lunar surface," referencing 1967's "The Moonbase." They state that they had attacked the moon because the Doctor had destroyed their home planet, Mondas (in 1966's "The Tenth Planet"), and they were in danger of becoming extinct.

Who is the Doctor? The new Doctor is remarkably different from his predecessor. He's impish and clown-like, appearing cowardly and uncertain, until his moments of steel shine through. He's 450 years old, in Earth terms. (This is the only time his age is ever specified in context.) When everyone else needs anoraks due to the cold, he only needs a cloak. He talks for the first time about his family, but says he lets them sleep in his mind, suggesting that they're long dead. The Doctor is far from saintly in this story — he manipulates everyone from Klieg to Toberman, and even strong-arms Victoria into the tomb — but he does all these things while seeming goofy and avuncular. The deaths of several crewmembers are a direct result of his actions, as are those of any passersby who inadvertently get electrocuted from the death-trap doors he resets.

Companion Chronicles Victoria Waterfield joined the TARDIS crew in the previous adventure. She's in Victorian dress in the opening scene, but she changes into a dress that shows off much more of her legs than a Victorian lady would be used to. Surprisingly, she's an excellent shot, hitting a tiny Cybermat across the room on the first attempt. The Doctor's other companion, Scottish highlander Jamie McCrimmon from 1746, remains with this incarnation of the Doctor until his regeneration, making Jamie the longest-running companion in *Doctor Who* (in terms of total number of stories). And yes, he wears that kilt the entire time.

Monster of the Week The Cybermen did not die out years ago, as was believed, but found a new planet, Telos. They have a Cybercontroller, a much taller Cyberman, whose brain is partly visible through an opaque, vein-covered bulb on top of his head; unlike the other Cybermen, he has no chest unit. They also have Cybermats, small silverfish-like creatures, about the size of a hand. The Doctor says that these are a form of metallic life and they home in on human brainwaves.

Stand Up and Cheer The awakening of the Cybermen is magnificent. As the ice melts, the Cybermen slowly, almost agonizingly, come to life. Cutting through the plastic film that covers their individual capsules is weird, but effective. But the most brilliant aspect is the sound design: with a haunting theme and a combination of odd noise and unearthly scratching, the atmosphere is incredibly effective. And then the Cybercontroller emerges and says, "You belong to us. You will be like us." Cue cliffhanger . . . and an entire generation of terrified children.

Roll Your Eyes Captain Hopper's outrageous "Gee whiz" accent is something you can only marvel at in disbelief. It's easily the worst American accent in the entirety of *Doctor Who*. And we've seen "Daleks in Manhattan." He gets lines like "It's quiet . . . too quiet," "Some character has balled up the lot!" and "It's not exactly peaches back on the ship." There's a great drinking game to be had here. Actually, for his scenes, alcohol is absolutely essential.

You're Not Making Any Sense In the cliffhanger to episode three, Klieg shoots the Doctor at point-blank range. The Doctor only survives because Callum jumps in front of the gun. Two seconds later (in episode time, although a week has passed for the viewer), Klieg decides not to shoot the Doctor after all. So what the heck happened?

Interesting Trivia This story opens the fifth season of the Classic Series, which became known as "the monster season," as it featured monsters in every story but one, a litany of bases under siege and commanders with a shaky grasp on reality. This story only really features the monster aspect (although the tomb set does share some of the characteristics of the bases to follow, as one prominent location where almost all of the action takes place), but it also has the feel of an "event" story, the way season openers these days do (and it also follows the climactic season finale that was "The Evil of the Daleks"). While it's commonplace now, what we're seeing here is *Doctor Who's* first attempt at it. This is partly because the seasons had just been made shorter (running at 34 episodes a year, instead of 48 or so), and the production team was interested in streamlining the program this way.

We're not told much about the planet Telos, except that the Cybertomb is apparently an entire city, also called Telos. A later story, 1985's "Attack of the Cybermen," has Telos as the Cybermen's adopted home planet; its original inhabitants, the Cryons, have been almost totally destroyed. One thing we do learn here, upheld in the sequel as well, is that Telos is extremely cold, especially at night.

The foam coming out of the dead Cyberman in episode four was deemed too horrifying for children, and director Morris Barry had his knuckles rapped over it. Although it's just foam spurting out of a chest unit, what sets this moment apart from the violence elsewhere in the story is the biological nature of it. Like the Dalek mutant being glimpsed under a cloak in 1963's "The Daleks," it's the hint of a biological entity within the robotic shell that truly sells the horror of what these creatures are. The foam generator was a new device in the arsenal of the special effects team at the BBC; the next two seasons use it extensively.

After decades missing from the archives, this story was found in 1991 and rush-released on video (with an early example of an "extra" feature: a specially recorded introduction by director Morris Barry). It almost didn't happen, because Shirley Cooklin objected, but Equity negotiations stipulated that a single actor objection could not prevent a video release (unlike a writer objection, which could — and almost did for later stories written by Douglas Adams). "The Tomb of the Cybermen" went on to top the U.K. video charts for several weeks, the only release from the Classic Series that did.

If you have trouble understanding the Cybermen's electronic speech, don't worry, you're not alone. Voice actor Peter Hawkins was fitted with a special electronic device that sat under his palate (with electrical leads trailing out of his mouth; don't try this at home, kids!) and relayed the vibrations in his mouth when he spoke. While it created a disturbing sound, it wasn't so great for distinguishing different syllables. It was later discovered that Hawkins could make similar voices just as well on his own without the aid of electrical appliances in his mouth!

Unlike in the Hartnell era, the opening titles in (most of) the Troughton era stories feature the Doctor's face, a practice that was kept for the remainder of the Classic Series.

This was one of the stories that Matt Smith watched in preparation to play the eleventh Doctor — and it profoundly influenced how he approached the part. Steven Moffat's original conception of the eleventh Doctor was more of a hipster and a dashing young hero, dressed in a pirate-like jacket. However, Smith looked at Patrick Troughton's portrayal and decided he wanted to play it like an eccentric old professor in a jacket and bow tie. As a long-time fan of the Classic Series, Moffat could hardly protest.

The TARDIS Chronometer A quarry on the planet Telos. The Doctor says the Cybermen have been sleeping for five centuries and the Cybermen state that they invaded the moon because they needed the energy. The clear implication is that this is set five centuries after the events of "The Moonbase," so around 2570.

Oh My Giddy Aunt? (RS?) Out of the depths of improbability came the discovery that "The Tomb of the Cybermen" still existed. Long held up as the pinnacle of all that *Doctor Who* could hope to aspire to, there was no earthly way that it could live up to its reputation. Nothing could hope to achieve the heights of grandiosity that fan lore had placed upon this story, so —

Oh, forget all that. "The Tomb of the Cybermen" is really good.

Is it perfect? Of course not. But it mostly holds up really well. The single setting is very effective, the characters vivid, the delayed suspense about the Cybermen appearing is used to good effect — and when they finally do turn up, they're suitably imposing and given a great overseer in the Cybercontroller.

Patrick Troughton is incredible in his earliest surviving story. By turns devious, childlike, kind and ruthless, he makes his multi-faceted take on the character look easy, when it's anything but. Whether you're used to the Doctor as a wise old man (from watching Hartnell) or as a dashing hero (from the New Series), this take on the central character is unlike anything seen elsewhere. Even Matt Smith's oddball portrayal isn't like this, although you can see the antecedents.

The two companions work very well. Jamie is a solid right-hand man to Troughton's Doctor, as often providing the setup to jokes as he does the punchline. (Witness the Doctor saying, "Anyone who wants to leave should do so now" and Jamie walking away, to be followed by the Doctor saying, "Not you, Jamie.") Victoria is shoehorned into the role of the woman left behind, but she does get a great foil in Kaftan and acquits herself well. Oh, and the "sleep in my mind" scene is an absolute triumph.

All in all, this is a pretty excellent story. Not the be all and end all of what *Doctor Who* could ever achieve, but something very impressive in its own right . . .

Hang on, there's one small thing I need to mention. Something that gets in the way of enjoying this story. That's right, I'd like to talk about race. So hold onto your hats, because this isn't going to be pretty.

For all its dramatic strengths, this story is deeply and fundamentally flawed. Number one, all the good guys are white, while all the villains are not. This is not a good look. Number two, Shirley Cooklin is in blackface as Kaftan. Yes, blackface. And Number three, there's Toberman.

Ah yes, Toberman. Here we have the first major part in *Doctor Who* for a person of colour, and he's a) almost mute, b) a servant and c) defined entirely by his physical prowess. In fact, the very first line in the story proper, after the initial TARDIS scene, is someone telling Toberman how stupid he is.

Most of the time, he stands silently, except when he's called upon for a display of strength (opening the exterior doors) or to intimidate someone (and oh, how we're supposed to laugh when the Doctor backs away from his towering presence). To deal with Toberman, the Doctor addresses Kaftan. Toberman is fiercely devoted to her, despite being her servant, so much so that his grief over her death allows him to break his Cyberconditioning. And his only meaningful contributions to the story are through his strength: he hurls the Cybercontroller across a room, beats a Cyberman to a foamy death and makes the ultimate sacrifice in closing the doors.

This is pretty horrendous stuff. In an earlier version of the script, the character was going to be deaf, to make a point about the nature of body replacements and disability, which is partly why he has so few lines. That would have at least provided some context.

The worst of it is just how limited the thinking is. This story is set more than 500 years in the future, yet the writers didn't conceive of a role for a black man that's anything other than somebody's mute servant. Viewed today, when there's a black president of the United States, a mere 45 years after it was written, this is hard to stomach.

In the end, "The Tomb of the Cybermen" is a great piece of drama, with some very questionable aspects. It might appear to be of its time, but that's also its tragedy, in so many ways.

Second Opinion (GB) While I agree this is a story that should be watched, I vacillate in my opinions regarding "The Tomb of the Cybermen." There was a time in my life when I thought it was the greatest Cybermen story ever and the jewel in the crown of Patrick Troughton's tenure as the Doctor. Now I'm not so sure.

It's a story where, bizarrely, the fancy restoration work done to *Doctor Who* for the DVDs might have done it a disservice. When you see it fully cleaned up with the video look Auntie Beeb originally intended, "The Tomb of the Cybermen" looks kind of cheap and nasty and dated. George Roubicek's American accent should be put in a museum of dialect badness; Shirley Cooklin's swarthy, Middle Eastern–type is something out of panto; Roy Stewart's grunting stereotype is really embarrassing because you can see moments when Stewart genuinely tries for pathos only to be swept away in what was expected of him.

It doesn't help that, honestly, the plot of "Tomb" could be written on the head of a pin with room for a host of Cybermats: Cybermen are entombed. Then released. Then entombed. Then released. Rinse, repeat. This story could have been resolved by episode two.

And yet, "The Tomb of the Cybermen" is saved by lots of brilliant little moments, like the Doctor and Victoria talking about their respective families — a rare moment of looking back on previous *Doctor Who* stories, an even rarer look at the Doctor and his family, and a tender character moment all rolled into one. Or the ways Kit Pedler and Gerry Davis try to prevent ennui by writing in a Cybermat invasion, and intrigue with Kaftan and Klieg.

But the real revelations are in two performances. Victoria is one of those characters best understood as someone who really doesn't want this lifestyle of danger and terror, but is stuck with it because the Doctor has adopted her. To be sure, she's the original screamer, but she's also unbelievably shrewd: one of the delights of watching "Tomb" is seeing her outsmart Kaftan multiple times (using her screaming!) and dryly putting down Hopper at every opportunity. Deborah Watling doesn't get enough credit for pulling all that off. And George Pastell is delightfully loopy and maniacal as Eric Klieg. Klieg is a character who never, ever loses his delusion that he's the smartest man in the room. It could have been a one-note portrayal, but Pastell is great in adding a sense of desperation as Klieg holds on to his delusions even when he's been given multiple reality checks. Troughton, Watling and Pastell (and to a lesser extent Frazer Hines) make this story work. The rest? Not really.

They say the devil is in the details. "The Tomb of the Cybermen" is proof that *Doctor Who* is in there too. Take away the great moments and three great performances, and what's left is a pantomime of a story that hasn't dated well. But thankfully those things are there. It's a classic, but only just.

The Psychic Papers: The Missing Episodes

Between the start of the William Hartnell era on November 23, 1963, and the end of the Patrick Troughton era on June 21, 1969, 253 episodes of *Doctor Who* were broadcast. Of those episodes broadcast, only 147 episodes are in the BBC Archives. That means 106 episodes, a whopping 42% of those made in the 1960s, are missing — including William Hartnell's final episode, Patrick Troughton's first story, the debut story of Brigadier

Lethbridge-Stewart and popular stories featuring the Daleks and Cybermen.

So what happened?

Episodes of *Doctor Who* were originally shot and broadcast on video-tape. Videotapes were expensive and took up a lot of space in the BBC engineering department. General practice was to wipe the tape as soon as it was practical to do so. By the mid-1970s, no 1960s *Doctor Who* existed on videotape.

However, *Doctor Who* was sold by the BBC to foreign countries for broadcast, along with its other programs. In order to avoid dealing with the various standards for broadcast from country to country, BBC Enterprises (now known as BBC Worldwide) arranged to have 16mm black and white film prints made of the videotaped episodes and distributed those to ter-ritories abroad. The early William Hartnell episodes had a wide distribution to 34 countries. The number of purchasers waned to just seven countries by the end of the Troughton era.

As the 1970s progressed, the commercial viability of old *Doctor Who* decreased, as there was less and less foreign-sales interest in black and white television from the 1960s. (Furthermore, the necessary rights and clearances for foreign sales were beginning to lapse.) Domestic home video was a con-cept not even yet thought of in science fiction. The British actors' union, Equity, had severe strictures on how many programs could be repeated during the course of a year on British television (which changed in the 1980s as the concept of residuals came into play). In short, there was no market for these old episodes. There was little space for storing them — worsened by a turf war where the BBC Film Library refused to hold materials not made on film — and there was a shocking lack of interest in keeping the material heritage of British television. A few episodes were consigned to the British Film Institute for historical interest, and the order came for the episodes to be "withdrawn, deaccessioned and junked" from the archival holdings: the film cans were pulled from the shelves and consigned to landfill.

Doctor Who probably would not have had more than a handful of epi-sodes to show from the 1960s were it not for Ian Levine. Levine, a record producer and diehard fan, wanted copies of the episodes from the 1960s he had watched as a boy, and he was in talks with the BBC to obtain those fea-turing William Hartnell and Patrick Troughton. (Levine was prepared to pay the astronomical sums required for them, and had even finessed a special release with Equity.) Levine was shocked one day in 1978 when he arrived at the BBC Film Library, armed with contracts to purchase episodes, only to find several old *Doctor Who* episodes in a pile on a skip, ready for junking. Included in this skip was the very first Dalek story from 1963, "The Daleks."

Levine worked quickly to get a moratorium put on junking episodes, saving "The Daleks," and the Film Library had its mandate expanded to include videotaped material. Eventually, an audit was done of the various repositories, including the Film Library, the videotape collection, the British Film Institute and BBC Enterprises, and 152 episodes — well over half the output of the 1960s — were missing. Individual episodes and only a handful of complete stories were missing from the Hartnell era, thanks to the greater number of countries the series had reached. The Troughton stories, distributed to fewer countries, were missing almost entire seasons. (Colour versions of several Jon Pertwee stories from the early 1970s were also missing from the archives, although black and white prints were retained.)

By the 1980s, the BBC, along with fans like Levine, mobilized in a search to find missing episodes, contacting foreign broadcasters and film collectors alike. Over the next 30 years, episodes were returned from disparate places, including Australia, Nigeria and Cyprus. Film collectors in Britain and New Zealand turned in episodes. Former BBC engineers returned the film cans they had been ordered to dispose of at work but had taken home instead. Members of a Latter Day Saints church operating on a former BBC property found they had two episodes in their basement! Most of these findings were of single episodes; these finds sometimes completed stories with gaps in them.

Probably the most celebrated find was in 1991 when ATV in Hong Kong informed the BBC that it was returning several episodes of *Doctor Who*, presumably in response to the BBC's appeal to foreign broadcasters several years earlier. These turned out to be all four episodes of "The Tomb of the Cybermen," the only complete story fully missing from the archive ever to be returned. ATV broadcast the episodes in Hong Kong in June and July 1970 and had held on to them ever since. The arrival of "The Tomb of the Cybermen" increased the number of complete Patrick Troughton stories to a grand total of six.

The missing stories are not completely lost, however. In the 1960s, *Doctor Who* fans who were early adopters of technology audio-recorded episodes using reel-to-reel tape recorders. (Some fans were very inventive in how they did this, even hooking up the tape recorder direct to the audio output wires inside the TV set to avoid having to keep the room silent while watching!) There are at least three sources of off-air recordings of 1960s stories; between them, there are audio-recordings of every single episode of *Doctor Who*. The sound has been cleaned up and the stories made available to purchase as part of the BBC's AudioGo label, with linking narration by *Doctor Who* actors.

There is even a partial visual record. In the 1950s and 1960s, a photographer named John Cura offered a service he called "Tele-snaps," where he took pictures of television programs during broadcast, largely to sell the pictures to television producers and directors. A large number of 1960s *Doctor Who* serials were photographed by Cura, providing what are essentially 80 or so screen-grabs per episode. Clips from *Who* that appeared in other programs (such as the children's series *Blue Peter*), film rushes and censored trims from foreign broadcasters also add to the visual record. Another more unusual source of material was provided by an anonymous fan in Australia, who had 8mm footage (from filming his TV set) of several key scenes from the Hartnell and Troughton eras, notably William Hartnell's final scenes as the Doctor in "The Tenth Planet" (1966).

In 2004, all of the rediscovered individual episodes were released on the compilation DVD set *Lost in Time*. There are several almost-complete stories, missing one or two episodes, and these are being released with animated versions of the missing episodes, using the original off-air soundtrack. Even today, missing episodes are being found. In December 2011, a single episode each from "Galaxy 4" (1965) and "The Underwater Menace" (1967) were returned by a film collector who had purchased them (along with other films) sometime in the 1980s at a school fête. At the time of writing, there are rumours that the most exhaustive missing episode search ever is underway and there may be even bigger finds to come. Who knows what else still may be out there?

· ·

The Mind Robber (1968)

Written by Peter Ling, Derrick Sherwin (uncredited)

Directed by David Maloney

Featuring Patrick Troughton (Doctor Who), Frazer Hines (Jamie), Hamish Wilson (Jamie), Wendy Padbury (Zoe)

Supporting cast Emrys Jones (The Master), Bernard Horsfall (Gulliver), Christopher Robbie (The Karkus), Sue Pulford (The Medusa), Christine Pirie (Princess Rapunzel), John Greenwood (D'Artagnan/Sir Lancelot), David Cannon (Cyrano), Gerry Wain (Blackbeard)

Original airdates September 14, 21, 28, October 5, 12, 1968

The Big Idea To escape destruction by a lava flow, the TARDIS moves outside time and space, eventually arriving in a place where fictional characters live.

Roots and References The 1966 *Batman* TV series (the Karkus); *The Nutcracker* (the clockwork soldiers). In the Land of Fiction, the Doctor, Jamie and Zoe meet Lemuel Gulliver from Jonathan Swift's *Gulliver's Travels*; Rapunzel; schoolchildren similar to the ones from E. Nesbit's books; and mythical creatures such as the unicorn, the Minotaur and Medusa. Inside the castle, Jamie looks at a page from *Treasure Island* and listens to a passage from Louisa May Alcott's *Little Women*; the filing cabinets there include William Makepeace Thackeray's *Vanity Fair*, Edgar Allen Poe's "The Pit and the Pendulum," Cervantes's *Don Quixote*, Arthur Ransom's 1930 novel *Swallows and Amazons* and Charles Dickens's *Martin Chuzzlewit*. Jamie and Zoe are trapped in a French book of animal fables, *Scènes de la Vie Privée et Publique des Animaux* (in a chapter that translates to "A Fox Is Caught in a Trap"!). The final battle features Cyrano de Bergerac, D'Artagnan, Blackbeard and Sir Lancelot. The Master of the Land of Fiction is a writer for the *Boys' Own*–esque children's magazine *The Ensign*; his greatest creation is Captain Jack Harkaway, who was actually a character in the magazine *Boys of England*, introduced in 1871.

Time And Relative Dimensions In Space You have to really pity *Doctor Who* script editor Derrick Sherwin, who suffered several bad weeks during the making of this story. The scripts by Sherwin's former colleague from the British soap *Crossroads*, Peter Ling — with the tantalizing premise of "where does all fiction eventually wind up?" — were working out (a rarity during this season), but the story immediately before it, 1968's "The Dominators," had developed problems (including a falling-out between the production team and writers). That story needed to be shortened by an episode, adding an episode to Ling's story. However, "The Mind Robber" pretty much had its story locked in; furthermore, its budgetary allocation had already been spent in realizing Ling's ambitious script.

Sherwin was left with no choice but to write an episode-long prologue to Ling's story himself. He had no budget for additional speaking parts and no sets other than those of the TARDIS and the studio's all-white cyclorama. Sherwin discovered some disused robot costumes, originally made for a 1967 episode of the BBC science-fiction anthology series *Out of the Unknown*, which allowed him something to work with. He wrote the prologue, which became the first episode of "The Mind Robber" (the only *Doctor Who* episode broadcast without a writer credit), under the limitations of what he had on hand to produce it.

But Sherwin's problems were far from over. Already frustrated by his workload (and soon to quit over it), Patrick Troughton threatened revolt when he found out the three lead actors alone would have to carry the first episode. Consequently, the individual episodes were shortened, some by as many as five or six minutes. (Episode five bears the shortest running time of any episode in the history of *Doctor Who*, at 18 minutes.) Even with that straightened out, episode two, the first of Ling's script, ran into trouble straight away when actor Frazer Hines came down with chicken pox. The Land of Fiction's fantasy setting fortunately allowed the part to be temporarily recast. On short notice, actor Hamish Wilson was called in and a scene was hastily added to explain Jamie's new face.

Adventures in Time and Space The story follows from the cliffhanger at the end of "The Dominators" where the TARDIS was about to be buried under the lava created in the wake of the detonation of one of the Dominators' seed devices. The TARDIS's fluid links ("The Daleks") start boiling, creating mercury vapour (as it had done in 1968's "The Wheel in Space"). Jamie mentions to Rapunzel that his father was a piper (1966's "The Highlanders").

Who is the Doctor? The Doctor has clearly read a great deal of classical Earth literature; he knows myths and legends and can even recite *Gulliver's Travels* by heart. He's been to the year 2000, but apparently he doesn't read the comics sections of newspapers. Pity.

Companion Chronicles Zoe Heriot is a parapsychology librarian from the far future of the 21st century. She's a genius and would like to think herself the Doctor's equal, though this aspect toned down as she travelled with him. She's still quite impressed when she has the opportunity to show the Doctor up, such as when she remembers Jamie's face.

Monster of the Week The clockwork soldiers are robots that look like windup toy soldiers, only they're full-sized and have a camera mounted in their hats. They, along with the white robots, are controlled by the Master (of the Land of Fiction; he's not the evil Time Lord we'll meet later in the series).

Stand Up and Cheer The Doctor's defeat of Medusa is an exciting moment in the story (with some great Harryhausen-esque stop-motion animation). It becomes something stranger, and altogether post-modern, when Jamie reads about those events in the castle, revealing that the encounter with the Medusa is an attempt to turn the Doctor and Zoe into fiction. All this draws attention to the fact that Jamie, Zoe and the Doctor are (meta)fictional characters. It's an attempt to make fiction within a fiction, which illustrates how different and unusual this story is from anything that came before. Or indeed after.

Roll Your Eyes During episode four, actor Emrys James has a piece of spittle sticking to the corner of his mouth that is both gross and highly distracting.

You're Not Making Any Sense The Land of Fiction, it turns out, is controlled by a computer that intends to use humanity's imagination against them and render them all fictitious, leaving Earth uninhabited. Leaving aside the fact that it seems a rather ridiculous and needlessly overcomplicated use of such incredible power, there's a more basic question: who created the computer in the first place?

Interesting Trivia The whole story is predicated on an unusual premise: when you write about events after they've happened, it's history. If you write about them before they've happened, it's fiction. And when you write about fictional events, where do they happen, and where does fiction actually go when it's created? It's a charming idea. But what is the Land of Fiction? Is it another dimensional plane? A shared psychic space? There's no clear answer given.

In fact, the first episode of the following story, 1968's "The Invasion," picks up precisely where this leaves off (even starting with this story's final scene of the TARDIS reassembling). However, no one mentions anything that happened, there's no sign of the Master in the TARDIS and no mention of where he went nor any mention of the Land of Fiction. (They just continue on to their next port of call on the dark side of the moon). Which means either the Master disappeared when they did and was returned to his own time — a fact that no one feels the need to comment on — or else "The Mind Robber" may have been some sort of dream.

Gulliver's dialogue is supposed to be comprised of passages from *Gulliver's Travels*; in actuality, Peter Ling made up more and more material as the story progressed. Gulliver speaks about the Yahoos, the base humans he met when he was in the kingdom of the Houyhnhnms (a race of highly intelligent horses that Gulliver regarded as creatures of perfection) from book IV, but his dialogue is mostly from earlier in the book. One advantage to using Gulliver was that, as Swift's book was written in 1726, there weren't copyright issues to work around. At one stage, the script included characters like Zorro, but copyright prevented that from being realized onscreen.

The TARDIS Chronometer The Land of Fiction, outside time and space.

Oh My Giddy Aunt? (GB) For this story, we have the rare honour of having a special guest join me to review "The Mind Robber." Ladies, gentlemen and various multiforms, would you please welcome, direct from the Land of Fiction, Lemuel Gulliver.

"I am content to gratify the curious reader with some general ideas."

Well, thank you, Gulliver. Perhaps we could start by talking about what it was like to be in a story like "The Mind Robber" and work with the Doctor, Jamie and Zoe?

"It would not be proper, for some reasons, to trouble the reader with the particulars of our adventures."

Well, that's understandable and I applaud your desire to be circumspect. However, if I may be so bold, Gulliver, I must say that "The Mind Robber" is an example of *Doctor Who* at its most versatile and creative. The first episode is stunning almost because of all the creative challenges rather than in spite of them. For a story set on a dream world where the residents of fiction wind up, Derrick Sherwin's transitional first episode in a white void is such a perfect beginning you can't imagine the story any other way. I guess what I would ask is how do you feel the remaining episodes went, Gulliver?

"I know very well, how little reputation is to be got by writings which require neither genius nor learning, nor indeed any other talent. This may perhaps pass with the reader rather for an European or English story, than for one of a country so remote."

I see your point. Part of the charm of "The Mind Robber" is that it is so very erudite. The idea that fiction ends up in a strange land populated by a forest of words and literary characters is really clever. In a story full of outrageous, even camp, moments, one wonderful thing about it is that it's so straitlaced and natural. The strange and fantastic become even more dramatic.

"The Mind Robber" subsists on the surreal nature of the place, and a series of puns and cameos from literary characters. (Though not nearly enough. What about Hamlet? What about Robin Hood?) When the actual plot arrives, it seems like a half-hearted capitulation: a computer wants to render humanity into fiction and has chosen the Doctor to be its host. But there's no explanation.

"A strange effect of narrow principles and short views!"

Oi! Steady on there, Gulliver.

"Why nature should teach us to conceal what nature had given. This resolution perhaps may appear very bold and dangerous."

My point exactly. This is *Doctor Who* attempting to be pure fantasy: a story with its own dream-like logic. There's a swirl of images (Jamie standing atop the forest of words, Medusa stretching out towards Zoe) and riddles. None of the whys or hows are explained, but does it matter? The story doesn't so much progress as it follows things through to an inevitable if slightly incomprehensible solution.

"It is a truth much beheld by all that much of 1960s British genre TV contained surreal episodes that ended with things blowing up. Have you not experienced the delights of *The Prisoner*?"

What did you just say, Gulliver?

"This I mention as an instance of the great power of habit and prejudice."

Oh, okay. Are you sure you don't want to say something about what happened during the making of "The Mind Robber"?

"They would often strip me naked from top to toe, and lay me at full length in their bosoms . . ."

And I think we're out of time. Thanks so much, Gulliver.

Second Opinion (RS?)

Freeze Gulliver's words, he doesn't exist.

(Sorry, co-author, I couldn't resist.)

This story's fine plot, prepared by two cooks

Is something quite odd; it's all about books!

Episode one gives us nothing but white

Sure Zoe screams — but her catsuit is tight.

They're making it up as they go along

On thruppence, four droids, a wing and a song.

The land is a place where fiction is real

Where riddles play tricks and soldiers reveal

The plot to the Master (no, not that one).

He's a writer of tales; don't jump the gun.
The trees are plastic, like props of the time
But that's the whole point; they're part of the rhyme.
Rapunzel has hair that falls to the ground
Lucky for him, that's where Jamie is found.
Medusa has snakes made from stop-motion
Scotched by a mirror; what a fine notion.
The Karkus appears, Zoe's trapped in a jar
Minotaurs, swordsmen . . . How very bizarre!
If told today, it would feature a host
Of actors from movies, or TV at most
Like Buffy or Batman or good Captain Jack.
(Well, actually, kind of; this story's on crack!)
This is much wilder, a tale about words
Hugely delightful, for library nerds.
The Doctor explains, "It's fiction, my dear"
Postmodern Zoe: "Then why are we here?"
When Frazer's replaced (a case of the pox)
The show carries on; it's out of the box!
Hamish impresses, but how very mad
That Jamie's just swapped for some other lad.
The Doctor and Z return to the cave
Not filmed but read out; it's so very brave.
The ending is quick: the actors just fade
The credits roll once the TARDIS is made.
There's no final scene we all get to see
These cuts are so fast for '60s TV.
It's madness, bonkers, completely insane
Self-referential, for fictional gain.
Not just old-fashioned, the form is quite new
Cam'ras are looked at and so I'll review
This tale in the style of Shakespeare's iamb
Because hey, why not? At least it's not spam.

Patrick Troughton

Born in Mill Hill, Middlesex, in 1920, Patrick Troughton began acting on stage while still in school. Troughton's emerging career was interrupted by World War II; he joined the navy and survived the sinking of his vessel, winning a medal for bravery in the process (it was the second such disaster for him; he survived an earlier sinking in the first few days of the war while still a civilian). After the war, Troughton resumed his career, moving to films with a small part in Laurence Olivier's *Hamlet* (1948). But it was on television that Troughton really made his mark. He was in demand as a character actor throughout the 1950s; in 1953, he was the first person to portray Robin Hood on TV.

Troughton was approached to play the Doctor while he was working on the film *The Viking Queen* (1967). He was initially hesitant because his children were fans of *Doctor Who* and he didn't see how he could replicate William Hartnell's performance. Troughton's initial reimaginings of the role were to appear in blackface wearing a turban, or as a grizzled windjammer sea captain, before deciding upon a Chaplin-esque tramp as his inspiration (a "cosmic hobo," according to Sydney Newman).

Doctor Who was his only lead role in a television series. After *Who*, he went back to appearing in episodic television, miniseries and film (1976's *The Omen* is probably his most widely known work outside of the U.K.). He returned to play the Doctor in 1972's "The Three Doctors," 1983's "The Five Doctors" and 1985's "The Two Doctors."

Troughton was a private man who gave very few interviews. It was later revealed that, for much of the 1960s and 1970s, he was maintaining the fiction (for his mother's benefit) that he was still married, while he was actually in a common-law relationship with another woman. At *Doctor Who* conventions, he tended to wear his costume and acted (somewhat) in character as the Doctor while answering questions. It was at an American *Doctor Who* convention in Columbus, Georgia, that Troughton died of a heart attack on March 28, 1987.

The War Games (1969)

Written by Terrance Dicks and Malcolm Hulke **Directed by** David Maloney

Featuring Patrick Troughton (Doctor Who), Frazer Hines (Jamie), Wendy Padbury (Zoe)

Supporting cast David Savile (Lt. Carstairs); Jane Sherwin (Lady Jennifer); Noel Coleman (General Smythe); Richard Steele (Commandant Gorton); Terence Bayler (Major Barrington); Hubert Rees (Captain Ransome); David Valla (Lt. Crane); Esmond Webb (Sgt. Major Burns); Brian Forster (Sgt. Willis); David Garfield (Von Wiech); Gregg Palmer (Lt. Lucke); Philip Madoc (War Lord); Edward Brayshaw (War Chief); James Bree (Security Chief); Vernon Dobtcheff (Chief Scientist); Bill Hutchinson (Sgt. Thompson); Terry Adams 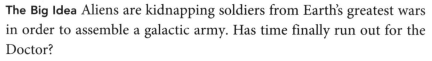 (Cpl. Riley); Leslie Schofield (Leroy); Rudolph Walker (Harper); Michael Lynch (Spencer); Graham Weston (Russell); David Troughton (Moor); Peter Craze (Du Pont); Michael Napier-Brown (Arturo Villar); Stephen Hubay (Petrov); Bernard Horsfall, Trevor Martin, Clyde Pollitt (Time Lords); Clare Jenkins (Tanya Lernov)

Original airdates April 19, 26, May 3, 10, 17, 24, 31, June 7, 14, 21, 1969

The Big Idea Aliens are kidnapping soldiers from Earth's greatest wars in order to assemble a galactic army. Has time finally run out for the Doctor?

Roots and References Literature about World War I, particularly Erich Maria Remarque's *All Quiet on the Western Front* (the initial setting, carrying on fighting a war without remembering why you're doing so and a superior class using troops for their own games); the Nuremberg trials (making sense of the aftermath, the War Lord rejecting the validity of the Time Lords' court); Greek mythology (God-like beings living among humans and playing games with their fate).

Time And Relative Dimensions In Space *Doctor Who*'s sixth season was in flux. One story lost an episode (1968's "The Dominators") while another had one added ("The Mind Robber"). Planned stories fell through at the scripting stage, necessitating last-minute replacements (1968's "The Krotons"). As the season neared its end, pretty much everyone associated with the show, both onscreen and off, decided to leave. A six-part and a four-part story were planned to close out the season, but both fell through. A ten-part replacement was written at the last minute and taped a mere two weeks before broadcast. "The War Games" was the result.

Malcolm Hulke had previously co-written 1967's "The Faceless Ones," while Terrance Dicks was the incoming script editor (he was an assistant script editor on this season). As they lived near each other and were fast typists, they were able to turn the scripts around relatively quickly.

Producer Derrick Sherwin decided that the Doctor's people should be introduced and that they were to be called the Time Lords. Until this point, we'd only met one of the Doctor's people (the Meddling Monk, seen in "The Time Meddler" and "The Daleks' Master Plan," both 1965). The Doctor's exile to twentieth-century Earth at the end of this story sets the stage for the next several years of *Doctor Who*.

Adventures in Time and Space At the Doctor's trial, he shows images of monsters he's faced in his era: Quarks (1968's "The Dominators"), the Yeti (1967's "The Abominable Snowmen" and "The Web of Fear"), the Ice Warriors (1967's story of the same title, 1969's "The Seeds of Death"), Cybermen (1967's "The Moonbase" and "The Tomb of the Cybermen," 1968's "The Wheel in Space") and Daleks (1967's "The Evil of the Daleks"). Footage of the TARDIS landing on the sea (1968's "Fury From the Deep") or in space engulfed in cobwebs (1968's "The Web of Fear") is reused, but presented as new. Jamie is returned to his own time (and dons his original costume from 1966's "The Highlanders") and Zoe is as well (1968's "The Wheel in Space"; a set from that story is rebuilt and Clare Jenkins reprises her role as Tanya).

Who is the Doctor? For some reason, he can't speak French, despite being able to speak most other languages in the universe. Including Spanish, as he does when talking to Arturo Villar later in the story. In the first episode, he briefly kisses Zoe on the forehead before being taken to the cells; this is unusual behaviour for the Classic Series Doctor, who rarely kisses anyone.

We finally learn the reason he left his home planet and went on the run: because he was bored and wanted to travel. He carries pieces of a white cube with him that can be used to contact the Time Lords.

Companion Chronicles Zoe is familiar with World War I, knowing that it took place in the early twentieth century. At the story's conclusion, she's returned to the Wheel, with memories of the Doctor and Jamie only from the events of her debut story and a lingering sense of having forgotten something.

Jamie's reaction to a redcoat (his sworn enemy) is one of immediate compassion, showing how far he's come. In a clever move, he pretends to fight with the redcoat, but they're actually cooperating to overpower the guards. At the story's conclusion, he's returned to the Highlands (with only the briefest memory of the Doctor) and is shot at by that same redcoat, whom he pursues, knife in hand.

Monster of the Week No actual monsters in the final story of the 1960s, but there are villains. In fact, in the final episode, there are two. The first, the ones running the war games, are simply called "aliens." They have no names, only titles, and plan to take over the galaxy. The second — and much more terrifying — are the Time Lords, the Doctor's people. They are immensely civilized, but also immensely powerful, dematerializing people (so that they never existed), remote-controlling the TARDIS and imprisoning planets in perpetuity. They can live forever (barring accidents) and have the secret of space-time travel, but are content to observe and gather knowledge.

Stand Up and Cheer When placed on trial by his own people, the Doctor's defence is passionate, showing a slideshow of monsters and arguing that his "crimes" are entirely justified because he did good. He challenges the very core of the Time Lords' policy of non-interference, forcing them to rethink their attitudes.

Roll Your Eyes The bitch-fest between the War Chief and the Security Chief is one long eye roll. They appear to be having some sort of marital dispute, culminating in the ridiculous "What a stupid fool you are"/"What a stupid fool YOU are!" exchange.

You're Not Making Any Sense The aliens use human wars to find the most disciplined and courageous fighters for their galactic army, but wars aren't natural selection. You can be as disciplined and courageous as the next man, but if you catch a stray bullet from a machine gun, you're not going to be joining the aliens' galaxy-conquering army any time soon.

Interesting Trivia The aliens do not cherry-pick from wars later than 1917, as greater technological knowledge would be dangerous. This detail was probably added to avoid World War II, still fresh in everyone's minds; featuring such a recent conflict would have been in poor taste. That said, the opening titles — featuring bombs and machine guns with the title cards in flashes — do seem very reminiscent of World War II.

The trench scenes were shot on a location near a rubbish tip. The location didn't impress Patrick Troughton, who saw a rat and threatened to quit on the spot if he saw any more (he'd had rat-shooting duties in the war); given their filming location, there were likely hundreds nearby!

If you're familiar with the sonic screwdriver from the New Series or even the colour era of the Classic Series, you might be in for a bit of a shock. The sonic screwdriver had made its debut at the end of the previous season and is seen quite clearly here. Instead of the elongated tool with bits on it that we're used to, Troughton's sonic screwdriver is just a plain cylinder with a large light at one end, rather like a laser pointer. He also holds it in a fist, rather than between his fingers and thumb, as later Doctors do.

The revelation that the Doctor is a Time Lord caps off six years' worth of hints about the nature of the Doctor. We knew from "An Unearthly Child" that the Doctor comes from "another time, another world" and he was "cut off" from his own people. "The Daleks" revealed he had spent time as a pioneer, suggesting that perhaps he'd been a colonist on another world. The Doctor mused about returning to his home planet in "The Massacre" (1966) but concluded emphatically, "I can't." The Doctor's alien nature emerged after his first regeneration in 1966's "The Tenth Planet" (though this was portrayed as a "renewal") and in the discussion of his age in "The Tomb of the Cybermen." Now we know his race, though we don't know the name of his home planet. (That is revealed in 1973's "The Time Warrior.")

You might notice that this is a regeneration story without an onscreen regeneration. There's a very good reason for that: at the time of filming, Jon Pertwee hadn't been cast. As a result, this is the only Classic Series changeover we don't witness. The new casting was unveiled to the press only four days before the screening of episode ten of this story, something hard to imagine happening today.

The TARDIS Chronometer An alien planet and the various war zones contained within. When fleeing from the Time Lords, the TARDIS makes quick jumps, landing on the sea, in outer space, in a pit of alligators and finally on the home planet of the Time Lords.

Oh My Giddy Aunt? (RS?) The problem with being a long-time *Doctor Who* fan is that the show starts to become an anthology series. With so much of it, you dip in and out, sampling some eras more than others or finding niches to study. Even if you do contemplate a watch-through from the beginning, there's that intractable problem of 106 missing episodes to deal with.

But if you can do "the pilgrimage" (as we like to call it), or at least a close approximation of it — such as the one we've helpfully outlined in this book — then you're in a much better position to appreciate "The War Games" than if you viewed it in isolation. Seen as the culmination of a mystery six years in the making, it's utterly superb.

What really makes this work is the slow burn of the narrative. Only the first episode plays its cards too quickly: imagine how much more effective the story would have been if the first episode had contained no explicit science-fiction elements at all, instead fooling the viewer into thinking this was an historical story set in the trenches of the Great War. Instead, we have view-screens and hypnosis, so that viewers are reassured that Something Is Going On. Historical stories had become not just passé but apparently unexploded storytelling devices, which must be disposed of immediately.

That said, the first episode is otherwise just about perfect, leading us into the mystery with aplomb. The episode is quite brutal: within minutes, Jamie cuts himself on barbed wire; the TARDIS crew is shelled and then captured by Germans; subsequent refuge in the Allied trenches leads to a death sentence based on no evidence; and the episode ends with the Doctor in front of a firing squad. *Doctor Who* will rarely be this grim again. The missing memories of the soldiers are a great hook and, cleverly, the Doctor is put on trial in a kangaroo court, foreshadowing where the story eventually ends up.

The middle episodes have been criticized as a lot of running around, being captured and escaping. Which is true as far as it goes, but what gets forgotten is just how exciting these are! The cliffhangers are especially effective; this is quite a feat, given how many of them we get.

Best of all though is just how subtle the clues are about what's really going on. Hearing the TARDIS materialization sound in episode two is really shocking. It's followed by the appearance of a box — later called a SIDRAT, which is TARDIS backwards — in a corner where there was previously nothing. This is edge-of-the-seat stuff.

What's nice is that the nature of the SIDRATs isn't overdone. We figure out that they're bigger on the inside because they hold so many soldiers, not because someone exclaims it in shock. The Doctor is genuinely thrown by the appearance of the SIDRAT, trailing off and becoming distant, in contrast to his usual manner. And he's evasive about just how he's able to operate them so easily.

And then the Doctor recognizes — and is recognized by — the War Chief.

This is an astonishing moment, because it's when you realize that, for once, this is personal. The Doctor is someone who has no name, no backstory and is always jumping in and out of situations — and suddenly all his chickens are coming home to roost.

From there, it all spirals out. The first-ever mention of the Time Lords is in a throwaway line by a man with his back to us, where we're casually told these are the War Chief's people (in a conversation during which neither the Doctor nor the War Chief are present), almost daring us to put the pieces together. And the Time Lords as a threat have been built up by other characters over several episodes. The terror on the War Chief's face when the Doctor threatens to call them in speaks volumes, while the War Lord taunts the Doctor by suggesting he'll wish he'd been shot in the back when the Time Lords finally catch up with him.

And then they do. Suddenly, the Doctor has nowhere to run and nowhere to hide. Even before we see them, they're able to impose force fields, control the TARDIS and find the Doctor wherever he runs.

As a result of all this buildup, episode ten is a tour de force. The War Lord has spent three episodes being icily calm in his villainy, so when he screams in pain — as the result of a mere glance from one of the Time Lords — we realize just how powerful the Doctor's people are. And they completely annihilate the War Lord: his planet is imprisoned in perpetuity and he himself is retroactively erased from existence.

You do not mess with these people.

Then it's the Doctor's turn. Placed on trial by beings even more powerful than those we've spent nine episodes watching, all he can do is plead morality. That he succeeds in changing their minds feels less like a response to his triumphant argument than that he happened to catch them in a benevolent mood. However, this benevolence nevertheless results in exile, forced regeneration and the loss of his friends.

The final goodbyes to Jamie and Zoe are thus very moving. Jamie's still in denial about escaping from all this, but it's all the Doctor can do to have a fond farewell to his two friends. Their subsequent fate

— losing all memories of him except for their first encounter — is surprisingly brutal, in part because we actually witness it.

And so the '60s — and the black and white era — draws to a close. It's as resoundingly gratifying a close as you could possibly imagine, finishing a chapter in the Doctor's life in preparation for the next one. "The War Games" isn't just a rollicking *Doctor Who* adventure; it's a triumph of storytelling that provides an incredibly satisfying answer to the show's central mystery. The series will never be the same again.

Second Opinion (GB) I still remember with absolute clarity the first time I saw "The War Games." It was July 1987. I was 17 years old. At the time, *Doctor Who* was being shown as edited movies on the local PBS station, WNED Buffalo, on Saturday afternoons.

By late June, we were at the Patrick Troughton episodes. Unfortunately, I was often away from home and I was reliant on the Burk family VCR to tape the episodes. It came equipped with a timer, but it was the days before complex remotes; you had to program the timer using three buttons on the VCR. It was a process so complex that today I remember it better than the Apostles' Creed: press "program"; press "set check" until the day of the week was set, then press "enter." You repeated the process for the hour, the minute, then the channel. When all that was done, you pressed the big "TIMER" button on the bottom left of VCR.

WNED showed "The War Games" in two installments. During the first, I was at a pool party, but I successfully program/set-check/entered my way into being able to watch it later. It was glorious. I loved David Maloney's direction; how it looked and felt more like 1970s *Doctor Who* than the program it started out as in 1963. I adored the pop-art design of the alien headquarters (which included weather balloons!). I found the pace surprisingly fast for a ten-part story and loved the variety of set pieces that showcased Patrick Troughton's Doctor.

But I was going on a camping trip with my church youth group the following weekend. (I hated my church youth group, which was a microcosm of my high school). Before I left, I programmed the VCR to record *Doctor Who*. Pressed the big "TIMER" button. Goodbye.

While I was away, my mom and dad rented a video. They turned off the timer, watched *Out of Africa*, put my tape back in — and forgot to press "TIMER" again.

Three insufferable days later, I came home to watch the final episodes of "The War Games," the episodes that revealed the true nature of the Doctor and gave us the first appearance of the Time Lords. And found myself denied.

Bitter was my sorrow.

I wouldn't see the rest of "The War Games" until it came out on VHS in January 1992. By this time, I was a university student living in Toronto; I went to Sam the Record Man on Yonge Street on release day, before the videotapes were even out of the shipping boxes. The first thing I watched was the second tape of "The War Games" and its remaining episodes, picking up where I had left off.

Just two weeks before that, I had kissed a girl for the first time. This was almost as sweet.

The second half of "The War Games" was as good as, if not better than, I thought it would be. Philip Madoc was incredible. The Time Lords were awesome, in the truest sense of the word. The end of the second Doctor, Jamie and Zoe was unbelievably sad. I would forgive it James Bree, the limited number of extras, the bad accents, everything. It was *Doctor Who*'s true epic.

Every time I watch "The War Games," I think about my five-year wait to watch the second half and think it can't be as good as it was when I watched it for the first time at 17 and 22 years old. And every time, I am wrong. It's even better.

. . . .

Restoration

When *Doctor Who* episodes from the 1960s and early '70s were rebroadcast in syndication and released on home video in the 1980s and early 1990s, the condition of them was shockingly bad. Made from dirty, scratchy film prints with soundtracks full of noise and hiss, the poor quality took viewers out of the experience of watching *Doctor Who* and gave certain 1960s stories the reputation that they were downright unviewable.

Starting in 1992, a group of fans that worked in the BBC behind the scenes as engineers and technicians started to change that. The first challenge they took up was the colourization of the 1971 Jon Pertwee story "The Daemons." Thanks to its original colour videotape being wiped, it only existed as a black and white film recording, so they decided to figure out a way to colourize it. Their method was ingenious: the colour signal was taken from an off-air videotape of the story (when it aired on PBS in the mid '70s, before the colour version was wiped), the geometry warped so it matched the black and white film print, and then added to the luminosity signal of the film print. It was painstaking work, but they did it. They used this technique for two other Pertwee stories, "Doctor Who and the Silurians" and "Terror of the Autons" (1971).

By 1997, this group of boffins, who called themselves the Doctor Who Restoration Team, expanded their work to restore episodes to the best possible condition for home video release. One of their first projects was the VHS version of "The War Machines," which suffered from film prints of variable quality and a number of missing scenes due to foreign censor cuts. Using off-air audio recordings, footage recovered from various sources (including *Blue Peter*), the recovered censored footage (which had been sitting in an archive in Australia, along with other missing footage) and some ingenious cutaways (to distract from what was missing), they managed to restore "The War Machines" to its original length. The Doctor Who Restoration Team employed a variety of technical processes, removed dirt and scratches, and made the film print almost pristine-looking. Audio restoration took out all the noise and hiss. The team employed similar techniques for all stories released on VHS and DVD for the next decade and a half.

The great leap forward came in 2002 with a process that had a profound impact on the way we watched 1960s *Doctor Who*: the video field interpolation restoration effect, or VidFIRE. The process utilized computer-motion estimation and added frames between existing film frames; the film played back at normal speed, only now had 48 frames per second instead of 24. The result effectively recreated the look and feel of the original broadcast. It was revolutionary. Instead of being marbled in near unwatchable film, stories featuring Hartnell and Troughton's Doctors now looked as good as they once had. In fact, they probably look better now than on the 405-line television screens of the time!

A further discovery called reverse standards conversion enabled stories that only existed in the poorer North American NTSC format to decode the higher quality PAL information they were originally taped with, ensuring better quality source material on several Jon Pertwee stories (the only copies of which were NTSC versions recovered from Canada).

But the most incredible process was yet to come. In 2007, some BBC engineers watching black and white film prints of Jon Pertwee colour stories from the early 1970s noticed dots within the film that were minuscule flashes of colour. They discovered these dots were artefacts from the film recording of the colour videotape; even though recorded in black and white, they contained the chroma (colour) information of the original. Using variants of the reverse standards conversion process, they managed to decode the information in these "chroma dots" and, with much labour-intensive work, recover the colour from the black and white film print. The first full results of this were seen in the 2012 DVD release of "The Ambassadors of Death" (1970), which now exists in colour thanks to a process that can be likened to creating diamonds from barbecue charcoal briquettes.

The restoration process on *Doctor Who* could be glibly called a massive attempt to make stories look like they were made on crappy videotape. But this process is the result of incredible technical advances and film restoration techniques that are at the forefront of the industry. Some *Doctor Who* DVDs have more restoration work done to them than the high-quality Criterion Film releases. And that achievement came from a group of fans who wanted to see the stories as they remembered them from childhood. That's pretty neat.

· ·

The 1960s

The 1970s

Starring
Jon Pertwee (1970–1974)
Tom Baker (1974–1981)
as the Doctor

Tips for Newbies

- **Space out the longer stories.** The '70s stories move faster than those from the '60s, but some of them are quite lengthy, extending to six and seven episodes. You don't need to be quite as rigid about only watching a single episode at a time as in the '60s, but do remember that they were made to be viewed that way. A couple of episodes at a time should be quite watchable. Only gorge on an entire story in one sitting if you're feeling particularly brave.

- **Watch it like it you are at the theatre.** The same rule applies as in the '60s. The pacing is faster and there are more cuts, but nowhere near as many as today. Scenes are long and talky. But the production team know this, so they've put a lot of effort into both the script and the actors.

- **Don't worry about the effects.** The special effects are sometimes worse in the '70s than they were in the '60s. Monochrome hides a multitude of sins that colour simply can't. The early days of the '70s also saw the use of significant amounts of greenscreen, which hasn't held up too well. Remember that they were experimenting with the limitations of the era's technology — and are often on the cutting edge of it — so try to be forgiving. Or laugh now and again, but don't let it ruin the rest of the story.

Spearhead From Space (1970)

Written by Robert Holmes **Directed by** Derek Martinus

Featuring Jon Pertwee (Doctor Who), Caroline John (Liz Shaw), Nicholas Courtney (Brigadier Lethbridge-Stewart)

Supporting cast Hugh Burden (Channing), Derek Smee (Ransome), John Woodnutt (Hibbert), Neil Wilson (Seeley), Betty Bowden (Meg Seeley), Hamilton Dyce (General Scobie), John Breslin (Captain Munro), Clifford Cox (Sergeant), George Lee (Corporal Forbes), Tessa Shaw (UNIT officer), Antony Webb (Dr. Henderson), Henry McCarthy (Dr. Beavis), Allan Mitchell (Wagstaffe), Talfryn Thomas (Mullins), Prentis Hancock (second reporter)

Original airdates January 3, 10, 17, 24, 1970

The Big Idea An alien intelligence that controls plastic intends to take over the world by replicating key figures and slaughtering the populace with its Autons. Fortunately, the Doctor has just been exiled to Earth by the Time Lords.

Roots and References The 1955 BBC science fiction series *Quatermass II* (the hollow meteorites containing an alien intelligence); *The Avengers* episodes "The Cybernauts" and "Return of the Cybernauts" (the Autons); *Invasion of the Body Snatchers* (infiltration by alien facsimile); *Thunderball* (Scobie opening the door to find his duplicate, and Sam Seeley's name for the meteorites); the 1953 film *House of Wax* (Scobie being a part of a waxwork display). Robert Holmes also borrowed from his storyline for the 1965 film *Invasion* (particularly the Doctor's arrival in the hospital). The Fleetwood Mac song "Oh Well (Part One)" plays over a sequence in the factory in episode two.

Time And Relative Dimensions In Space As the 1960s came to a close, *Doctor Who*'s ratings had seriously tapered off. Patrick Troughton had been playing the Doctor for three years and, after the arduous demands of shooting more than 40 weeks a year, he wanted out. Producers Derrick Sherwin and Peter Bryant had wondered if the run of futuristic space adventures was really the way to go, given *Doctor Who*'s meagre resources. During the fifth season, they'd had some success with a story set on near-contemporary Earth: in 1968's "The Web of Fear," the Doctor fought the Yeti in London, aided by Colonel Lethbridge-Stewart and his military forces. Sherwin and Bryant decided to try out a new structure that capitalized on that format. "The Invasion" (1968) brought back Lethbridge-Stewart, only now he was a brigadier and the leader of the United Nations Intelligence Taskforce (UNIT), an agency that deals with extraterrestrial threats (in that case, an invading force of Cybermen). The mixture of a contemporary setting and monsters was a bold experiment that worked, and plans developed to change the series radically. The new Doctor was exiled to Earth where he would work with Brigadier Lethbridge-Stewart and UNIT.

Writing the first story to establish this new format was easy enough, but when it came time to tape the first *Doctor Who* story to be made (and broadcast) in colour, they faced a problem: a strike prevented anyone from using the facilities at the BBC Television Centre. *Doctor Who* was granted permission to make the story on 16mm film (the only story made entirely on film until the 1996 TV Movie) and shot on location in lieu of on sets (primarily the BBC's training and emergency broadcast facilities at Wood Norton).

Adventures in Time and Space The Brigadier tells Liz that the Earth has been twice before saved by the Doctor ("The Web of Fear" and "The Invasion"). The Doctor obliquely mentions that the Time Lords have taken the secret of time and space travel from him and marooned the TARDIS ("The War Games").

Who is the Doctor? Much of what we now know about the Doctor's alien physiology is established here: it's revealed he has two hearts, his body temperature is very low, his blood is nothing like a human's, and he can put himself in a coma where brain and heart activity are almost nil.

Companion Chronicles The Doctor finds himself working for UNIT under Brigadier Lethbridge-Stewart as its scientific adviser. The Brigadier trusts the Doctor enough to accept his transformation at face value. The Brigadier has already seconded Dr. Elizabeth (Liz) Shaw, a scientist from Cambridge, to investigate the Nestene invasion. Liz is skeptical of the Brigadier's claims (even though the Brigadier turns out to be right), but she gets along well with the Doctor.

Monster of the Week The Nestenes are a disembodied intelligence contained in plastic spheres. They can control plastic and have created an army of drones, called Autons, who are armed and lethal, as well as facsimiles of key figures in government.

Stand Up and Cheer The Auton shop window dummies suddenly waking and slaughtering people in the street is such an iconic sequence that Russell T Davies stole it wholesale and put it in the first episode of the 2005 revival of the series, "Rose." For good reason: it's chilling in how it juxtaposes a sleepy dawn and people queuing for buses with the unexpectedness of mannequins coming to life and then shooting people. It loses a point for not showing the shop window being broken (by cutting to another location where it's only heard), but it gains that back by showcasing in just two minutes what *Doctor Who* is now capable of doing not only in 1970 but thereafter.

Roll Your Eyes The scene where the Nestene creature emerges, tentacles flailing and strangling the Doctor, actually had to be reshot due to technical concerns. Watching Jon Pertwee pulling faces during this scene makes us think they probably should have done one more take.

You're Not Making Any Sense While there might be a logical rationale for keeping the real Scobie alive (2005's "Rose" states that the Nestenes keep the people they duplicate alive in case they have further use for them), why put him in a London landmark like Madame Tussauds? Surely it would be better to keep him prisoner in the plastics factory.

Interesting Trivia Regarding the previous alien invasions that the Brigadier helped the Doctor repel, he says, "A policy decision was made not to inform the public." Presumably he's referring to guidelines around first contact with aliens devised by the United Nations, which are mentioned in "The Sound of Drums" (2007). We also learn in this story that the soldiers in UNIT forces are comprised of seconded personnel from its signatory countries' military forces (in the U.K., from the British Army), which means that Captain Munro has to follow faux–General Scobie's orders.

The shower scene is the first time we see the Doctor semi-naked, revealing he has a tattoo of a cobra on his left forearm, which none of his predecessors or successors appear to have. Of course, the reason for that is it's Jon Pertwee's own tattoo from his days in the navy. However, on the third Doctor, the tattoo calls for more speculation: is it the brand of a Time Lord criminal? Your suggestion is as good as ours.

A number of production staff played roles in this story. The commissionaire at the UNIT gate being browbeaten by the Doctor is actually producer Derrick Sherwin. Sherwin was unimpressed by the actor cast for the role — especially as all he had to do was react to the Doctor — and so he fired him. Sherwin himself had been an actor (most recently in the 1968 film *The Vengeance of She*) and was still an Equity member, so he recast himself in the part. Robin Squire, an assistant at the *Doctor Who* office, was also pressed into service to play the lead Auton when the actor cast found the plastic mask claustrophobic. Unlike Sherwin, Squires did not have an Equity card, so he was given the punning pseudonym "Ivan Orton." (Think about it for a minute. You'll get it.)

The TARDIS Chronometer Several locations around the Epping forest and London, near to the present day.

Hai? (GB) While we generally speak of post-2005 *Doctor Who* as the "New Series" (a term that is starting to fall out of favour, admittedly, the less new it becomes), it could be argued that the "new series" of *Doctor Who* really begins here. "Spearhead From Space" is a stunning reboot of *Doctor Who* into a show about a military force with an outlandish alien scientist that investigates strange phenomena and prevents alien invasions. Long gone are the historicals, and even the future is more or less out of the picture. It's a show set in the present (or near enough).

And yet, in the same way that the post-2005 *Doctor Who* is the same program as the one that aired from 1963 to 1989, so too is this 1970 remodelling connected to the program made from 1963 to 1969. The Doctor is a little better dressed and less tramp-like, but he's still the same charming eccentric we love. The monsters are just as inventive as ever: spheres that form a collective intelligence fall from the sky and use plastic to create an infiltrating army? Yeah, that's *Doctor Who* all right. And the Autons are super creepy in how they move and look. Definitely *Doctor Who*.

Some of this story hasn't worn well (particularly comedy poacher Sam Seeley in his broad West Country accent; you have to love the BBC's patronizing attitude towards the lower classes). But the rest of this remodelling is dazzling. In a funny way, the strike that allowed the entire story to be made on film was the happiest of accidents, as it only adds to the shock of the new. Derek Martinus makes it work in such bold and imaginative ways, filming the Brigadier's impromptu press conference in the hospital with a handheld camera to give the whole thing a vérité look and feel. (He even had his own film crew stand in the shot for added realism!)

The whole of "Spearhead From Space" is played realistically. From the sweat on the brows of the UNIT radar station operators, the blood on the windscreen of the jeep that's been run off the road and the aforementioned scrum with reporters to the location work in the factory (with Fleetwood Mac playing) and Ransome's state of shock (complete with water proffered by Munro dribbling down his chin), it's all designed to add a sense of verisimilitude to a story where plastic men try to take over the world. And it works beautifully. The scene where the shop window dummies attack is even better here than when it was remade 35 years later.

The other big change (which sadly doesn't last long) is the series moving towards an ensemble cast. While the Doctor is unmistakably the lead, the other cast members aren't mere assistants. Nicholas Courtney's Brigadier Lethbridge-Stewart is the epitome of cool. I love the first scene between Liz and the Brigadier: he talks to Liz with a knowing smile the entire time, utterly unfazed by her skepticism. The Brigadier is a leader you believe in. He's open-minded, observant, decisive and nobody's fool.

Caroline John as Liz Shaw gets all the great caustic lines. Nobody does haughty wit better than John. When the Brigadier says Liz has six academic degrees, we believe him. She's intelligent but not imperious and is able to adjust her thinking where needed. She's Scully from *The X-Files* about 23 years earlier. Refreshingly, Liz doesn't treat the Doctor as competition, but she doesn't exactly defer to him either. She just gets on with working with him as a colleague. In other words, she's a professional. How often do you see that on television?

The real weak link is Jon Pertwee, but it's not his fault; it's the production's. They thought that since Jon Pertwee was a popular comedian, the script should be designed to exploit that, with a comedy chase sequence in episode one, where the Doctor escapes his abductors on a wheelchair set to jaunty music by Dudley Simpson, and an escape sequence in episode two full of silent comedy bits. (Shooting on film with a single camera does Pertwee no favours either: each closeup is specifically shot and therefore designed for maximum goofy impact.) Pertwee seems happy to go along with it for now, but, as will be seen shortly, he'll commit himself to a completely different course.

In many ways, "Spearhead From Space" is a pilot for the new series that is to follow: much of it is discarded (like Scobie being liaison to the regular army) or refined (like Pertwee's portrayal of the Doctor, the comedy influences and the Doctor's car), but much of it is kept and synthesized. And with it, *Doctor Who* becomes a show of the now, as well as the past and the future. Here's to the new series.

Second Opinion (RS?)

A review of the BBC's new science-fiction show, 26/1/70

It's the start of the 1970s, and the BBC has decided to launch a brand new science-fiction show. Starring comic actor Jon Pertwee as a mysterious alien and featuring an ensemble cast of soldiers and scientists, this fresh TV show is full of action and adventure. Recorded on glorious film, it looks fantastic and showcases the BBC's new colour transmission abilities.

The first episode of this new show hits the ground running. By withholding its central character for over half the episode (it's a full 14 minutes before we see Pertwee's face!), viewers are forced to rely on the very human interactions of the supporting cast. This gives the story room to breathe, while (very necessarily) establishing the format of the series. There's so much going on in the first episode: meteorites crashing to Earth, Liz recruited to UNIT, the mysterious patient, reporters, Channing, the poacher. This is television for right now!

Some have criticized this new show as derivative of the old black and white series, *Doctor Who*, but such criticisms don't really hold up. While it's true that the central character is a mysterious alien and co-star Nicholas Courtney did indeed play a similar supporting role in two *Doctor Who* stories a few years before, that's about where the similarities end. There's no travelling in time, no alien planets and no studio sets. The roles for women are far superior and there's a sense of realism that would be untenable in the old show.

For example, having Pertwee's alien encounter the medical system is exactly the sort of thing you simply couldn't have done in *Doctor Who*. It works because everyone reacts in a very human and realistic way: some with disbelief, others with an eye to making a profit. And then there's Pertwee himself. Cast for his comic background, he uses comedy to showcase a likeable and endearing alien trapped on Earth. I, for one, am looking forward to laughing along with his antics every week!

This new show is an unqualified success, proving that the powers that be were right to cancel *Doctor Who* in its favour. Only by switching to an entirely new series can BBC science fiction cast off the embarrassments of the past. And, thanks to an ensemble cast, high production values and a grounded format, that's exactly what this new series has achieved. I give it five years.

Jon Pertwee

Jon Pertwee was born in 1919 in Chelsea in London. His father, Roland Pertwee, was a prominent British screenwriter and occasional actor (who, with his other son Michael, later created the first soap opera for British television, *The Grove Family*). Jon's first work onscreen was as an extra in the 1938 film *A Yank at Oxford* (which his father worked on as a writer, uncredited).

The acting bug stuck with him and, in spite of a spotty academic record, Pertwee briefly attended the Royal Academy of Dramatic Art before being expelled. Pertwee found theatre and film roles (including a bit part in 1939's *The Four Just Men* alongside his father) before joining the Royal Navy at the start of World War II. After the war, Pertwee developed a reputation for his comedic work, particularly on radio, where his repertoire of funny accents and voices served him well. In 1957, Pertwee became part of the popular radio comedy series *The Navy Lark* (a series that continued even through his time on *Doctor Who*, ending in 1977), which cemented Pertwee's reputation as a comedic actor.

It was Pertwee himself who suggested his name be put forward for the role of the Doctor. To Pertwee's surprise, producers Peter Bryant and Derrick Sherwin already had him on their short list. (Their first choice, Ron Moody, had declined.) Bryant and Sherwin hired Pertwee because they thought the character should be even more comic than the second Doctor.

When Bryant and Sherwin departed early in Pertwee's tenure as the Doctor, the actor had to find his own way in the role. He famously asked his friend Shaun Sutton, who was head of drama at the BBC (and production executive in charge of *Doctor Who*), how he should play the Doctor. Sutton said, "Play it as Jon Pertwee." As Pertwee noted many times, that answer terrified him: after relying on so many comedic personas over the years, he didn't know who Jon Pertwee was. He decided to play the role straight, but brought in his own love of vehicles and gadgets. Pertwee played the Doctor for five seasons, longer than any actor up until that point.

After *Doctor Who*, Pertwee was still in demand as an actor and a presenter. Pertwee was quite active in bringing an adaptation of Barbara Euphan Todd's *Worzel Gummidge* children's books to television; he played the role of Worzel in an ITV series that ran from 1979 to 1981 (with a revival based in New Zealand from 1987 to 1989). He reprised his role as the Doctor in the 1983 story "The Five Doctors," the thirtieth anniversary sketch "Dimensions in Time" (1993) and the BBC radio stories "The Paradise of Death" (1993) and "The Ghosts of N-Space" (1996). He wrote two memoirs, *Moon Boots* and *Dinner Suits* (1984) and *I Am the Doctor*, a book co-written with David J. Howe about his *Doctor Who* career, which was published posthumously in 1996.

Jon Pertwee died of a heart attack while on holiday in Connecticut on May 20, 1996, two months before his 77th birthday. The U.K. screening of the 1996 TV Movie (shown a week later) was dedicated to his memory.

. . . .

Doctor Who and the Silurians (1970)

Written by Malcolm Hulke **Directed by** Timothy Combe

Featuring Jon Pertwee (Doctor Who), Caroline John (Liz Shaw), Nicholas Courtney (Brigadier Lethbridge-Stewart)

Supporting cast Fulton Mackay (Dr. Quinn), Peter Miles (Dr. Lawrence), Ian Cunningham (Dr. Meredith), Norman Jones (Major Baker), Thomasine Heiner (Miss Dawson), Ian Talbot (Travis), Geoffrey Palmer (Masters), John Newman (Spencer), Bill Matthews (Davis), Roy Branigan (Roberts), Gordon Richardson (Squire), Nancie Jackson (Doris Squire), Paul Darrow (Captain Hawkins), Richard Steele (Sergeant Hart), Alan Mason (Corporal Nutting), Harry Swift (Private Wright), Dave Carter (Old Silurian), Nigel Johns (Young Silurian), Pat Gorman (Silurian scientist), Peter Halliday (Silurian voices)

Original airdates January 31, February 7, 14, 21, 28, March 7, 14, 1970

The Big Idea A scientific research base accidentally awakens an underground race of reptiles who were the original inhabitants of Earth — and who are determined to reclaim the planet as their own.

Roots and References Jules Verne's *A Journey to the Centre of the Earth* (discovering an entire civilization underground, especially the opening scene); the 1957 BBC science-fiction serial (and its 1965 film remake) *Quatermass and the Pit* (aliens found underground that lived with humans in the past, unlocking the primal race memory); Arthur Conan Doyle's *The Lost World* (the dinosaur); the then-ongoing smallpox eradication campaign (the worldwide plague and efforts to create a cure). The Doctor sings, "'Twas brillig and the slithy toves did gyre and gimble in the wabe," from the poem "Jabberwocky."

Time And Relative Dimensions In Space With the new "exiled to Earth" format, writer Malcolm Hulke argued that there were only two possible story types: mad scientist or alien invasion (the latter having been seen in the previous story). To invert this, Hulke and script editor Terrance Dicks proposed an alternative: what if the aliens were already here and the rightful owners of the planet?

Who is the Doctor? The Doctor now has a car, a yellow Edwardian roadster, which he spends some time fixing up and names Bessie. He covets the scientific knowledge in the Silurian bunker. He seems unconcerned about changing future history by negotiating a planet-sharing arrangement between humans and Silurians. (2010's "Cold Blood" suggests that such an agreement is not a fixed moment of time and hence possible.)

Companion Chronicles Liz is noticeably cheerier than she was in the previous story. She's initially quite apologetic on the Brigadier's behalf, defending him to the Doctor, although she and the Brigadier clash later in the story. She's able to decipher the Doctor's formula for the antidote when he's kidnapped, meaning she puts the final touches on saving humanity from the plague.

The Brigadier is mostly on the Doctor's side, although he's slightly more eager to mount a frontal assault on the Silurians. However, at the story's end, acting on orders from on high, he destroys the Silurian base, apparently killing everyone within. The Doctor explicitly calls this murder.

Monster of the Week The reptilian Silurians (although there's no indication they call themselves that) were the original inhabitants of Earth, but went into hibernation to avoid the impending collision of an asterioid that ultimately became Earth's moon. Since the expected catastrophe never happened, they failed to awake. They have three eyes, with the top one showing a red spectrum that they use to operate things remotely and also kill people.

Stand Up and Cheer Masters's plague-inducing journey through London isn't exactly a cheerful moment, but it is incredibly harrowing. Unusually, we see the larger implications of what's happening in a story, as random passersby are infected, the police are just too late to stop Masters and he finally keels over against a railing. The montage of people collapsing in the station cross-fading to the Brigadier on the phone, the Doctor in the lab and Liz taking blood is a directorial triumph.

Roll Your Eyes "She was found in the barn, paralyzed with fear. She may have seen something." Thanks for that, Doctor.

You're Not Making Any Sense Liz states that the Van Allen belt is a protective belt around the Earth that filters out the sun's radiation and that destroying it would mean the Earth would heat up and we'd all die of sunstroke. However, it's not protecting us at all; it's full of dangerous radiation (and this was known in 1970). In fact, removing it would be beneficial for both humans and also artificial satellites. In 1996, it was even proposed that we try to deliberately remove it using high-voltage tethers attached to satellites. Presumably Malcolm Hulke mistook it for the ozone layer. He also named the monsters "Silurians" even though they can't possibly be from the Silurian age!

Interesting Trivia The Doctor says his life covers several thousand years, which is vastly more than the 450 Earth years stated in "The Tomb of the Cybermen." He may be referring to the span of time he's visited (although millions would be more accurate in that case) or possibly using Gallifreyan years. If he means Earth years, then this suggests a vast gap in what we've seen, which can only reasonably take place between "The War Games" and "Spearhead From Space" (we'll come back to this in "The Five Doctors"). On the flipside, the fourth Doctor later says that he's in his 750s, suggesting that the "thousand" years stated here isn't right.

The cyclotron, the central feature of the Wenley Moor base, is a nuclear reactor that's being developed; its inclusion in the story reflects the growing energy crisis of the 1970s, the backdrop for many stories in this era. At the end of the '60s, petroleum production in many parts of the world (including the United States) peaked. This resulted in higher prices, the oil crisis of 1973, runaway inflation and complicated negotiations with the Middle East for supplies. The writing was already on the wall by the time this story was made: in 1970, the U.S. congress told the Atomic Energy Commission to broaden its nuclear horizons to include other energy sources.

This story's official title is indeed "Doctor Who and the Silurians." Don't let anyone tell you otherwise. It's right there onscreen. We don't have to like it, but we do have to acknowledge it. The camera script was usually titled "Doctor Who and . . ." but the director or producer would remove that precursor before the title captioning. Here, that wasn't done, probably because there was no one minding the store: the *Doctor Who* production office was in turmoil as a new producer, Barry Letts, was brought in at the last minute after his predecessors left during pre-production on this story. However, in response to the error, scripts stopped being titled "Doctor Who and . . ." after this.

The TARDIS Chronometer Wenley Moor (in Derbyshire) and London, near to the present day. Interestingly, the TARDIS is neither seen nor referred to in the entire story.

Hai? (RS?) "Doctor Who and the Silurians" can be summed up in one word: epic. At seven episodes long, it's not even the longest story of the previous 12 months, although it kind of feels like it. But not in a bad way.

"Doctor Who and the Silurians" is determined to tell a long-form narrative. Everything is drawn out: except for glimpses, we don't see a Silurian until the very end of episode three; the manhunt, using helicopters and dogs, feels massive; and the Doctor's work on the antidote to the plague is so painstakingly slow, it actually feels like real science. We even see the Doctor driving through city streets on his way to the countryside (foreshadowing the later devastation that comes to that city). By the time random extras are dropping like flies at Marylebone station, it genuinely feels like it's been a long, long time since that magnificent shot of the Silurian silhouetted against the sunset.

This sense of scale also permeates the story's background and potential: we're dealing with history on the order of millions of years, while the moral dilemma is predicated not just on the future of the human race, but of two civilizations, both with a rightful claim to Earth. The epic nature of the story effectively lays the groundwork for the moral dilemma. Since the Silurians are revealed so slowly, by the time they make their case for ownership of the Earth, we can't help but at least listen to their arguments.

And those arguments are fascinating! We're the interlopers, not them. It's an intractable problem, helped enormously by the fact that the British Empire was winding down and colonialism no longer looked like the right thing to do. The drama is also given legs because both groups have dissenters, meaning the arguments get played out in quattro: humans for and against, and Silurians for and against. That's structural genius. Best of all, neither side is presented as morally wholesome: the Silurians only kill in self-defence, but then they unleash a plague, whereas the humans first try to make peaceful contact in exchange for scientific progress, then they destroy the Silurian base, murdering an entire species.

That ending is a triumph for the show. We're reminded that these people the Doctor hangs out with are soldiers and part of what soldiers do for a living is kill people on the orders of governments. The Brigadier has thus far been a steadfast friend, a cool head in a crisis and the man to save the Doctor more often than not. Here he's portrayed as exactly what he is: a man willing to murder others, if that's what his orders require. This sting in the tail of the story is brilliant, only undercut by the fact that there's almost no follow-up. (The Doctor briefly complains about the Brigadier's actions in the next episode, but then they patch things up and remain BFFs thereafter.)

There's only really one downside to "Doctor Who and the Silurians," but it's a particularly unfortunate one. The third Doctor is brilliant, inquisitive and sees the bigger picture, but if there's one characteristic that defines him above all else, it's that he's rude. He's rude to the Brigadier on multiple occasions (although he can take it), he's rude to Dr. Meredith (pulling UNIT rank on him as soon as he meets him), dismissive of Major Baker (resulting in Baker's distrust), rude to Masters and even revels in Dr. Lawrence's impending death ("I'd be very happy to lose him"). Even worse, this behaviour has drastic consequences: had he not been so offensive to Dr. Quinn when visiting him at his cottage, Quinn might have trusted him and revealed the Silurian he had locked away, very likely resolving the crisis much sooner. After the fresh and likeable take on the Doctor we saw in "Spearhead," here Pertwee establishes the character he plays for the rest of his tenure . . . and it's not very nice.

That aside — and, fortunately, there's enough going on that we can, in fact, cast aside the Doctor's character and still love this story like a brother — "Doctor Who and the Silurians" is an amazing piece of television. Episode six is probably the highlight, with the incredible plague scenes and the laborious efforts to find a cure (something TV series would be afraid to show today, but this is exactly the pace of real science). But that episode is really just the payoff to the setup: the careful buildup, the gripping central dilemma and a story determined to keep making it bigger and bigger, without ever losing the sense of realism. Epic, indeed.

Second Opinion (GB) Seven episodes. Viewed today, when the average *Doctor Who* story is done in three-quarters of an hour, the idea of a story taking place over seven 25-minute episodes is mindblowing.

There are four-part stories in the Classic *Doctor Who* canon that are a difficult slog to watch. These days, finding a watchable seven-part story just doesn't seem possible.

But it is.

"Doctor Who and the Silurians" is proof positive that *Doctor Who* can thrive in the long-form storytelling format. Not a single one of its episodes is wasted. Malcolm Hulke knows that intrigue is the grease that keeps the engine of storytelling going and he builds up intrigue better than most: secretive characters, double-crossing aliens, double-crossing humans, a plague that threatens humanity . . . Each episode has a new twist that cannily builds on what took place before.

The result is one of the most solidly constructed *Doctor Who* stories of any era.

At its base is probably the best idea for a *Doctor Who* monster, ever: millions of years before humanity, bipedal reptiles ruled the Earth. And now they want it back. It's such a simple idea, but it upends everything we've seen when it comes to alien invasions in *Doctor Who* before or since. The Silurians have a noble purpose behind them.

The result is not a traditional invasion tale but a clash of values, with the Doctor caught in the middle. The whole story is riddled with such ambiguities as the characters — reptilian and ape-descendant — are neither good nor bad, but driven by personal motivations. Dr. Quinn (played with a colourful palette of qualities by Fulton McKay) is charming and friendly, but also fuelled by his need for success; Miss Dawson just wants to be loyal to the man she loves, even in death; the Brigadier wants to do what is right for the public good; the Old Silurian wants peace; and the Young Silurian wants the planet that's rightfully theirs. Each is prepared to do whatever it takes to get what they want. And that, my friends, is how you create unforgettable drama.

The actors put their all into it. I disagree with my co-author's knee-jerk reaction to the Doctor's supposed rudeness. I think something much more interesting is going on. This is a Doctor driven by his need to bring about the greater good no matter what anyone — human or Silurian — thinks, and if he's abrasive, so be it. Jon Pertwee is never better than here. His Doctor is at once a solid hero and flawed protector. Pertwee, to his great credit, doesn't try to hide the Doctor's huge blindspots and that very arrogance drives many of the conflicts in the story and indeed much of Pertwee's tenure as the Doctor. As a result, the Doctor is more compelling than ever. Nicholas Courtney also captures the qualities that made the Brigadier great — his loyalty, his cunning, his charisma — but isn't afraid to take the character to darker places as the downbeat ending, a triumph of *Who* in any era, demonstrates. Fulton MacKay, Peter Miles and Geoffrey Palmer also make the most of the meaty roles given to them.

Where "Spearhead From Space" showed us that the "exiled to Earth" reformatting could make exciting television, "Doctor Who and the Silurians" demonstrates that this new format could also be challenging, thoughtful and full of moral complexity — and keep the audience on the edge of their seats for seven episodes. This is *Doctor Who* at its finest.

Inferno (1970)

Written by Don Houghton **Directed by** Douglas Camfield, Barry Letts (uncredited)

Featuring Jon Pertwee (Doctor Who), Caroline John (Liz Shaw), Nicholas Courtney (Brigadier Lethbridge-Stewart), John Levene (Sergeant Benton)

Supporting cast Olaf Pooley (Professor Stahlman); Christopher Benjamin (Sir Keith Gold); Sheila Dunn (Petra Williams); Derek Newark (Greg Sutton); Ian Fairbairn (Bromly); Walter Randall (Harry Slocum); Derek Ware (Private Wyatt); David Simeon (Private Latimer); Keith James (Patterson); Dave Carter, Pat Gorman, Walter Henry, Philip Ryan, Peter Thompson (Primords)

Original airdates May 9, 16, 23, 30, June 6, 13, 20, 1970

The Big Idea An attempt to drill through the Earth's crust goes awry, resulting in the release of toxic slime that turns men into monsters and an accident that sends the Doctor sideways into a parallel universe.

Roots and References *Quatermass II* (the oil refinery); John Wyndham's 1961 short story "Random Quest" (the alternate universe); *Nineteen Eighty-Four* (the Big Brother–style poster); World War II (what if the Nazis won?). The Doctor sings "La donna è mobile" from *Rigoletto* and talks about Batman (presumably the 1960s TV version).

Time And Relative Dimensions In Space Don Houghton had been story editor on the soap *Crossroads* when Terrance Dicks was writing for it. When Dicks transferred to *Doctor Who*, Houghton pitched a story about a drilling project inspired by recent attempts by both the Russians and the Americans to drill through the Earth's crust. Houghton had asked the U.S. embassy for information, but was told that it was top secret. He decided they were covering something up and decided to write a story about such a scenario.

Letts' and Dicks' predecessors had committed the story to a seven-episode slot. However, Letts and Dicks had hated Houghton's story, originally entitled "The Mo-Hole Project," and were concerned it didn't have enough storyline to sustain its massive running time. Terrance Dicks suggested the idea of a parallel universe plotline to bulk up the centre of the story.

Adventures in Time and Space Liz checks both of the Doctor's hearts, the first time this is referred to since "Spearhead From Space."

Who is the Doctor? He says he's a scientist "of sorts" and is using the project's nuclear reactor to run his own experiments on the TARDIS console, which he removed from the ship. He uses Venusian karate a number of times to immobilize his opponents (this would become a regular feature of the third Doctor). He also continues to display his propensity for singing, both at the beginning and the end of the story.

Companion Chronicles "Inferno" arguably sees the beginning of what's often termed "the UNIT family": the close-knit connections between the Doctor, his companion, the Brigadier and recurring members of UNIT. Sergeant Benton, previously seen in 1968's "The Invasion" (where he was a corporal), was added to the previous story, 1970's "The Ambassadors of Death," when it was decided to make him part of the "UNIT family" here. He continues to appear as a UNIT everyman throughout the remainder of the third Doctor's era and into the fourth Doctor's era.

In the alternate universe, Lethbridge-Stewart has an eyepatch, a scar running beneath it, and is brigade leader of the Republican Security Forces. He's also missing his trademark moustache and is a man on the edge, barely able to cope when the chips are down. Elizabeth Shaw (not Liz) is a section leader in the Republican Security Forces, although she studied physics and thought about becoming a scientist. As a result, she's won over by the Doctor's arguments and even shoots the Brigade Leader in order to enable the Doctor's escape.

Monster of the Week Green liquid oozes from the drilling shaft and, when touched, turns its victims violent, hairy and blue. When exposed to sufficient heat, these creatures grow full beards and sport a buffalo hump. They're incredibly hot to the touch and resistant to bullets, but can be slowed by the CO_2 in fire extinguishers. They're named "Primords" in the credits, but never onscreen.

Stand Up and Cheer After the Doctor has returned to our world, Sir Keith Gold enters the hut, very much alive, unlike his counterpart in the parallel world. After witnessing all manner of harrowing death and destruction (including of the entire planet), the Doctor realizes that free will is not an illusion after all. It's an absolutely triumphant moment that gives the story hope when it's desperately needed.

Roll Your Eyes The Doctor and the Brigadier decide to climb a 20-foot-tall ladder to have a meeting on top of a catwalk . . . that they could have had just as easily on the ground (and indeed they'd had a very private conversation in a room full of technicians just moments before). It's like a comedy routine out of *Get Smart*: the catwalk of silence.

You're Not Making Any Sense When the console slips sideways in time, the Doctor goes with it, as he's at the controls. Makes sense. But why does Bessie (the Doctor's vehicle) travel as well? She's not physically attached to the console and is, as far as we know, just an ordinary — if slightly souped-up — car. Worse, when the Doctor manages to dematerialize at the story's conclusion, Bessie stays exactly where she is!

Interesting Trivia The alternate universe has all manner of differences, some obvious and some subtle. The minor changes include the books on the shelves by the console changing to filing boxes, "Unity is Strength" posters, Liz's hair, the three-arrow logo, "Stahlman" being spelt "Stahlmann" and the professor lacking a beard. Sutton goes from dressing in hip fashions to dressing like it's the early 1960s. Major changes include Britain having been a republic since 1943, the royal family having been executed and UNIT being replaced by the Republican Security Forces. There is a ruling party, and dissidents, like Sutton, are used as slave labour. Furthermore, events are slightly more advanced than in the real world: the rate of drilling is faster and Sir Keith is already dead.

You may notice that the TARDIS console appears rather green. That's because it was the original prop, appearing for the final time. To create certain visual results in black and white footage, props were painted. In this case, the TARDIS was painted green, which read as white in monochrome, but didn't flare as much as an actual white object would on video cameras. The prop was retired after this story and a new (white) one built for the following season.

This is Liz Shaw's last story, although you'd never know it from the final scene. Instead of being written out in this story, there's a line in the next season saying that she returned to Cambridge. Producers wanted a less intelligent character as companion, to whom the Doctor could more readily explain the plot. (Caroline John was pregnant and would have had to leave in any event.)

Director Douglas Camfield had been offered the producer's job before Letts. He'd worked on a number of *Doctor Who* stories and had a reputation for meticulously planning his shoots. However, after the second episode of "Inferno," he suffered a minor heart attack and was admitted to hospital. Barry Letts took over as director, although he followed Camfield's detailed notes. The incident was kept quiet, for fear that Camfield might not find work again, but it was particularly worrying to Camfield's wife, Sheila Dunn, who was playing Petra.

While filming this story, Jon Pertwee played a practical joke that has since passed into convention anecdote lore. During the scene where Nicholas Courtney swivels in his chair to reveal he's wearing an eyepatch, Pertwee arranged for the entire cast to be wearing eyepatches. Courtney had the last laugh: he continued the scene, completely ignoring them, at which point the cast fell over laughing. That's not the only in-joke in this story: the Big Brother–esque leader, seen in posters around the project, is Jack Kine, the head of the BBC special effects department (itself following an in-joke from the BBC's 1954 production of *Nineteen Eighty-Four* where special effects man Roy Oxley was used for Big Brother).

Ratings for *Doctor Who* had been precarious and the show's seventh season was in danger of being its last. So this was very nearly the final story ever. However, by the time "Inferno" aired, things had stabilized somewhat, thanks largely to Barry Letts's steady hand on the rudder, and the production team were given the go-ahead to continue.

The TARDIS Chronometer At a drilling project, near to the present day. A deleted scene (available as a DVD extra) placed the project in the fictional town of Eastchester.

Hai? (RS?) You're running *Doctor Who*. Your predecessors have lumped you with a format you don't like, consisting of multiple seven-part stories in a row. Your latest script is making all the problems clear: the story is dragged out far longer than it should be. What do you do?

Why, insert another story inside it, of course!

The genius of "Inferno" is in its structure. It takes a solid four-part story of a drilling project gone wrong and replaces what should have been episode three with an entirely new four-part story of a drilling project gone wrong. What's even better is that in the alternate-universe story the Doctor fails utterly: he can't defeat the monsters, he can't even save Earth. And everybody dies.

People have complained that episode six, which finishes on a cliff-hanger where the world actually ends, is so grim that episode seven can only be a letdown. These people are wrong. Episode seven is a triumph precisely because what's come before it has raised the stakes so high. The Doctor might look like a madman, attacking machinery with a wrench, but his behaviour is a result of the trauma he's just witnessed. And we understand, because we've seen it too.

The structure doesn't just carry the day on its own, however. The early episodes are sustained by some very innovative direction. A shot of a Primord attacking a man cuts immediately to Benton hammering a nail into a wall, which is an astonishingly effective way to convey violence without actually showing it. The burn mark on the wall after Slocum has leaned against it is a perfect way of illustrating how hot the Primords are. And when we get to the alternate universe, the pace is noticeably faster and more brutal. The scene of the Doctor being tortured is particularly harrowing for something originally broadcast at 5:15 on a Saturday afternoon.

"Inferno" is also an actors' triumph. Honours go to Nicholas Courtney, who clearly relishes his role as the Brigade Leader and makes an actual character out of him, not just a cipher in an eyepatch. It's an uncomfortable role that turns our cuddly soldier friend vicious and unlikeable. Courtney's delivery of the line "We'll all be roasted — alive!" (with a tremor in the final word) is incredible. And we're even given a scene back in the real world of the Brigadier ordering Benton to bring Stahlman to him by any means necessary. For once shouting at his underlings, we see the Brigadier's potential to become the Brigade Leader. Courtney knows just how to shade both characters so they are linked and yet distinct.

Jon Pertwee is much more likeable here than he was in "Doctor

Who and the Silurians," partly because he gets to be compassionate (such as in the scene where he asks the alternate Liz if she ever thought of being a scientist) and partly because when he is insulting, it's almost always towards Stahlman. This works because a) Stahlman fires first and b) he can take it. The Doctor also plays the role of the only reasonable man in an unreasonable world: even Liz doubts him until almost the final minute. There's no better way to make your central character likeable than to make him the only one viewers could possibly relate to.

Perhaps one of the most interesting of all the changes the alternative world presents is that Petra gets a promotion. She's a personal assistant in the real world, whom men talk of borrowing, but she's Dr. Williams in the alternate universe, second in command of the project. That's just awesome. She and Greg Sutton end up carrying much of the story — not dissimilar to Ian and Barbara in the early days — and even manage a low-level romance, twice over.

And this is where we see the structure playing out beautifully. Greg has to win over Petra twice under very different circumstances: one where she's the office secretary, the other where she's a loyal party member, even threatening to report him for treason. As a result, their relationship anchors the drama of both storylines in a very human way, matching the philosophical highs of the Doctor's "free will is not an illusion" speech and the plot mechanics of the drilling turning Stahlman into a Primord all over again.

Everything in between is also firing on all cylinders. We have just enough of a taste for the drilling project before being thrust sideways into its alternate. This is followed by a smackdown of exposition on what makes this world tick. Then we watch that world start to fall apart . . . and then it actually does! This is *Doctor Who* on a scale never attempted before or since.

"Inferno" is gritty, uncomfortable and brutal. But that doesn't matter in the slightest, because it's figured out the solution to its biggest problem: the sheer length of the thing. By playing with the structure, this seven-part story feels like a high-octane thriller. You won't believe three hours have passed . . . in large part because it feels like the middle half of them seem to pass at the same rate as the rest. Only sideways.

Second Opinion (GB) The problem with watching "Inferno" now is that parallel universe stories have become so very common. Just about every science-fiction series has an episode where the series regulars encounter alternative versions of themselves with a beard, or as a lesbian (never both, oddly enough), or as a sneering idiot (in the case of Mickey and Ricky in 2006's "Rise of the Cybermen"). But back when "Inferno" was being made, there was only one other example of it on television — *Star Trek*'s "Mirror Mirror" — which aired on British TV the week episode six was broadcast, so it's doubtful it influenced this production. They made this story from a completely blank page.

Keep that in mind while watching "Inferno," because I believe it's probably the finest parallel universe story in the history of television.

"Inferno" has the familiar tropes we know and love from this sub-genre: oh look, the Brigadier has a scar and an eyepatch, Liz has brown hair and Benton is a thug. But Nicholas Courtney, Caroline John and John Levene have clearly thought about the differences between the two characters they each play. Courtney as the Brigade Leader is particularly stunning. At first he plays the character with the cool cruelty of Mussolini, but that's just a façade; as the story progresses, we see the key difference is that the Brigadier is truly a leader who can inspire people, while the Brigade Leader, ruling by fear and the power of his rank, has none of those qualities. He's a useless, desperate man once his rank and power is gone. Caroline John is even more complex: Elizabeth Shaw keeps to the party line, but the inquisitiveness of Liz is always there, just beneath the surface. John even brings Liz's trademark sarcasm to bear (towards the Brigade Leader!) once the world ends. The result is believeable characters rather than just an opportunity for the actors to appear in drag.

The story is impressively constructed because the world created is so well thought-out. They devote the whole of episode four to establishing the parallel reality which anywhere else would feel like filler, but here it gives a background to the nightmare scenario that unfolded in the previous episode: we discover how the iconoclastic Sutton still survives (on sufferance because he's a good engineer, though it's implied he's soon for the firing squad), and learn from Petra, Elizabeth and the Brigade Leader how this world works.

And then that world dies. The characters lose their hold on everything, but decide to sacrifice themselves so the Doctor can save his world — and it makes for beautiful, exciting drama.

I love Douglas Camfield's direction, particularly the location sequences. The whole of episode three, which features the Doctor trying to survive this parallel world, is gorgeously tense.

"Inferno" is one of the few stories in 1970s *Who* where whole subplots are given to the minor characters. Derek Newark's edge-of-your-razor machismo is well suited to the role of Sutton (on both Earths) and he's one of the most memorable supporting characters in *Doctor Who*. His romance with Petra is charming, though Sheila Dunn seems a bit old for the ingénue role she's playing. Olaf Pooley is superb: his Professor Stahlman is pompous, obsessed and later tortured by the evil mutation he's undergoing, but he's never, ever a mad scientist, which is an approach a lesser actor might have taken. Caroline John really deserved a better exit, though.

"Inferno" basically concludes the more adult, super-sophisticated ensemble drama era of *Doctor Who* that began with "Spearhead From Space." If this had been the final story of *Doctor Who*, it would've been one hell of an ending.

The Psychic Papers: UNIT Dating

For a series with many a fan debate like *Doctor Who*, there has been no debate more contentious than the question of when the stories featuring UNIT from the late 1960s and early-to-mid 1970s are set. Simply put, do they take place in the then–present day or in the future?

Brigadier Lethbridge-Stewart's first appearance (as a colonel) was in 1968's "The Web of Fear," a sequel to 1967's "The Abominable Snowmen." The latter was set in 1935. In "The Web of Fear," characters explicitly state that the story's events take place 40 years later, making it 1975. The Brigadier talks about the events of "The Web of Fear" (and its follow-up from 1968, "The Invasion," set four years later) as taking place "several years ago" in "Spearhead From Space," which puts that story in the late 1970s at least.

The producers' original intention was that these "contemporary" stories were set in the near future: the late 1970s, if not the early 1980s. However, there's only one onscreen reference to this, in 1975's "Pyramids of Mars" (a non-UNIT story) when Sarah Jane Smith, who started travelling with the Doctor during the UNIT years, says she's from 1980.

This dating only became a problem in 1983 when "Mawdryn Undead" was broadcast. That story is set in 1983 and has the Brigadier retired as a maths teacher at an English public school. It's explicitly stated (indeed it's a plot point, with part of the story set in 1977 during the Queen's Silver Jubilee) that the Brigadier left UNIT in 1976 (around the time the last story featuring UNIT aired on television), the implication being that the UNIT stories were set in the 1970s, around the time of their airdates.

So which is it? Are the UNIT stories contemporary or in the near future? Are they set in the 1970s or the 1980s? The trouble is, there are equally compelling arguments for both. On the one hand, the UNIT stories feature a British space program (1970's "The Ambassadors of Death"), videophones (1971's "The Claws of Axos"), different prime ministers (1973's "The Green Death"), female prime ministers well before Thatcher (1975's "Terror of the Zygons"), all indicating that these are set in the future. On the other hand, the fashions are definitely of the same era the stories were made, there's signage for pre-decimal currency in "Doctor Who and the Silurians" (which would place it before decimalization in 1971) and "The Green Death" features calendars for 1972 (when the story was made).

Some fans have suggested that Sarah was rounding up to 1980 in "Pyramids of Mars," though this would seem a very odd thing to do. It's also possible that Sarah could have travelled for five or six years with the Doctor, and it would be 1980 if she were to return to the point where her age properly reflected the date, though that also seems pretty thin. (She says, "I'm from 1980," as though it were the year she came from and not something more theoretical.) That said, Sarah being from 1980 would mean that all the UNIT stories from "Spearhead From Space" onward take place within about 18 months, which seems equally implausible. (Muddying the waters is the 1981 spinoff *K9 and Company*, which in a story set in 1981 has Sarah back from travelling with the Doctor for several years.)

The New Series sidestepped the whole issue, with the Doctor glibly remarking in 2007's "The Sontaran Strategem" that he couldn't remember whether he was scientific adviser to UNIT in the '70s or the '80s. However, a 2008 episode of the spinoff series *The Sarah Jane Adventures*, "The Temptation of Sarah Jane Smith," establishes that she was born in 1951, which suggests her stories in the UNIT era took place in the 1970s, close to when they were broadcast, or else Sarah is older than she appears. (In fact, she is, since actress Elisabeth Sladen was born in 1946!)

Perhaps there's a speculative explanation: UNIT stories were originally set in the late 1970s and early 1980s, but an event like the Time War (as referenced during the Eccleston and Tennant years) or the crack in the universe (2010's "The Eleventh Hour") or the "Big Bang Two" that reset the universe (in 2010's "The Big Bang") moved it back to the 1970s somehow. That said, making events take place ten years earlier (and making people born ten years earlier) seems like an awfully complicated method of rewriting causality.

Given that "Mawdryn Undead" is the more explicit argument and is supported by *The Sarah Jane Adventures*, we're siding with the UNIT stories being set in the time they were made in. (Actually we've hedged it to "near to the present day.") But we freely acknowledge that there is really no correct answer. The truth is indeterminate: in the 1970s, the UNIT stories were set in the 1980s, and in the 1980s, the UNIT stories were set in the 1970s. No one said time travel would be easy.

The Mind of Evil (1971)

Written by Don Houghton **Directed by** Timothy Combe

Featuring Jon Pertwee (Doctor Who), Katy Manning (Jo Grant), Roger Delgado (The Master), Nicholas Courtney (Brigadier Lethbridge-Stewart), Richard Franklin (Mike Yates), John Levene (Sgt. Benton)

Supporting cast Fernanda Marlowe (Corporal Bell), Patrick Godfrey (Major Cosworth), Simon Lack (Kettering), Pik-Sen Lim (Chin Lee), Kristopher Kum (Fu Peng), Tommy Duggan (Senator Alcott), Raymond Westwell (prison governor), Michael Sheard (Summers), Roy Purcell (Powers), Eric Mason (Green), Neil McCarthy (Barnham), William Marlowe (Mailer), Hayden Jones (Vosper), David Calderisi (Charlie), Johnny Barrs (Fuller)

Original airdates January 30, February 6, 13, 20, 27, March 6, 1971

The Big Idea The Doctor and Jo are at Stangmoor Prison investigating the Keller Machine, which takes the evil from hardened criminals' brains. How is it connected to a world peace conference? Easy: the Master is involved . . .

Roots and References Anthony Burgess's 1962 novel *A Clockwork Orange* (the psychological conditioning of antisocial elements of society; Stanley Kubrick's film version came out almost a year after this story was broadcast); the 1954 film *Riot in Cell Block 11* and the 1962 film *The Birdman of Alcatraz* (the prison); *Dracula* (the Keller machine's vampiric nature; Jo also compares Stangmoor to Dracula's castle); *Thunderball* (the theft of the Thunderbolt missile). The Master plays King Crimson's "The Devil's Triangle" on his transistor radio.

Time And Relative Dimensions In Space Producer Barry Letts spent most of his first season on *Doctor Who* making stories his predecessors had commissioned. When it came time to plan *Doctor Who's* eighth season, he was determined to put his stamp on it. Letts made three major innovations. The first was to make shorter serials in order to ensure that there were more "first nights," which acted as jumping-on points for viewers and usually increased ratings. The second was to replace Caroline John's scientist Liz Shaw with a more traditional assistant figure who could feed the Doctor questions about the plot; the result was Jo Grant.

The third and most interesting development was a regular villain for the earthbound Doctor. Seizing upon the idea of a Moriarty figure for the Doctor's Sherlock Holmes, Letts and script editor Terrance Dicks came up with the character of the Master, a Time Lord who was in every way the Doctor's equal, except he was evil. Every story in Season Eight featured the Master, played by Roger Delgado. "The Mind of Evil" was the Master's second appearance in the series. The brief for the character was given to Don Houghton, fresh off his success in writing "Inferno."

Adventures in Time and Space The Doctor has already had one skirmish with the Master in the previous story, 1971's "Terror of the Autons," and the Doctor is still holding on to the Master's dematerialization circuit, which he stole from the Master's TARDIS. The Keller Machine makes the Doctor re-experience the death of a world in flame, which, given this is a story by Don Houghton, presumably refers to the events in the parallel world in "Inferno." Later, the Keller Machine shows a variety of images of the Doctor's past enemies, which include some rather odd choices (presumably the production team had a quick rummage through their files of still photographs). These include a Dalek (with a poor attempt at a Dalek voice to go with it), Koquillian (1964's "The Rescue," although he was actually a human in disguise), a Zarbi (1965's "The Web Planet"), a Silurian ("Doctor Who and the Silurians"), a War Machine (who knew the Doctor was so traumatized by them?) and the Ice Lord Slaar (1969's "The Seeds of Death").

Who is the Doctor? The Doctor speaks Chinese fluently (see also "The Talons of Weng-Chiang") and claims to be a personal friend of Mao

Zedong. He brushes away the pills given to him by Dr. Summers, claiming they would upset his metabolism and kill him. (Fans assumed for decades that these pills were aspirin, but they're never identified.)

Companion Chronicles The Doctor's assistant is now Josephine (Jo) Grant, who got the job with UNIT thanks to an influential uncle at the United Nations. Jo is plucky and courageous, and something of an action star here, clobbering prisoners and using firearms with the best of them. Captain Mike Yates showed up the same time as Jo in "Terror of the Autons." He's charming and somewhat impetuous. The character was intended to give the Brigadier an officer to liaise with the lower ranks (as a brigadier-general wouldn't do that sort of thing) and possibly to be a romantic interest for Jo. (The latter detail never quite worked out, especially as Katy Manning's chemistry with Jon Pertwee was quite strong.)

Monster of the Week The Keller Machine is presented as a device that absorbs the evil from the human brain. It's actually an alien mind parasite brought to Earth by the Master, who uses the negative psychic energy it absorbs to interfere at the peace conference. A side effect is that people who encounter the machine fatally re-experience their worst fears. As the creature inside grows in strength, it is capable of teleporting itself and physically consuming its victims as well.

Stand Up and Cheer The UNIT forces retaking Stangmoor Prison is exciting stuff, full of action and great stunts. But, honestly, why we like it so is the sight of the Brigadier pretending to be a cockney van driver.

Roll Your Eyes Jo laments Barnham's death saying, "We should never have left him there." To which the Doctor replies, "Well, how do you think I feel?" Yes, because it's all about you, Doctor.

You're Not Making Any Sense It's such a cool idea that we feel somewhat guilty faulting it, but there's no way that the human body can physically manifest the symptoms of drowning and rat bites.

Interesting Trivia "The Mind of Evil" has one of the two subtitled conversations in the Classic Series (the second is in "The Curse of Fenric"). The Chinese dialogue between the Doctor and Fu Peng was coached by Pik-Sen Lim, who played Chin Lee. Lim, a Chinese-British actress born in Malaysia, was married to writer Don Houghton, who wrote the Chin Lee character to give his spouse an acting gig. Kristopher Kum, who played Fu Peng, was from Singapore and was frequently sought after for parts requiring a variety of Asian nationalities. The fact that the Asian roles are played by actual Asians is rather unusual, as we will see in a little while.

Just how long has the Master been operating on Earth? According to Professor Kettering, the Keller Process has already been performed 112 times in Switzerland. That presumably means that the Master has been operating as Emil Keller for quite some time. At this point, the Doctor has the Master's TARDIS dematerialization circuit, so he can't travel in time. So either there have been quite a few months between "The Mind of Evil" and the previous story, "Terror of the Autons," or the Master was already posing as Keller prior to "Terror of the Autons." (As a side project in case the Nestene invasion in that story didn't work out, perhaps?) Or maybe the Master simply hypnotized Kettering and others into believing the process had been performed in Switzerland in order to gain access to Stangmoor.

To people new to British television of the 1970s, there are some very strange credits, like "fight arranger" (a stunt person who choreographs fight scenes). Probably the most unusual *Doctor Who* credit is "Action by HAVOC." HAVOC was a stunt crew organized by Derek Ware. (The name is not an acronym; it just appears in all caps.) Their speciality was large-scale action scenes featuring multiple stunt people, quite handy for an action-based series like *Doctor Who*. They appeared in several Jon Pertwee–era stories, often ones where action sequences went over budget! On this story, director Timothy Combe went over budget with the storming of Stangmoor and the addition of a helicopter in episode six, and was consequently never asked back to *Doctor Who*. In spite of all the elaborate stunt work, some of the film sequences were damaged, which meant that further shooting needed to be done — this time with Combe and members of the crew filling in (in less hazardous ways) for HAVOC!

The Thunderbolt rocket was a real (though unarmed) ground-to-air missile supplied by the Royal Air Force, who were happy to pitch in once it was mentioned that the army cooperated during the making of 1968's "The Invasion." (The air force also supplied several men to pitch in on the hijack sequence, though they were wearing standard-issue uniforms instead of the prison garb the hijackers should have been wearing; a hasty rewrite was made to mention that several prisoners had fake uniforms.)

Until the 2013 DVD release, this story only existed in black and white, as the colour masters were wiped in the '70s. The colour recovery process for episodes two through five used chroma dot colour recovery while episode one was manually colourized.

The TARDIS Chronometer Stangmoor Prison and throughout London, near to the present day.

Hai? (GB) Here's why I love the Master: he's the only villain I know who would casually call someone on the phone and ask, with the nonchalance of someone calling his broker, "Would the Doctor be there by any chance?" One wonders what he might have done had Benton told him the Doctor was out: "Would you mind leaving a message? Just let him know my TARDIS is working and I plan to destroy the universe. Yes, that's right. Thank you so much."

But that's the brilliance of Roger Delgado's portrayal of the Master. He hardly ever goes for histrionics, instead playing the character with a charming, conversational quality. The Master finds everyone and everything faintly amusing; as a result, he's great company, the sort of guy you would enjoy hanging out with if you met him a wine bar . . . before he killed you without a second thought, obviously.

Part of the fun of "The Mind of Evil" is just watching the Master, as he drives in the back of a chauffeured car, smoking a stogie, running rings around the Doctor and UNIT. He knows everything his adversaries are up to, and pretty much routs them at every turn. My favourite sequence is his taking of Stangmoor: he gives Mailer an attaché case full of weapons, helps take over the prison and then says, "Right, Doctor, now I'm ready for you." The great thing about Don Houghton's script is that the Master is so incredibly competent (his propensity for revealing his plans to the Doctor aside). It's only when the Keller Machine runs rampant that he's undone.

The Doctor, comparatively, doesn't have a lot to do. He's great in the early episodes when he deduces the connection between the Keller Machine and the peace conference, and thoroughly charms Fu Peng. But later episodes see him on the back foot, constantly reacting to the Master's plans and the Keller Machine — when he's not being imprisoned and tortured. But that actually works in the story's favour: in spite of the enemy having the advantage, the Doctor manages to win anyway.

The victory costs a lot, though. Barnham's death is perhaps inevitable, but also unbelievably harsh. Dr. Summers calls Barnham "an idiot . . . or a saint" and Neil McCarthy's performance magnificently captures both aspects. His murder makes the Master look brutal — and the Doctor, who put the guileless man at risk, looks brutal as well. The Doctor's response that he feels terrible comes off as very hollow. And dickish, when it comes down to it, as he seems to ignore that Jo is actually upset about all this.

My co-author has occasionally railed against the rudeness of the third Doctor. I'm not particularly bothered by it (indeed, the Doctor is rude and arrogant to varying degrees in all his incarnations), but even I found myself annoyed with his behaviour here. He spends most of Kettering's demonstration making grouchy asides; he tells off Jo for not delivering a report instead of thanking her for saving his life when he first encountered the Keller Machine; the Brigadier shoots Mailer and the Doctor remonstrates him for showing up almost too late. The Doctor is a bit of a jerk. It's like this incarnation of the Doctor has some form of Time Lord Asperger's syndrome, demonstrating little empathy, misunderstanding non-verbal cues and speaking without any filter whatsoever. Certainly, the Doctor's friends make allowances for his behaviour: Jo either ignores him or defends him to others, while the Brigadier seems to have opted for increasingly wry smiles.

"The Mind of Evil" is a frustrating story in that, once the connection between the peace conference and Stangmoor is made, all the interesting stuff with Chin Lee terrorizing the conference delegates disappears and we're exclusively dealing with Stangmoor and the threat of the Thunderbolt as the Master becomes more directly involved. But that frustration is mitigated by how great of an ensemble piece this story is. Each UNIT character gets a wonderful moment: Yates tracks down the hijackers and escapes, Benton attempts surveillance, and the Brigadier leads the raid on Stangmoor. They have a familiar interaction with each other, sharing in-jokes and demonstrating the easy relationship co-workers can have (the exchange when the Brigadier makes Benton acting prison governor is a lot of fun to watch). The story also does what *Doctor Who* does best: assembles a fantastic cast of character actors and lets them loose. McCarthy has been already singled out, but Michael Sheard and William Marlowe get far more mileage out of playing Dr. Summers and Mailer than seems possible.

That's not to say that the story doesn't show its age. In many ways it does, quite badly. Yates's assessment of Chin Lee is that she's "quite a dolly." The Master has a black chauffeur (a non-speaking part). And the Brigadier and the Doctor can't stop talking about the "Chinese girl." While having Chinese adversaries was admittedly quite topical in 1971 ("The Mind of Evil" was broadcast a year before Richard Nixon's visit to China), viewed 40 years later, it opens the question of why Pik-Sen Lim, who is great here, couldn't have played a character other than a representative of the People's Republic?

But where it still impresses is in the overall spectacle. The hijacking of the Thunderbolt, and the taking and retaking of Stangmoor are thrilling. Add to this a brilliant ensemble cast and a fantastic villain, and we have the epitome of the exiled-on-Earth/UNIT era of *Doctor Who*. If only the Master would phone the Doctor more often.

Second Opinion (RS?) The Keller Machine might just be my favourite *Doctor Who* monster ever.

It's never really explained what it is, other than an alien psychic parasite. We don't even get a proper look at it, so it simply sits in its container, being menacing. But the wheeze is delightful: it sucks the evil from men's hearts and, in turn, is afraid of the purity in their souls. Or something.

This is awesome. You might as well have an alien that eats publicity and is deathly afraid of J.D. Salinger.

Then, just when you think you have the measure of it, it starts teleporting. Despite the fact that this talent might have come in handy on any number of occasions previously, the Keller Machine is so nefarious that it simply doesn't bother to do so, until it causes maximum impact, conveniently at a cliffhanger.

The reason this works, of course, is because the silent, menacing killer, with ever-changing rules of conduct, is supplemented by a mouthpiece, in the form of the Master. So six episodes worth of sparring can be sustained, even when the creature at the core of the story can't walk, touch or speak.

We're at a transition point in the series: no longer in the monster era of the '60s, when just having something scary lumbering down the corridor was enough, but not yet at the point where the monster itself is an articulate but disfigured humanoid who can spar with the Doctor.

So what we have here is one of the most streamlined ideas for a monster ever. Something sinister in a box. It lives on evil and is killed by good. You can't get any more pure in a *Doctor Who* monster than that. In fact, somewhere out there is a BBC script that feeds off convoluted villains, that mysteriously starts teleporting itself about the television centre, devouring plot contrivances, but is finally stopped when it encounters the Keller Machine itself. You know it makes sense.

And is it just me, or does it look a little bit like a TARDIS console?

Carnival of Monsters (1973)

Written by Robert Holmes **Directed by** Barry Letts

Featuring Jon Pertwee (Doctor Who), Katy Manning (Jo Grant)

Supporting cast Michael Wisher (Kalik), Terence Lodge (Orum), Peter Halliday (Pletrac), Leslie Dwyer (Vorg), Cheryl Hall (Shirna), Tenniel Evans (Major Daly), Jenny McCracken (Claire Daly), Ian Marter (Lt. John Andrews), Andrew Staines (Captain)

Original airdates January 27, February 3, 10, 17, 1973

The Big Idea The Doctor and Jo think they're on a steamship in the 1920s, but they're actually specimens in an intergalactic peepshow run by a travelling showman.

Roots and References The 1968 British drama *The Year of the Sex Olympics* (the functionary class, the use of television to amuse the masses with horrifying images); E.M. Forster's 1924 novel, *A Passage to India* (Major Daly and Claire); *The Lost World* (the plesiosaurus attacking the steamer). Vorg attempts to communicate with the Doctor in *palare*, the language of carnival people.

Time And Relative Dimensions In Space By 1972, the producers responsible for changing the show's format and exiling the Doctor to Earth were long gone. The current team decided the exile had run its course. During Pertwee's fourth year in the role — the tenth season of *Doctor Who* — the Doctor was given the freedom to travel through time and space once again.

This story was the first to take the Doctor out into the stars. But writer Robert Holmes had to work within the strictures of how *Doctor Who* was now being filmed. Scenes were shot according to specific sets or locations in separate recording blocks. In order to save money, the cast members in one recording block could not be used in the other (save for Jon Pertwee and Katy Manning). Holmes came up with a script where the S.S. *Bernice* and the Miniscope's inner workings were shot in one block, and the scenes on Inter Minor were shot in another.

Adventures in Time and Space The Doctor has been freed from his exile in the previous story, "The Three Doctors" (1972), and has promised to take Jo to visit the planet Metebelis Three. (He'll spend the rest of the season attempting to get there.) The Miniscope contains Ogrons (last seen in 1972's "Day of the Daleks"; they appear in the following story, 1973's "Frontier in Space") and Cybermen (the lone Cyberman is wearing a headpiece from 1968's "The Invasion").

Who is the Doctor? It is revealed here that the Doctor was something of a firebrand on his home planet and managed to get the Time Lords to interfere and put a stop to the use of Miniscopes. The Doctor's propensity to namedrop various historical figures begins in earnest with the third Doctor's era; here he claims to have learned boxing from John L. Sullivan.

Companion Chronicles Jo takes all the oddness she encounters — from the Doctor talking to chickens to having to be repeatedly captured as a stowaway — completely in her stride. She's a good lateral (and literal) thinker. The Doctor is very protective of her; she even pretends he's her uncle when they try to talk their way past the S.S. *Bernice* passengers.

Monster of the Week The chief attractions of the Miniscope are the Drashigs, gigantic serpentine creatures with massive teeth. They have no intelligence centre, act purely out of instinct, eat omnivorously (even metal) and mostly hunt by scent. (Incidentally, the model puppet was created with the skull and teeth of a fox terrier!)

Stand Up and Cheer The end of the first episode, with Vorg's hand reaching in and pulling the TARDIS out of the hold of the S.S. *Bernice*, is stunningly imaginative. It takes the story, and *Doctor Who* itself, into completely new territory. As Paul Cornell, Keith Topping and Martin Day write in 1994's *Doctor Who: The Discontinuity Guide*, "TV naturalism crawls into a hole and dies." We couldn't have put it better ourselves.

Roll Your Eyes While we won't hear a bad word about the Drashigs, which are probably the most impressive model-based monsters created in the 1970s, we will pour buckets of scorn on the plesiosaurus, which is embarrassingly bad.

You're Not Making Any Sense One understands Kalik's plan to hide the power source for the eradicator to discredit Vorg when the Drashigs break free. However, had one been in Kalik's place, one would have kept the power source about one's person (and planted it later), just in case one became a source of food for the Drashigs.

Interesting Trivia The scale of everything inside the Miniscope is puzzling. In order for it to fit a steamship and ocean, the vast expanse of marshland for the Drashigs and all the other spaces containing specimens, all of it must be incredibly miniaturized. However, Vorg can stick his hand into it and pull out things or stab around with an object. Given that Vorg just puts the TARDIS somewhere in the top of the Miniscope to keep it from growing, it's quite likely that its compression field shrinks anything inside it, so perhaps Vorg's arm shrinks down (while still attached to his body) as he tries to remove the "bric-a-brac" TARDIS in circuit three. In which case, no wonder Vorg doesn't want to stick his hand inside too often!

Then there's the constant cycling through the same sequence of events. The Doctor talks about it as though the specimens are brainwashed (the people on the S.S. *Bernice* don't remember having performed the sequence before, and they can't see the plating on the deck floor), but the precision with which they repeat the same sequence again and again indicates there must be some kind of playing with time at work. (It would also account for why the people don't age or fatigue.) This might also explain why the Time Lords were able to ban the Miniscope: they had the authority, since a Miniscope manipulates time.

Even so, there's a lingering question: was the S.S. *Bernice* put back in its proper time, changing established history? Because it was routed through the TARDIS, it's equally possible the S.S. *Bernice* wound up on Metebelis III or Skaro!

Ian Marter, who plays Lieutenant Andrews, was producer Barry Letts's first choice to play regular guest star Captain Mike Yates, but the actor had to turn down the role. Letts later cast him as the fourth Doctor's companion Harry Sullivan. It's one of seven instances where an actor played another role before becoming a regular on the series. (The others were Nicholas Courtney, Peter Purves, John Levene, Lalla Ward, Colin Baker, Freema Agyeman and Karen Gillan.)

During the making of this season, producer Barry Letts wanted to try a new arrangement of the theme song with modern synthesizers. And so Delia Derbyshire, who realized the original tune in 1963 (making loops of oscillator noises and mixing them together), along with Brian

Hodgson, made an attempt using a Delaware synthesizer. The higher-ups at the BBC hated the result and it was scrapped. But that version was already on the early edit tapes for "Carnival of Monsters"; this version of episode two made it to Australia and in 1978 it was shown in a repeat broadcast there. (This extended cut, rejected theme song and all, can be found in the special features on the DVD release.)

The TARDIS Chronometer Inside a Miniscope and on the planet Inter Minor, presumably sometime in the future.

Hai? (GB) The success of "Carnival of Monsters" is chiefly the result of two people who, in many ways, set the tone of *Doctor Who* for the remainder of the 1970s and whose legacy continues today.

The first of these is its writer, Robert Holmes. Holmes had written four stories for *Doctor Who* prior to this. All of them possess moments of brilliance and cleverness, but they are mostly potboilers. "Carnival of Monsters" is the point in *Doctor Who*'s history where Robert Holmes emerges as its resident genius, with a unique voice.

And what a place for it to emerge! Had things gone according to the tradition of past outer space stories in 1970s *Doctor Who*, the Doctor's first foray as a free agent in space and time would have been a space-opera runaround, full of social commentary, space travel and honest-to-Alvin-Toffler futurism. (If you don't believe me, put on 1971's "Colony in Space" and 1973's "Frontier in Space" some time.)

Thankfully, *Doctor Who* doesn't stick to tradition and "Carnival of Monsters" is a complete change: we have a loopy comedy, smack dab in one of the straightest eras of *Doctor Who*. The Doctor and Jo land in the 1920s on a steamer in the Indian Ocean. Only it's not quite like that, there's a monster. Only it's not quite like that, they're actually inside a futuristic reality TV device that's run by a showman visiting a planet of bureaucratic grey people who speak of themselves abstractly. And with that, *Doctor Who* suddenly becomes the program we knew it would become: satirical, wild, bizarre, full of suspense and monsters, and just plain entertaining.

You know this story is something special from the first lines of dialogue where the Inter Minorians discuss their lot in life. ("Reluctantly, one must agree.") But that's just Holmes warming up. There's the double act of Vorg and Shirna: the former ebullient and shifty, the latter weary of the other's stunts. Best of all, there's the gorgeously strange world-building with references to the unseen President Zarb, humans referred to as "Tellurians" (a term that will reoccur in Holmes's work), the gambling-addicted Wallarians, the Eternity-Perpetuity company and "Voldale's theory that life is infinitely variable" (which is apparently proven wrong by the existence of humans). *Doctor Who* frequently travelled to other planets in its first ten years of existence; this is one of the first times it went to another *world*.

It's Holmes's brilliant sense of satire that really makes this story. Throughout is a subtle but brilliant parallel between the Raj-era imperialism of Major Daly, and the hostility of Kalik, Orum and Pletrac towards the functionaries. ("Give them a hygiene chamber and they store fossil fuel in it.") None of the functionaries is given any kind of voice, but at the same time, the Inter Minor ruling elite who do speak are blithering idiots. Pletrac is a stuffed-shirt who hopes appeasement will make everyone happy, Orum just wants whatever the dominant character wants, and Kalik is paranoid to a Nixonian level but doesn't have an ounce of self-preservation.

These twits are the ones trying to deal with the greatest threat to their existence: television. And here's where the satire really comes into play. The Drashigs are "always a favourite with the children" (which borders on Holmes biting the gigantic hand that feeds him). Vorg defends the Miniscope to Kalik saying, "It's nothing serious, nothing political." (But it is. The Inter Minorians believe that by amusing the functionaries they could make them a more docile workforce.) Oh, and did you notice that, for all Vorg's protests that he can't tell the Tellurians apart, when it comes down it, Vorg doesn't know there are extra humans in Circuit Three because he doesn't actually watch the programs he promotes! It's funny, wry and incisive.

The other person who defines this story, and *Doctor Who* in this era in general, is the producer. Barry Letts directed this story and produced *Doctor Who* from 1970 to 1974, almost the entirety of the Jon Pertwee era and one story with Tom Baker. He co-created the Master. He cast Tom Baker, Elisabeth Sladen, Roger Delgado and Katy Manning in roles that made them icons. He made *Doctor Who* a weekly television spectacle, a template that Russell T Davies and Steven Moffat emulate even today.

Letts understood what *Doctor Who* was capable of doing and that his job was to make it as exciting as possible so people watched. That's not to say his predecessors didn't do that either, but Barry Letts made it a vocation. His task was to get bums on seats watching at teatime on Saturday afternoons and to do whatever it took to get them there. He achieved this in so many ways that now seem commonplace but at the time were huge innovations. He made the episode length of stories shorter. He experimented with an early version of greenscreen technology and used models to give *Doctor Who* stories a cost-effective but grand scale and scope, comparable with film instead of stage. And as a former actor, he understood the importance of the performances.

You can see all of this on display in "Carnival of Monsters," a story with great scope and ambition. "Carnival of Monsters" is not content to just have a guy in a rubber suit, but the sort of gigantic, terrifying monster you'd see at the cinema (and made with one-twentieth of Ray Harryhausen's budget). Episode three has an incredible sense of spectacle to it: the Drashigs aren't perfect, but they blend in with the locations incredibly well and they invoke real menace. It's stunning to watch.

"Carnival of Monsters" is a triumph of two people's visions of *Doctor Who*: a writer who thought the show could be smarter, funnier, bolder and more imaginative than anything else, and a producer/ director who thought the show should be the most exciting spectacle on British television. That *Doctor Who* is still watched today is because of what these two people attempted to do here.

Second Opinion (RS?) In a complex television production, a show excels when the ancillary pieces — not just the writer and producer — don't just bring the script to life, they actually enhance it.

Take the costumes and makeup, for example. The S.S. *Bernice* crew and passengers look exactly the way you'd expect: Claire's dress and hairstyle are perfectly 1920s; Andrews is impeccable in his uniform and his own hairstyle is quite accurate, even though it's only seen once; and Major Daly looks every inch the colonialist in his off-white suit and striped tie. The result is the BBC doing what it does best: recreating the past to perfection.

It's when the story looks forward, rather than backwards, that costume and makeup really come into their own. On Inter Minor, the officials are appropriately grey-faced, which adds shading to their bureaucratic dialogue. Even better, their costumes are subtly pinstriped. We know who these people are, even before the script tells us: despite being aliens on a futuristic planet, they're civil servants.

This frees up the dialogue to really shine. Instead of wasting valuable time telling us who these people are, the script concentrates on its witty dialogue and world-building. Pletrac wears judge's robes, because he's head of a tribunal, something that you'd otherwise probably forget.

In contrast to the Inter Minorian greyness, Vorg and Shirna are a burst of colour. Their outfits are as bright as you can imagine, with baubles and beads adorning them. The reveal of the costumes is a clue to what's going on here: they start off in grey spacesuits and then expose the colour beneath. Once again, costume tells us who these people are before the script does: they're travelling performers, with a wardrobe to match.

As for the Doctor and Jo, their palette is somewhere in the middle. Not as flashy as the performers or as precise as the ship's inhabitants, they're halfway between uniform and showy. Jo's blue jacket gives her a more formal look than she usually has and is stylistically similar to the Doctor's outfit. For his part, the Doctor is mistaken for a carnival performer solely because of the way he dresses.

The Functionaries are dressed in an appropriately drab manner, reminding the viewer of the visual similarities between them and the Indian crew aboard the S.S. *Bernice*. That connection is strengthened when you realize that neither group has any dialogue and are seen in entirely subservient roles. The most advanced task that each group performs is to man weapons.

And thus, expressed solely through the visuals, we see a connection that the dialogue never makes explicit. The Functionaries are lower-class workers, who vastly outnumber their masters and create an ever-present threat of revolution. The imaginative leap to how the ship's crew must view their servants isn't very difficult at all; it would have had even more resonance in 1973, with viewers seeing reports of rebellions in British colonies on a regular basis.

Without doubt, the visuals help enormously in adding depth to the story and, in at least one instance, draw a connection that Robert Holmes may not have even been thinking of while writing it. That's the magic of television.

- -

Making *Doctor Who* in the 1970s and 1980s

The start of the 1970 season of *Doctor Who* marked a number of important changes in the way the program was made. Though the vast majority of households in Britain still had black and white TV sets, and would for much of the decade, the advent of *Doctor Who* in colour meant that more sophisticated cameras, lighting setups and recording equipment were required. Consequently, with only a few exceptions, *Doctor Who* was made at BBC Television Centre in London. The days of small studios like Lime Grove were over.

Videotape editing facilities had also become more sophisticated. Tape editing in the '60s was no more complex than physically cutting the videotape and splicing it together, but by the early '70s it was possible to edit by dubbing the raw footage onto a new tape. Stories were no longer required to have single episodes shot in script order.

It was the second story of the 1970s, "Doctor Who and the Silurians," that bridged the transition from old methods to new. In the fashion of the 1960s stories, each episode was shot separately in scene order. However, the cave set was badly damaged between shoots. Incoming producer Barry Letts decided that, from then on, the show would be shot on a set-by-set basis.

The *Doctor Who* filming schedule now encompassed the whole story, not just individual episodes. It was based on the particular sets being used and took place in two or three studio sessions (depending on the length of the story), split a week or so apart. In addition to this was the location filming, which became more extensive during the 1970s. This practice continued until the Classic Series ended in 1989.

While studio sessions were still performed in real time with a vision mixer to switch between multiple cameras, improved editing facilities and out-of-sequence recording meant the pace of production was much faster and retakes were feasible. Not only were flubbed lines (mostly) a thing of the past, but the best take of a sequence would be chosen. There were still time constraints to manage: union regulations required that a studio session conclude by 10 p.m., after four or five hours of taping. (Literally. The engineers would turn out the studio lights at 10:01 p.m.!) Even so, in the 1970s and 1980s, *Doctor Who* was made more like film than recorded theatre.

The '70s and '80s also saw an increase in special effects, done in-house by the BBC's special-effects department. One of the great innovations of the '70s was a process known within the BBC as colour separation overlay (CSO), but known elsewhere as chromakey. It was essentially a progenitor of the modern-day greenscreen process, where figures against a coloured background (sometimes blue, yellow or green) were composited against another video image. This allowed for the Doctor and his companions to see and interact (on a limited basis) with outer-space vistas or giant monsters — or sometimes even location footage! In the 1980s, computer-controlled cameras and post-production effects software added certain visuals and colours, so that, by the final story of the Classic Series, "Survival," an entire alien vista could be created in the background without resorting to greenscreen.

During the 1960s, *Doctor Who* had used stock music, original work by composers or, in the occasional episode, no music at all. The vast majority of 1970s *Doctor Who* episodes had soundtracks composed by Dudley Simpson, who employed a combination of small orchestras, or played organs and electronic instruments himself. His last score for *Doctor Who* was the final story completed in the 1970s, "The Horns of Nimon." During the 1980s, the responsibility for scoring *Doctor Who* was given to the BBC Radiophonic Workshop, who performed scores using state of the art synthesizers (and sampling sounds digitally) before they were replaced by contracted musicians who used similar instruments.

The Green Death (1973)

Written by Robert Sloman, Barry Letts (uncredited)

Directed by Michael Briant

Featuring Jon Pertwee (Doctor Who), Katy Manning (Jo Grant), Nicholas Courtney (Brigadier Lethbridge-Stewart), Richard Franklin (Mike Yates), John Levene (Sgt. Benton)

Supporting cast Stewart Bevan (Professor Clifford Jones), Jerome Willis (Stevens), Mitzi McKenzie (Nancy), Ben Howard (Hinks), John Rolfe (Fell), Tony Adams (Elgin), Roy Skelton (James), John Dearth (voice of BOSS), Richard Beale (Minister of Ecology), Talfryn Thomas (Dave), Roy Evans (Bert), Mostyn Evans (Dai Evans), John Scott Martin (Hughes)

Original airdates May 19, 23, June 2, 9, 16, 23, 1973

The Big Idea In Wales, a chemical factory's waste is getting into the nearby coal mine — creating giant, deadly maggots.

Roots and References The 1970 film *Colossus: The Forbin Project* and *2001: A Space Odyssey* (a sentient, talking computer with its own agenda). Much of the story was "ripped from the headlines," including the emerging ecological crisis of the 1970s (the overall theme) and the 1972 British miners' strike (the unemployed miners and the government's need for a cheap energy source). The Nuthutch took its inspiration from the early days of Greenpeace.

Time And Relative Dimensions In Space Producer Barry Letts was a man with a distinct point of view. He was a Buddhist and tended to lean to the left on most political issues, including environmentalism. Script editor Terrance Dicks suggested Letts put his thoughts into a *Doctor Who* story. Letts had co-written the two previous season finales with his friend Robert Sloman, a sometime playwright who worked in the circulation department at the *Sunday Times*. (With BBC politics preventing production team members from commissioning themselves to write, the stories went out under Sloman's name alone or under a pseudonym.) Letts and Sloman set to work on their environmental story for the finale of the tenth season. Early on, they had to accommodate one important change: Katy Manning was leaving the series after three years, so writing out Jo became a major focus for the pair.

Letts expected all kinds of controversy when the program went out. In the end, the only complaint was a humorous letter complaining that Jon Pertwee had mispronounced, at Letts's instruction, the word "chitinous"!

Adventures in Time and Space The Doctor finally gets to Metebelis III, a quest he started back in "Carnival of Monsters." Jo's first scene with Cliff deliberately echoes the first time she met the Doctor in 1971's "Terror of the Autons." Jo's uncle at the United Nations, who got her the job at UNIT in "Terror of the Autons," gets the Nuthutch UN funding.

Who is the Doctor? By now, the Doctor is an expert in Venusian aikido (he's moved on from their form of karate — mostly because the production team thought karate sounded too violent!), and he delivers a beatdown on several guards who bar his way. The Doctor is a master of disguise, fooling the guard by posing as an elderly Welsh milkman and dressing in drag as a cleaning woman! He's clearly shaken by Jo's decision to marry Cliff and quietly departs from the party, showing a loneliness hardly ever seen in one of the most convivial Doctors.

Companion Chronicles The Brigadier is given a rare opportunity to wear civvies for much of the story, but is still very much the thoughtful professional. While he disagrees with Jo's decision to join Cliff and the protesters, he respects her choice and even offers her a ride. A class act. Mike Yates is brought in by the Brigadier to spy on Global Chemicals (the

Brigadier points out to the Doctor that he doesn't just shoot at things). Mike looks briefly saddened when Jo announces her engagement.

However, this story is really about Jo's departure from UNIT and life with the Doctor. In some ways, the decision was already made at the end of the previous story, 1973's "Planet of the Daleks," when Jo spurned the advances of a Thal, telling the Doctor her life was on Earth. She decides to take a stand by staying on Earth to help Clifford Jones in his cause in Wales, leaving the Doctor to wistfully say, "The fledgling flies the coop." Her decision to marry Cliff only confirms this.

Monster of the Week The chemical waste from Global Chemicals is deadly to humans, but it mutates maggots to become gigantic. One of them even metamorphoses into a giant insect.

Stand Up and Cheer The Doctor and Jo have their return route blocked by a cave-in — and the way forward is a tunnel filled with giant maggots. That is exciting television in any era.

Roll Your Eyes The first utterance of "boyo" and you know you're not in Wales, but some notional place that the English think Wales is really like.

You're Not Making Any Sense BOSS's plan wouldn't really pass scrutiny at an average investors' meeting. The computer connects worldwide and takes over even more employees. And then what? And what about the giant maggots that would grow into giant insects that could reproduce and kill much of the populace?

Interesting Trivia The joke at the start of this story is that Metebelis III isn't the beautiful planet the Doctor has described, but a hostile dump! The Doctor's one souvenir, the blue crystal of Metebelis III, returns in Jon Pertwee's final story.

When the Minister of Ecology puts on the prime minister, he calls him "Jeremy." It's a bit of a joke on the part of Barry Letts: Jeremy Thorpe was the leader of the Liberal Party, the third party in Britain (it would later merge with the Social Democratic Party in the 1980s and become the Liberal Democratic Party). The Liberals had a tiny number of seats in Parliament. Letts was making the joke that, in the near-future world of the UNIT stories, Thorpe somehow managed to win!

The Doctor is seen repairing the space-time coordinate programmer, which will (slightly) improve his accuracy from this point on and enable him to travel more often to places he selects. The Doctor seemed to have no real idea of how to fix it in his first and second incarnations, so either regaining the knowledge of time travel in "The Three Doctors" came with a few added extras, or the Doctor has spent a lot more time figuring out how his TARDIS worked during his exile.

If you're wondering why Elgin abruptly disappears from the action, only to be suddenly replaced by James as a brainwashed employee, there's a good reason: actor Tony Adams burst his appendix between studio sessions, necessitating a last-minute replacement by Roy Skelton. Skelton took on Elgin's part, hastily renamed James.

This isn't the last we'll see of Jo Grant: the character returned in 2010 (still played by Katy Manning) in *The Sarah Jane Adventures* story "Death of the Doctor." In that story, Jo is still married to Cliff, has children and grandchildren, and continues her lifestyle of travelling and protesting. She meets the eleventh Doctor, who tells her that, while he never visited her, he always kept track of her and was proud of her. Katy Manning, on the other hand, followed up her *Doctor Who* career more controversially: in the mid-1970s, she appeared nude on the cover of a men's magazine with a Dalek!

The TARDIS Chronometer Llanfairfach, South Wales, near to the present day, with visits to Metebelis III and the Doctor's lab at UNIT headquarters.

Hai? (GB) About 12 or so years ago, when my goddaughter, Cadence, was seven years old, I started showing her episodes of *Doctor Who*. (I told her, "It's just like Harry Potter." Yes, I lied.) This being well before the New Series debuted, I showed her Tom Baker stories to begin with and she really enjoyed them. I canvassed friends on what other ones to show her. My friend Eva suggested "The Green Death": "It's big and it's colourful and has a scary monster. She'll love it."

Cadence did indeed love it. To this day, it's her favourite *Doctor Who* story. In fact, when I told her I was writing this book, she responded, "'The Green Death' better be in there."

Truthfully, I probably would have included it anyway. Eva was right: it is big and colourful and has the scariest of monsters. Even if SFX technology has since progressed, the maggots are still frightening. I can't think of a monster in the history of *Doctor Who* that generates a more visceral reaction than the giant maggots. Even writing this has me squirming in my chair.

I remember when my best friend, Rob, described "The Green Death" to me when I was a teenager. He said, "Of course, being *Doctor Who*, it turns out a computer is behind it all . . ." I take his point. Having BOSS turn out to be a computer seems like the middle-aged dad version of science fiction and a terribly unsubtle way to talk about how companies value efficiency over protecting the environment. But . . . I love BOSS. Characterizing the computer not as an efficient logical calculating machine like Colossus or HAL but rather as an English capitalist is genius. The Doctor's not battling an automaton but an ego (one that might be bigger than the Doctor's!), one who is fond of the sound of his own voice (the humming is a great touch) and who treats Stevens affectionately like some kind of a pet (I love how BOSS calls Stevens his "little Nietzschean"). It completely subverts expectation, like all good *Doctor Who*.

"The Green Death" is a taut thriller with science-fiction overtones. Take out the Doctor and it would still hold up well on its own as a movie, which I don't think I can say all that often about *Who* stories. The characters are vivid and well defined, the slow reveal of BOSS and his role is well done, and there's a brilliant ensemble of characters: Cliff's commune, the miners, the Global Chemical employees, Stevens, the Brigadier. And all of them get wonderful moments. The climax where Stevens destroys BOSS, the camera zooming in on him as a tear streams down his face, is haunting.

That's not to say the Doctor is superfluous; quite the contrary, no Doctor instigates trouble better than this incarnation. Pertwee is sublimely suave here, whether he's beating up Stevens' thugs (a scene that evokes in me equal measures of *Kill Bill* and the 1966 TV *Batman*) or facing down Stevens and BOSS. (As BOSS and Stevens have the Doctor in their clutches and put the brainwashing headphones on him, the Doctor just casually works out a few sums, nonchalantly resisting the attempt to take over his mind.) Okay, Pertwee camps it up as a pantomime widow a little too much when dressed as a cleaning woman, but I'll forgive that because of his final scene. The idea of the Doctor as a lonely god, always losing the ones he loves, didn't originate in the New Series; it starts here.

One of the subtle touches to this story is that it addresses, at least indirectly, the fact that Jo and the Doctor's relationship is a complicated one. He's avuncular towards her — he calls her a "fledgling"

— but he also cares for her a great deal in ways that seem more than avuncular, as witnessed by his quiet but significant departure once Jo's mind is made up to marry Cliff. On the one hand, the relationship seems asexual, but is there more motivating the Doctor? Ambiguity like this is something we expect to see in the New Series: is the Doctor's derailing of Cliff's nighttime assignation with Jo paternalistic meddling, deliberately obtuse, or actual cockblocking? Or all three?

As for Jo, she marries the first man her own age who resembles the Doctor — and there's nothing subtle about it, either. Even before she's met Cliff, she tells the Doctor that Cliff reminds her of a younger version of him. Her first scene with Cliff copies almost exactly the circumstances of the Doctor's first meeting with Jo. And Clifford Jones himself is eccentric, morally self-righteous, funny, charming and a rabble rouser. (He doesn't know Venusian aikido, but I'm sure he could learn.) What does this say about Jo's relationship with the Doctor? Were they in love with each other but incapable of acting on it for some reason? Or was Jo interested but the Doctor never reciprocated? We'll never know.

It's a shame that the convention of the age when this story was made meant that Jo couldn't just be with Cliff, but had to marry him. Not only because it reinforces the usual sexist tropes, but because it obscures the fact that the character had really made her choice in going to the Nuthutch instead of Metebelis III. Jo wants a life of her own, not to be ordered around by the Doctor or the Brigadier. True, she is following another man's dream, but it needs to be said that she chooses to go exploring the Amazon even before Cliff has proposed. She really does want to find a life for herself.

That's "The Green Death": it's big and colourful and exciting for a seven-year-old, but it's also full of suspense, drama, great characters and subtle undertones that make it something adults can appreciate as well. Give it a try. Cadence will be pleased if you do.

Second Opinion (RS?) You never forget your first time.

I was five years old and my TV schedule was full. I was already following way too many programs and had no time for another. Come on, I had priorities! Monday was *Skippy*. Tuesday was *Flipper*. Wednesday was *Mr. Squiggle*. (Hey, I grew up in Australia. Don't judge me.) My father had been a fan of William Hartnell and had watched the early days of *Doctor Who*. One day — later research reveals it was June 12, 1978 — he was watching episode six of "The Green Death," for old times' sake.

I tried not to watch, I really did. The maggots had me intrigued, but I was determined not to get hooked on yet another show. I only had so much time, you understand. I went back to my room to build some paper planes.

However, something drew me out again and I stood watching from the doorway. Benton throwing food to the maggots was pretty good, but I wasn't going to get sucked in. Not with my TV schedule so overbooked.

After a while, I finished my paper planes and thought I might just wander back and see how it was progressing. It couldn't do any harm, surely? And then I saw it. The moment that would change my entire life.

That's right, I saw the giant fly. And oh, what a thing of beauty it was!

I was hooked then and there. My TV schedule may have been packed, but nothing — nothing! — could possibly be as exciting as this. I sat and watched the rest of the episode with wide eyes. I could have sworn I saw Stevens' body flying over the factory in the explosion, even though I now know that was actually a piece of the model.

The next day, I tuned into episode one of "The Time Warrior" and met Sarah Jane Smith and Sontarans in the Middle Ages. I never looked back.

Since then, I've lived with *Doctor Who* my entire life. It's made me friends and lovers, and taken me around the world. When I moved to a new hemisphere and knew no one, the language of *Doctor Who* allowed me to make friendships with people as soon as I met them (including that Burk guy). And I've seen amazing episodes of this TV show — including falling in love all over again with the New Series — that I continue to adore.

But no experience in my life has been or ever will be as profound or worldshaking as watching the thrilling finale of "The Green Death" at five years old and losing my *Doctor Who* virginity. I went in as a boy and came out a fan.

The Ark in Space (1975)

Written by Robert Holmes **Directed by** Rodney Bennett

Featuring Tom Baker (Doctor Who), Elisabeth Sladen (Sarah Jane Smith), Ian Marter (Harry Sullivan)

Supporting cast Wendy Williams (Vira); Kenton Moore (Noah); Richardson Morgan (Rogin); John Gregg (Lycett); Christopher Masters (Libri); Gladys Spencer (High Minister's voice); Stuart Fell, Nick Hobbs (Wirrn); Peter Tuddenham (voices)

Original airdates January 25, February 1, 8, 16, 1975

The Big Idea On board a space station in the far future, an alien insect intends to lay its eggs in the surviving members of the human race.

Roots and References The 1958 film *The Fly* and Franz Kafka's *Metamorphosis* (a human mutating into an insect), *Quatermass and the Pit* (projecting thoughts onto a screen), then-current fears about nuclear war (hiding survivors away in a secure environment).

Time And Relative Dimensions In Space John Lucarotti, who wrote several episodes in the first Doctor era, was commissioned to write a story set on a space station. He formulated a tale involving floating disembodied superminds called the Delc. The incoming production team — producer Philip Hinchcliffe and script editor Robert Holmes — wanted to skew *Doctor Who* slightly older, with more sophisticated stories and enhanced horror, and found Lucarotti's more juvenile scripts wanting. However, Lucarotti lived on a boat in the Mediterranean and, thanks to a postal strike, was unavailable for rewrites. Robert Holmes stepped in and started from scratch. Lucarotti received no credit, but he did receive an *ex gratia* payment.

The space-station setting was devised as a cost-savings exercise. Two stories in the season were filmed on the same set; this story and 1975's "Revenge of the Cybermen" both take place on *Nerva*. (In the latter story, the TARDIS crew end up on *Nerva* in an earlier era.)

Adventures in Time and Space The story continues on from the previous story, 1974's "Robot," where the Doctor offered to show an incredulous Harry the inside of the TARDIS. Harry later mentions the Brigadier telling him to stick with the Doctor (from the same story). Sarah references her first time travelling in the TARDIS (1973's "The Time Warrior").

Who is the Doctor? The fourth Doctor is noticeably more alien than his predecessors. He veers between aloof and moody, commanding and childlike. Here he uses a yo-yo to take a gravity reading and also carries a cricket ball, antenna and jelly babies. He states that his doctorate is purely honorary and that humans are his favourite species. His brain can withstand the kind of shock that would kill a human, allowing images from the dead Wirrn to be projected on a screen. Sarah also notes that the Doctor talks to himself sometimes, because he's the only person who understands what he's saying.

Companion Chronicles Sarah Jane Smith is a journalist who met the Doctor when she impersonated her own aunt, a virologist. Along with the Brigadier, she witnessed the third Doctor's regeneration into the fourth. Surgeon Lieutenant Harry Sullivan was assigned to the fourth Doctor following his regeneration in the previous story, "Robot."

Harry and Sarah engage in full-on banter here, not dissimilar to Amy and Rory travelling with the eleventh Doctor. They constantly tease each other around chauvinism, with Harry calling her names like "old girl" and noting how proud Sarah must be that there's a woman in charge of Earth. Sarah gives as good as she gets, telling him off whenever he calls her sexist names and generally standing up for herself.

Monster of the Week The Wirrn, space-borne insects the size of humans, recycle waste into oxygen using enzymes in their lungs. They only visit planets occasionally, for food and oxygen, like a whale rising from the ocean. They can absorb human knowledge by infecting someone and also pass on their race memories to the infected. Humans destroyed their breeding colonies on Andromeda, forcing them to become wanderers.

Stand Up and Cheer The Doctor's "indomitable" speech is one of the all-time greatest speeches in *Doctor Who*. Or indeed anywhere. In a stark future, the Doctor discovers the human race preserved in a single room and delivers a speech celebrating their achievements ("only a few million years since they crawled out of the mud and learned to walk") and their ability to survive anything ("and now here they are, out among the stars . . . ready to outsit eternity"). Watch it and see if you don't get shivers. Ladies and gentlemen, Tom Baker is the Doctor.

Roll Your Eyes In 1975, there was a new product on the market, mainly used in industrial packing. It wouldn't have been familiar to the vast majority of viewers at home, especially if spray-painted green. We get that. But sadly, no matter how much you try to disguise it, there's absolutely no way that bubble wrap looks like anything but bubble wrap.

You're Not Making Any Sense The inhabitants of the space station *Nerva* were supposed to awaken 5,000 years ago, but overslept because the dying adult Wirrn cut through the cables. Just before it died in a cupboard, it laid its eggs inside technician Dune. When the TARDIS arrives, what was once Dune has just moved to the pupal stage. So do the Wirrn really gestate for 5,000 years, then?

Interesting Trivia The backstory to the launch of the Ark isn't explicitly revealed, but there are enough clues to piece it together. Solar flares threatened Earth's destruction, so they adapted *Nerva Beacon* (as it used to be called) into *Nerva* space station. Humans were chosen based on their genetic material to ensure the human race would survive. Records of all human learning were placed on the Ark, along with animal and botanic specimens. A few other groups may have survived: Vira assumes the Doctor and Harry are from a colony (we see such survivors in the next story, 1975's "The Sontaran Experiment") and there's also talk of thermic shelters.

Other *Doctor Who* stories also deal with the near-destruction of Earth in the far future, most notably the first segment of 1986's "The Trial of a Time Lord" (also by Robert Holmes). In that story, Earth was nearly wiped out and civilization lost as a result of the Time Lords forcibly relocating the planet to another galaxy. It's tempting to think that these might be the same event (especially if the planet was returned afterwards, although that's not clear from "The Trial of a Time Lord"). The final destruction of Earth happens much later, which we saw in 1966's "The Ark." Some of the survivors from that period headed to a new planet, while others ended up on colonies, as we see in "Frontios."

"The Ark in Space" had among the highest ratings of the Classic Series. The second episode scored 13.6 million viewers, a record for the series to date and one that would only be bested in 1979 up against, literally, no competition (more on that a little bit later). It also reached number five on the U.K. charts, the series' highest position until 2007's "Voyage of the Damned" reached number two.

When the DVD was released, an option was added to watch the story with updated special effects, remodelled by the BBC visual effects department. The space station doesn't wobble and the transport ship looks like an actual rocket, rather than something out of a build-your-own-plastic-spaceship kit. We're of two minds about it. The original effects were of their time and obviously fit in with the story overall, in a way that 21st-century CGI simply can't. On the other hand, if you're showing this to a non-fan as their first exposure to the Classic Series (which is a great idea, actually), then it might not be a bad idea to switch these on.

Unusually, most of the twelfth season's stories were linked — something that hadn't happened much since the 1960s. This story ends with the Doctor, Sarah and Harry transmatting down to Earth. In the very next story, 1975's "The Sontaran Experiment," they find the planet rehabilitated since the solar flares but also discover human explorers being experimented on by the Sontaran Styre. Naturally, the Doctor defeats Styre and prevents the Sontaran from invading before the travellers transmat back to *Nerva*. Or so they think . . .

The TARDIS Chronometer Aboard space station *Nerva*, many thousands of years in the future. The space station was built around the thirtieth century (approximately the year 3000) and the solar flares were 10,000 years ago. Since other stories have Earth inhabited up to at least the year 5000, this has to take place sometime after the year 15,000.

What? (RS?) "The Ark in Space" has only one thing on its mind: what does it mean to be human? Everything pivots around this question.

Right from the get-go, it doesn't look like previous *Doctor Who*. It's not just Tom Baker's alien Doctor, although that's a part of it. This feels grown up, a confident and adult story, where everything comes together, from the set design to the costuming. *Doctor Who* isn't a kid's show anymore; it's happy to have them along for the ride, but children aren't the primary audience.

The plotting is incredibly tight, starting from a simple incident: the Doctor repairing the cables. From this, the automatic guard — a key factor in the eventual defeat of the Wirrn — appears, Sarah is transmatted to the cryogenic chamber, the inhabitants begin to awake and the Wirrn infest the solar stacks. The subsequent reveal of the backstory involving Dune is carried off with considerable aplomb, partly because it takes some time before we get to see it and partly because the flashback is intimately connected to the very present danger of the Doctor's brain potentially overloading and the Wirrn larva attacking. That's brilliant.

In some ways, the second story of any Doctor could be a Hartnell story. This is probably the ultimate example of that: the first episode sees the TARDIS crew exploring a location without any other characters present; the Doctor is primarily an observer, at least initially; and the premise is a magnificent idea, of the sort you don't see in any other kind of television program.

That idea is quite simple in its enormity: the entire human race, in one room. Having the fate of our species hang in the balance, with the bare minimum of survivors under immediate threat, is the story's engine. Humanity is something worth celebrating and too precious to be lost.

However, it's the sub-theme of possession that really brings the issue of humanity to the fore. The second cliffhanger sees Noah's hand transformed, but it's the following pause in the drama that's really telling. The (long dead) high minister's voice rings out, making a sweeping speech about the grand efforts that have been achieved here, while we see all the aspects of the station: the exterior of the Ark, the wonderful windowed corridors, the cryogenic room. Here in this metal vessel, humanity stands at a precipice. The events here matter.

Furthermore, when Noah wrestles with being possessed, we're treated to an astonishingly effective portrayal of a man at war with himself. Kenton Moore is superb, carrying off a difficult scene on his own, largely through vocal and facial expressions. Indeed, the third cliffhanger doesn't involve our heroes in danger, it involves Noah completing his transformation into a Wirrn. That's horrific, because his humanity has now been completely eliminated.

The Doctor tries to appeal to Noah through his memories of the sun and the sky, but he no longer has memory of such things. Humanity is intimately tied to the Earth itself, which has become a proxy for what the Ark's inhabitants are striving for. They don't just want to go on as a species; they're desperate to return to Earth. Rogin even suggests it would have been preferable to die on Earth in the solar flares than to live on the Ark in the cold.

The solution to the Wirrn infestation is a mix of the elegant (electricity) and futuristic (the transmats are reversible). This is quite stunning, because it allows the viewer at home to connect to the story, but it also takes its established sci-fi rules and turns them on their head. Either solution alone would have been quite poor. But combining them is the Goldilocks of plot resolutions: where electricity is too simple an answer and reversible transmats too complex, what we get is just right.

There's even a working definition of precisely what it is that makes us human: self-sacrifice for the greater good. Between Rogin taking the brunt of the thruster blast so the Doctor won't and the last vestige of humanity in Noah resulting in the destruction of the Wirrn in the transport ship, we see the most important aspect of the theme: that there are some things bigger than an individual life and they're worth dying for.

Both Russell T Davies and Steven Moffat have claimed "The Ark in Space" as their favourite Classic Series story. The fact that two very different people, with diametrically opposed ideas about what *Doctor Who* is all about, can agree on this story's quality should tell you everything you need to know. "The Ark in Space" is the flag-bearer for what *Doctor Who* is capable of. It looks incredible. It's acted to within an inch of its life. It stars a leading man you cannot take your eyes off. And it has fundamental things to say about what it means to be human.

It really doesn't get much better than this.

Second Opinion (GB) Rogin really bothers me. A whole episode is spent establishing that Vira and Noah are from the future and don't understand or use slang, and then an episode later you have Rogin saying things like "I reckon" and generally talking in twentieth-century colloquialisms that would be archaisms by the standards of Vira and Noah.

It would be simple to claim Rogin as a mistake: Rogin is there because it's easy to write a character like him — sarcastic, humorous and cowardly, but in the end noble and full of pithy wit — and it's harder to write someone more formal like Vira. And perhaps it is a mistake on Robert Holmes's part. Or it may be something more interesting, more thematic: perhaps Rogin's very existence indicates that, in this rarifed world, humanity will win out no matter what.

My co-author quite rightly states that "The Ark in Space" is legendary for its optimistic humanism, but it's an odd thing to say about a story set on a space station where humanity has become almost hivelike. Like Rogin, "The Ark in Space" is a story full of contradictions. It's a story about how humanity redeems itself by banishing the insect-like race that they were in danger of becoming, both metaphorically and literally. Noah and Vira start out as autocratic pragmatists and wind up as romantic heroes. The warm smile on Vira's face at the end (a smile that was inconceivable when the character was introduced in episode two) conveys everything: the human race now has its humanity back.

What's even more fascinating is how all this warm humanism serves as fodder for the horror. There's no denying that it's a little embarrassing to see Kenton Moore holding up his arm wrapped in bubble wrap. But here's the thing: the effect doesn't matter. What matters is Noah's reaction. The revulsion is wonderfully realized by Moore. This is *Doctor Who*'s first foray into body horror (essentially making *Alien* about five years before Ridley Scott) and it effectively sets the agenda for Philip Hinchcliffe and Robert Holmes's tenure producing *Doctor Who*, with a more adult treatment of horror and suspense, and superior production values.

The performances are superlative. Tom Baker is everything my co-author says and so much more. I love watching the relationship between Harry and Sarah, which seems combative and yet flirtatious as well. And Elisabeth Sladen already has a wonderful connection with Tom Baker: the scene with Sarah stuck in the ventilation duct is lovely as the Doctor uses her anger to motivate her. The looks on both characters' faces when she's finally free are priceless. And the first episode (carried, effortlessly we might add, only by the regular cast) gives Ian Marter some great scenes with Tom Baker as well. Harry is stodgy, but Ian Marter never makes him foolish.

But it's Wendy Williams who really deserves plaudits, taking Vira from someone cold and logical to warm and open in a small space of time. It's done through a series of tiny shifts (watch Williams as Vira admits that she and Noah were "pairbonded") and it's not a random change but a steady evolution. Because, at the end of the day, humanity will win out. It always does.

Tom Baker

Tom Baker was born in working-class Liverpool in 1934, the son of a Catholic woman and a Jewish sailor, the young Tom hardly knowing the latter. Baker says his interest in acting developed when he was an altar boy at the local Catholic church. While serving at a funeral and crying from the bitter cold, a mourner thought he was affected by grief and gave him a coin. Baker claimed he honed his performance, so it was no longer accidental and it continued to be lucrative.

Baker was drawn to the church and at 15 he left school to become a monk. He stayed in monastic service for another seven years. After departing the monastery, Baker served his National Service requirement in the army, where he enjoyed acting during Christmas party shows. Once discharged, Baker studied acting for a short time, then briefly married and had two children before abandoning them. He caught the attention of the National Theatre (then headed by Laurence Olivier) for his performance as a dog in a revue show. Baker became a contract player at the National Theatre and also began to work in film and television.

Olivier himself recommended Baker play Rasputin in the 1971 film *Nicholas and Alexandra*. It was a breakout role for Baker. While it led to other film roles (most notably in 1973's *The Golden Voyage of Sinbad*), parts were still scarce and Baker worked as a day labourer on a construction site. Annoyed about being out of acting work, Baker wrote a letter to his friend Mary Slater, the wife of Bill Slater, the incoming head of serials at the BBC. At the time, Jon Pertwee was leaving *Doctor Who* and Bill Slater suggested Baker to producer Barry Letts for the part of the Doctor. Letts immediately caught a screening of *The Golden Voyage of Sinbad* and agreed.

Baker went from being an out-of-work actor to having one of the biggest roles on television. He played the Doctor for an unprecedented (and still unbeaten) seven years. During his time in the role, he became a dominant force in the studio and was increasingly difficult to work with. When John Nathan-Turner took over as producer in 1980, it was agreed by mutual consent that Baker would leave. Around this time, Baker married his *Doctor Who* co-star Lalla Ward, though the pair separated after 16 months.

Baker continued to be popular on television, playing Sherlock Holmes in an adaptation of *The Hound of the Baskervilles* in 1982 and Puddleglum in the 1989 BBC adaptation of C.S. Lewis's *The Silver Chair*. He also had a key role in *The Life and Loves of a She-Devil* in 1986 and a rare American TV guest spot in a 1984 episode of *Remington Steele*. Baker continued to do theatre work, most notably an acclaimed stint in a touring version of *Educating Rita*.

During the 1990s, Baker became much in demand as a voice actor, and was heard in many commercials. This led to him becoming the narrator in the BBC comedy series *Little Britain* (2003–2006). Baker credited his popularity to children who had loved him in *Doctor Who* and were now old enough to produce and cast work. His well-received autobiography, *Who on Earth Is Tom Baker?*, was published in 1997, followed in 1999 by a dark children's novel, *The Boy Who Kicked Pigs*.

Baker has always been reluctant to reprise his role as the Doctor, refusing to take part in 1983's "The Five Doctors" (footage from an abandoned story was used instead) and only making a cameo in the thirtieth anniversary sketch "Dimensions in Time." In 2008, he surprised fans by agreeing to return to the role in a series of BBC audiobooks, followed by performances in full-cast audio plays by Big Finish productions in 2012 — a full decade after other living actors who played the Doctor reprised their parts.

Genesis of the Daleks (1975)

Written by Terry Nation **Directed by** David Maloney

Featuring Tom Baker (Doctor Who), Elisabeth Sladen (Sarah Jane Smith), Ian Marter (Harry Sullivan)

Supporting cast Michael Wisher (Davros); Peter Miles (Nyder); Stephen Yardley (Sevrin); Harriet Philpin (Bettan); Denis Chinnery (Gharman); James Garbutt (Ronson); Jeremy Chandler (Gerrill); Drew Wood (Tane); Andrew Johns (Kavell); Ivor Roberts (Mogran); John Franklyn-Robbins (Time Lord); John Scott Martin, Cy Town, Keith Ashley (Dalek operators); Roy Skelton, Michael Wisher (Dalek voices)

Original airdates March 8, 15, 22, 29, April 5, 12, 1975

The Big Idea The Time Lords send the Doctor on a mission to Skaro to avert the creation of the Daleks.

Roots and References World War I (trench warfare, especially the opening scene), World War II (the bunker, the Kaleds' Nazi salute, the Kaled uniforms, Nyder's Iron Cross), the July 20 plot to kill Hitler (the failed rebellion against Davros in the bunker), the 1957 film *The Seventh Seal* (the Time Lord's appearance resembles Death). Sarah quotes from "Good King Wenceslas."

Time And Relative Dimensions In Space Terry Nation had returned to write Dalek stories during the Jon Pertwee era: 1973's "Planet of the Daleks" and 1974's "Death to the Daleks" featured slight tweaks to the Daleks' abilities, grizzled space veterans fighting against them on an alien planet and a background of the ever-expanding Dalek empire. He pitched a similar story to the departing producer, Barry Letts, but Letts felt it was too derivative of his earlier work and suggested writing about the Daleks' origins instead. Nation was keen to introduce a mouthpiece for the Daleks, a character who could deliver speeches that their monotones could not. The result was Davros, their heretofore unmentioned creator.

Adventures in Time and Space This story continues from 1975's "The Sontaran Experiment," which ends with Sarah, Harry and the Doctor transmatting back to *Nerva* station (from "The Ark in Space"). It's ostensibly a prequel to "The Daleks" (and, by definition, every subsequent Dalek story) and ends with the Daleks being entombed in their city, setting up their original TV appearance. It features Thals, who were seen in both "The Daleks" and 1973's "Planet of the Daleks." The Doctor mentions the Dalek invasion of Earth (1964's "The Dalek Invasion of Earth," later made into the 1966 AARU film *Daleks — Invasion Earth 2150 A.D.*).

Who is the Doctor? The Time Lords have allowed the Doctor his freedom to roam time and space in return for (they stress) occasional favours. He almost murders Davros in order to halt the Daleks' production process and prepares to commit genocide, by destroying the incubation chamber. However, when faced with the decision, he ponders the implications of his actions, wondering if future worlds will become allies, asks a philosophical question (could you kill a child if you knew it to be evil?) and wonders whether this action would make him the same as the Daleks. Fundamentally, he's taking on the inherent responsibilities of being a Time Lord, in a way his own people don't.

Companion Chronicles Sarah leads an escape plan from the Thal workforce, but is terrified of heights. She argues with the Doctor that he should kill the embryonic Daleks, not agreeing with his belief that they are equivalent to children. Both she and Harry plead with the Doctor not to reveal information about the future when being tortured by Davros. For his part, Harry refuses to back away from the landmine the Doctor's stepped on, calmly wedging it in place and holding onto it when the Doctor releases his foot.

Monster of the Week Davros, the creator of the Daleks, is a mutated Kaled scientist (a race that is entirely different to humans and Time Lords, except for outward appearances), confined to a wheelchair, with only the use of one hand. He's kept alive by the life-support system in his chair and apparently sees through a blue third eye wired to his forehead. He creates the Daleks in order to provide a vehicle for the species the Kaled race will ultimately mutate into. However, he genetically alters the mutants inside, removing conscience and feeling, so that they are conditioned to survive — which they believe is only possible by becoming the dominant species in the universe.

Stand Up and Cheer The "Do I have the right?" speech. After all the horrors of war, torture and the inability to stop Davros from creating the Daleks, the Doctor wires up the incubator room with explosives. However, at the crucial moment, he's unable to commit genocide, even of Daleks, because he sees that as being akin to killing a dictator when he was a child. The speech is full of power, in large part because it also asks the question of us. Faced with the same situation, would we go through with it or not?

Roll Your Eyes The comedy clam has to be seen to be believed. It's not so much that it looks too stylized to be real. It's not that the Doctor hits it with an obviously lightweight polystyrene rock. It's not even that Harry "accidentally" steps in it, which involves taking an especially large step into the very precise gap that is the clam's mouth. No, it's the comedy scuttle the thing does after the Doctor pokes it, shuffling from side to side, that has us gawking in disbelief.

You're Not Making Any Sense Why would Davros have a switch on his chair that will kill him in 30 seconds if pushed? Worse, it's the closest switch to where he likes to tap the console and his hands aren't that steady, so surely there's every chance he might accidentally press it himself.

Interesting Trivia Russell T Davies has claimed that the Time War that destroyed the Doctor's people started here — and that the Time Lords fired first. It's not hard to see what he means. The Time Lords send the Doctor back to the dawn of Dalek civilization with the explicit intent of averting the Daleks' creation. It's easy to see the subsequent escalation in the Classic Series: 1984's "Resurrection of the Daleks" has the Daleks plotting to duplicate the Doctor in order to assassinate the High Council of Time Lords, while "Remembrance of the Daleks" has the Doctor . . . we'll talk about that later on. It's tempting to think that the Time Lord who appears early in the first episode is from the era just before the Time War, using the most assured of all Doctors to make a first strike in a four-dimensional war.

When talking of the future history of the Daleks, the Doctor mentions the Dalek invasion of Earth in the year 2000. This is clearly meant to be a reference to the 1964 story of the same name. However, that story took place in the 22nd century. Was there another invasion we don't know about in the early 21st century? (The story makes it clear the Doctor isn't lying.) Or is there something else going on here? At the story's conclusion, the Doctor states that he's delayed Dalek development by a thousand years, which suggests he changed history somehow, perhaps restoring the date of the Dalek invasion to one we're familiar with.

Did the Doctor create the Daleks (again)? We saw in "The Daleks" that the Doctor may have been inadvertently responsible for creating the Dalek empire. As it turns out, he may have even had a hand in their creation. Here he convinces the Kaled government — who already had doubts about Davros's work — to stop Davros (using knowledge from the future), which forces Davros to destroy the Kaled people and unleash the Daleks. Subsequently, Davros removes their conscience and pity. Had the Doctor not forced the Kaled government to act, Davros would not have accelerated the process and may have been stopped, or may not have removed the Daleks' conscience. So the Daleks as we know them are a direct consequence of the Doctor's actions.

"Genesis" is a direct prequel to "The Daleks," but the two only line up in a vague way: there's a war and the Daleks are entombed underground. However, many of the details from the previous story aren't addressed here. The Daleks don't run on static electricity. The 1963 story implied that the Thals had never had contact with the Daleks. The Thals here aren't exactly the blond supermen of later on and the Daleks look considerably different too. Most oddly of all, where's the nuclear war? "The Daleks" featured a petrified forest and such high levels of radiation that just walking around without medication was lethal. There's a chance the Thal rocket fulfills that role — the distronic toxemia that the workers suffer suggests a form of radiation poisoning — but for the planet to have such high radiation levels thousands of years in the future suggests a massive, planet-wide catastrophe . . . and we don't really see that here.

"Genesis of the Daleks" also presents a slightly different origin story to that given in "The Daleks." In the original 1963 tale, the Dals and the Thals are similar humanoid races that eventually evolve into the Daleks and the genetically superior Thals after a Neutron War. Here, Davros creates the Daleks as separate beings based on the Kaleds' inevitable genetic evolution. However, since the Daleks' origins in the former story was read from an historical record, it may have been faulty or incomplete, particularly if a nuclear war happened during the intervening time.

Director David Maloney contributed to this story in several key ways, rewriting several sequences, including the opening scene (which Nation felt was too violent) and the cliffhanger to episode five (which features the Dalek mutant wrapped around the Doctor's neck). The latter cliffhanger was supposed to be the "Do I have the right?" speech, but the timing of the episode was such that it had to be moved into the final episode.

Michael Wisher took playing Davros quite seriously, even wearing a bag over his head during rehearsals to get used to wearing the prosthetic mask and using his voice to convey the character. When shooting the story, Wisher took to wearing a kilt to save his trousers from being worn out by the Dalek-like base he sat in — an incongruity noted by many who were in the studio!

The Nazi references are obvious throughout this story — the uniforms, the salutes — but one of them, Nyder's Iron Cross, was deemed too close for comfort. (It's one thing to suggest Nazis, it's another to wear their apparel.) Between the first and second studio sessions for this story, producer Philip Hinchcliffe and David Maloney decided that the Iron Cross should be quietly left off Nyder's costume for the rest of filming.

The TARDIS Chronometer On the planet Skaro, in the distant past.

What? (RS?) "Genesis of the Daleks" is fundamentally about one thing: war.

In the opening moments, we see the horror of the trenches, with a creeping barrage, a minefield, a gas attack and soldiers machine-gunned to death. The dead are an integral part too, not just propping up the numbers, but also providing the gas masks to save our heroes. We see the war of attrition moving in both directions: the devolution of armaments and clothing on the one hand, and the buildup of more and more advanced weaponry (such as the Thal rocket) on the other. Generals plot troop movements, scientists toil away in secret bunkers developing ever more gruesome weapons and ordinary soldiers simply die.

The war analogy also gives us Bettan's resistance, combining various races (Thals and Mutos) allied against a common enemy, the destruction of an enemy state using a new superweapon (20 Daleks wipe out the Thals almost entirely) and the aftermath of the war resulting in a sudden interest in democracy. There's some kind of subtle analogy here, but I can't quite place it . . .

The direction is on exactly the same page as the scripting. From the fog-laden, slow-motion killing and the handheld camera in the opening to the Kaled uniforms (their monochrome results in the Doctor's and Harry's splashes of colour standing out even more) and the low camera angles, this is a production where everything is firing on all cylinders. And you can understand why: this was made by a generation for whom World War II was still fresh. The thinly veiled analogy seen here shows that everyone is instinctively singing from the same songbook.

There are some unforgettable images, the most vivid of which is probably the Dalek silhouetted against sandbags and the burning sky, towering above Bettan. Seen out of context, you have a BBC backdrop lit with odd colours and a fake-looking wall. Suspend your disbelief, however, and what you have is an indelible image that burned its way into millions of childhoods.

The acting is also top drawer. Look at Peter Miles, who creates the definitive loyalist in Nyder with a calm tone and banal evil at every moment. Compare that to his portrayal of Dr. Lawrence in "Doctor Who and the Silurians," where every line was dripping with over-the-top rage, and you can see the difference. Somebody — almost certainly David Maloney — has a firm hand on the rudder, getting superlative performances out of even the weakest actors.

Even the *Doctor Who* periphery is less safe than usual. Without the TARDIS, the Doctor is forced to rely on the time ring, something that's taken from him early in the story and that motivates him towards the end. Combine that with the tape of future history that must be destroyed and the stakes are continually raised. Nothing about this story feels safe.

And sitting at the centre of this story is the man around whom everything revolves: Davros.

The first episode builds up his arrival, with Ravon's protests about supplies being silenced as soon as Nyder mentions Davros's name. And yet, although his first appearance is at the end of the episode, the cliffhanger isn't about his shock reveal, but rather his behaviour. His experiments create the Daleks, of course, but for once the pepperpots aren't the focus of the story, appearing in a grand total of 15 minutes out of 135.

Instead, it's Davros's actions that drive the entire story. He meets with the Thals in secret and engineers the destruction of the Kaled dome, then uses that as a means to seize power for the Daleks. When the rebellion starts in the bunker, he allows it to play out because he knows you can't kill an idea. Even when given an ultimatum, he still orders Gharman and the others around. This is a man who casually commits genocide, twice over. His philosophy is simple but brutal: achievement through power, and power through strength.

The genius of Davros as a concept is that he's not just a ranting villain — even though he rants better than just about any villain in any medium, ever. He's capable of calm, reasonable conversation, in addition to power-mad speeches. After interrogating the Doctor and torturing his friends, he then wants to sit down and have a chat with the Doctor, as fellow men of science. He sweet-talks Mogran, before immediately signing the death warrant of his whole race.

He's also capable of admitting when he's wrong, changing his mind about time travel and the non-existence of life on other planets in response to the Doctor's presence. All this makes for an extremely dangerous opponent, because he isn't some narrow-minded dictator who can't see subtleties, but rather somebody in full possession of his faculties, who can follow a chain of logic and change his mind . . . and still craves ultimate power. That's terrifying.

And then, at the end, he's only undone because he underestimated the single-mindedness of his creations. Having unleashed a monster upon the universe, he neglected to consider that the monster might turn on him. In the Shakespearean version of this story that has Davros as a heroic central character, that's an exquisite tragedy.

Usually voted in the top stories of all time, "Genesis of the Daleks" rightly sits at the apex of *Doctor Who* at its very best. From a script that was forced to work harder than usual and first-rate acting to direction determined to bring the horrors of war to life, this is a story that hits the ground running and doesn't let up for 135 minutes. A story where the best the Doctor can manage is to slow down the Daleks slightly and hope that something good can come out of their evil. But it's fundamentally a story of war and how the singular vision of one maniac with a gift for seizing political power can rain countless horrors down on everyone — and the best you can hope for is survival.

Second Opinion (GB) Remember when I reviewed "The Daleks" and said that it was an exciting three episodes followed by four episodes of tedium? "Genesis of the Daleks" simply reverses that order. Everything memorable from this story — the "Do I have the right?" speech, the embryo strangling the Doctor, the Doctor being forced to admit the Daleks' future defeats, the Daleks usurping Davros — comes from the end of episode four onwards.

Before the end of episode four . . . not a lot happens. There's a visually arresting opening sequence and a couple of stabs at excitement (the Doctor in the minefield, Sarah's escape attempt ending in a brilliant freezeframe cliffhanger) and a couple of good moments with Davros, but otherwise it's far from an all-time classic. Rather, it's a bog-standard runaround. There are lots of games of capture/escape/capture and several trips between the Kaled and Thal cities, which, as near as I can tell, are separated by a distance of about five city blocks. Once we're past the end of episode four, we're cooking with gas. Tom Baker is incredible, particularly in the scenes where the Doctor's talking to Davros about the morality of having power over life and death. Here we have the incredible, raw intensity of an actor with everything to prove. (And Michael Wisher, a pretty unremarkable actor in stories like "Carnival of Monsters," is electrifying as Davros.) The scene with the Doctor holding the wires is also a tour de force for Baker.

However, I would like to back up the bus here and point out something. Everybody, it seems, loves this scene where the Doctor asks, "Do I have the right?" And watching just a clip of Tom Baker's wonderful speech, it is a glorious moment that elevates *Doctor Who* from a simplistic morality play to something broader and more complex. But . . . it doesn't really, in context. The Doctor doesn't decide against destroying the incubator room. Gharman comes and *interrupts him*, telling him Davros has accepted their terms. There is no decision; in fact, the Doctor tells Gharman he's grateful, the implication being he is saved from the choice.

And here's the thing that has perplexed me about this story and the reaction to it for decades: *the Doctor goes back to do the job after all.* He says, "I'm going back to the incubator room. This time I'm going to blow it up." The same incubator room that 20 minutes earlier he was agonizing over the moral implication of blowing up. His intent is clear: the Doctor is going back to commit genocide as the ultimate sanction.

Only he doesn't. He's about to use the very same explosive again, but a Dalek inexplicably connects the two wires (you would think they'd have insulated bases, but okay). The Doctor then tells Sarah, "I'm afraid I've only delayed them for a short time. Perhaps a thousand years." Um, how? If I squint really hard at all the evidence, I could theorize that it's because the Daleks now have total sentience and they will figure out how to replicate themselves down the road. But the Doctor doesn't know this when he goes to blow up the room. His intent is still genocidal. He's only stopped by some kind of authorial fiat. So there's not all that much moral complexity.

I think you should watch "Genesis of the Daleks" because of Michael Wisher's Davros (and everything my co-author says about him) and the origin story it tells. But — heresy I know — I don't think this is a classic. It's grossly padded (though a great director distracts us from that), makes little sense when reconciling it with "The Daleks" and is cowardly in how it raises compelling issues but studiously avoids dealing with them. It's considered a classic because it provides most of the great clips of the Tom Baker era, not because it's actually great.

Pyramids of Mars (1975)

Written by Stephen Harris (actually Robert Holmes, from a story idea by Lewis Griefer) **Directed by** Paddy Russell

Featuring Tom Baker (Doctor Who), Elisabeth Sladen (Sarah Jane Smith)

Supporting cast Gabriel Woolf (Sutekh); Bernard Archard (Marcus Scarman); Michael Sheard (Laurence Scarman); Peter Copley (Dr. Warlock); Michael Bilton (Collins); George Tovey (Ernie Clements); Peter Mayock (Namin); Vik Tablian (Ahmed); Nick Burnell, Melvyn Bedford, Kevin Selway (mummies)

Original airdates October 25, November 1, 8, 15, 1975

The Big Idea The TARDIS is drawn off course to a gothic mansion in 1911, where a warning is given from the stars: beware Sutekh the destroyer.

Roots and References *The Mummy,* both the 1931 and 1959 versions; the 1970s Egyptian fad (the interest in Egyptology, "pyramid power"), Erich von Däniken's *Chariots of the Gods?* (the Osirians being the source of Egyptian mythology). The two guardians' challenge to free Sarah is taken from the "Knights and Knaves" logic problem. The Doctor and Sarah walk into a room and, seeing the villains, wheel around

The 1970s

simultaneously before they're seen, a deliberate homage by Tom Baker and Elisabeth Sladen to the 1931 Marx Brothers' film *Monkey Business*.

Time And Relative Dimensions In Space Television shows often get made in spite of disasters behind the scenes. Such was the case when Robert Holmes commissioned experienced television writer Lewis Griefer to write a script that riffed on Egyptian mythology and *The Mummy*. In Griefer's draft storyline, the Doctor battled various Egyptian gods (first in the British Museum and then on Mars) in a story motivated by alien grains and rice. It disappointed Holmes and producer Philip Hinchcliffe, and they tried to fix the problems in rewrites. But Griefer had taken ill and then he took a teaching position in Tel Aviv. Holmes — assisted by director Paddy Russell — started over, retaining only the original concept Holmes had supplied Griefer. The story was broadcast under the pseudonym "Stephen Harris," after Griefer requested his name be removed.

Adventures in Time and Space The Doctor claims Sarah is wearing one of former companion Victoria's outfits (albeit not something Victoria was seen wearing onscreen). Sarah remarks that the tests in the Martian pyramid are reminiscent of similar tests in the city of the Exxilons seen in 1974's "Death of the Daleks." The Doctor is headed back to UNIT headquarters after the events of 1975's "Terror of the Zygons." The site of the priory is where UNIT headquarters is later built (and first seen in 1973's "The Three Doctors"). For the second time since 1973's "The Time Warrior," the Doctor mentions that his home planet is called Gallifrey.

Who is the Doctor? The Doctor is brooding initially; feeling separate from humanity, he says, "I'm a Time Lord, I walk in eternity." He's lost interest in being part of UNIT. He can sense Sutekh's influence, declaring that "something is going on contrary to the laws of the universe." His seemingly callous reaction to Laurence's death leads Sarah to call him inhuman — a charge the Doctor accepts but also reframes in the context of the many deaths that will occur under Sutekh. The Doctor's physiology includes a respiratory bypass system, and this story features the first of many times it inexplicably keeps him from choking to death. He states that he's 750 years old.

Companion Chronicles Sarah is travelling alone with the Doctor again, and the pair have become practically inseparable at this point. She pricks the Doctor's pomposity, and they mock each other affectionately. Sarah is apparently a crack shot with a rifle. When she's imprisoned by the guardians, the Doctor regrets having taken Sarah with him at all, but the moment quickly passes.

Monster of the Week Sutekh, last of the Osirians, is a being of unimaginable power who seeks to bring death and darkness to all of humanity. He has been imprisoned in perpetual paralysis inside a tomb in Egypt. But, even weakened, he's capable of projecting his will into the cadaver of Marcus Scarman and the living body of the Doctor, and he can remotely prevent the box of gelignite from exploding. He also uses service robots that look like mummies to do his bidding.

Stand Up and Cheer The last ten minutes of episode three, which see the Doctor and Sarah enacting their plan to blow up the rocket, are glorious. It leads to an amazing cliffhanger as Sutekh's wrath is unleashed on the Doctor. (That's actually Tom Baker in the mummy costume, by the way!)

Roll Your Eyes In one of the all-time great gaffes in *Doctor Who*, Sutekh rises . . . and a production assistant's hand can be seen attempting to keep the cushion on Sutekh's chair.

You're Not Making Any Sense You have imprisoned a being that wants to destroy all life. So why have an automated prison management system that uses logic games an average 12-year-old nerd could solve without even breaking out their slide rule?

Interesting Trivia Marcus Scarman claims the tomb of Sutekh dates back to the first dynasty of the pharaohs, or the period from 3100 to 2800 B.C., so presumably Sutekh has been imprisoned for almost 5,000 years. The Doctor states that the "Osirian pattern" became subsumed into Egyptian mythology. Those facts about the Osirians that became Egyptian myths are remarkably specific: Sarah points to the 740 Osirians who defeated Sutekh as being the same 740 gods who appear on the tomb of Tuthmosis III, who died some 1,400 years after the first dynasty and Sutekh's imprisonment.

The story of Set, or Seth, is a fascinating — if grim — one. Set, the god of darkness and chaos, sought to usurp his brother Osiris, ruler of Egypt, by murdering him, dismembering his body and scattering the remains around Egypt. Osiris's wife (and sister) Isis recovered the remains, reassembled them and embalmed Osiris, where he was resurrected as a mummy and became god of the afterlife. With her undead king, Isis conceived Horus, who would become a sky god. The conflict with Set and Horus is not for the squeamish: the tale includes Horus beheading his mother in a fit of pique while Set sexually abuses Horus. It ends, depending on the version, with Horus and Set being reconciled or Horus being utterly defeated.

The trip to 1980 answers a question that *Doctor Who* viewers (and its producers) had been asking for over a decade: if an adventure happens in history, why doesn't the Doctor just leave? The future still exists, after all. Here the Doctor shows that isn't the case: the future can be fashioned and shaped, and every point in time has an alternative.

Filming on location was by this point a regular part of the program, particularly in historical stories where old buildings lent a timeless quality that was impossible to replicate in-studio. The Scarman estate is actually Stargroves, one of Mick Jagger's homes. Jagger was in Munich at the time, recording the Rolling Stones' album *Black and Blue*, so sadly fans of both *Doctor Who* and the Stones were denied the possibility of a photo of Tom Baker with Mick.

The TARDIS Chronometer Sutekh's tomb in Egypt, the Scarman estate in England and a pyramid on Mars, 1911. The TARDIS also briefly visits an alternate future in 1980.

What? (GB) My co-author is right. You never forget your first time. Mine was in May 1984. I was 14 years old, and I was sick. I was lying on the couch in our family room in Oakville, Ontario, Canada, wrapped in an afghan my grandmother made. My eight-year-old sister was watching something — probably *Vegetable Soup* — on the Buffalo PBS station, WNED. She left the room partway through to do something else but didn't turn off the TV.

Six o'clock came, and with it *Doctor Who*. "Pyramids of Mars" by Stephen Harris. Episode two.

My best friend had been trying to get me to watch *Doctor Who* for ages. I'd like to say it was his recommendation that kept me from changing the channel; it was more likely a lack of energy from the flu. What I can say is that, 23 minutes and 53 seconds later, after the inevitable cliffhanger, I desperately wanted to see what happened next.

I don't want to merely wallow in nostalgia here. I want to figure out what it is about *Doctor Who* that attracted me so much on that first viewing (and the next day, when episode three sealed the deal for me).

First of all, it's so well put-together. *Doctor Who* stories are always better set in the past because they benefit from great location work. This is no exception. The forest, the mansion, the cottage . . . it's so sumptuous looking. It feels like a good English horror film. The mummies are great: all they can do is lumber around, but they are quite menacing. Paddy Russell uses closeups to great effect, so the focus is always on the characters.

The other thing I remember loving was the trip to 1980 to witness a landscape desolated by Sutekh. (I have qualms about the characters' motivation in doing that. I just can't see Sarah simply giving up and saying, "That's not our problem, let's go.") This moment gives this time-travel story (and, by extension, all time-travel stories in *Doctor Who*) real consequences. The imagination behind it continues to be breathtaking to me. It's so simple, so logical and so very bold.

The thing I really adored, and still adore, about "Pyramids of Mars" is Tom Baker and Elisabeth Sladen as the Doctor and Sarah. The pair remain the definitive Doctor/companion pairing for me; they've never been bettered. The fourth Doctor and Sarah (and with the fourth Doctor, it's always "Sarah," never "Sarah Jane") were friends: proper friends, best mates backpacking around the universe on an eternal road trip, cracking jokes and taking the piss out of each other. (I love how she gently mocks the Doctor about being a Time Lord who walks in eternity.) They're charming, witty and near equals.

I will forever cherish the moment when the Doctor tells Sarah to hit her target, the box of gelignite, and Sarah says, "Don't worry, I know what I'm doing," as she picks up the rifle and checks the sights. It's a throwaway piece of stage business designed to emphasize an odd bit of storytelling: that Sarah would suddenly be an expert marksman. But it's the simple matter of factness to the moment that sells it. As a 14-year-old, I believed Sarah could do it, because Sarah seemed more perturbed that the Doctor is nagging her about getting it right than about hitting the bull's eye. And when she hits the target and it doesn't go off, due to Sutekh's intervention, she lets out an annoyed growl of "I got that." And I believed her all the more. It's such a wonderfully thought-out performance.

And Tom Baker is at his zenith here. He's become such a larger-than-life character that people forget his first few seasons of *Doctor Who* when he was a relative unknown, like David Tennant or Matt Smith, putting his all in his performance. And, like Tennant and Smith, Tom Baker was a heavyweight actor in those days. As a teenager, I loved what I called "the Tom Baker pain expression" and we see it in all its glory at the end of episode three. Baker just goes for it: the Doctor is not in discomfort or actorly pain, but undying agony. His portrayal of the Doctor is never more nuanced than here: he's detached from the immediate horror, but not unaffected or unemotional. It is, as Sarah says, inhuman, but only because he's a man with a mission to save all life everywhere. And then the Doctor jokes with Sarah. (When dressed as a mummy: "How do I look?" "That must have been a nasty accident." "Don't provoke me.") And suddenly everything is thrown into sharp relief.

No wonder I fell in love with *Doctor Who*. The Doctor himself is the most compelling character ever: intense, brooding, funny, detached, passionate. And all of it feels real.

Sutekh spooked the hell out of me. Gabriel Woolf never goes above a whisper, never moves in a hood ornament of a costume and yet is the scariest *Doctor Who* villain, ever. Lines like "Your evil is my good" and "Where I tread, I leave nothing but dust and darkness; I find that good" are blood-chilling thanks to his vocal performance. This is a program with a bold imagination that encourages the same in its viewers.

The story has another macabre double act fuelling it. The Scarman brothers are masterpieces of characterization: one is a figure of pathos, the other is the creepiest character in *Doctor Who* (and thank you, Bernard Archard, for all the nightmares). Michael Sheard's Laurence is so achingly human: what brother could ever embrace the idea that their sibling is a cadaver animated by a demigod? In one of the saddest but most horrific scenes in *Doctor Who*, he's killed while trying to convince his brother he's still human.

"Pyramids of Mars" is an inversion of the standard format of 1970s *Doctor Who*: rather than a gradual reveal of the menace, the Doctor knows Sutekh is trying to escape his prison at the ten-minute mark of episode one. The rest of the story is a series of attempts to stop him, and it works by being continually entertaining: there's always a tense set piece, a puzzle, a character moment, a frightening scene, a tender piece of drama, a bit of heroism. (Even the weakest part, episode four, which puts the Doctor and Sarah through a series of tests similar to the one in 1974's "Death to the Daleks," has the clever idea of having them desperately trying to catch up to Scarman.)

"Pyramids of Mars" was my first *Doctor Who* story. It's my favourite

Doctor Who story. And frankly, it's the best *Doctor Who* story. I under-stood that as 14-year-old. I still understand that today.

Second Opinion (RS?) I'm sorry, what? You don't like "Genesis of the Daleks"? Have you no soul? Look, I know this is the "Pyramids" entry, but this is the first chance I have to respond to my co-author's frankly baffling assessment of "Genesis" and I really feel the need to get it off my chest. The first three episodes are wonderful! There's tons going on (politics, world-building, character establishment), the set pieces only up the stakes and so what if the two domes are close together? No man's land in World War I was a matter of metres wide in some places. I'd like to apologize to anyone with good taste anywhere.

Okay, okay. Now that that's out of the way, let me tell you about something else I love: the first cliffhanger of "Pyramids of Mars."

We spend the entire episode knowing something is up, though we don't know how it connects to Scarman opening the tomb at the begin-ning. Namin is clearly set up as the villain: he's eloquent and sinister, and his playing of the organ is magnificently creepy.

And then he summons the creature from the tomb. The effects are simply awesome: the carpet burns with every footstep. Namin pros-trates himself, saying he is Sutekh's true servant. Then the creature corrects him, saying *he's* the true servant of Sutekh — and that he brings Sutekh's gift of death to all humans. And then he kills Namin, for no reason at all.

It's stupendous.

What's particularly brilliant is that Namin has been set up to be the subordinate to Sutekh. He's like Nyder foreshadowing Davros in (the quite wonderful, I might add) "Genesis of the Daleks."

But this cliffhanger does something different from "Genesis." It adds a second servant, making Namin number three in the hierarchy. And by making the servant so powerful — his every step burns and his touch is death — you can't help but wonder just what on Mars we're going to get with Sutekh himself. This is powerful writing and shows why Robert Holmes remains the undisputed master of Classic *Doctor Who*.

I'm not the only one who loves this cliffhanger. Russell T Davies is with me on this. In the British version of *Queer as Folk*, broadcast in 1999 when *Doctor Who* was apparently long dead, never to return, Davies made one of the main characters, Vince, a *Doctor Who* fan. To

The 1970s

141

illustrate Vince's lot in life, the first episode contrasts Vince's best friend (and secret crush), Stuart, having wild sex with a minor while Vince is at home, watching *Doctor Who*. Hilariously, Vince even watches it like porn, ripping off his shirt and rewinding the tape. The footage used for the *Queer as Folk* episode was this cliffhanger, and cutting between the wild sex and *Who* is inspired.

But here's the thing. As much as I laughed along watching that scene in *Queer as Folk*, I loved it. What's telling is the scene that Davies chose: he didn't use an embarrassing clip that poked fun at *Doctor Who* when seen out of context. Instead, he went for the very best: a moment that encapsulates what was — and, thanks to Davies, happily still is — so great about *Doctor Who*.

And that's "Pyramids of Mars" all over. *Doctor Who* in its purest form, the kind of thing that fans and the general public adored — and that so inspired the man who would eventually resurrect the show that he used it to say something fundamental about character, decades after its time. My co-author is absolutely right. Except about "Genesis," of course.

The Seeds of Doom (1976)

Written by Robert Banks Stewart **Directed by** Douglas Camfield

Featuring Tom Baker (Doctor Who), Elisabeth Sladen (Sarah Jane Smith)

Supporting cast Tony Beckley (Harrison Chase), John Challis (Scorby), Michael Barrington (Sir Colin Thackeray), Kenneth Gilbert (Dunbar), Sylvia Coleridge (Amelia Ducat), Mark Jones (Keeler/Krynoid voice), Seymour Green (Hargreaves), Michael McStay (Moberley), Hubert Rees (Stevenson), John Gleeson (Winlett), John Acheson (Major Beresford), Ray Barron (Sgt. Henderson)

Original airdates January 31, February 7, 14, 21, 28, March 6, 1976

The Big Idea An alien pod found in Antarctica infects human beings and turns them into plants, threatening to destroy all animal life on Earth.

Roots and References The 1951 film *The Thing From Another World* (a plant-like alien found in the Antarctic), *The Quatermass Experiment* (transforming into a plant), *Day of the Triffids* (plants taking over), the *Avengers* episode "The Man-Eater of Surrey Green" (rich English eccentric, killer alien plant). The exchange regarding the Daimler and Amelia Ducat is lifted from *The Importance of Being Earnest* ("The car is irrelevant!"). Writer Robert Banks Stewart was also influenced by the "Banks" in his name: it comes from a family connection to famed botanist Joseph Banks.

Time And Relative Dimensions In Space Originally, a six-part version of Bob Baker and Dave Martin's "The Hand of Fear" was to close out *Doctor Who's* thirteenth season. However, problems with the script saw it pushed back (where it was reworked considerably and appeared in the next season as Sarah Jane Smith's swansong), and a new story was commissioned from veteran writer Robert Banks Stewart (who had previously contributed 1975's "Terror of the Zygons"). Stewart wrote the scripts quickly and they were approved by the production office without incident. (You may notice from other entries in this book how rarely that happens!) Stewart's solution to a six-parter was a two-episode story at the start, set in the Antarctic, that served as a prequel to the four remaining episodes set in England.

Adventures in Time and Space A UNIT team shows up at the end and the Brigadier is mentioned briefly (said to be in Geneva). The humanoid version of the Krynoid costume is the same monster costume from 1971's "The Claws of Axos," only painted green. You can tell in the publicity photos, but director Douglas Camfield covers it very well onscreen.

Who is the Doctor? He's noticeably more eccentric in this story, getting other people to do things he could easily do (like read out a report), making big pronouncements often from an unusual point of view (such as with a chair over his head) and refusing to let anyone use Winlett's name after he's been infected. He's also angrier, screaming at Scorby on multiple occasions, and more violent. He punches the chauffeur, viciously twists Scorby's neck and carries a gun (although he says he'd never use it). However, he's also commanding (instantly taking over at the cottage, despite the fact that the guards had been trying to kill him moments before). He carries a toothbrush and doesn't need a jacket in Antarctica. He's president of the Intergalactic Flora Society.

Companion Chronicles The Doctor describes Sarah as his best friend. She has a tender scene with Keeler when he's first turning into a Krynoid, offering him the compassion no one else has. However, she also stands up to Scorby repeatedly, despite the implied threat of violent reprisal, and even berates him for his sexism.

Monster of the Week Pairs of Krynoids travel through space as pods and two were embedded in the Antarctic permafrost 20,000 years ago. They can grow without nitrogen, only needing ultraviolet light. When they germinate, the pod opens and a shoot infects whomever is nearby. They consume animal life, eventually extinguishing it from any planet they inhabit. They can also control other plants, speak and mentally possess humans.

Stand Up and Cheer Harrison Chase has captured Sarah and is holding her arm next to the about-to-germinate pod. We've seen how dangerous the situation can be, from the Antarctic episodes. And then the Doctor crashes through the skylight, beats up Scorby and rescues Sarah. When Chase asks him what he does for an encore, the Doctor — gun in hand, unusually — replies, "I win!" It's about as unlikely a *Doctor Who* scene as there ever was, but for sheer chutzpah, it's magnificent.

Roll Your Eyes The Antarctic scene at the end is very poor. Sarah emerges from the TARDIS in a swimsuit and, rather than immediately freezing to death, she and the Doctor launch into a bad comedy routine that's capped by forced laughter. It's like a terrible last scene from a kids' show that always ends with everyone laughing, for no real reason. (Plus, there's no reason for the TARDIS to have travelled there; they originally arrived by helicopter!)

You're Not Making Any Sense Why does Winlett change faster than Keeler? Keeler spends a long time in the cottage, slowly changing and still able to speak, whereas Winlett changes very rapidly. It's made clear that cold slows the process (which is why Keeler accelerates his growth once he's out of the cottage, whereas Winlett doesn't because he's running around in the Antarctic). Just how warm is it in that base?

Interesting Trivia This story sees the last regular appearance of UNIT, the paramilitary organization that the Doctor has worked alongside since the late '60s stories. Philip Hinchcliffe and Robert Holmes wanted the Doctor back in space and time, and saw UNIT as an unnecessary encumbrance. UNIT's last appearance with Brigadier Lethbridge-Stewart had been in 1975's "Terror of the Zygons," which started Season 13, and they were phased out over the course of the season: the Brigadier was missing from UNIT's next appearance in 1975's "The Android Invasion" (Nicholas Courtney was touring in a theatrical production), though Benton was around. This final appearance saw no recurring guest stars, and UNIT's role is limited to the final battle in episode six.

Shortly before broadcast, the master tape of the first episode was lost, causing a panic. Producer Philip Hinchcliffe even began preparations to re-edit the second episode to allow the story to begin there. Fortunately, the tape was found, having been wrongly numbered in the tape-storage system. It was clearly a story that had its share of misfortunes: the police box TARDIS prop collapsed on top of Elisabeth Sladen while shooting the ending. The prop, which was built in 1963 (with slight redecorations over the years), had become quite tatty and was barely stable. For the following season, a new, slightly smaller version of the police box was built.

The TARDIS Chronometer Antarctica and England, near to the present day.

What? (RS?) "The Seeds of Doom" has two problems. First, it simply isn't *Doctor Who*. And second, it's extraordinarily good.

Listen to the evidence for the first charge: the Doctor and Sarah travel to Antarctica by helicopter, not TARDIS; the Doctor's primary opponent is a thug, and they engage in multiple fistfights; the Doctor's greatest contribution to the story is convincing a bunch of bureaucrats to take action; the Doctor carries a gun and punches people into unconsciousness; and the resolution to the story involves sending fighter planes to blow the threat to smithereens. These are textbook examples of what not to do in a *Doctor Who* story.

The second charge just makes it worse: although it shares the theme of possession with its recent predecessors, this isn't a treatise on what it means to be human like "The Ark in Space" or a fundamental examination of war like "Genesis of the Daleks." Instead, it's content to be nothing but a high-octane thriller.

And it's magnificent. Everything about this story is designed to thrill. The two-part prequel is there solely to make the cliffhanger to the third episode more terrifying, because we've already seen what happens when the pod opens. Having frightened us twice with the body-horror possession, Keeler's transformation then accelerates so that the final third of the story is spent facing a gigantic plant monster devouring a mansion. Plants come to life! Super-weapons don't work! The only way to escape is to make a Molotov cocktail! It ends with a fight in a composting machine! The plot is like a checklist of everything a ten-year-old boy would find exciting.

However, what makes this work for adults are the characters.

They're utterly superb. They might be drawn with broad brushstrokes, but Douglas Camfield knows how to cast and the result is the perfect synergy of actor and character. With personalities like Harrison Chase (a man who takes his prisoners on a house tour before executing them), Amelia Ducat (an elderly spy who smokes like a chimney and relishes the excitement of seeing guards with machine guns) and Sir Colin Thackeray (who's even invited to become a companion at the story's end) competing for attention, the result is unmissable drama. Even the lesser characters, like Dunbar (flawed, but ultimately noble), Keeler (a man in over his head if ever there was one) and Hargreaves (the unflappable butler, calmly serving raw meat to a man in the process of turning into a vegetable) stand out.

Of all of them, though, it's probably Scorby who deserves the most attention. What should be simply an unlikeable thug is instead vicious and layered thanks to John Challis's portrayal. There's a real nastiness to him, on full display when he beats up the Doctor. The story takes a brilliant turn when it forces him to align with the Doctor. Their subsequent interactions are no less intense and it feels like a genuine tragedy when Scorby finally snaps and is drowned in a fit of hysteria.

Oh, and the whole thing looks absolutely gorgeous, at least once the action moves to England. Chase Manor is a marvellous location, full of nooks and crannies, and the grounds, with plants filling the backdrop everywhere we look, are the perfect setting.

Back in my undergraduate days, I was watching this story when my roommate wandered into the living room. He wasn't a *Doctor Who* fan and he desperately had to get a good night's rest before a big exam the next day. He watched until the end of the first episode. And then the second. And the third. With every passing episode, he kept saying, "I really have to get to bed!" But he didn't go. "The Seeds of Doom" had him captivated. He couldn't tear his eyes off it.

Do I care that a story that isn't really *Doctor Who* was the one to hook a non-fan, rather than something that showed what the series has to say about the human condition? Hell no. Not when it's this good.

Second Opinion (GB) World-building, shmorld-building. "Genesis of the Daleks" is still really boring and ordinary during much of the first three episodes . . .

Never mind. Back to "The Seeds of Doom."

At first you wonder if it's even *Doctor Who*. "The Seeds of Doom" seems more like *The Avengers* (the British TV series, not the Marvel comic) at first blush, with the Doctor being summoned by a random bureaucrat and the appearance midway through of a random eccentric and a plot pretty much taken from the *Avengers* episode "The Man-Eater of Surrey Green." But it's thankfully bigger, and better, than that.

The first two episodes set in the Antarctic are a brilliantly suspenseful two-part story that you think can't be topped, and then it is by a further four episodes set on Chase's estate. And even if all four episodes are just running around in various states of capture and escape, it doesn't matter. It's so exciting and engrossing.

And that's what's so great about "The Seeds of Doom." It really shouldn't work, but dammit, it does. As my co-author says, it does all the things that should be in the no-no column for *Doctor Who*, with a thuggishly violent Doctor and a heavy whiff of sadism to the whole proceedings. But Tom Baker, against all odds, continues to be charming and heroic, probably because he amps up the eccentricity surrounding the thuggish moments. And the sadism just makes the horror more delicious, as the cliffhanger to episode three with Sarah and the pod shows us.

"The Seeds of Doom" is also stylish, thanks to direction by Douglas Camfield that looks so incredible you think location footage shot on video was actually made on film. The composition is that gorgeous. (Look at the scene where Chase is lying in the grass if you don't believe me.)

The story is also supported by some brilliant casting, particularly Tony Beckley as Harrison Chase, who manages to be at once obsessed, oblivious and cruel. And, let's face it, "I could play all day in my green cathedral" is one of the filthiest megalomaniacal exclamations in 50 years of *Doctor Who*.

If you haven't noticed by now, *Doctor Who* is capable of being pretty much any kind of program it wants to be. In these six episodes, it gets to be a phenomenally good modern horror story, with lots of gritty action sequences and overtones of *The Avengers*. Do I mind? As my co-author says, hell no.

The 1970s

The Deadly Assassin (1976)

Written by Robert Holmes **Directed by** David Maloney

Featuring Tom Baker (Doctor Who)

Supporting cast Peter Pratt (The Master), Bernard Horsfall (Goth), Angus MacKay (Borusa), George Pravda (Spandrell), Erik Chitty (Engin), Derek Seaton (Hilred), Hugh Walters (Runcible), Llewelyn Rees (the President), Peter Macock (Solis)

Original airdates October 30, November 6, 13, 20, 1976

The Big Idea The Doctor is summoned to his home planet when he foresees the death of its president. But his old adversary, the Master, is waiting for him . . .

Roots and References The 1962 film *The Manchurian Candidate* (the Doctor as an unwitting would-be assassin); JFK's assassination (the death of the president, framing the man found on the balcony, the mention of the CIA); *The Phantom of the Opera* (the Master lurking in the upper reaches); the 1935 film *The 39 Steps* (a wrongly convicted man trying to prove his innocence); Richard Connell's short story "The Most Dangerous Game" (the Doctor being hunted by Goth).

Time And Relative Dimensions In Space After the departure of Elisabeth Sladen as Sarah Jane Smith, Tom Baker suggested the Doctor travel alone and talk to himself, in lieu of having a companion. Producer Philip Hinchcliffe instead suggested a single companionless story to show Baker why it wouldn't work. His idea was something based on *The Manchurian Candidate*, despite never having seen the movie. Robert Holmes felt that such a political thriller might work best within Time Lord society, with the Doctor returning to his home planet. From there, the idea led to a revival of the Master.

This story ran into problems not in production, but in broadcast. Mary Whitehouse, leader of the National Viewers' and Listeners' Association (NVLA), a right-wing pressure group, complained to the BBC director general, Sir Charles Curran, about the violence in "The Deadly Assassin." For a decade, Whitehouse and the NVLA had been regularly lodging complaints with the BBC, against everything from *Till Death Us Do Part* (for the swearing) to *Doctor Who* (for its horrific content and violence). Recent complaints against *Who* included the violent war imagery in "Genesis of the Daleks" and the sequence in "The Seeds of Doom" where viewers are shown how to create a Molotov cocktail. Philip Hinchcliffe and Robert Holmes believed that the majority of their audience was skewing older, and the kids who were watching were capable of discerning the fantastic settings of *Doctor Who* as distinct from real-life scenarios. However, with "The Deadly Assassin," Whitehouse managed to demonstrate that the cliffhanger to episode three, which ends on a freezeframe of the Doctor being drowned, contravened the BBC's policy of not ending programs viewed by family audiences with violent or disturbing imagery.

Hinchcliffe, who was soon to leave *Doctor Who*, protested, noting that a cliffhanger with the Doctor in jeopardy was a regular occurence. Nonetheless, the director general felt forced to apologize to Whitehouse and the NVLA, a first for the BBC in respect to Whitehouse. Incoming producer Graham Williams was told to tone down the horror and the violence.

Adventures in Time and Space This is the first story fully set on the Doctor's home planet, Gallifrey, which was seen briefly at the end of "The War Games" and named in 1973's "The Time Warrior." We get a summary of the Doctor's sentence and exile ("Spearhead From Space" onwards), as well as a mention that the sentence was remitted (1972's "The Three Doctors"). Goth is played by the same actor who played the unnamed Time Lord judge in "The War Games," suggesting that they may be the same character.

The Master was last seen in 1973's "Frontier in Space." (A planned showdown at the climax of the third Doctor's era never occurred, due to the untimely death of actor Roger Delgado.)

Who is the Doctor? The Doctor willingly returns to Gallifrey for the first time and we get more details on his background here than anywhere else. He's a member of the Prydonian chapter of the Time Lords, notorious for the cunning and intelligence of its members. Borusa confirms that, as an Academy student, the Doctor had a "propensity for vulgar facetiousness" (which viewers have been well aware of for a while!). Runcible asks, "Weren't you expelled or something?" which could be referring to the Doctor's exile, but could also hint at another scandal that led to his departure from Gallifrey. (The Doctor coyly answers, "Something like that.") The Doctor also has a formidable grasp of Gallifreyan law, knowing the loophole that saves his life. His brain has an unusually high level of artron energy (possibly from his extensive travel in time and space). He's a competent artist, drawing caricatures at his trial.

Monster of the Week The Master, now withered and decayed, looks almost skeletal and claims that hate keeps him going. (It's implied that the Doctor is responsible for his current condition, although the details are never disclosed.) He met Goth on Tersurus, when he was dying, as he'd passed his twelfth regeneration, beyond which no Time Lord can survive.

Stand Up and Cheer The president is dead and the Doctor has been caught red-handed, still clutching a weapon. He offers no defence during his interrogation and sits silently at his trial, merely sketching. And when his guilt seems overwhelming, with a rushed execution to follow . . . he stands up and offers himself as a candidate for the presidency. It's an absolutely stunning move.

Roll Your Eyes In the Matrix, Goth manifests himself like a samurai, sporting a dodgy Kabuki mask for good measure and making a stereotypical "oriental" cry that is just downright embarrassing.

You're Not Making Any Sense After the Doctor has eluded the chancellery guards for some time, they finally have the bright idea to use a tracker to find him. This device is startlingly accurate . . . in locating the Doctor's clothes. Once they trace his outfit to a museum, they appear to give up on the device entirely. Was it only programmed to search for Earth fibres or something?

Interesting Trivia We learn all manner of Time Lord history here, from exposition and throwaway lines (like Pandak III and his nine-century term as president). The most crucial detail is the existence of Rassilon, the engineer who founded Gallifrey by stabilizing a black hole known as the Eye of Harmony, which appears to contradict what we learnt in 1972's "The Three Doctors." In that story, Omega was responsible for inventing time travel (the result of which was his becoming trapped in a universe of antimatter). From this point on, Rassilon becomes far more integral to Time Lord history than Omega (although we hear more about both, in due course).

The wooden console room seen here is the secondary console room, introduced in 1976's "The Masque of Mandragora." It replaced the white console room for one season.

Of the many changes to established mythology that this episode makes (the Master as a skeleton, Time Lords as pedantic old men, their technology considered prehistoric junk), there's one that's caused no end of grief. We're definitively told that Time Lords have only 12 regenerations (and hence 13 lives). This overwrites the previous assertion that Time Lords were immortal, barring accidents (as stated in "The War Games"). More worryingly, it also suggests that we may be running out of Doctors: with Matt Smith the eleventh, this means there are only two to go and then the series must wrap itself up once Justin Bieber calls it quits as the thirteenth Doctor, no matter how high the ratings are. Or at least, that's how the argument appears to run among a number of fans (conveniently ignoring the competing piece of evidence that states that Time Lords are immortal). There are several outs to this dilemma: one is that the production team that created the "13 lives" rule considered Tom Baker to be about the twelfth Doctor, so the rule's already been violated. Another is that the Master is offered a new regeneration cycle in "The Five Doctors," so it's possible to go beyond 13. A third is that the Time Lords are wiped from history in the New Series, suggesting that their rule may have died with them. Finally, Russell T Davies already dealt with this one: in the *Sarah Jane Adventures* episode "Death of the Doctor" (starring Matt Smith as the eleventh Doctor), Davies snuck in a line saying that Time Lords had 508 lives. So we shouldn't be writing the series' eulogy any time soon.

When this story first aired, there was fan outcry. It was voted the worst story of the season in the Doctor Who Appreciation Society poll, and lengthy diatribes were written about how it betrayed the spirit of *Doctor Who* by the founder and then-president of the fan club, Jan Vincent-Rudzki. Depending on your familiarity with *Doctor Who*, you may be wondering what all the fuss is about. If you're watching the Classic Series for the first time, in order — or watching the stories in the order we suggest in this volume — then you might have some sympathy: the Time Lord society presented here is rather less powerful than the one glimpsed in "The War Games" and "The Three Doctors"; that was the heart of Vincent-Rudzki's argument, and it's indisputably true. However, what we get here is far richer (and sets the stage for further return appearances of the Time Lords); Robert Holmes knows that there's more dramatic mileage to be had in showing the ultimate empire as something that's steeped in tradition and political infighting (q.v. the British Empire) than in a society of godlike aliens. Holmes took his inspiration for the Time Lords from British universities and their seeming inability to change, regardless of the world around them.

If you're paying careful attention, you might notice that there are only two candidates for the presidency (the Doctor and Goth), one of whom ends up dead. So does that mean the Doctor ends the story as president-elect of the Time Lords? You betcha! In fact, this is an ongoing plot point for the series, that gets taken up in the following year's season finale, "The Invasion of Time," which sees the Doctor return to Gallifrey to claim the presidency.

Just as 1966's "The War Machines" predicted the internet, this story predicts virtual reality. The Matrix is a place where the brains of deceased Time Lords are stored, able to predict future events. The environment can be shaped to resemble an entire world, where the rules can be altered, but it mostly plays out as though real. And if the virtual body dies inside, then so does the real body. It's all so similar to the 1999 movie *The Matrix* that you wonder if someone wasn't taking notes.

The TARDIS Chronometer Gallifrey, the planet of the Time Lords, time-frame unknown.

What? (RS?)

Crust

- One Master, pre-baked
- Pinch of psychopathic hatred
- The planet Gallifrey
- Time Lord society (this can be made to order, given the paucity of information doled out previously)
- Time Lord history, the older the better

Stewed filling

- Scroll text, with narration
- A companionless Doctor (it's true that the flavours of the Doctor and companion usually complement each other, but in this recipe we've found that it tastes better without the latter!)
- Political intrigue
- Costumes (preferably by future Oscar-winning designer)
- Dotty old men (women not required for this creation, except in voiceover)

Chocolate ganache

- Interrogation
- Torture
- News broadcast
- Courtroom drama
- Pseudo companions
- Matrix foreshadowing

Cream layer

- Train
- Dinosaur egg
- Surgeon
- Clown
- Biplane
- Giant spider
- Poison
- Marsh gas

Maple frosting

- Rassilon
- Time Lord lives
- Extonic circuitry (or any old prehistoric junk)
- Symbols of office
- Heroes (if you have them)
- Eye of Harmony

Festoon the planet Gallifrey with pomp and circumstance. Slowly add Time Lords, and dust with Time Lord history, a little at a time. Take the Master and add a pinch of psychopathic hatred. This should be as predictable as ever. Place in the centre of the Gallifrey mixture and fold the other ingredients around him. Allow to settle.

Once the crust has hardened, insert the Doctor into the mixture. Layer in the scroll text. (This isn't strictly necessary, but improves the flavour.) Add political intrigue, a generous helping of costumes and dotty old men. Heat in warm oven for 23 minutes.

When the first part is hot enough, mix together all the ingredients for the chocolate ganache. Although these are standard ingredients, the combination of flavours here will come together nicely. Dust with a hint of Matrix foreshadowing.

Meanwhile, prepare the cream layer to one side. This layer is the crucial one: its flavours provide a dramatic contrast to the rest of the dessert, but it's the very boldness of the concept that gives this its tang. These ingredients can be mixed in any order, except for the marsh gas, which should be kept until the end. When you're done, flambé the marsh gas for a short time. Add water at the end. (Although some people have complained about this step, so you can cut it if you are so inclined.)

When the cream layer is in place, the final step is the maple frosting. This should be carefully aged. The aim here is to assemble an impressive number of ingredients, but to make people mostly forget about them. (If you have no heroes, feel free to invent them.) The result may initially seem less impressive than previous creations, but in fact has much better staying power. This step has also received complaints from some readers, but is an absolutely crucial part of the recipe. Without it, the entire creation has no verisimilitude.

Allow all the layers to settle and refrigerate overnight. Recipe can be made ahead of time and frozen. In fact, we highly recommend this, as the flavours need time to be absorbed. The recipe is never more tasty than when the odds are against it.

When everything is done, serve to an unsuspecting audience. They may be surprised at first, but they'll eventually come to appreciate the sheer mastery of assemblage that you have here. In fact, this is such an inspired creation that you'll never make another recipe the old way again.

Second Opinion (GB) Or, to put it another way . . .

This is the first story in *Doctor Who*'s history to visit the Doctor's home planet for more than just a passing vignette. It's the first story to feature the Doctor without a companion. It's the culmination of Philip Hinchcliffe's vision of a *Doctor Who* that is more adult and gritty. It's all these things, and it's also just a brilliant hour and a half of television.

It is also, probably more than any *Doctor Who* story before it, a perfect union of all the elements of television production. Everything combines to make Gallifrey seem dark, mysterious and awe-inspiring. There's Roger Murray-Leach's design — with its large, cavernous structures — working with Dudley Simpson's organ music to add a sense of grandeur and cathedral-like awe; all this works with David Maloney's direction, which makes the most of both of these elements and gets the actors, particularly Tom Baker, to underplay their roles and make the stakes seem so much higher.

Robert Holmes's superb script takes *Doctor Who* and puts it into a hard-boiled mould: outsider/loner returns home to be accused of a crime he didn't commit and has to prove his innocence. And if all that isn't enough, the third episode is a giant spectacle, shot entirely on film on location, of the Doctor being hunted by the killer. The gambit is brilliant: the Gallifrey setting is so claustrophobic that when you're finally outside it's even more menacing. And we see the Doctor vulnerable in a way we've never seen before, which makes the drama all that more compelling and the ending all the more shocking.

Then there are the Time Lords themselves. Some have suggested their portrayal here has peeled away their mystery by making them petty and cynical. I think it's where all the previous appearances were inevitably leading: if you have all this power, you probably would be a cynical society obsessed with internal politics. But I will grant its detractors the point: I can't help watching "The Deadly Assassin" and thinking it might have been a cul-de-sac. Others will not have Holmes's flair for making the Time Lords at once impressive and corrupt.

About the only thing that really frustrates me about "The Deadly Assassin" is the cliffhanger to episode three. For decades, I'd only seen the PBS version, which simply cuts to black after Goth says, "You're finished," and it's just as effective. I truly love Philip Hinchcliffe's work as producer and I think Mary Whitehouse is a fanatical nutjob, yet here I agree with her: I think the freezeframe on the drowning Doctor is somewhat gratuitous.

That said, "The Deadly Assassin" is an important story in *Doctor Who*'s annals. It's also television at its most exciting. Excuse me while I sample some more of this lovely confection.

The Face of Evil (1977)

Written by Chris Boucher **Directed by** Pennant Roberts

Featuring Tom Baker (Doctor Who), Louise Jameson (Leela)

Supporting cast David Garfield (Neeva); Victor Lucas (Andor); Brendan Price (Tomas); Leslie Schofield (Caleb); Colin Thomas (Sole); Lloyd McGuire (Lugo); Leon Eagles (Jabel); Mike Elles (Gentek); Peter Baldock (Acolyte); Tom Kelly, Brett Forrest (guards); Rob Edwards, Pamela Salem, Anthony Frieze, Roy Herrick (Xoanon); Harry Fielder (assassin)

Original airdates January 1, 8, 15, 22, 1977

The Big Idea The Doctor finds himself reviled by a primitive tribe as their "evil one" — and in case there's any dispute, he even finds his likeness carved in a rock face.

Roots and References Walter Miller's 1960 novel *A Canticle for Leibowitz* (the post-apocalyptic society treating ordinary things as holy relics); several *Star Trek* episodes, particularly "The Apple" (a computer worshipped as a god); the Book of Common Prayer (the litany); *Forbidden Planet* (the projection of Xoanon's id); *Goldfinger* (the laser threatening to destroy the Doctor and Leela). The Doctor whistles the "Colonel Bogey March" (made popular in the 1957 film *The Bridge over the River Kwai*) and quotes Rudyard Kipling's "The Young British Soldier," though he claims it as the work of Gertude Stein. (The Doctor misattributing literary quotes was something of a running gag during this era.)

Time And Relative Dimensions In Space For a five-year period, roughly between 1971 and 1976, *Doctor Who* had virtually no new writers. Bob Baker, Dave Martin and Robert Sloman were brought on during the eighth season, but everyone else had written for (or worked on) the show during the 1960s. The first new writer after this period was Robert Banks Stewart in 1975, though it must be said that Stewart was a veteran writer and TV producer. The first truly "new" writer — new to television writing and to *Doctor Who* — was Chris Boucher. Boucher was mentored by script editor Robert Holmes, who thought his work had promise. Unusually for the era, where writers tended to work from

The 1970s

155

briefs supplied by Holmes and producer Philip Hinchcliffe, Boucher brought his own idea for "The Face of Evil" (far more daringly titled "The Day God Went Mad") to the production team.

The major addition to the script was creating a new companion. It was thought that this character, a "savage," would be vastly different to the standard "English rose" young female: she would be violent, aggressive and instinctive, and part of her relationship with the Doctor would be him "civilizing" her, similar to Henry Higgins and Eliza Doolittle in *Pygmalion*. Boucher created Leela, whom he named after Palestinian hijacker Leila Khaled, a figure in the news at the time.

Adventures in Time and Space While this story is based on a past trip the Doctor made to a planetary survey team called the Mordee expedition, it was never depicted on television. He says a communications device is "dead as a Dalek."

Who is the Doctor? The Doctor is talking to himself because he's alone, and he's becoming forgetful (tying several knots in his hanky as a reminder). He's a crack shot with a crossbow (and was taught by William Tell). He wonders if he left his personality print on Xoanon out of vanity — an interesting avenue of inquiry that isn't further explored.

Companion Chronicles Leela is a young warrior in the tribe of the Sevateem. She's a skilled huntress and knows how to kill with a knife or janis thorns (a local plant that can paralyze). She is also quite brave and prepared to challenge her tribe's allegiance to Xoanon in order to prevent bloodshed. Leela is inquisitive, asking things that others, even the Doctor, haven't considered. While the Doctor objects to Leela killing, he also takes a liking to her, encouraging her to ask questions.

Monster of the Week Xoanon is a computer that was used by the Mordee expedition. It is capable of independent thought, though the Doctor was unaware of its sentience many years ago when he tried to repair it using his own brain and forgot to wipe his personality print. Consequently, Xoanon developed split personalities; over the years, it began to think of itself as a god, projecting its id as invisible creatures that roam the planet. It kept the descendants of the expedition's technicians (the Tesh) and the planetary survey team (the Sevateem) at war with each other as part of a twisted eugenics experiment.

Stand Up and Cheer After the Doctor cures Leela from the janis thorn toxin, Leela wakes up and asks the Doctor, "Do you know the answer to everything?" and the Doctor answers, "Yes. Well . . . no. Answers are easy. It's asking the right questions that is hard." This is why the Doctor is our hero.

Roll Your Eyes There's no polite way of saying this: the Tesh are just plain embarrassing. Psychic powers or no, it's hard to consider people who look like sous-chefs in the Eurozone at EPCOT as a credible threat. That said, the Sevateem aren't exactly prizes; the males aren't particularly toned and it seems as though the tribe's entrance qualification is to look like one of the Bee Gees.

You're Not Making Any Sense Where are the women? Leela is a full-fledged warrior, but there are apparently no other women in the Sevateem. In fact, there are no women other than Leela to be seen anywhere: no warriors, no civilians, no female Tesh even. It's an utterly bizarre omission. We can only presume the entire society will die off in one generation, now that she's gone.

Interesting Trivia Throughout the story, Xoanon is characterized as "schizoid." As in much of television and popular culture of the 1970s, the assumption here is that schizophrenia and multiple personality disorders are one and the same thing, which is wrong. Schizophrenia is a disorder that's characterized by the breakdown of thought processes, resulting in delusions, hallucinations and paranoia. Multiple personality disorder is a condition that is characterized by developing disassociated identities.

The interesting question this story asks is who were the Sevateem. Were they the descendants of the original survey team from long ago, or were they indigenous to the planet being surveyed by the Mordee expedition? (Or, as Caleb puts it, "Are we their captors or their children?") The question is never really answered. The Sevateem's complete ignorance of the technology that surrounds them and how they turn the process of checking the seals on a spacesuit into a form of genuflecting indicates a society who watched more technologically advanced people do things they didn't understand. The Tesh know the purpose of the equipment and yet have turned everything into a sacred process as well, which suggests a society who became what they were after generations of doing the same thing and making a religion out of it, encouraged by a mad computer with a god complex.

Louise Jameson drew inspiration for playing Leela from several sources, including the child of a neighbour (her openness and naïveté) and Jameson's dog, Bosie (her instinctive nature and tendency to slightly cock her head when she perceives something). Jameson had to wear brown contact lenses (more on that in a couple of stories) for the role and, of course, the abbreviated costume. (Jameson requested the flap on the back of it because she was self-conscious about her bottom!) During makeup tests, Leela had darkened face paint, pictures of which exist, but it was decided to have Leela sport only a slightly darker skintone to Jameson's own.

The addition of Leela did not sit well with Tom Baker, who didn't want the Doctor to be saddled with a companion. Baker was also very conscious of the influence *Doctor Who* had on young children (he refused to smoke or drink alcohol if a child was within view), and he objected to Leela's violence and her skimpy costume. Baker was mollified by the production team's assurances that she would only be around for the three stories that ended the fourteenth season. Of course, the production team had no intention of replacing her, but Philip Hinchcliffe was departing as producer and, according to Louise Jameson, left it to his replacement, Graham Williams, to run interference with Baker!

The TARDIS Chronometer An unknown planet, sometime in the future.

What? (GB) Shortly after *Who Is The Doctor*, our guide to the New Series, came out, I was on a panel at Toronto ComicCon. An audience member asked what Classic Series story I would recommend to someone who hadn't watched it before. I didn't hesitate. "The Face of Evil" had been released on DVD a week or so before. I still think it's the perfect story to see if you're new to old-school *Doctor Who*. It's not that there aren't other great candidates: "The Ark in Space" is fantastic for that, and "The Brain of Morbius" worked with my wife and goddaughter. But "The Face of Evil" is so intelligent and exciting, and the Doctor is never better.

The first episode alone is a stunning piece of work. Not only does it drop the viewer into the deep end of a fully realized world of a tribe obliviously worshipping the relics of a spacefaring survey team (unusually for this era, it starts *in media res*); not only does it introduce a wonderfully proactive and fascinating character in Leela; not only does it give us an incredible mystery with the Doctor known to the "savages" as an evil god but Tom Baker's opening scenes are unbelievably funny and delightful.

Those scenes where the Doctor eccentrically talks to himself (and the viewer) almost seem like a manifesto of what's to come with Tom Baker's ascension to a larger-than-life Doctor. He never crosses the line into outright outlandishness, but Baker's Doctor is wittier and sillier from the get-go. It's almost as though Baker, Philip Hinchcliffe and Robert Holmes realized that, without Elisabeth Sladen as Sarah, Baker would need to bring more of the Doctor to bear in the stories. And he does. The Doctor is an explosive series of contradictions here. He's charming and funny (threatening people with a jelly baby, his reaction when his bluff is called), but he's also brutal and thuggish (his move with Caleb is right out of *Get Carter*). Baker keeps these different aspects together and makes it all seem so light and fresh and funny. It's wildly compelling.

"The Face of Evil" is all about strong characterization. The Sevateem are not the usual stock-ignorant savages but guileful characters who are manipulative, cynical, and driven by competing motives within the group and with each other. The roles are brilliantly cast, particularly Leslie Schofield's double-dealing Caleb. (His delight when Andor is killed and he ascends to leader is astonishing.) David Garfield as Neeva is great. Garfield relishes the opportunity to portray a man who worships — and then seeks revenge on — the god who betrays him.

But it's the supernova intensity of Louise Jameson's debut as Leela that demands our attention. Jameson doesn't so much portray Leela as embody the part. It's such an incredible performance. Even when she's not the focus of the scene, she's fascinating to watch; even if it's just her posture, she's constantly inventive in her performance. The glorious thing about it is that it's unmannered and feels totally natural.

What's more, the story is gorgeously designed (there are ducting coils mixed in with jungle, suggesting that the spaceship has become a part of the environment) and the story is hugely exciting. Chris Boucher gives us a roller-coaster ride with jeopardy at every turn. Just as one threat is diminished, a bigger one comes, piled on like a thinking person's Bond film on a BBC budget. This is laid bare for us in the final two episodes in the Tesh's domain: while the setting and the characters are not as compelling as in the first two episodes, the thrills are amped up. And the cliffhanger to episode three, with the Doctor under siege from all of Xoanon's personalities, kicks it up a notch and becomes genuinely haunting when the child's voice utters, "Who am I?"

On paper, "The Face of Evil" reads like a shopping list of every science-fiction trope of the '70s: planet inhabited by now-savage descendants of space travellers, worshipping their ancestors' technology as a god. But it's so much more than that. The Doctor seeing his own face in the rock immediately takes those tropes and puts them at a 45-degree angle: full of mystery and perplexity and real possibility. With its central idea of a super-computer afflicted by the Doctor's personality that consequently becomes a god, "The Face of Evil" is a pure science-fiction story, which everyone assumes *Doctor Who* is all the time, but it hardly ever is. Seeing this, one wonders why *Doctor Who* doesn't try this more often. (Was a 16-year-old Steven Moffat taking notes while watching? The notion that the Doctor's interference has unintended consequences is right in his wheelhouse.)

In the best tradition of science fiction, "The Face of Evil" is a beautiful piece of world-building and it works because of its lacunae. Who carved the Doctor's face in the rock? Are the people the descendants of the Mordee expedition or of the planet's original inhabitants? How long has it been since the Mordee expedition? How did Xoanon get to this state? These gaps in the story are not flaws in the plot, but rather blemishes that make the world seem real. A world where history is a series of found objects and people don't know where they came from or where they are going — a world without end.

The central mystery is beautifully realized in what must be the greatest articulation of *Doctor Who*'s secular outlook. Neeva putting a giant spacesuit glove on his head is silly, but is it any sillier than the vestiges of the first-century vestments worn by priests in church? The litany, which tells the story of achieving landfall and a survey team venturing out only in the language of Cramner, is a similar dig at religion. And we have Xoanon creating the world in his own image, only Xoanon's a computer with a personality disorder performing a bizarre eugenics experiment only it can understand.

But this exploration of philosophical themes is so much more than a couple of good Pythonesque jokes. It's a state of mind. Leela says, "I don't know what to believe" and the Doctor responds, "Well, that's a good sign, anyway." The Doctor encourages Leela to ask questions, to never let anything stand just because others say it's so. And Leela already has the courage of her convictions: while many within her tribe don't believe in Xoanon but are content to prop up the system, either to obtain their own ends (Caleb) or because they won't speak up (Tomas), the first scene has her standing firm in the conviction that

Xoanon doesn't exist and the random slaughter of her people must stop. "The Face of Evil" is a song of praise for the questions "why" and "how." It embodies one of the qualities of the *Doctor Who* universe that I love: everything should be explicable. Or as Tomas says, "With proof, you don't have to believe."

It's no wonder I think "The Face of Evil" is one of the best gateway stories to *Doctor Who*. It's intelligent. It's funny. It's exciting. It has great actors doing wonderful things with a great script. It says something meaningful about how we should look at the world around us but in a bold and imaginative way. It's everything I love about *Doctor Who* in four episodes.

Second Opinion (RS?) What he said. Except for the . . . no, what he said.

The Talons of Weng-Chiang (1977)

Written by Robert Holmes **Directed by** David Maloney

Featuring Tom Baker (Doctor Who), Louise Jameson (Leela)

Supporting cast Christopher Benjamin (Henry Gordon Jago), Trevor Baxter (Professor Litefoot), John Bennett (Li H'sen Chang), Deep Roy (Mr. Sin), Michael Spice (Weng-Chiang), Chris Gannon (Casey), Alan Butler (Buller), Tony Then (Lee), Vincent Wong (Ho), John Wu (Coolie), Conrad Asquith (PC Quick), Judith Lloyd (Teresa), Dudley Simpson (conductor), Patsy Smart (ghoul)

Original airdates February 26, March 5, 12, 19, 26, April 2, 1977

The Big Idea In Victorian London, women are disappearing off the streets. What does a Chinese magician at the Palace Theatre have to do with it?

Roots and References The "yellow peril" genre fiction of the late nineteenth and early twentieth centuries, particularly Fu Manchu (Li H'sen Chang and the Chinese villains); *The Phantom of the Opera* (the masked Magnus Greel hiding beneath the theatre); the 1953–1983 BBC series *The Good Old Days*, the 1960 film *The Entertainer* and music halls of the nineteenth century (the theatre and Jago); the Jack the Ripper murders (the missing girls). The song "Daisy, Daisy" is sung at the theatre (and composer Dudley Simpson uses a few bars from it in his score). Litefoot quotes from John Bunyan's *Pilgrim's Progress*, while the Doctor attributes the first line of J. Milton Hayes's poem "The Green Eye of the Little Yellow God" ("There's a one-eyed yellow idol to the north of

Katmandu") to Henry Champion, continuing the running gag of misquoting people. The Doctor is dressed up like — and acts in a manner similar to — Sherlock Holmes (Tom Baker would play the great detective for the BBC in 1982) and several Holmes references occur throughout, most notably Litefoot having a housekeeper named Mrs. Hudson.

Time And Relative Dimensions In Space Script editor Robert Holmes thought he had left the final story of *Doctor Who*'s fourteenth season in safe hands with veteran writer Robert Banks Stewart. Stewart had been briefed to write a story set in the Victorian era inspired by the Whitechapel murders, with Holmes suggesting that the killer could be from the future. Stewart wrote a storyline for this under the title "The Foe From the Future" and Holmes went on vacation with his family. Unfortunately, Holmes's wife suffered a perforated ulcer while in Munich, which meant an enforced extended stay. When Holmes finally made it back to the office, he found a note from Stewart indicating he had taken a script editing job at ITV and was unable to write the script after all. With no time to commission a replacement, Holmes was forced to write it himself.

This was the final story produced by Philip Hinchcliffe and the last to be directed by David Maloney (who went to produce the BBC science-fiction series *Blake's 7*). As it was his last hurrah, Hinchcliffe was not so tight with the purse strings, encouraging Maloney to do extensive location shooting and expensive night filming.

Adventures in Time and Space Leela uses a janis thorn (from "The Face of Evil") to kill one of Chang's men. The Doctor shows off his knowledge of Chinese languages (he apparently speaks Mandarin, Cantonese and all the local dialects), which he demonstrated in "The Mind of Evil" and mentions having been to China before (1964's "Marco Polo").

Who is the Doctor? The Doctor is immediately accepted by the police (and later Litefoot and then Jago) as a figure of authority, largely just by virtue of being knowledgeable.

Companion Chronicles The Doctor continues to educate Leela by having her dress up in Victorian clothes and showing her the place where her ancestors lived. She's still quite unworldly when it comes to nineteenth-century living: she's never seen anyone smoke a pipe and eats rather crudely. (Litefoot manages to score a small victory when he gets her to use a napkin and not the tablecloth to wipe her mouth!)

Monster of the Week Magnus Greel, a.k.a. "The Butcher of Brisbane," is a war criminal and scientist from the 51st century, posing here as the Chinese god Weng-Chiang. The zygma experiment that enabled him to travel back in time left half his face melted out of shape. He needs energy from living things to survive and has been kidnapping girls for this purpose. Long ago, he imparted mental powers to Li H'sen Chang, a peasant. He has increased the size of London sewer rats to act as guards to his inner sanctum.

Stand Up and Cheer The first meeting between Litefoot and Jago may be the funniest scene in *Doctor Who* not featuring the Doctor. Litefoot, who is sweeping up, is mistaken by Jago for the butler. Once corrected, Jago proclaims, "By dash me optics," and pronounces Litefoot to be the "peerless premiere professor of pathology." Litefoot is non-plussed, showing Jago to the parlour while keeping his stick at the ready to clobber him. Lovely.

Roll Your Eyes The giant rat is something of an embarrassment. Its hair isn't oily, like a real sewer rat's, so it looks instead like a fluffy gerbil and . . .

Hold on. Wait a minute. Never mind that. There's a Caucasian man wearing prostethics to look like he's Chinese, speaking in a stereotypical Chinese accent. Forget the rat; this guy is the actual embarrassment.

You're Not Making Any Sense How wonderful that the Coincidence Fairies have come to visit, ensuring not only that the time cabinet has been left in the home of the pathologist the Doctor has befriended, but that Greel leaves behind the key for it in his underground lair once he finally obtains the cabinet. That was very kind of them.

Interesting Trivia Almost 30 years after this story, Russell T Davies and Steven Moffat drew from its details — Greel being from the 51st century and worried about pursuit from Time Agents — in creating Captain Jack Harkness (a former Time Agent) and the future society seen in the eleventh Doctor era.

The subterranean River Fleet starts near Hampstead and winds underground through the sewer system before emptying in the Thames some six kilometres away. The Doctor claims to have fished with the Venerable Bede on the Fleet, though Bede, who lived from 673 to 735 AD, apparently never travelled to London.

During the making of this story, it was suggested that Robert Holmes's ultimate double act, Litefoot and Jago, would make an excellent *Doctor Who* spinoff. The idea was never seriously developed, though Trevor Baxter and Christopher Benjamin reunited in 2010 to record audio adventures, for Big Finish productions, featuring the premier pathologist and the impunicable impressario. Not bad for two characters who don't meet until the penultimate episode!

The portrayal of the Chinese in this story owes a strong debt to the "yellow peril" genre of late nineteenth- and early twentieth-century pulp fiction. The genre was characterized by intelligent, evil and invariably "oriental" masterminds intent on destroying the West. Trading in stereotypes of long-dead Mongol warlords and submissive coolies, the most popular examples of the genre are the tales of Fu Manchu, who was not created until 1913. "The Talons of Weng-Chiang" is set in a fantasy London overrun with the secret Chinese Tongs and opium dens that feature in "yellow peril" stories, and Robert Holmes has acknowledged in interviews his debt to Fu Manchu. The "yellow peril" genre arose from reactionary hysteria to Chinese immigration to the U.S., but in Britain there were a scant 582 people of Chinese origin on the census rolls in 1891; the London fictionalized here never existed. The Tongs were barely more than fraternal organizations. Opium was still an over-the-counter item available from the local pharmacist. The whole story is, essentially, predicated on this racist genre of fiction.

That Li H'sen Chang was played by a Caucasian man cuts to the heart of the British sensibilities regarding casting. There is a mindset in Britain that sees portraying another ethnic group as a form of "dressing up." Thus you have John Bennett playing Li H'sen Chang, Jonathan Price playing a Vietnamese character in *Miss Saigon* or Ben Kingsley playing Gandhi (and Caucasian actors portraying Chinese characters in 1964's "Marco Polo" or Mexicans in "The Aztecs"). Assuming another ethnicity in a role is viewed as no different than playing a different nationality. At the other end of this scale lies the racist underbelly of British entertainment: from 1958 to 1978, one of the most popular light-entertainment shows from BBC television was *The Black and White Minstrel Show* where music-hall songs were performed by white actors in blackface. (Indeed, a non-blackface version was tried and ratings actually went down.) Such stereotyping was frequently found in British comedy and light entertainment. Far from being mere "dress-up," the practice relies on racist stereotypes and propagates them. Such attitudes undergirded British television in 1977.

Public broadcaster TVOntario was slated to air this story in December 1980. Anticipating a problem, they sent the episodes to a Chinese

Canadian citizens group, now known as the Chinese Canadian National Council (which had been formed a year earlier after succesfully protesting a racist report on the news program *W5*). The council was not, to put it mildly, impressed with what they saw. They felt the story "associate(s) the Chinese with everything fearful and despicable" and chided the story for its "dangerous, offensive, racist stereotyping." William Wong, the president of the council, stated to the *Toronto Star* that it "includes everything from an evil Fu Manchu character to pigtailed coolies and laundrymen who submissively commit suicide on their master's orders." Based on this assessment, TVOntario pulled the story from broadcast. Other Canadian television stations later showed it (PBS stations in the U.S. had since the stories became syndicated in 1978), but these stations never bothered to ask viewers of Chinese heritage what they thought about it.

The TARDIS Chronometer Victorian London. The date is never stated, though it is some time after the Whitechapel murders of 1888.

What? (GB) There are always aspects to things you love that make you uncomfortable. There's the beloved aunt who makes inappopriate remarks at Christmas dinner. There's the boyfriend who reveals he's intolerant about something you never thought him capable of. And there's the really brilliant episodes of your favourite television series that feature racist stereotypes.

Let's get this out of the way because it's unavoidable. Yes, "The Talons of Weng-Chiang" is a stunning tour de force and undoubtedly one of the greatest *Doctor Who* stories of all time. And yes, "The Talons of Weng-Chiang" is almost unbearably racist.

Long-time readers will know I'm the polite moderate of the two of us regarding politics. But when it comes to "The Talons of Weng-Chiang," I think it would do a disservice to the story, you the reader and myself to ignore the problem.

Let's count the stereotypes in the first episode alone. Pigtailed, silk-pyjama-dressed henchmen: check. Martial arts: check. Villainous figure with "oriental" goatee: check. Chinese characters being remarked upon for their inscruitable behaviour: check. And, in case we forget, lead Chinese character being played by a white actor: check. Through the next five episodes, we continue to cycle the stereotpes: opium dens, Chinese laundries, pithy aphorisms, tales of peasantry . . . it's like some form of bad stereotype bingo. (The Chinese aren't the only ones: the Irishman Casey is either cowardly, drunk or both.)

No, I won't play the game of "in the context of the times it was made . . ." or "but it's pure fantasy . . ." or "the writer, director and producer didn't intend it to be racist . . ." While all three points are true, and I agree with most arguments that have been thus made, "The Talons of Weng-Chiang" is still racist.

The story does attempt to undercut the stereotypes. In the same way that "Pyramids of Mars" subverts the mummy story, so does "The Talons of Weng-Chiang" subvert the "yellow peril" story. Li H'sen Chang certainly looks the part of a Fu Manchu, but "Talons" isn't about an educated Chinese megalomaniac destroying the West; it's about a time-travelling monster who manipulates a Chinese peasant into doing his bidding. And, in tragic fashion, the peasant is elevated above his lot and then cast down by that monster. However, this doesn't let Robert Holmes off the hook: Li H'sen Chang might not be Fu Manchu, but it can be argued that he is merely a cut above being a "submissive coolie."

Also, to the story's credit, the Doctor seems unconcerned by race and either ignores or derides how others speak about the Chinese. When Litefoot says, "What has it come to when a man can be attacked by ruffians in his own home?" the Doctor replies, "Yes, but they were *Chinese* ruffians!" The line delivery just drips with irony, undermining the casual racist attitudes expressed throughout the episode.

And John Bennett's performance, to give him his due, has a charming twinkle that covers a deep well of pathos: the scene where Li H'sen, now disgraced, tells the Doctor of being rejected by his god is beautiful and heartbreaking. He doesn't play Chang badly; quite the opposite: he imbues him with real sophistication, charm and even nobility. But it's hard to watch this on a modern, big-screen TV where the prosthetic slant eyes are so obvious. And the first Asian actor with a speaking part doesn't appear until episode five.

It's impossible to know if the stereotypes would have been lessened by casting a Chinese actor as Chang, but the decision to cast a white actor (ironically, a more expensive choice, given their use of prosthetics) certainly exacerbates the problem. I don't think anyone involved had sinister motives in casting John Bennett; in fact, I think if they were questioned, they would claim no qualified Asian actor was found to play that part. But that response only identifies the systemic discrimination at the heart of British television in the 1970s: there were no roles for minorities and no minorities could allegedly portray such a role anyway. It's a subtle racism underpinning a broader one.

Okay. That's the bad news.

Here's the good news. "The Talons of Weng-Chiang" is incredible and might be Tom Baker's two finest hours in his tenure as the Doctor.

The look and feel is near perfect. In fact, I would argue that this story influenced the post-2005 New Series more than any other: high production values, great use of location, night shooting . . . it's lush and sumptuous. But it's no hollow confection. It smartly filches the best bits of various Victorian genres and gives us a Doctor who is truly Sherlockian: authoritative, brilliant and one step ahead of everyone else. (Did I mention Tom Baker is wonderful at it?)

Litefoot and Jago are both sublime supporting characters. (The Doctor looks as though he's about to laugh himself silly every time he's with Jago; I swear the Doctor keeps him nearby just because Jago and his pompous perigrinations amuse him so much.) When the two actually come together, it seems divinely preordained. Robert Holmes is so confident with their pairing that he effectively stalls episode five to allow for the comic bit with the dumbwaiter, instead of pushing the plot forward with the Doctor and Leela.

It's a story that only dials down from exciting in order to give us either comedy or atmosphere, and that's a great thing. The dialogue is wonderful. I could have spent this whole review quoting things like, "My dear Litefoot, I've got a lantern, a pair of waders and possibly the most fearsome piece of hand artillery in all England. What could possibly go wrong?" Or Greel questioning Litefoot and Jago, where a panicked Jago basically repeats either Greel's questions or Litefoot's answers. It's razor sharp and witty, on top of everything else.

Make no mistake, "The Talons of Weng-Chiang" is incredible. It's everything great you want *Doctor Who* to be. But there are often aspects to things you love that don't make you comfortable. Acknowledge them. Be aware of them. You can still love the end result.

Second Opinion (RS?) My co-author is right: "The Talons of Weng-Chiang" is racist. The fact that we both feel the need to state this so clearly is because of fandom's response to the story. Countless articles and books have been written extolling the virtues of "Talons," except for that one flaw: the giant rat. When it comes to the racism, fandom either ignores it altogether or apologizes for it, desperately placing it in context in a way that (say) Toberman in "The Tomb of the Cybermen" isn't.

I disagree with my co-author on the claim that "Yes, but they were *Chinese* ruffians" is not a racist line. Litefoot hasn't been expressing any attitudes that the Doctor needs to pillory, and the line draws attention to the race of the ruffians in a way that wasn't necessary. People have tried to apologize for that line for years, but there's no getting away with it. The Doctor's being racist.

But I'm more interested in asking a different question: why exactly do we love "Talons" and its ilk so much, even to the point of wilful blindness?

For all our bluster, it isn't actually the intelligent writing that draws fans to *Doctor Who*. And no, it isn't the competency of the special effects either. Or the costuming. Or the design work. Rather, it's the acting.

It's always been the acting.

This is the real reason "Talons" embodies the '70s and hence the entirety of *Doctor Who* for us, and why we're so loath to let it go, despite its obvious flaw (whichever one you adhere to). In essence, Classic *Doctor Who* is a stage play performed against a black backdrop, with minimal props and not nearly enough explosions. Nevertheless, an entire alien culture or history or galactic war can be convincingly presented to us by three British character actors performing their hearts out to make it real for us. Nothing else matters.

"Talons," like *Doctor Who* as a whole, is flawless, because to admit any of its flaws is to give up the realism those actors have given us. Lose that and we lose it all. Lose "Talons" and *Doctor Who* isn't a genre unto itself that rose out of pop-culture entertainment for children to defy gravity and last indefinitely, it's just a TV show. Intellectually, we know this, but we don't really believe it.

So if "Talons" has one flaw, it's that it's simply too good. It's the standard we think of when we imagine the '70s (and most of televised *Who*, including the New Series) and that's extremely dangerous, because the majority of the show can't compete in some ways and shouldn't be trying to in others. It forces us to ignore or apologize for the racism, when we should be discussing and acknowedging it. We've put "Talons" on a pedestal from which we dare not remove it. It's the culmination of the Hinchcliffe/Holmes era and thus the Classic Series itself. It's only the acting that really makes the difference.

But that's all the difference in the world.

Horror of Fang Rock (1977)

Written by Terrance Dicks **Directed by** Paddy Russell

Featuring Tom Baker (Doctor Who), Louise Jameson (Leela)

Supporting cast Colin Douglas (Reuben), John Abbott (Vince), Ralph Watson (Ben), Alan Rowe (Skinsale), Sean Caffrey (Lord Palmerdale), Annette Woollett (Adelaide), Rio Fanning (Harker)

Original airdates September 3, 10, 17, 24, 1977

The Big Idea The lighthouse of Fang Rock comes under siege from a Rutan scout.

Roots and References The Ray Bradbury 1951 short story "Fog Horn" (an aquatic creature attracted to a lighthouse); *Upstairs, Downstairs* (the Edwardian class politics between Palmerdale's people and the lighthouse crew). The Flannan Isle incident of 1900 where three lighthouse keepers disappeared in mysterious circumstances (the keepers' deaths); the Doctor quotes extensively from the Wilfrid Wilson Gibson poem "Flannan Isle" (about the missing lighthouse keepers) at the end of the story. Terrance Dicks drew heavily from the 1975 reference book *Lighthouses: Their Architecture, History and Archaeology* by Douglas J. Hague for his information about Victorian and Edwardian lighthouses.

Time And Relative Dimensions In Space Script editor Robert Holmes commissioned his predecessor, Terrance Dicks, to write a flashy vampire story to open the show's fifteenth season, called "The Witch Lords." (Holmes clearly felt classic monster film pastiches were in Dicks's wheelhouse, having had him riff on *King Kong* in 1974's "Robot" and on *Frankenstein* in 1975's "The Brain of Morbius.") Dicks was some way into writing the script when the higher-ups at the BBC informed incoming producer Graham Williams that "The Witch Lords" had to be cancelled; they were planning a high-profile production of *Dracula* and didn't want *Doctor Who* to produce something that could be considered a parody of that.

Holmes suggested a historical story set in a lighthouse, which Dicks thought was Holmes's revenge for Dicks having him write a historical set in the Middle Ages (1973's "The Time Warrior"). Dicks told Holmes he knew nothing about lighthouses, so Holmes told him to go buy "a boys' book of lighthouses." As none existed, Dicks relied upon a recently published reference book on the subject. Holmes also suggested the monster should be the Rutans. Dicks's vampire story eventually appeared in 1980 as "State of Decay."

The 1970s

169

Adventures in Time and Space This is the first time we see a Rutan, but they've been mentioned before in 1973's "The Time Warrior" as the enemy of the Sontarans. Surprisingly, this is their only onscreen appearance in all of *Doctor Who*. The Doctor reminds Leela that she saw ships on the Thames (in the previous story, "The Talons of Weng-Chiang"). Leela says she's not a "tesh-nician," referencing the Tesh from her home planet ("The Face of Evil"). The Doctor mentions that they have lighthouses on Gallifrey (the planet was seen most recently in "The Deadly Assassin").

Who is the Doctor? The Doctor becomes much more eccentric here. He announces the grim news of everyone's impending death with a huge smile on his face, is incredibly rude to Adelaide and hangs out a window to evade the Rutan. When asked if he's in charge, he says, "No, but I'm full of ideas," summing up the character very nicely. He appears to know H.G. Wells personally (calling him "Herbert"), although he later meets him (apparently for the first time) in 1985's "Timelash."

Companion Chronicles Leela's disregard for social niceties again manifests itself, in this case getting changed in front of Vince, threatening to kill Palmerdale and slapping Adelaide (whose helplessness increasingly exasperates Leela). She used to believe in magic but, thanks to the Doctor's influence, now believes in science. She goes outside to hunt for the creature and later gloats over its body as it dies. (The Doctor mentions his disapproval of this in passing.)

Monster of the Week The Rutan scout crash lands on Earth while evaluating it as a potential base, as part of their war with the Sontarans. The Rutans evolved in the sea and adapted to land; they have the ability to affect the local weather, summoning fog and causing a drop in temperature. They are high voltage, giving off electric shocks that kill humans on contact and even fish at a distance of several yards. The Rutan scout makes a detailed study of Ben's body so it can impersonate Reuben. It's specially trained in the latest metamorphosis techniques (implying that not all Rutans can change their form). The Rutan home planet is Ruta 3.

Stand Up and Cheer The Doctor has just told everyone to stay put in the crew room. Lord Palmerdale refuses and makes to go downstairs. Suddenly, Leela pulls out a knife and says, "You will do as the Doctor says or I will cut out your heart." The shock on the Edwardian man's face speaks volumes.

Roll Your Eyes The model of the ship is very poor indeed. What's even worse is when it crashes onto the rocks, tearing apart like cardboard.

You're Not Making Any Sense Episode three's cliffhanger has the Doctor realizing he's locked the Rutan in the lighthouse with them. Except that, as episode four proves, the "lock" is ridiculously easy to undo. (Indeed, when the mothership is approaching, the Doctor and Leela have 117 seconds to escape from the lamp room; when they reach the door, the Doctor opens it immediately.)

Interesting Trivia This story opened the fifteenth season of *Doctor Who* and saw a new producer, Graham Williams, assume the helm of the show. At the time, inflation was starting to spiral out of control. *Doctor Who*'s budget was kept constant, but the prices of everything sky-rocketed, meaning that in real terms the budget was shrinking. The show looks a lot cheaper from this point on (especially through the remainder of the '70s). Adding to this story's budget woes was the fact that the season's second story, "The Invisible Enemy," was shot first and cost more than expected. When the vampire story "The Witch Lords" was spiked (sorry, we couldn't resist . . .), it was decided to keep this story's cast small and limited to a single location.

Another issue that arose was that there was no space available to shoot in studio at the BBC Television Centre. Filming moved to Pebble Mill Studios in Birmingham, which had never handled as complex a production as *Doctor Who*. The cast and crew were unhappy about having to move out of London, but it turned out for the best: the technical staff in Birmingham were eager to prove themselves (hoping to attract further big productions to their studios) and went out of their way to be professional. Even so, this was the only British-made *Doctor Who* story to be made outside of London until the New Series began production in Cardiff, Wales.

The production was also beset with interpersonal problems. Tom Baker had been upset with the character of Leela since her introduction and took his frustrations out on Louise Jameson. She finally stood up to him during this story, forcing him to apologize; as a result, their working relationship improved. Baker was also unhappy with director Paddy Russell, finding her too uncompromising and constantly calling her "sir." They went head to head on several occasions. Although she won the major fights with him, she vowed never to work on *Doctor Who* again and left the BBC shortly afterwards.

Louise Jameson had initially been contracted for three stories. When she was asked to stay on, she agreed, under one condition: that her eyes change colour. Jameson had worn brown contact lenses for several stories, but found them very uncomfortable. As a result, the story ends with Leela's eyes changing to blue, due to her witnessing the explosion of the Rutan mothership.

The TARDIS Chronometer The lighthouse and its surroundings on Fang Rock, circa 1900 (it's been 80 years since the story of the beast of Fang Rock and that was said to be in the 1820s).

What? (RS?) If you've only been watching the stories we've been discussing, "Horror of Fang Rock" might seem like a little bit of a comedown. But only a little bit. This isn't one of the mega-classics of *Doctor Who* . . . but it's an extremely good second-tier story. This is the kind of thing most non-fans think of when they imagine Classic *Doctor Who* — and, in a way, there's no better compliment.

Faced with a reduced cast and a single location, the production team went overboard in making this atmospheric. The lighthouse setting helps enormously: the curved walls and doors give it a unique look, while the cramped sets help with the claustrophobic feeling. The conceit that the Rutan causes the lights to go out and fog to rush in is a brilliant one: with the lights low, the menace is heightened. The dead fish add to the creepiness. Clever directorial touches, like the foghorn drowning out Ben's screams, are perfect.

All this taps into what the BBC does best: making things look old. The lighthouse feels lived in, with all manner of little details, from the racy postcards in the crew room to the communications system, that evoke a sense of reality. The three settings — the boiler room, crew room and lamp room — add to that realism. There's no doubt whatsoever about the geographical arrangement of these rooms; you genuinely believe they are on top of each other, rather than side by side as the sets probably were.

The elegant dialogue conveys things like the time period not through exposition, but through humour (such as when Reuben tells Vince he's King Edward) or arguments over the benefits of electricity.

The characters work well too, partly by being such clearly defined tropes. In the lighthouse, you have the old superstitious mule, the young and inexperienced rookie, and the competent, modern-thinking leader, who's killed off early in the proceedings. From the ship, you have the rich aristocrat, his posh but weak secretary, the working-class sailor and the solid, upright military man. The characters should come off as clichés — and they do, in a way — but what saves them from staleness is all the details. The gentlemanly rivalry between Palmerdale and Skinsale not only fleshes out their characters, it contributes to the plot. Harker blames Palmerdale for the loss of the ship and then effortlessly takes over running the lighthouse. Palmerdale bribing Vince is a neat moment, made even stronger when Vince burns the money after Palmerdale's death. Everyone's motivation is crystal clear. Small touches like Adelaide's astrologer also make the characters seem richer.

Which only makes it all the more shocking when they're killed. The Rutan picks them off slowly, every one in a slightly different way (my favourite is Palmerdale's death, when the Rutan climbs up the outside of the lighthouse and electrocutes him from the balcony). And then, once the Rutan has enough strength, it mounts a frontal assault on the crew room. Cleverly, every death slightly alters the power dynamics among the characters, saving the story from becoming a gore-fest.

And then, at the end, everyone is dead. This is the only *Doctor Who* story where only the TARDIS crew survives. Even the fish are killed. This gives the story a resonance that punches above its weight: without a supporting character to have learned a lesson or remembered the Doctor, what we have is a bittersweet ending. The Doctor may have saved the planet from a Rutan invasion, but everyone who helped him along the way has perished.

"Horror of Fang Rock" is a small and claustrophobic story, but it's no poorer for that. It's the kind of *Doctor Who* story that never quite makes anyone's top-ten list, but is usually just outside it. With rich characters, a stupendous setting and buckets of fog-laden atmosphere, this is *Doctor Who*'s equivalent of business as usual. And if you're going to judge a series not on its absolute highlights, but on the kind of workmanlike story that shows you what sort of program it is, you could do a lot worse than this one.

Second Opinion (GB) "The Horror of Fang Rock" really pales in comparison to its immediate predecessor, "The Talons of Weng-Chiang": it looks cheaper and the horror itself is really toned down (odd to say of a story where everyone dies, but they all seem to die in such perfunctory ways). You can tell the production team is spooked by the tussle with Mary Whitehouse: there isn't a single cliffhanger that shows any character in actual jeopardy; it's just model ships crashing and dramatic pronouncements.

The story seems similarly tentative. There clearly aren't enough people in the lighthouse to sustain four episodes, so they have a shipwreck to bring in exemplars of the Edwardian class system in episode two as cannon fodder, complete with a pre-existing conflict between Palmerdale and Skinsale, which both pads out the story and helps engineer everyone's downfall. The plot is very predictable, with every character doing exactly what you expect they'll do: oh, look, Skinsale's sabotaged the telegraph. Adelaide's being useless. And Palmerdale isn't listening to the Doctor at all. Ho bloody hum.

And then there's the ending. Or rather the endings. The Doctor kills the Rutan, but Leela goes back to cheer its death. (It's a stirring, though very uncomfortable, character moment, showing Leela at her most alien; the Doctor's disapproval is a fascinating counterpoint.) Then there's the destruction of the mothership. And then Leela's temporary blindness. It feels like they ran out of story 15 minutes into episode four and they keep stalling . . . but every scene they add on is beautifully done. It's stalling, but it's stunning.

And yet, Terrance Dicks has, in many ways, written the textbook on how to make *Doctor Who* and you can see his influence even today in the New Series: this story is a collection of dramatic set pieces that range from the funny (Leela freaking out Vince) and the dramatic (Palmerdale's unravelling) to the terrifying (Reuben, revealed as the actual menace, standing and glowing with a malevolent yet mischievous expression), all building to a spectacular climax that works not only in terms of the plot but gives a great character moment with Leela.

On the whole, I don't think "Horror of Fang Rock" holds up as well as it could or should, but when it does it's stunning. It's part curate's egg and part Fabergé egg.

The Psychic Papers: The Novelizations

In 1964, somebody at Frederick Muller publishers had a bright idea: produce books based on the popular TV show *Doctor Who*. They hired script editor David Whitaker to write the first one and chose, as their starting point, the original Dalek story. Produced in hardcover, the book was called *Doctor*

Who in an Exciting Adventure With the Daleks (yes, really). Two more books followed: *Doctor Who and the Crusaders*, also by Whitaker (based on his 1965 script, "The Crusade"), and *Doctor Who and the Zarbi*, based on 1965's "The Web Planet" (and written by its scriptwriter Bill Strutton).

As well as changing the titles to varying degrees, the books were intended to be standalone adventures with no knowledge of the television series required by the reader. Thus the first book had its opening restructured to provide an introduction to *Doctor Who*, ignoring "An Unearthly Child" altogether. Whitaker wrote the book from Ian's perspective, but made him a research scientist studying rocketry; Barbara is Susan's tutor. They meet at an accident site on Barnes Common and stumble into the TARDIS as a result. The books were illustrated with artwork depicting images from the TV show throughout the pages. The books didn't sell all that well, though there were paperback reprints (even one in the U.S.).

However, in the early '70s, another publishing house, Universal Tandem, was starting a new imprint, called Target, and wanted something popular that would sell. They stumbled across the old novelizations and bought the rights to reprint them with new covers. They also decided to continue the novelizations with the then-current Doctor, Jon Pertwee.

Target approached the *Doctor Who* production team and was put in touch with script editor Terrance Dicks, who became the liaison. Script writers were asked if they might like to novelize some of their stories. Some, such as Robert Holmes, were uninterested, but others, including Dicks himself, Malcolm Hulke and producer Barry Letts, were on board.

Target's first two titles, published in January 1974, were *The Auton Invasion* and *The Cave Monsters*, retitled adaptations of the 1970 stories "Spearhead From Space" and "Doctor Who and the Silurians" by Dicks and Hulke, respectively. While close to the televised stories, a number of changes were made to flesh out character motivations, smooth out plot holes and the like. Dicks had never written a book before and worked so hard on it that he was a week late in delivering the manuscript. When he didn't hear back from the publishers, he assumed they must have cancelled it, so he called them, only to discover that it had already gone to the printers and they were eager for the next one!

Thus began the process of regularly turning *Doctor Who* stories into novelizations. The pay was apparently quite poor, which is why most of the early writers only contributed a few. However, Terrance Dicks saw a career opportunity. When he left the *Doctor Who* production team, he turned to freelance writing, penning both *Doctor Who* novelizations and also original novels. He became a children's author, with over 200 novels to his name, about a third of which are *Doctor Who* books.

During the 1970s, most of the novelizations were by Terrance Dicks, although Malcolm Hulke, Barry Letts, producer Philip Hinchcliffe and even Ian Marter (who played Harry Sullivan) were also commissioned to adapt scripts. As *Doctor Who* grew in popularity during the 1980s, more and more writers of the original television scripts adapted their own work instead of having others do it for them. (Even Robert Holmes finally adapted one of his own scripts, turning 1985's "The Two Doctors" into a novelization in 1986.)

The impact of the novelizations were enormous. In the days before video recording, people could only watch a *Doctor Who* story once (perhaps twice with the occasional repeat) and then that was it. Novelizations, however, were a permanent record. They were a connection to past adventures (and past Doctors) that fans might never see (particularly since so many stories were missing). They expanded upon stories that needed it and slashed others to fit into 144 pages (their standard book length).

The novelizations, particularly those written by Terrance Dicks, gave fans memes that they can still recite decades later: Jon Pertwee had "a shock of white hair" and "a young-old face." The TARDIS control room was always "impossibly big"; it reliably "sped through the vortex" at the beginning of each story and was off to the next adventure at the end. Pockets were "capacious," jackets "voluminous" and scarves "ridiculously long." Most memorably of all, the TARDIS always materialized with a "wheezing groaning sound."

The novelizations could take a complex plot, which had been spread over a number of weeks on TV, and condense it into a single, satisfying reading experience. (1984's "The Awakening," a two-part story, resulted in a longer novelization than 1969's "The War Games," which had ten parts!) The writers smoothed over the rough edges and sorted out minor flaws, while nevertheless introducing their own series of bizarre contradictions. Jo first meets the Doctor in *Doctor Who and the Doomsday Weapon* (1971's "Colony in Space") and then again for the first time in *Doctor Who and the Terror of the Autons*, published only a year later (this time adapting the TV story where they first meet). Meanwhile, in *Doctor Who — Black Orchid*, the Doctor fondly recalls the events of *Doctor Who — The King's Demons* (which occurred later in his life, but was published earlier and both novelized by the same writer who'd penned the TV episodes).

Later novelizations probed ever more deeply into their source material, so that those from the final season of the Classic Series were deeply literate and complex works in their own right. *Doctor Who — Remembrance of the Daleks* was such an important work that elements in it were referred to in the TV series (in "Ghost Light") and set the path for the original novels of the '90s.

Eventually, all but four stories were novelized (those were not because of complicated rights issues: two stories by Douglas Adams and two 1980s stories featuring the Daleks). They were a cash cow, selling millions and inspiring generations. Even today, long out-of-print Target novels are being released as audiobooks by the BBC AudioGo label.

When they finally ran out of stories to novelize, in 1991, Target's owners, Virgin Publishing, began producing original *Doctor Who* fiction, which sustained the series through the wilderness years when the show was off the air. For a long time, the last official *Doctor Who* novelization was BBC Books' adaptation of the 1996 TV Movie, written by Gary Russell. In 2012, Gareth Roberts wrote an adaptation of Douglas Adams's uncompleted 1980 story "Shada," providing a glimmer of hope that the remaining four Classic Series novelizations might one day be released.

The novelizations are deeply loved. Fans even went back and wrote the missing novelizations themselves, self-publishing them out of New Zealand (and later online) to round off the collection. Many people, especially those who lived outside of Britain, read the novels before seeing the episodes themselves, as mid-to-late 1980s novelizations often appeared in stores well before the stories were broadcast. What's more, for many fans, the pictures in their head were always superior, making the TV series seem even stronger than it was.

The New Series dispensed with the novelizations (although not *Doctor Who* novels: there are a range of original novels skewed to a younger demographic that have been running since 2005), but the concept hasn't disappeared entirely. When the kid-friendly *The Sarah Jane Adventures* spinoff went into production, a series of novelizations followed, many (although not all) written by the script writers.

And guess who wrote the first one, 33 years after the first Target novelization? Terrance Dicks.

The Stones of Blood (1978)

Written by David Fisher **Directed by** Darrol Blake

Featuring Tom Baker (Doctor Who), Mary Tamm (Romana), John Leeson (K9)

Supporting cast Beatrix Lehmann (Amelia Rumford); Susan Engel (Vivien Fay); Nicholas McArdle (de Vries); Elaine Ives-Cameron (Martha); David McAlister, Gerald Cross (Megara voices)

Original airdates October 28, November 4, 11, 18, 1978

The Big Idea In an English stone circle, some of the stones appear to be moving. And drinking blood.

Roots and References *The Devil Rides On* (an occult group comprised of seemingly ordinary people committing animal and human sacrifice); *Night of the Demon* (Stonehenge and magic); Druidic lore (de Vries and the stone circle); the legend of the Rollright stones (being unable to count them); Arthurian legend (Vivien's various identities include Lady Morgana Montcalm, which echoes Morgain le Fay, as does Vivien's current surname). The Doctor mentions Gog and Magog from Biblical legend and British iconography.

Time And Relative Dimensions In Space For *Doctor Who*'s sixteenth season, producer Graham Williams decided to have a series of linked stories around the quest for the Key to Time. New script editor Anthony Read approached his old friend David Fisher to join *Doctor Who* as a new writer. Fisher had first been asked to write for the show in 1963 by David Whitaker, the original script editor. Fisher was asked to pitch a supernatural story and instructed to include strong female roles. He had been fascinated by legends of the Rollright stones moving about the countryside. His work delighted the production team so much, he wrote the following story as well.

The Key to Time season consolidated Graham Williams's response to the BBC's edict that the violence and horror be toned down, which he did by replacing it with a stronger vein of humour and greater reliance on the comic potential of the series' star, Tom Baker.

Adventures in Time and Space "The Stones of Blood" is the third in a six-part story arc centred on finding the Key to Time. But don't worry if you haven't seen the previous episodes, as the general idea is explained in the opening scene: the Doctor and Romana must find all six segments of the Key, which are in disguise. Assembling them will enable the

White Guardian (a powerful entity above even that of the Time Lords) to restore balance to the universe. We briefly hear the voice of the White Guardian (previously seen in 1978's "The Ribos Operation") warning us to beware the Black Guardian. We haven't seen him yet, but he shows up at the end of the season, in 1979's "The Armageddon Factor."

A dead Wirrn appears in one of the cells ("The Ark in Space"). The android chained to the wall is from 1975's "The Android Invasion." Romana mentions the planet Calufrax, referring to the previous story, 1978's "The Pirate Planet." (A scene was recorded with a Sea Devil, from 1972's "The Sea Devils," but was cut in editing.)

Who is the Doctor? He denies being from outer space and instead says he's from inner time. He's become quite eccentric by this story: he brings a multi-coloured umbrella from the TARDIS, but throws it away as soon as he realizes it'll be a nice day after all.

Companion Chronicles Romanadvoratrelundar is a Time Lady from the Doctor's home planet, Gallifrey. Currently in her first incarnation, she was assigned to the Doctor by the White Guardian (although until now she believed it was the Time Lord president) to help him search for the Key to Time. She's good at puzzles, assembling the recovered pieces of the key when the Doctor can't. She can repair K9, based on a lecture she once heard, but believes hyperspace to be a theoretical absurdity.

Also travelling in the TARDIS is K9, a mobile computer in the form of a robot dog. The original K9 was a gift from his designer, Professor Marius, in 1977's "The Invisible Enemy." When Leela elected to stay on Gallifrey, in 1978's "The Invasion of Time," the original K9 stayed with her. However, the Doctor had already built a second version, seen here. K9 is pedantic and quite literal: he mentions that he is not programmed to bark and erases all memory of the game tennis when Romana tells him, casually, to forget about it.

Monster of the Week The Ogri, mobile stones who drink blood, are a silicon-based lifeform, with a globulin deficiency (hence the need for blood). Their home planet is Ogros, in Tau Ceti; it's covered in swamps of amino acids and is in the same star system as Diplos.

Stand Up and Cheer It's actually horrific, rather than cheerful, but the scene with the two campers is astonishing in its bravery. The Ogri leave the circle to "recharge," which involves finding blood to drink. We then see two people — who don't appear in any other scenes or interact with any other characters — camping in a tent. What's brilliant is that the Ogri don't crush them or their tent; they just stand there. Two immobile stones, just waiting menacingly for someone to touch them . . . as the campers do. Horrifically, Pat's hand turns into a skeleton, before the scene ends with a fade to blood red. This is about as adult as *Doctor Who* ever gets.

Roll Your Eyes Vivien's dress and makeup when on the spaceship have to be seen to be believed. Cessair of Diplos appears to be attending some sort of fancy-dress cocktail party, wearing an incredibly slinky, low-cut dress and with layers of silver face paint. Why exactly does she change into this outfit? Is the silver face paint supposed to indicate her true alien form? Why does it disappear entirely when the Megara transport her back to Earth in the final scene?

You're Not Making Any Sense Does Romana really believe the Doctor pushed her over the edge of the cliff? So much so that she refuses his help when clinging to the side? *Really?*

Interesting Trivia This was the series' hundredth story (and the fifteenth anniversary), so to mark the event a scene was scripted and rehearsed where Romana presents the Doctor with a cake to celebrate his 751st birthday. Producer Graham Williams felt this was too indulgent, so he cut the scene before it was recorded. However, the cake had already been ordered, so the cast was at least able to eat it.

If the first cliffhanger seems a bit odd, it's because it had to be constructed largely in editing. Tom Baker felt the idea of the Doctor as a doppelgänger was such a *Doctor Who* cliché that he refused to appear in the scene, only lending his voice. He also didn't feel it was suitable that children fear the Doctor. So the scene has to be sold through reaction shots and audio, giving it a disjointed feel.

Vivien mentions three stone circles in Britain: Stonehenge at Salisbury, one in Wales and the one we see here. Stonehenge is rightly famous for its history and druidic rituals, but there are a number of stone circles throughout the country. The stone circle seen here is the Rollright Stones. Its three separate monuments (the King's Men, the King Stone and the Whispering Knights) are thought to be about 5,000 years old. Interestingly, on the day of filming, a group of schoolchildren had come to count the stones and were most put out when there appeared to be too many, believing that the counting legend may have come true. They were even more puzzled when one of them fell over, but then Tom Baker appeared and everything made sense.

The Megara were written as flying orbs, but later changed to the more ethereal flickering lights, to avoid any similarity to the recently released *Star Wars*. This was the first instance of the show reacting to that movie (although the production team were proud that their robot predated R2D2 and was actually mechanical). For the next several years, unfairly or not, *Doctor Who* was often judged against that blockbuster and its sequels, despite having a tiny fraction of its budget.

The TARDIS Chronometer Boscombe Moor, England, and a spaceship in hyperspace (but in actuality occupying the same location), present day.

What? (RS?) Classic Series *Doctor Who* has always been a boys' club. Largely written, produced and directed by men, the Classic Series was not only centred on its dominant male character, it was mostly populated by supporting male characters. When female characters appeared, they did so as sidekicks and assistants, usually someone for the Doctor to explain the plot to. Attempts were made to alter this dynamic — Sarah Jane Smith is a feminist, while Liz Shaw is an intelligent scientist — but the show's female characters too often devolved to helpless, screaming and in need of rescue by the Doctor.

Given that he's a superintelligent Time Lord, you can understand why this happens: no human can come close to knowing as much as him and the show emphasizes his brilliance, forcing everyone else into subsidiary roles.

However, in 1977, incoming producer Graham Williams had an idea for a companion to replace Leela (who admittedly wore a hypersexualized outfit, but continued the trend of otherwise intelligent and empowered female leads). He decided to give the Doctor an equal. The result was Romana, a Time Lady whose introduction specified that she scored higher than he did at the Time Lord academy, who knows details of his life (such as his age) and the TARDIS better than he does, and who basically treats him as her assistant, not the other way round. In short, she's River Song, decades ahead of her time.

"The Stones of Blood" sees that conceit taken even further. There are only three male characters: the Doctor, de Vries (who's immediately identified as a servant to the true power, shown to be weak and quickly killed off) and the unnamed male camper. Everyone else is either female or a robot. And these women — with the exception of de Vries's partner, Martha, who doesn't last long — are no shrinking violets.

Take the idea of Amelia Ducat from "The Seeds of Doom" (an elderly eccentric who becomes gleefully embroiled in the action) and make her into a central figure. Hire an extremely experienced and capable actress (in what was to be one of her last roles, shortly before her death) and let her loose on the Doctor. Amelia Rumford should get some sort of award for the most eccentric supporting character imaginable. Beatrix Lehmann is a delight from start to finish, as adept at comedy as Tom Baker and playing the sort of character that we don't usually see in *Doctor Who*: a smart, capable woman with a massive ego and a willingness to throw her lot in with the madness around her. She even rescues the Doctor!

Then there's Vivien Fay, an equally strong character, who isn't diminished by being revealed as the villain (in a hilarious scene where Amelia is convinced she knows the figures in the paintings, only for it to be the woman she lives with). The lesbian subtext is so obvious it's almost text, especially for the '70s, but the cliché of the evil lesbian is avoided. Indeed, all the deduction that Romana and Amelia do involving citric acid turns out to have no relevance to the plot — by the time it's delivered to the ship, the Doctor's already convinced the Megara to scan Vivien — meaning it's actually about the close relationship between the two women after all.

The backstory is explicitly female: the circle has always been owned by women, while the Doctor is dismissed as a "typical male." Upon discovering that one of Vivien's former aliases was Señora Camara, the Doctor immediately wonders if there was ever a Señor Camara. And Amelia's notes, which must date back years, are all kept at Vivien's cottage. You do the math.

With the women driving the plot, the Doctor goes in a different direction: outright comedy. From covering K9's "eyes" when they stumble across the bodies and the bullfighting (where even the incidental music gets in on the act) to giving K9 mouth to mouth and saying, "Run as if something very nasty were after you, because something very nasty will be after you," the Doctor acts the fool, largely disengaging himself from the mechanics of the plot. This isn't a weakness, because it allows the women to step up (repairing the machine, for instance), while he appears to be at a 45-degree angle to the rest of reality.

What doesn't quite work are the Megara. The latter episode and a half of the story is caught up in a legal drama that's funny, but tonally too dissimilar to what came before. It does come together at the end — the reason the Megara are there in the first place is the same reason Vivien is, which is all related to the segment of the Key to Time — but too much time is spent on the Doctor being tried for an inconsequential crime.

Modern-day television is highly dependent on emphasizing relationships as a means of emotionally engaging the viewer. Modern Doctor Who has embraced this in its own way, by often emphasizing the Doctor/companion dynamic in a romantic way in the New Series (or mixing it up with variants like unrequited love or love triangles). There is a school of thought that argues such an approach appeals to female fans. But, when you think about it, that narrowcasts women as a demographic niche, who will be satisfied so long as there's a Harlequin romance somewhere. However, way back in 1978, Classic Series Doctor Who did something more revolutionary: it created female-centric Doctor Who not by throwing the Doctor and Romana into a romance but simply by populating the story with clever, competent women, who were good at what they did and who weren't diminished by being in a series that revolves around a dominant man.

Now that's feminist.

Second Opinion (GB) I'm not completely convinced Vivien and Amelia have some kind of a lesbian relationship. (And I'm not sure how it's supposed to be so especially obvious for the 1970s. Or how people of the same gender who are, seemingly, 40 years apart in age living together is rife with industrial-grade subtext.) If they do, then the drama onscreen completely betrays it: Amelia seems more nonplussed than anything that Vivien is actually an alien criminal with a line in killing people with vampiric rocks.

And while I agree it's an important change-up to what surrounds it, and points the way forward, I'm not sure if "The Stones of Blood" is the all-singing, all-dancing feminist celebration my co-author wants it to be. A female villain and a lack of male parts is one thing, but I do think it's largely window dressing, thanks to the switch to the Megara storyline that makes Vivien a passive observer (she spends most of episodes three and four lounging around in the ridiculous cocktail dress).

A story directly motivated and influenced by the female characters would be much more interesting, rather than them simply reacting to offscreen action. It doesn't help that Vivien being the Cailleach, who is in turn really Cessair of Diplos, is left as a surprise revelation, so we never see much of her as a villain. I'd have loved to have seen a female twist on, say, Harrison Chase or Magnus Greel. But she's pretty much sidelined.

The rest of the triumphs and problems of "The Stones of Blood" are very nicely summed up by my co-author. Well, except for how occasionally frustrating it can be watching Tom Baker — that incredibly intense, brilliant actor who made "The Talons of Weng-Chiang" and "Pyramids of Mars" reasons to live — become the chief operating ham. And how dreadful the direction has become: Darrol Blake is competent, but not particularly surprising or interesting. To say nothing of the ridiculous sight of Beatrix Lehmann pretending to ride a bicycle.

The Psychic Papers: The Guardians and the Key to Time

In 1977, incoming producer Graham Williams had a bold idea: a season-long story arc. This might not seem so bold today, but it was a big deal at the time. Television didn't do that kind of thing then, because it simply wasn't practical. Repeats often meant episodes were screened out of order or only part of a season aired. (Terry Nation, creator of the Daleks, once told Chris Boucher during the making of Blake's 7 that he always wrote the first and last episodes of a season, because those were more likely to be repeated.) Sometimes even the original broadcast of a season wouldn't have the story running order set until very late in the day. (As late as the final season of the Classic Series, all four stories were designed so they could be shown in almost any order and were broadcast in a different order than they were shot; overseas stations broadcast them in a different order again.) Trying to coordinate six stories in a season-long arc was no mean feat.

Williams was unable to make his idea work for his debut season, but he was successful in his sophomore season, which centred on the quest for the Key to Time. But what is the key, and who controls it?

Since their introduction, the Time Lords had grown steadily less impressive. The godlike beings of "The War Games" had devolved into the squabbling old men of "The Deadly Assassin." They were further diminished in 1978's "The Invasion of Time," which saw Gallifrey invaded by Sontarans and the Time Lords saved by their own outcasts.

Williams's big idea was to go above the Time Lords. He posited that there were two higher beings, the Black and White Guardians. One was the guardian of order, the other of chaos. One light, one dark, but neither dominant over the other.

The season arc was predicated around the fact that the universe was out of balance, and things would soon become dangerously unstable. And so, in the season opener, 1978's "The Ribos Operation," the White Guardian sends the Doctor on a mission: to locate the Key to Time.

The Key to Time was a device that could bring the universe to a halt, allowing the White Guardian to restore the balance. Being so powerful, the key was split into six segments, each disguised in some way. These segments were scattered throughout time and space. Those who managed to find them could use them as a source of power, for abilities like transforming into other beings or growing unnaturally large.

Every story during the season featured the Doctor and Romana seeking a segment of the Key to Time. Often it would tie in to plot (1978's "The Pirate Planet" or "The Stones of Blood"); other times it would be largely ignored: 1978's "The Androids of Tara" has Romana finding the fourth segment in the first ten minutes!

The quest came to an end in 1979's "The Armageddon Factor" with the Doctor and Romana finding and briefly assembling all six segments of the Key before scattering the segments again. (Curiously, though, no mention is made whether or not the balance of good and evil is restored while the Key to Time is assembled, so there's no indication whether the Doctor's quest had any positive result!)

Fearful of the Black Guardian's wrath, the Doctor fitted his TARDIS with a randomizer, so that even he wouldn't know where he was landing next. This set up a loose backstory for the next season and a bit, although the randomizer was also overridden on occasion. The Doctor abandoned using it in "The Leisure Hive."

The Black Guardian did eventually catch up with the Doctor, in his fifth persona. The Black Guardian recruited a new companion, Turlough, to be his agent aboard the TARDIS. However, after a number of attempts, Turlough found himself unable to kill the Doctor and ultimately rejected the Black Guardian.

This was the last we saw of the Guardians (especially as the actor playing the Black Guardian, Valentine Dyall, died not long afterwards). However, in theory they're still out there, with the Black Guardian presumably still plotting revenge on the Doctor.

Graham Williams had one final thought in his original pitch. Just as the Time Lords seemed godlike, but now had their own higher beings, he suggested it was possible that even higher beings than the Guardians existed — and, indeed, that this hierarchy had no ultimate being. Every level of Guardian had some higher Guardian.

Who knows, this could be a story arc for a season still to come . . .

• •

City of Death (1979)

Written by David Agnew (Douglas Adams, David Fisher and Graham Williams) **Directed by** Michael Hayes

Featuring Tom Baker (Doctor Who), Lalla Ward (Romana)

Supporting cast Julian Glover (Count); Catherine Schell (Countess); David Graham (Kerensky); Kevin Flood (Hermann); Tom Chadbon (Duggan); Peter Halliday (soldier); Eleanor Bron, John Cleese (art gallery visitors); Pamela Stirling (Louvre guide)

Original airdates September 29, October 6, 13, 20, 1979

The Big Idea The Doctor and Romana are on holiday in Paris, but dangerous experiments in time are being conducted by Count Scarlioni, and the *Mona Lisa* is involved — all seven of them.

Roots and References Herman Cyril McNeile's Bulldog Drummond novels (Duggan); the Raffles series of stories by E.W. Hornung, *The Pink Panther* and a host of "gentleman thief" stories and films (Scarlioni); the 1968 film *The Thomas Crown Affair* (the theft of the *Mona Lisa*); Salvador Dali's work (the drawing of Romana with a clock-face) and Douglas Adams's own *The Hitchhiker's Guide to the Galaxy* (the soldier's attitude towards his job). The story, of course, features the *Mona Lisa* prominently.

Time And Relative Dimensions In Space This is the story of "City of Death." More popular than "The Creature From the Pit," better selling than *The Dalek Survival Guide*, and more controversial than Russell T Davies's trilogy of blockbusters, "Where the Face of Boe Went Wrong," "Some

More of Boe's Greatest Mistakes" and "Who Is This Face of Boe Person Anyway?" To better understand "City of Death," it is best to tell the story of some of the minds behind it. A human from the planet Earth was one of them, a six-foot-tall ape descendant named Douglas Adams . . .

Adams had come to the attention of the *Doctor Who* office, where he submitted his still-in-development radio script for *The Hitchhiker's Guide to the Galaxy*. He was commissioned to write "The Pirate Planet" (1978), part of the Key to Time season. Adams's work was much loved by producer Graham Williams, who asked him to become script editor when Anthony Read left. At this point, Adams was still a jobbing writer (though he was becoming quite busy: the first season of *Hitchhiker's* aired on BBC Radio 4 in 1978 and Adams juggled script editing duties on *Doctor Who* with writing the first *Hitchhiker's* novel) and he was happy for the steady income. One of the first crises he presided over was that of a David Fisher script called "A Gamble With Time."

During the Key to Time season, Fisher had done a send-up of Anthony Hope Hawkins's novel *The Prisoner of Zenda* (and its various film adaptations) called "The Androids of Tara." It was very popular with the production team and Fisher was commissioned to write another literary parody for *Doctor Who*'s seventeenth season. This time, he took his inspiration from the Bulldog Drummond novels (a popular series about a private detective from the 1930s). "A Gamble With Time" had a Drummond stand-in facing trouble in a casino in Monte Carlo in 1928. The casino is being plundered by Count Scarlioni, a Sephiroth who has splintered himself across time. "A Gamble With Time" ran aground for two reasons: the first was Graham Williams's frustration that the parody of Bulldog Drummond was too prominent and the Doctor less so (he was also not enamoured with the casino setting). The second was a location opportunity: production unit manager John Nathan-Turner realized that the story could be shot in Paris, provided there was a limited cast and crew — but this would mean a rewrite to set the tale in contemporary France.

Fisher was embroiled in a divorce and couldn't do the extensive rewrites. With little time left, Williams effectively locked Adams and himself in his apartment for a weekend to write a new script in three days, subsisting mostly on coffee and Scotch. The completed serial was broadcast under a BBC in-house pseudonym "David Agnew," mostly to shield Adams and Williams from BBC management, who took a dim view of the producer and script editor writing scripts. (Williams and Anthony Read had used the same pseudonym for the same reason with their last-minute script for 1978's "The Invasion of Time.")

Adventures in Time and Space The randomizer, the device that the Doctor built into the TARDIS to elude the Black Guardian at the end of 1979's "The Armageddon Factor," is mentioned. The Doctor muses that the sonic screwdriver might have been broken on their last adventure on Skaro with the Daleks (1979's "Destiny of the Daleks"). When Duggan fixes the screwdriver by bashing it against the wall, the Doctor asks Duggan if he would like to stay on as his scientific adviser — a sly reference to the Doctor's exile with UNIT.

Who is the Doctor? We have the first tacit admission that the Doctor is somewhat unworldly when it comes to women when he tells the Countess, "You're a beautiful woman, probably." He's a good friend of Leonardo da Vinci and Shakespeare. When he tells the Count that he can't meddle with time, the Count speaks on behalf of millions of viewers when he says, "What else do you ever do?" To which the Doctor replies, "Well, I'm a professional, I know what I'm doing."

Companion Chronicles After their search for the Key to Time ended, Romana decided to regenerate (no reason or life-threatening need was indicated; it seemed to be purely for fashion) and chose the likeness of Princess Astra, whom the Doctor and Romana met in 1979's "The Armageddon Factor." (Lalla Ward played both characters.) In her second incarnation, Romana is less haughty than her predecessor, though still quite aristocratic (she comes by it naturally; Lalla Ward is more properly known as the Honourable Sarah Ward, the daughter of the seventh Viscount Bangor) and is more intellectual. Romana says she's 125. She and the Doctor seem to have a very happy relationship (not surprising, since she and Tom Baker started dating while making this story; more on that later!).

Monster of the Week Count Scarlioni is the human disguise for Scaroth, the last of the Jagaroth, a tentacle-headed cyclops who, because of his ship's accident that created all life on Earth, has splintered himself across human history. He can still contact his other aspects through time and has spent millennia aiding human development (and profiting from it) so he can get the technology necessary to send him back to stop the accident that splintered him.

Stand Up and Cheer The entirety of episode two, which is the funniest, wittiest, smartest 24 minutes and 33 seconds of *Doctor Who*, ever.

Roll Your Eyes The Paris sequences are so sublime that the studio sequences with wobblier-than-usual walls (even by the standards of *Doctor Who*; Duggan's crash into the walled-up room is embarrassingly bad) and British power outlets are a bit of a letdown.

You're Not Making Any Sense Paris seems to be a place where thugs in fedoras can stage armed robberies and abductions in broad daylight without any sign of the police, and an odd man with a scarf can chat with gendarmes and even traipse around a crime scene at the Louvre without any problem. Those wacky French.

Interesting Trivia The Doctor has gone back to stating that history cannot change, at least where Scaroth preventing his earlier self from pressing the button is concerned. It could be that it's (as we later discover in the New Series) a fixed point in time (well, it pretty much has to be!) and therefore cannot be changed. However, much of the dialogue is pointing towards another problem: if Scaroth prevents himself from pressing the button, then life on Earth won't have existed for him and he can't have influenced human history and travelled back in time in the first place. It's essentially the universe's biggest version of the grandfather paradox.

Da Vinci painted the *Mona Lisa* roughly around the time stated here, between 1503 and 1506. Whether or not Lisa del Giocondo had eyebrows is still subject of some debate: it has been said the fashion of the era was plucked eyebrows, though a recent art researcher has suggested that the eyebrows were on the original painting, though very thin, and have worn off the painting over time.

Scarlioni's plan to forge the *Mona Lisa* by having the original painter duplicate the works sixfold is clever — except that it's easily the most photographed painting in the world, so the level of duplication would have to be *really* exact. Plus, the painting warped when it was taken out of its frame, causing a crack in the top of it. This too would have to be duplicated.

How does Scarlioni's mask work? That's a pretty massive head he has under there, so presumably there's some kind of compression field involved, similar to that used by the Slitheen in 2005's "Aliens of London"/"World War Three." However, the mask doesn't seem to include any kind of a dental appliance to fake a mouth. Perhaps it's some kind of a holographic projection. The Countess seems to think he's gay, which presumably is why there hasn't been any . . . closer inspection of the Count.

One of the cleverest sight gags in the episode is watching Romana while she modifies the time machine. She's working on the plug! In the U.K. and Europe, which have higher voltages than North America, there are fuses in the electrical outlets. The implication is that she's changed the fuse, which is why it burns out after two minutes.

This story had the highest ratings of any *Doctor Who* story of all time, with 14 million viewers. While we would like to credit the brilliant scripts and performances, the reason is far more basic. ITV and its constituent networks were on strike, and broadcasting a test pattern; there was simply no competition.

If some of the plot seems vaguely familiar, it's probably because you read it in Adams's 1987 novel, *Dirk Gently's Holistic Detective Agency*. In it, a Salaxian ship blows up four billion years ago, creating life on Earth, and a ghost of a Salaxian influences human history (including adding an ending to Coleridge's poem "Kubla Khan") in order to prevent the ship from blowing up. Adams recycled that plot strand from "City of Death," while another plot strand — a time traveller living as a Cambridge don — was taken from "Shada," the six-part story written by Adams that was to be the finale to the seventeenth season, but was cancelled midway through filming due to a BBC strike.

Yes, that was John Cleese in a cameo as a pretentious art lover in episode four. Douglas Adams knew Cleese from the Cambridge Footlights, the university revue that generated several generations of British comedic talent, and Adams had contributed some sketches to *Monty Python*'s final season on TV (albeit after Cleese left). Learning that Cleese would be at BBC Television Centre around the same time the episode was filming, Adams arranged the cameo for Cleese and fellow Cambridge Footlights alum Eleanor Bron. Cleese suggested they perform the cameos under the pseudonyms "Helen Swanetsky" and "Kim Bread" (which Cleese later used on Adams's *Starship Titanic* videogame), but the BBC demurred.

The TARDIS Chronometer Paris, 1979 (what the Doctor describes as more of a "table wine" in terms of its vintage); Leonardo da Vinci's studio in Florence, 1505; and around 400 million BC, somewhere in the middle of the Atlantic Ocean ("He's out of his depth") at the start of life on Earth.

What? (GB) I tried — in vain it seems — to decline writing any review. Good work speaks for itself. Great works have fabulous lines like "Ah. Well, it's my job, you see. I'm a thief. This is Romana, she's my accomplice. And this is Duggan. He's the detective who has been kind enough to catch us. You see our two lines of work dovetail beautifully." Surely after that, a review is superfluous?

However, after consultation with my co-author, my editor, my lawyer and our publisher's lawyers, apparently I am still obliged to write a review. And one that's longer than "'City of Death' is one of the greatest *Doctor Who* stories ever written. Full stop. That is all."

Honestly, what do you want me to say? Tom Baker at the height of his already larger-than-life portrayal of the Doctor. Douglas Adams writing at the height of his power, fuelled by Scotch and a firm deadline (one he actually met!). Lalla Ward in a schoolgirl outfit (which she chose because she wanted young girls to see that school was okay) being clever, compellingly aloof and cute as a button. A plot that stretches like a slinky. (It's a caper to steal the *Mona Lisa*! Led by a disguised alien! Who is splintered throughout history! Who will stop all life on Earth if he succeeds in travelling back in time to stop the accident that splintered himself!) Dialogue that has to be the wittiest in *Doctor Who*, ever. ("You know what I don't understand?" "I expect so.") The all-time best villain in *Doctor Who*. ("You're going to help me ... And if you do not, it'll be so much the worse for you, this young lady and for thousands of other people I could mention if I happened to have the Paris telephone directory on my person.") The finest comedic scenes in *Doctor Who* (the Doctor and the Count's scene giving one-word answers to the other deserves to be cast in platinum and hailed through the ages). A glorious Paris setting. A cameo by John Bloody Cleese. Dudley Simpson rising above his usual fare and producing a gorgeous score. What more do you want?

It's a funny world. (And not necessarily ha-ha funny in this instance.) There are people who honestly, even after 50 years, have not received the memo that *Doctor Who* is, by and large, a comedy (or, at the very least, has a rich comedic sensibility). There are people who think that *Doctor Who* is a serious science-fiction series. But "City of Death" does the incredible: it's a serious science-fiction story that's also an incredible comedy. There are lots of jokes: the sort of great jokes you'll repeat at parties and embarrass your significant other with for the rest of your life. ("Where are we going?" "Are you talking philosophically or geographically?" "Philosophically." "Then we're going to lunch.") The jokes are like the astounding flourish at the end of a Mozart symphony. The premise is pure Adams-inspired lunacy (even if David Fisher came up with it), but the implications are gobsmackingly fascinating. (And here we have Adams to thank: the idea that Scaroth wanted to prevent the explosion that started human life and commit genocide by grandfather paradox was his.) Kerensky and Scarlioni's time machine, with its separate time continuum, is really, really brilliant. It's the sort of idea that could be the basis of a good SF novel or film and it's just thrown out off-handedly like a da Vinci sketch.

Even the comedic dialogue is a method of delivery for thoughtful ideas. The Doctor's conversation with Kerensky about temporal theory and the size of the universe is a really clever exchange. But then, all the jeopardy in this story happens through imaginative ideas. The actual onscreen action is limited to a few too many sequences where it's obvious that Tom Baker, Lalla Ward and Tom Chadbon are the only cast members they could afford to bring to Paris, a few captures and escapes, and an art theft of which we only see the dress rehearsal. But what drives the story along is pure intrigue: Why is the Count conducting time experiments? Why are there six *Mona Lisa*s in the Count's cellar? How can the Count be in 1505 Florence?

As we can see from a few too many Matt Smith stories and their over-reliance on cleverness (see my treatise on "A Christmas Carol" in *Who Is The Doctor*; hush, co-author), this should be the kiss of death for a *Doctor Who* story. But "City of Death" works staggeringly, incredibly well because all of those riddles lead to something bold, imaginative and just plain fun. Plus, it helps that the whole story is like a family science-fiction serial written by Oscar Wilde. ("The Terror of Being Earnest"?) It's so beautiful and funny that the story just breezes along effortlessly.

Or, to put it another way: since it has no call to be here, the art lies in the fact that it is here.

My work here is superfluous. "City of Death" is exquisite. Absolutely exquisite.

Second Opinion (RS?) *Who's 50* is a wholly remarkable book. In many of the more relaxed civilizations on the Outer Edges of Fandom, it has already supplanted the great 1983 work *Doctor Who: The Unfolding Text* as the standard repository of all knowledge and wisdom, for though it has many omissions and contains much that is apocryphal, or at least wildly inaccurate, it scores over the older, more pedestrian work in two important respects.

First, it is slightly larger. And second, it has the words THE 50 DOCTOR WHO STORIES TO WATCH BEFORE YOU DIE inscribed in large, friendly letters on its cover.

Here's what *The Unfolding Text* has to say about "City of Death": it says that "There was a certain appropriateness in the Parisian 'Art' context of 'The City of Death,' with its play on notions of artistic 'authenticity' and criticism, since Tom Baker's 'bohemian' look . . . had been based on a portrait by Toulouse Lautrec."

Who's 50 also mentions "City of Death." It says that the Doctor confronting Scarlioni in his drawing room is the best scene in existence. Not just of *Doctor Who*, but of everything. It states that the art theme is brilliantly constructed to be both central to the plot and transcending the usual concerns of *Doctor Who*. And that the appearance of John Cleese and Eleanor Bron is just about the most exquisite thing ever invented.

The companion guide also tells you that Lalla Ward is the daughter of the Viscount Bangor, the latest academic speculation about the eyebrows of the *Mona Lisa* and what Romana is really doing with that time machine.

"City of Death," it says, is about the most massively useful thing a Classic Series fan can have. Partly, it has great practical value. You can use it to amuse friends with the delights of the Tom Baker comedy half hour; you can use it as a companion to a fine wine you recently purchased at a new vintage outlet; you can use it to win online discussions with people who think late '70s *Doctor Who* is cheap and dull (a mind-bogglingly stupid group, they assume that if they can't see through you, then you can't see through them); and, of course, you can use it to relax with, enjoying its pleasant company like an old friend.

More importantly, "City of Death" has immense psychological value. For some reason, if a non-fan discovers "City of Death," he will automatically assume that the entirety of the rest of the series is just like this. Any fan who can face hiatus, cancellation, Big Finish audios and the New Series Adventures, and still know where his "City of Death" is, is clearly a fan to be reckoned with.

Who's 50 also says that the effect of watching "City of Death" is like having your brains smashed out by a Louis Quinze chair — wrapped around a large British detective.

Many people have speculated that if we knew exactly why a Louis Quinze chair was wrapped around a large British detective, we would know a lot more about the nature of the universe than we do now.

The 1980s

Starring
Tom Baker (1974–1981)
Peter Davison (1981–1984)
Colin Baker (1984–1986)
Sylvester McCoy (1987–1989)
as the Doctor

Tips for Newbies

- **Enjoy the special effects.** Okay, they're not perfect, but you can see that the production team keeps trying. And sometimes they're quite nifty.

- **Bear with the changes.** The 1980s were an experimental decade for *Doctor Who*: traitorous companions, an unlikeable Doctor, all manner of accents in the TARDIS. The theme music and the titles evolve as well. It settles down eventually, but the ride can be a bit wild.

- **Learn to love the music.** One of the most jarring things for people is the score, which solely uses synthesizers. This probably more than anything else dates the series. And yet, these scores are often among the most beautiful and evocative music written for the series. Give it a chance.

- **Remember that this is historical too.** Sometimes it's easier to watch older stuff, because it's safely in the past, whereas more recent fare can look embarassing. But it's been over 25 years since the '80s ended — about as long as the entire Classic Series run — so try to apply the same forgiveness to it you would to the earlier eras.

The Leisure Hive (1980)

Written by David Fisher **Directed by** Lovett Bickford

Featuring Tom Baker (Doctor Who), Lalla Ward (Romana), John Leeson (K9)

Supporting cast Laurence Payne (Morix), Adrienne Corri (Mena), David Haig (Pangol), Martin Fisk (Vargos), Nigel Lambert (Hardin), David Allister (Stimson), John Collin (Brock), Ian Talbot (Klout), Andrew Lane (Foamasi)

Original airdates August 30, September 6, 13, 20, 1980

The Big Idea The Doctor and Romana take a holiday on the Leisure Hive on Argolis, only to find its experimental work with tachyonics sabotaged.

Roots and References *The Godfather* trilogy of films (echoes of the original Mafia spoof storyline; "Foamasi" is also an anagram of "Mafiosa"); Yevgeny Zamyatin's *We* and Aldous Huxley's *Brave New World* (the walled-off society following an apocalypse; Pangol's eugenics).

Time And Relative Dimensions In Space In 1980, everything changed for *Doctor Who*. Graham Williams and Douglas Adams had departed as producer and script editor, so the search was on to find the person to bring *Doctor Who* into the '80s. The BBC brass's first choice was George Gallaccio, who had worked as a production unit manager (what would now be considered an associate producer) on the series back when Philip Hinchcliffe was producer (he had gone on to work as producer of the thriller *The Omega Factor*), but Gallaccio wasn't interested. The job was offered to the series' current production unit manager, John Nathan-Turner. Nathan-Turner's work on *Doctor Who* dated back to the Patrick Troughton era, when he worked as a floor manager on 1969's "The Space Pirates." Only 33, he was young by BBC standards and some feared he was perhaps not ready for the role. Barry Letts, who had produced *Doctor Who* in the early '70s, was brought back to act as executive producer and essentially supervise the new producer.

However, John Nathan-Turner was determined to put his stamp on the series as it entered its eighteenth season. There was a new version of the theme music and the title sequence. There was a new logo. There was a new costume for the Doctor. K9 would be on its way out shortly. Tom Baker, who had become more and more outlandish in his portrayal of his Doctor and had steadfastly refused to wear makeup on camera, was reined in. The score, primarily written by Dudley Simpson for over a decade, was given over to the BBC Radiophonic

Workshop to produce electronically. The high-camp jokiness that had punctuated the previous three years was replaced by a serious tone and a focus based on actual scientific concepts, thanks to Nathan-Turner and Letts's new hire for script editor, a science journalist and sometime scriptwriter named Christopher H. Bidmead.

Ground zero for all these changes was a story originally called "Avalon" by David Fisher that had begun under the previous regime: a Mafia parody in the mode of Fisher's recent work for the series. Barry Letts and Chris Bidmead immediately stripped the work of its humorous aspect; Fisher was happy to comply with the new edicts and even added tachyonics, which he had read about in *New Scientist* (though Bidmead insists this addition was his idea). K9 was written out of the story in its first scene.

John Nathan-Turner would be the producer of *Doctor Who* for the next ten years.

Adventures in Time and Space The Doctor mentions Gallifrey is in the constellation of Kasterboros, first established in "Pyramids of Mars." Numerous references are made to the randomizer, the device the Doctor added to the TARDIS to elude the Black Guardian starting in 1979's "The Armageddon Factor." The Doctor takes it out of the TARDIS (using the actual lighted panel from the TARDIS console prop) to use it in the recreation generator, saying he won't be bullied by a "galactic hobo" like the Black Guardian. This will have future ramifications . . .

Who is the Doctor? The Doctor seems more subdued, though just as quick-witted. (When told his scarf killed Stimson, he suggests, "Arrest the scarf, then.") Even when aged to a feeble 1250, the Doctor can still see the anomaly no one else can see: that Pangol is so young while every other Argolin is old.

Companion Chronicles Romana has started to think like the Doctor: she notices Hardin's experiments are a fraud by the necklace the subject wears (while the Doctor seems to have become more like her, noticing it through some technobabble explanation about the hologram). The Doctor got K9's seawater defences wrong, which takes the tin dog out of the rest of the adventure.

Monster of the Week The Foamasi are large reptilian creatures. Their homeworld has no private enterprise, but there is a thriving criminal gang called the West Lodge. The Foamasi can substantially compress their form to disguise themselves as humans, but — unusually in *Doctor Who* — their language is unintelligible without a translator.

Stand Up and Cheer The end of episode one is gorgeously directed and majestically cinematic: Romana goes back to the TARDIS thinking the Doctor is right behind her, only to discover he's in the generator. A Foamasi hand activates the generator and the Doctor pulls apart, his scream bleeding into the end credits. Ladies and gentlemen, *Doctor Who* has entered the 1980s.

Roll Your Eyes Pangol informs visitors at a futuristic resort that "Over the next hour and a half, we will study the wave equations that define tachyonics." No wonder bookings are bad at the Leisure Hive. There are two people in the whole universe who would consider this a holiday: one of them is this story's script editor, the other has a question mark at the end of his name.

You're Not Making Any Sense The Doctor's interference causes the generator to produce multiple beings that are outwardly Pangol, inwardly the Doctor. Um, how? Is there a setting that says "duplicate clothes from one, duplicate body from another"? While we're at it, did all the duplicates have the Doctor's scarf and coat tucked inside the helmet?

Interesting Trivia Tachyons are theoretical particles that can move faster than light. If you squint really hard, they could be responsible for ageing (or de-ageing) people, or for creating a "temporally coincident" duplicate (thanks to the Doppler shift, we would see two images of a tachyon particle as it passes by). However, when it comes to recreating something that can be manipulated or indeed creating full-scale copies of people, the relationship to actual science is nil.

Even though director Lovett Bickford made this story in the studio with the usual access to multiple video cameras, he elected to shoot the story with a single camera, like a feature film. This resulted in the kind of beautifully composed shots that are hardly ever seen in studio-based stories, with closeups, rack focus (where the focus shifts from foreground to background subjects), shots from low angles (many of the sets had actual ceilings!), lengthy static shots and more. It was incredibly labour-intensive to shoot this way, compared to a three-camera shoot from different angles with a vision mixer flipping between shots. The story not only went over budget, but each episode underran by three or four minutes (even with extra-long cliffhanger reprises).

Standard practice on the series was to never ask back any director who went over budget, so this was Bickford's only *Doctor Who* story.

Prior to this story, while the Doctors had a "costume," it was more a mode of dress that could be varied. For example, while the basic silhouette stayed the same, the Doctor might wear a different coloured coat or a scarf, or have a waistcoat on or not. One of John Nathan-Turner's decisions was to have the characters wear the same costumes week after week. It was a significant cost savings and also an attempt at branding, in a way: if the characters each had a regular costume, they would be more recognizable and help in marketing the series to merchandisers. (Even though the BBC was a public broadcaster, such commercial concerns could and did cross the *Doctor Who* producer's desk.) Thus Nathan-Turner had costume designer June Hudson create a new burgundy costume for the Doctor and, after later ditching the interior coat and replacing the brogues with buccaneer boots, this is what the Doctor wore in every episode. After Lalla Ward left, the companions also wore the same costume for extended periods.

Another of John Nathan-Turner's costume innovations was the addition of question marks to the Doctor's shirt. No one — not Tom Baker, not June Hudson, not Barry Letts, not Christopher Bidmead — particularly liked them, but Nathan-Turner was insistent. It would remain a part of the Doctor's costume design until the Classic Series ended in 1989.

The TARDIS Chronometer Brighton, England, sometime in the twentieth century, and the planet Argolis, in the year 2290.

What? (GB) The first episode of "The Leisure Hive" is one of the most stunning changes to the series since it switched to colour. The agenda is set from the start. A new version of the theme music. Completely new title graphics. A new logo. Fade into a slow, artful, silent pan along Brighton Beach, lasting precisely one minute and 38 seconds, to the strains of music that sound a bit like Philip Glass or Vangelis. Then there's a new TARDIS prop. The Doctor now wears a new burgundy costume. And K9 blows up!

John Nathan-Turner's predecessor, Graham Williams, was fond of talking about the "15% solution," which meant that viewers were prepared to accommodate changes of up to 15% every season compared to what was done before. With "The Leisure Hive," John Nathan-Turner worked out an 80% solution. It was all change. Gone is *The Tom Baker*

Comedy Half-Hour. In its place is something glossy, even stylish. There are sets with ceilings and cunning use of effects (thanks to a computer-controlled process called Quantel, the TARDIS now materializes on Argolis while the camera tracks out!). Did I mention the ceilings?! Tom Baker and Lalla Ward are still bantering, only this time it's about plot and technobabble.

It's the shock of the new that affects me every time I watch "The Leisure Hive." It's full of optimism and verve. The opening tracking shot is something that many ridicule — it wastes time doing nothing but establishing a scene — and yet after three years of indifferent and often incompetent directors, this little flourish signals the show's interest in arty little touches has returned.

It's the direction that really makes "The Leisure Hive" work. Lovett Bickford's decision to go single camera resulted in seriously under-length episodes but, damn, it's still gorgeous. Every shot is beautifully composed and the set feels like it's more than part of a TV studio for the first time in a very long while. There are all these lovely touches: the Argolin head pods dropping, signifying their rapid aging; Hardin discovering Klout is not what he seems; and the stunning cliffhanger to episode one, an ending that seems cinematic. Even stuck with a clunky monster design like the Foamasi, Lovett works around it, making the sequence where the Foamasi cut their way in from a cocoon attached to the Hive moody and atmospheric. Peter Howell's stirring synthesizer score (which only misfires on a couple of comedy cues) adds to the richness of the experience.

It's just as well that we have such a rich visual feast as it distracts from a somewhat anemic script that's really a runaround like in past seasons, only with the jokes stripped out to make room for a huge dollop of serious-minded technobabble. And yet, oddly, it works because Tom Baker and Lalla Ward treat such deadly dull, hard-science-fiction nonsense with an aloof detachment that makes you care even if you don't necessarily understand. (Oh, by the way: Lalla Ward in an Edwardian bathing outfit, complete with sailor top and straw hat? Best. Costume. *Ever.*)

The problem with the story is that technobabble does not equal science. Where something like "City of Death" (and even "The Stones of Blood") tingled the imagination with ideas of time travel and hyperspace, here we have leaden conversations about random field frames and FIFO stacks — replacing drama or even bold ideas with jargon. Tachyonics in this story are scientific MacGuffins (tachyons don't actually do any of the things suggested in this story; it's a massive extrapolation of a theoretical science at best) and the recreation generator is just a magic cabinet, no matter how often the new regime at *Doctor Who* said otherwise.

There are *some* lovely subtle touches to David Fisher's script. The relationship between Hardin and Mena gives the story a lot of heart precisely when it needs it (plus, Adrienne Corri and Nigel Lambert are really sweet). The Doctor as an old man gives Tom Baker something to do that involves acting and not chewing the scenery, which is delightful. And the underlying theme of eugenics is thoughtful, as Pangol, conceived through technology, becomes obsessed with preserving the purity of his dying species. David Haig threatens to go over the top, but he keeps it in check, mostly with a delicious sneer or a wry smile.

Technically and visually, "The Leisure Hive" is right at the cutting edge of television then. The frustrating thing is it never quite gives us a story with the same degree of deftness. It's arguably the slickest-looking story in the Classic Series, and it promises so many things the series never delivered during the 1980s — and could never hope to deliver. But it's still breathtaking to watch.

Second Opinion (RS?) *Doctor Who* has two ways of regenerating itself. The first is in front of the camera, whenever its leading man decides to move on. The second is behind. By throwing out what went before — no matter how successful — the show allows fresh blood to take over and create a new interpretation of the series. If we only saw the first kind of regeneration, the show would be very samey (and wouldn't have lasted anywhere near the length of time it has). It's the second that's the real secret to longevity.

"The Leisure Hive" is one of the few places where the behind-the-scenes regeneration doesn't coincide with the one on camera. And yet, everything else is new. From the title sequence and the (fabulous) music to the costumes and the science focus, this is a show almost entirely unlike its previous year.

The newness isn't just restricted to the production: the entire storyline revolves around the duality between the old and the new. Or, rather, between the old and that which is renewed.

There are the obvious markers: Pangol himself is a renewed Argolin, the Doctor is aged 500 years, the Argolins have a rapid rate of ageing (as shown by the beads falling from their head). But this duality is there in the backstory too: it's been 40 years since the war and the Leisure Hive, once a great tourist attraction, is now washed up. The Helmet of Theron is kept on display as a reminder of the past and the war leaves such a bitter memory that the Argolins won't sell the planet to the Foamasi.

The Argolins are sterile, so they have no future — and yet, rather than fade away, they're pushing the boundaries of both science and peace, trying to come to new understandings with other races. The crash into the '80s helps enormously here: the sets, lighting, music and direction simply don't look like those of the previous couple of years.

There's new science in tachyonics, Hardin's experiments apparently rejuvenate the elderly and the pun involving the recreation/re-creation chamber is worthy of Steven Moffat. Newness pervades everything. And then, at the end, the solution isn't to recreate the past (as Pangol wants to do with his army of clones), but a rejuvenation, which allows Mena to raise him better this time around.

"The Leisure Hive" stands as a testament to renewal. Taking something with great history and a rich past, it reinterprets it, puts it in a new light and brings the focus onto the present. And the result isn't something that dwells on the greatest hits of yesterday, but moves forward, rejuvenated.

That's the magic of *Doctor Who*.

Warriors' Gate (1981)

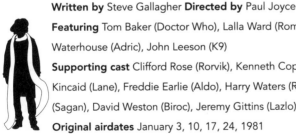

Written by Steve Gallagher **Directed by** Paul Joyce

Featuring Tom Baker (Doctor Who), Lalla Ward (Romana), Matthew Waterhouse (Adric), John Leeson (K9)

Supporting cast Clifford Rose (Rorvik), Kenneth Cope (Packard), David Kincaid (Lane), Freddie Earlie (Aldo), Harry Waters (Royce), Vincent Pickering (Sagan), David Weston (Biroc), Jeremy Gittins (Lazlo), Robert Vowles (Gundan)

Original airdates January 3, 10, 17, 24, 1981

The Big Idea Trying to escape E-Space, the TARDIS crew find themselves at a place of zero coordinates: the gateway between universes. But they aren't the only ones trapped in E-Space . . .

Roots and References *Alien* (making space travel ordinary); *Alice's Adventures in Wonderland* (the Doctor mentions the Cheshire Cat); *Star Trek's* "City on the Edge of Forever" (the Gateway); surrealist cinema of Jean Cocteau such as his 1946 film *Beauty and the Beast* (the Tharils) and his 1950 film *Orpheus* (the surreal environment, the mirror); Tom Stoppard's play *Rosencrantz and Guildenstern Are Dead* (the coin tossing and the jobsworth crew). The *I Ching* is quoted throughout (and its philosophy echoed throughout the story).

Time And Relative Dimensions In Space Award-winning science-fiction novelist Christopher Priest was originally commissioned to write Romana's final story, called "Sealed Orders." It concluded the E-Space trilogy of the eighteenth season and involved Gallifrey, but was eventually abandoned, as Priest was new to television drama and couldn't make his script fit the intricacies of *Doctor Who's* demands. (The production team hoped that the story could be resurrected later, but this was not to be.)

When problems with "Sealed Orders" were becoming apparent, script editor Christopher Bidmead contacted Steve Gallagher (who would go on to become about as famous as Priest as a horror novelist) to write "Dream Time." Had Priest's story worked out, "Dream Time" would have featured in the following season. Gallagher penned his script much like a novel, with extremely detailed descriptions and specifications (such as stipulating that the theme of one scene should be "rust"). It was deemed too complex to be filmed as written, so Bidmead and director Paul Joyce reworked the script.

Joyce wanted to push the boundaries of what could be accomplished on a *Doctor Who* production and tried to direct the story as though it were a film. Visual effects designer Mat Irvine even reported that, unique among any director he'd worked with, Joyce collaborated closely with the special effects crew, even commissioning an artistic rendition of the gateway, in order to more accurately capture its aged feel.

However, all this took time and frazzled the cast and crew. (Joyce fought with the lighting director, who objected to him using the lighting rig as part of the privateer set.) The experience took its toll on Joyce and memos flew among the BBC upper management. Joyce was, in fact, fired for half an hour but was reinstated as it was decided only he knew how to complete the story. When producer John Nathan-Turner finally saw the edited episodes, he praised Joyce for making four excellent episodes, but confessed that he had no idea what they were about.

Adventures in Time and Space This is the third and final story in the E-Space trilogy, which saw the TARDIS trapped in a pocket universe after passing through a Charged Vacuum Emboitment in 1980's "Full Circle." The Doctor mentions going back to Gallifrey, which was their intention at the start of this trilogy. The Doctor's old costume, including the multicoloured scarf, hangs on the hatstand in the TARDIS. It's not past continuity, but Packard expresses a fear of falling into a time rift, something seen in 2005's "Boom Town" and in the spinoff series *Torchwood*.

Companion Chronicles Romana has clearly matured during her time with the Doctor, as she doesn't want to return home to Gallifrey and, indeed, had been pondering leaving him for some time. Ultimately, she chooses to follow her own ideals, deciding to help Biroc free Tharil slaves throughout many planets. K9 is injured by the time winds and can only be restored by passing through the mirror — a one-way journey. Romana takes him with her when she passes through the mirror.

Adric, a boy genius in mathematics who stowed away in the TARDIS at the end of 1980's "Full Circle," was originally conceived as a mischievous "Artful Dodger" character; we see some of that original conception here as he saves the Doctor after cheekily pointing out that, while he doesn't know what he's doing, he's managed to turn the MZ machine against Rovrik and his men.

Monster of the Week The Tharils — tall, leonine bipeds with heavy beards and fur on their hands — are time sensitive, so they're used by the crew of the privateer to navigate the time winds. They're worth a fortune to others in this capacity. They're born with the ability to cross universes via the mirror in the gateway, whereas others have to be touched by the time winds in order to do so. They were once kings who ruled a thousand planets, keeping humans as slaves, but the humans revolted and developed Gundan robots to overthrow them. Now they're enslaved themselves, with the extremely heavy dwarf star alloy the only material able to bind them.

Stand Up and Cheer The lead up to the cliffhanger to episode three is stunning. The Doctor is attending a feast in the past, while Biroc recounts the history of the Tharils. In quick succession, the Gundans crash into the room, Romana in the present senses the Doctor's in danger, an axe crashes into the table and time jumps so that the Doctor's now sitting at the cobweb-covered table. This is artistic and clever, unlike any cliffhanger the show has ever produced.

Roll Your Eyes After being threatened with beheading by a Gundan robot, the Doctor survives when the two robots strike each other. However, one of them drops its axe onto the Doctor's back . . . only for it to bounce off harmlessly.

You're Not Making Any Sense The ship is so heavy because it's made of dwarf star alloy, on the grounds that that's the only substance that can bind the Tharils. So why not just make the manacles out of the stuff and use something lighter for the hull of the ship?

Interesting Trivia Steve Gallagher wrote the novelization of this story under his pseudonym John Lydecker. The story had been changed quite dramatically after his initial script, so he took the opportunity to resurrect his original vision. Target Books was happy with the manuscript and even made allowances to print a longer-than-usual novel. However, the *Doctor Who* production team was uncomfortable with such a deviation from the broadcast story and refused to approve it. Gallagher had four days to revise the novel and, in the days before word processing, had to do so by physically rearranging the text with scissors and glue! A few additional scenes survived this shredding, but it otherwise largely resembled the TV version. Gallagher claims to have retained the "off-cuts," so perhaps the full novel might be released one day.

Tom Baker was unhappy about Lalla Ward leaving the show, as the two were quite serious by now, although their relationship was tempestuous. (They were fighting during the filming of this story; notice how Tom almost never looks at Lalla.) They married shortly before this story aired, and the event was covered quite heavily by the press.

This story also saw the departure of K9, to much outcry. The *Sun* newspaper even ran a "Save Our K9" campaign, declaring victory when it was announced he'd appear in 20 of the 28 episodes this season (even though that had been the plan all along). The prop had caused problems right from the start, when the radio frequencies that controlled it interfered with those used by the cameras. The actors didn't like it, because it meant they had to crouch down whenever they needed to be in a tight two-shot. It couldn't traverse difficult terrains, but children absolutely adored K9. Producer John Nathan-Turner saw an opportunity to combine two repeated requests: more K9 and more Sarah Jane Smith. He'd approached Elisabeth Sladen about returning to the show as a companion, but she wasn't interested. However, he had a second idea: a spinoff series featuring the two, entitled *K9 and Company* (with the premise that the Doctor drops off K9 Mark III for Sarah, as the original had stayed on Gallifrey with Leela and the second version was in E-Space with Romana). Sladen was happy to be the star of her own show, so a 50-minute pilot was made, called "A Girl's Best Friend" and broadcast shortly after Christmas. It wasn't a huge success, and the series wasn't picked up. However, Nathan-Turner's idea wasn't without merit: 26 years later, something very similar was made, again starring Elisabeth Sladen and John Leeson as the voice of K9. It was called *The Sarah Jane Adventures* and ran from 2007 until Sladen's death in 2011.

The TARDIS Chronometer In the void separating E-Space from N-Space. It's likely the future, as the crew of the privateer navigate by limited time travel.

What? (RS?) In 1981, people watching this story either hated it or were downright bemused by it (not least of whom was the show's producer). But, like a fine wine, this tale has aged gracefully and now stands as an example of just how powerful *Doctor Who* can be when it puts its mind to it.

This isn't a simplistic adventure for children but is instead far more literate (using the *I Ching* as its starting point is mind-boggling) and interested in themes of enslavement, randomness, time and inaction. Those aren't things that necessarily go well together, but the story had a massive advantage on its side: an auteur director.

Paul Joyce, in his one and only *Doctor Who* outing, is as much an author as the script writer or editor (and, tellingly, all three contributed to the script). The camera is constantly moving. The sets are multi-level. Using the studio lighting gantry as the privateer ceiling is a breathtaking move. The artistic touches are incredible: the white void is an exceedingly strong background, the tossed coin freezing is great, the effect of vanishing into the mirror is amazingly strong and Biroc's phasing works very well to convey his disconnect in time.

These are astonishingly effective ways to convey what's happening; true, they're somewhat constrained by the limits of the technology, but that's actually something to be proud of. The production was pushing against the edges of what could be achieved on series television, so of course the white void looks a bit dirty in model shots and the coin doesn't mesh well against its background. If ever there was a *Doctor Who* story that isn't about its effects, it's this one.

That said, the black and white gardens of the gateway (with the actors filmed in colour) is a real highlight. It's sumptuous and artistic, especially because it has no cause to be there. Any other solution (a greenscreen garden in colour, location shooting) would have been ordinary. "Warriors' Gate" fights against ordinary with every fibre of its being.

This is a story that's extremely interested in time. (Check out the flash of the Gundan axe cutting into the table, which happens some time before the scene plays out and before the time shenanigans occur; even the storytelling itself is messing around with time.) Not in the usual science-fiction way of exploring nonlinearity (although the Doctor righting a cobweb-covered goblet that he'll later knock over many years earlier is divine), but in a way that's challenging for the viewer — and extremely rewarding if you look deeply enough. The Tharils' history moves from slavery to enslavement to redemption, like the rise and fall and rise again of a civilization bound to the wheel of history.

The Tharils believe that the weak enslave themselves; Biroc has a chilling line when one of their servants is mistreated ("They're only people") and yet he's never explicitly challenged on that, even when in the future. Instead, we're invited to think about it, because — as unpleasant as it might seem — there's nevertheless a grain of truth there. Do the weak enslave themselves? In a way, yes . . . but that doesn't mean it's right either.

Pervading the story is the idea of nothing being something. The Doctor wonders if the way out of E-Space is to just drift, the TARDIS coordinates are locked off at zero and even Romana's signal to Adric (where she raises both arms, one by one, very slowly, and . . . I'm sorry, where was I?) is designed to tell him to simply stay where he is. Rorvik fights against the inaction, finally "getting something done," but it isn't necessarily the right course of action (and, indeed, he pays for his action with his life moments later). Instead, we're told that the answer is to "Do nothing — if it's the right sort of nothing." What's the right sort of nothing? Very likely, it's letting history unfold as it should. The Tharils are at the point of freedom anyway and Rorvik's wrong actions are far more dangerous than inaction.

Yet the answer isn't to be idle either. Aldo and Royce are the kind of double act that Robert Holmes used to write, with comedic dialogue and the like, but they're also amoral. Not cruel like Sagan, but that doesn't excuse them. The rest of the crew is insubordinate, more interested in their bonuses and their lunches than following orders or examining the morality of their situation. This highlights the banality of evil, because some of them, like Packard and Lane, are even quite likeable. Nevertheless, like office workers in an evil corporation, they're still accountable for their actions.

Finally, there's Romana's departure. In a story that's all about inaction, this is one action that must be taken. Her fury at the idea of dematerializing while there are slaves on board shows that she's come an incredibly long way from the naïve theoretician we first met. That her departure happens so quickly and without too much emotion is somewhat surprising, but it fits within the story's mould: inaction is sometimes useful, but there are also moments when a choice must be made. And so she heads out to become the E-Space version of the Doctor, on a quest to free the Tharils from enslavement. It's a magnificent end for a companion who was crafted as a sort of apprentice to the Doctor.

"Warriors' Gate" is a complex meld of literary science fiction, the demands of series television and an artistic director, wrapped around a triumph of design. Its themes and storytelling style crash over one another like waves, each informing and reinforcing the other — and yet, it also makes perfect sense too. Television has come a long way since 1981, so this story, so ahead of its time, has finally come into its own. Like *Seinfeld*, it's a show about nothing. But, happily, it's the right sort of nothing.

Second Opinion (GB) "Warriors' Gate" is about the power of moments. It's like a beautiful series of haikus. Or a gorgeous Impressionist painting.

It's the unbelievably sexy way Lalla Ward raises her arms.

It's the stark image or Rovrik strangling the Doctor with his own scarf, the glamour of *Doctor Who* cast away from us.

It's the way the Doctor holds out a chair to keep the Gundan robot from killing him and a scene later winds up with an armful of sticks.

It's K9 repeating that mass is contracting such that ordinary viewers like me could say, "Oh my God! I actually understand the science-y bit!"

It's the Doctor talking through the mirror to Biroc.

It's the ludicrousness of phrases like "The backblast backlash'll bounce back and destroy everything." Or "Astral Jung." I don't even know what Romana is talking about in either instance.

It's sublime dialogue like, "One good solid hope's worth a cart-load of certainties."

It's the shot of the Doctor following Biroc along the path through the black and white painting. Beyond all the artsy things my co-author says, that's a bloody hard shot to achieve using video cameras and circa-1980 greenscreen technology — almost impossible, actually.

It's the whole third episode that takes the Doctor out of the story to show us how the world of the Tharils was made and unmade. It's lyrical and poetic and absolutely breathtaking in its scope, taking it from a runaround to the rise and fall of a civilization.

It's the less-than-half-hearted cheers that go up from Aldo and Royce in most circumstances.

It's the ending of episode three. It's always the ending of episode three, when it comes down to it.

That's "Warriors' Gate." A gorgeous swirl of images and ideas. *Doctor Who*'s first art-house film. It's got something to do with slavery and time winds and bored spaceship crewmembers and . . . I dunno. But it's gorgeous to look at. And it has Lalla Ward doing that put-her-hands-in-the-air thingie. And the ending of episode three.

It just . . . *is*.

Logopolis (1981)

Written by Christopher H. Bidmead **Directed by** Peter Grimwade

Featuring Tom Baker (Doctor Who), Matthew Waterhouse (Adric), Sarah Sutton (Nyssa), Janet Fielding (Tegan Jovanka)

Introducing Peter Davison (Doctor Who)

Supporting cast Anthony Ainley (the Master), John Fraser (the Monitor), Dolore Whiteman (Aunt Vanessa), Adrian Gibbs (the Watcher)

Original airdates February 28, March 7, 14, 21, 1981

The Big Idea Wanting to repair the TARDIS's chameleon circuit, the Doctor accidentally unleashes the Master on the planet Logopolis. The universe, and the Doctor, may never be the same again . . .

Roots and References Isaac Asimov's novel *The Gods Themselves* (shunting entropy into another universe); many of the terms are based on computers (e.g., block transfer, the central register). The Doctor misquotes Thomas Huxley's "The chessboard is the world; the pieces are the phenomena of the universe" as "the universe is a cheeseboard . . ."

Time And Relative Dimensions In Space Three things came together to create this story. The first was that John Nathan-Turner, anxious to have the Master come back as a regular villain, had cast Anthony Ainley to play the new version of the long-running villain.

The second thing was the idea of a TARDIS within a TARDIS. Bidmead claimed he was inspired by a moment in the season's penultimate story, 1981's "The Keeper of Traken," where the Master escapes destruction through a TARDIS parked inside his TARDIS. However, the concept was something explored in Christopher Priest's rejected script "Sealed Orders," indicating it may have been too good an idea for Bidmead to pass up.

Oh, and leading man Tom Baker had decided to depart the role after seven years. Each year, Baker threatened to leave, largely so the relevant producer would say, "Oh no, Tom, we love you, please stay," and he would. However, when Baker made his annual pronouncement to Bidmead and John Nathan-Turner, they immediately agreed. Nathan-Turner wanted to make his mark, and working with a new Doctor — and companion — would allow him to do so. For his part, Baker may have been more serious than usual. He was dismayed by Lalla Ward's departure and had realized it was time to go. "Logopolis" was thus constructed around the departure of the show's biggest-ever star.

Adventures in Time and Space Much of this story is a direct follow-up to the previous one, 1981's "The Keeper of Traken," which ends with the Master stealing the body of Trakenite Consul Tremas. Most of the plot for episode one revolves around the chameleon circuit being stuck, which echoes "An Unearthly Child." We're also told that the TARDIS was in repairs when the Doctor originally borrowed it. (We never saw this happen, but first heard that the Doctor stole the TARDIS in "The War Games.") There's also a reference to Totter's Yard ("An Unearthly Child"). With Romana and K9 in E-Space ("Warriors' Gate"), the Doctor decides not to return to Gallifrey after all (as he'd been instructed to do in 1980's "Meglos"). We see Romana's room (1980's "Full Circle"), although it's jettisoned to provide extra thrust. The Master is back to shrinking bodies, his modus operandi since 1971's "Terror of the Autons." The idea of pre-regenerative projection like the Watcher was seen in 1974's "Planet of the Spiders."

The Doctor's pre-regeneration flashbacks include the Master ("The

Deadly Assassin"), a Dalek (1979's "Destiny of the Daleks"), the Pirate Captain (1978's "The Pirate Planet"), Cybermen (1975's "Revenge of the Cybermen"), Sontarans (1978's "The Invasion of Time"), Zygons (1975's "Terror of the Zygons"), the Black Guardian (1979's "The Armageddon Factor"), and companions Sarah Jane Smith, Harry Sullivan, the Brigadier, Leela, K9 and both Romanas.

Who is the Doctor? The Doctor says that he and the Master have the same mind, in many ways. It's unclear precisely what this means, or whether this comment only applies to the Master or to Time Lords in general. The Doctor tries to console Tegan over the death of her aunt, but is woefully ineffective at doing so. He also notes that Time Lords have special responsibilities.

Companion Chronicles Nyssa was the daughter of Tremas on Traken and assisted the Doctor and Adric in their previous adventure. She didn't join the TARDIS at the end of that adventure but is instead brought to Logopolis by the Watcher. The destruction of Traken means she's the last survivor of her race.

Tegan Jovanka grew up on a farm in or near Brisbane, Australia. She's always loved planes and is on her way to becoming an air stewardess. She has a colourful vocabulary, with expressions such as "Rabbits!" and "Hell's teeth!" Her Aunt Vanessa is killed by the Master.

Adric demonstrates his expertise in mathematics by keeping up with the Logopolitans after being taught the humans' completely different numerical system.

Monster of the Week There are no monsters, only the Logopolitans, a bunch of old men whose brains stick out the back of their heads. They mutter in the language of numbers, using mathematics to create structure. Their city is laid out like a circuit board, and they've been responsible for holding back the entropic death of the universe for quite some time.

Stand Up and Cheer After seven long years, the fourth Doctor finally meets his destiny. Hanging by a cable from a radio telescope, he experiences *Doctor Who*'s first-ever flashback sequence and then falls to the ground, every bone in his body shattered. Surrounded by his companions, he looks up, smiles that famous smile one last time and goes out on a killer line: "It's the end, but the moment has been prepared for." And we all weep buckets of tears.

Roll Your Eyes The Master's message to the universe beggars belief. He holds the entire universe to ransom via . . . a portable tape recorder.

And, if they don't comply with his demands, he'll destroy the universe and everything in it, himself included. Um. No wonder he gives up and simply departs shortly afterwards.

You're Not Making Any Sense The Doctor's plan to flush out the Master just doesn't hold water. Thank you, we'll be here all week.

Interesting Trivia The police box on Barnet Bypass seen in the opening episodes was meant to be one of the last ones that remained in use, but it was removed due to vandalism shortly before the episode filmed. The production filmed on a different stretch of highway, using an older version of the TARDIS prop. By this time, police boxes had long been retired from use and the concept became inextricably linked with *Doctor Who*. In the 1990s, the BBC applied for a trademark on the image; the Metropolitan Police objected, on the grounds that they owned the rights. However, it was ruled that by letting police boxes lapse they had rescinded their hold on the concept, and the trademark belongs to the BBC.

Producer John Nathan-Turner devised the concept of an Australian companion with an eye to attract financing from the Australian national broadcaster, ABC. (It eventually worked too: see "The Five Doctors.") He was playing with potential first names and wrote "Tegan" (after a friend's niece) and "Jovanka" (the latter was the first name of the wife of the Yugoslavian president) on a piece of paper. Script editor Christopher Bidmead saw the paper and assumed "Jovanka" was her surname. At five-foot-two, actress Janet Fielding was too short for airline regulations to be a stewardess, but she argued that this regulation didn't apply in the southern hemisphere, where people from countries such as Indonesia were shorter, and thus got the role as Tegan. When Nathan-Turner later found out she was lying, he was amused at her brashness. To reflect her Australian character, family-friendly swearwords were invented for the program, including "Hell's teeth!"

Bidmead's idea was that events in this story were so dramatic that the universe sent a "fetch" version of the Doctor — the Watcher — back in time. Bidmead carefully specified that the character was not to be dwelt upon and given no dialogue. During editing, it was felt that the concept was unclear, so Sarah Sutton was asked to overdub the line "He was the Doctor all the time" to help explain the character.

This is the story with the largest death toll in all of *Doctor Who*. Whole planets are destroyed by entropy (including the entire Traken

Union, which must comprise billions of people). Most of them aren't onscreen, but it's hard to imagine any future story doing as much damage as this one.

The second law of thermodynamics does indeed state that, in a closed system, entropy increases. This is because closed systems tend to approach thermal equilibrium; it's a bit like putting a cup of coffee or an ice cube in a temperate room: both will eventually cool down or warm up to room temperature. That is, disorder tends to occur more than order. (The Earth isn't a closed system, as plenty of energy is provided from outside, thanks to the sun.) The universe is the ultimate closed system, so things will eventually fall apart.

Like tachyonics in "The Leisure Hive," block transfer computation was intended as an extrapolation of real science. Christopher Bidmead was an early adopter of technology and wrote his scripts using a word processor on his Vector Graphic MZ computer. Bidmead was fascinated by the fact that the inside of a central processor was effectively a sort of "logical space" inside which you could create other logical entitites, and copy them and move them around to other locations within that logical space. (Basically the ability to save, copy and paste we take for granted more than three decades later.) Bidmead extended that idea to its conclusion via a race of people who could create logical copies of whole space/time events.

The TARDIS Chronometer Earth, in the present (1982's "Four to Doomsday" would state the date was February 28, 1981) and Logopolis, also in the same timezone. The TARDIS is briefly taken out of time and space altogether.

What? (RS?) Some *Doctor Who* stories you can enjoy again and again. Others are throwaway fun. And then there are those that get you where it's personal. "Logopolis" is that story for me. And I'm not talking about Tom Baker's departure, as emotionally difficult as that was for me at nine years old. No, I'm talking about the mathematics.

"Structure is the essence of matter," says Monitor, "and the essence of matter is mathematics." Truer words have never been spoken. As a fairly gifted child, I could have gone in any number of directions. But it was *Doctor Who* — and "Logopolis" in particular — that set me on the path I'm on today. With its emphasis on recursion, hexadecimal code and numbers maintaining the universe, "Logopolis" fascinated me and drove me to study mathematics. That led to a Ph.D. in applied mathematics. Now I'm a professor of biomathematics. I use mathematical models to study the spread of infectious diseases — something incredibly useful, which has already had a meaningful impact on people's lives.

In short, "Logopolis" made me a mathematician.

You can whittle anything down to mathematics. Earthquakes, tsunamis, disease, marriage, a conversation . . . they can all be expressed by mathematics and the logic of analysis used to understand and predict the future. A great many of us are alive today as a direct consequence of mathematical modelling largely eliminating malaria from most of the world. Mathematics is probably the most powerful thing human beings have ever invented.

"Logopolis" gets this and makes it meaningful. Block transfer computation — creating solid objects via the power of muttering numbers — may not seem that scientifically likely, but it's a useful metaphor for just how powerful mathematics can be. Because mathematics takes chaos and turns it into order.

And this is what "Logopolis" is fundamentally about. Things are falling apart, from the TARDIS to Auntie Vanessa's car to the universe itself. Only by providing order, as the Logopolitans do with their mathematics, can the chaos of entropy be held back. This also explains the alliance between the Doctor and the Master, in the (shocking) cliffhanger to episode three. Their cooperation creates order, which is used to stabilize the chaos. Only when this alliance fails does chaos again threaten to take over.

However, the message isn't simply that order beats chaos. The police officers on Earth represent order, with the Doctor a chaotic element in their midst, but it's clear that their thinking is too limited to cope with the truth of the situation. Instead, their order is interrupted by the chaos of Adric's feigned bike accident. Another chaotic element is Tegan. Her presence interrupts the Doctor's plan to leave Adric on Logopolis and also demonstrates the role that human emotions play in disorder. Monitor makes it clear that something as ordered as a computer is no match for the chaos of the living mind, which is inherently superior.

This is true of mathematics as well: computers can solve some problems, but they cannot make the intuitive leaps that a human mind can. Computers also have no ability to link the real world to a mathematical representation of a disease or make the kinds of decisions about what factors are important and what can be safely ignored that allow mathematical models to be relevant and useful.

Then there's the recursion. Recursion is a mathematical tool that's used to solve equations by way of self-similarity. If the next thing looks like the previous thing, except for a small change, then that similarity can be extrapolated to provide a general understanding of the system as a whole . . . thus creating order out of chaos, yet again.

We see recursion take many forms here. There's the brilliant idea of a TARDIS within a TARDIS, which takes one of the central concepts at the core of *Doctor Who* (bigger on the inside) and asks fascinating questions. The story begins with a policeman (just as the very first *Doctor Who* story did, back in 1963) and the Barnet Bypass segment concludes with the police entering a police box. This is recursion at work in the storyline: similar, but different. Even the dialogue is recursive. In episode three, Adric says, "You said to be prepared for the worst." To which the Doctor replies, recursively, "Indeed I did. And I am prepared for the worst."

The Cloister Bell at the beginning portends doom. But this doom only happens because the Doctor takes the TARDIS to Logopolis, something he's dead set against until the Watcher tells him to. And the Watcher only exists because the fourth Doctor is heading to his death. So the Doctor's fate is recursive too: it creates itself.

"Logopolis" has often been described as having a funereal atmosphere. And yet, the funeral only happens at the very end. With the universe descending into chaos, the entire balance comes down to a simple cable, something very ordered. The Doctor breaks the cable, simultaneously acting as chaotic figure and also bringer of order to a universe threatened by the Master (whose subsequent dematerialization neutralizes the threat). The universe itself is destabilized by having a hole punched in it, but this in turn dissipates the chaos created by entropy.

And then the Doctor dies. The longest-serving Doctor, beloved of children, fans and the general public. In his place sits a new man, ready to start again. Similar, but different. Recursion has triumphed, because recursion is at the centre of everything. History repeats itself, only not exactly.

The message of "Logopolis" is clear: mathematics is all. From the sweep of history to the prediction of the future, mathematics is the essence of everything around us. Understand mathematics well enough and you can pretty much do anything. But as a mathematician, I have to ask myself a question: would I do it? To know that life and death on such a scale was my choice?

Yes, I would do it. That power would set me up among the gods. And through mathematics I shall HAVE THAT POW-ER!

Wait, was that out loud?

Second Opinion (GB) While I appreciate that this story made my co-author who he is today, could he have picked a story slightly less tedious or at least better written?

"Logopolis" could have its first episode taken away and nothing substantial would be missing. In any other era, the first 20 minutes is key to setting up the story and the characters. Here, as in so many stories during this era, the Doctor and companions spend the first episode wandering around the TARDIS, padding it out with cool but inconsequential set pieces. "Logopolis" ups the ante with its downright arrogant conceit that if two characters earnestly discuss a scientific concept the audience will somehow give a damn.

As arrogant conceits go, it's a doozy: there are high-minded conversations about entropy that go on forever without adequate illustration until the final episode, by which point the story is beyond the budgetary constraints of a program made in 1981 in the BBC Television Centre. It's much better to talk about closing CVEs and bubble memory and light-speed overdrives without showing what the hell these things are supposed to be. The Watcher keeps us hopeful that something good will happen, and the idea behind it is great, but it's so unclear we only end up finding out what he is through an overdubbed line.

Worse, there's no actual jeopardy; in fact, we get the opposite, with two characters pulled out of time so they can see what it does to other people. While I give credit to Christopher Bidmead for having it affect Nyssa — the shock value of destroying the planet the Doctor saved only a story ago is immense — the problem is it is only shock value.

But then the whole thing is just shock value for math and science geeks. What grates most is that none — and I mean *none* — of these leaden, high-minded "hard" science-fiction ideas actually make any sense in terms of the plot or story. The TARDIS-within-a-TARDIS scenario is a brilliant set piece in and of itself, but why does landing around the Master's TARDIS cause it to happen? (And what purpose does it serve other than to get episode one to 24 minutes, 30 seconds?) There is not a lick of sense in landing the TARDIS underwater to flush out the Master. Only the Doctor being shrunk in the TARDIS has any real impact on the story, but even then it's just to get him out of the way. The story only starts to get going in episode three: that's half the story lost to padding and inconsequential set pieces. But then we're in episode four, which mostly involves everyone running around the Pharos project.

For me, the true genius behind "Logopolis" is Peter Grimwade, who undermines the script's sober rationality and makes things seem odd and mystical, and creates a tone of inevitable doom and end-of-era gloominess (the "funereal atmosphere" mentioned by my co-author). But what Dr. Smith? doesn't get is that we sit through the tediousness and the plodding because we know right from the first shot of the Doctor brooding in the Cloister Room that something bad is going to happen. (Paddy Kingsland's score — full of brooding melodies and jarring, clanging bells — helps enormously.) It's totally counterintuitive to the padded math-geekery onscreen, but it works.

And everything inevitably leads to that final scene. I find myself agreeing with John Nathan-Turner: it was time for Tom Baker to leave. "Logopolis" underscores how uninterested Tom Baker was in playing the Doctor by his final season; everything about his performance is reduced to an aloof shorthand of avoiding eye contact with other actors and delivering lines in stentorian tones. If anything, it's a bittersweet ending to his time in the part.

> **DVD Note** We highly recommend selecting the CGI effects option on your DVD for the following story. This only matters for the last episode, but it really matters . . .

Kinda (1982)

Written by Christopher Bailey **Directed by** Peter Grimwade

Featuring Peter Davison (The Doctor), Janet Fielding (Tegan), Matthew Waterhouse (Adric), Sarah Sutton (Nyssa)

Supporting cast Richard Todd (Sanders), Nerys Hughes (Todd), Simon Rouse (Hindle), Mary Morris (Panna), Sarah Prince (Karuna), Adrian Mills (Aris), Lee Cornes (Trickster), Jeff Stewart (Dukkha), Anna Wing (Anatta), Roger Milner (Annica)

Original airdates February 1, 2, 8, 9, 1982

The Big Idea An expedition of the planet Deva Loka has been losing members. The native Kinda appear passive, but something evil haunts their dreams.

Roots and References Ursula Le Guin's 1976 novel *The Word for World Is Forest* (a forest planet with natives who have unexpected powers); Joseph Conrad's *Heart of Darkness* (finding truth among apparent savagery); James Herbert's *Dune* (the matriarchal order); the 1935 film *Sanders of the River* (Sanders); Buddhism (character names come from Buddist terms — Mara/temptation, Dukkha/pain, Panna/wisdom, Karuna/compassion — while many of the themes, such as meditation and the wheel of life, are drawn from Buddhist ideas); the Bible (the serpent in paradise, apples as temptation).

Time And Relative Dimensions In Space "Kinda" was originally commissioned by script editor Christopher H. Bidmead for Tom Baker's Doctor, who would have played the role of a "wise sage" in the story. When Baker departed, the story was rethought with a younger Doctor and two companions (as the plan had been at the time). Christopher Bailey wrote the scripts accordingly. The production team added Nyssa as a companion fairly late in the day and Bailey was reluctant to restructure the story again, so it was agreed that Nyssa would be written out of the main action of the story.

As the scripts came closer to realization, there was conflict among the creative personnel about the overall vision of the story. Christopher Bailey was more interested in the ideas and in leaving as much of the story as possible a mystery, feeling that the audience did not need to be spoonfed. Incoming script editor Eric Saward felt that this would leave the audience detached and the overall story was being lost in the general ambience (to the point where he added scenes when the story underran, filmed during the making of "Earthshock," that explained the nature of the Box of Jhana, something that was anathema to Bailey). Director Peter Grimwade, meanwhile, was concerned that the story lacked dramatic pacing. Consequently, "Kinda" was the result of a dialectic process, where the writer, the script editor, the director and, eventually, the actors all had very different agendas and different ideas about what should be done. What we see unfold onscreen is a turmoil where any one of those parties is winning or losing at different moments.

Adventures in Time and Space The Doctor briefly mentions K9, whom he last saw in "Warriors' Gate" (although the dog was seen by the general public the previous Christmas in the spinoff *K9 and Company*).

Who is the Doctor? Despite having the youngest body yet, this new Doctor tends to act like an old man, wearing half-moon reading glasses and getting tetchy with his companions. He has a (platonic) pseudo-romance with Todd, the closest he's been with a supporting character since 1964's "The Aztecs."

Companion Chronicles Adric has a habit of appearing to change sides in order to help out, but it rarely seems to work. (The Doctor even rolls his eyes at Adric's apparent defection.) He likes to eat.

When Tegan dreams in the forest, she confronts her inner fears. She's terrified of being alone and seems to dislike her own company.

Monster of the Week The Mara inhabits the dark places of the inside, appearing in the dreams of an unshared mind, but with the ability to become corporeal, so long as it's granted permission. Those possessed by it carry the mark of a snake on their arm. It appears to be a manifestation of pure evil and thus cannot face itself. Its true form is a giant snake.

Stand Up and Cheer The Box of Jhana cliffhanger is the sucker punch to end all sucker punches. The box has already altered Sanders, so we know it has some sort of power. Trapped in a cage by a madman threatening to have him shot, the Doctor is forced to open the box. Todd's anxiety sells the fear factor and the cliffhanger actually ends on her scream of pure terror. Viewers at the time had to wait almost a week to discover that what was in the box was . . . a jumping jack. This is an incredible punchline. Except that the sucker punch comes afterwards, as the box does indeed have a power (disrupting the electricity, opening the cage door) — and, indeed, proves key to the entire resolution.

Roll Your Eyes When Todd fears that Panna may be dead, the Doctor doesn't believe her, so he checks her over. Part of which involves waving a hand in front of her eyes and, when she doesn't react, he concludes that she must indeed be dead. As opposed to, say, blind, as she was before.

You're Not Making Any Sense When the Mara possesses Tegan, the snake on her arm is facing her elbow. When she wakes up, the snake tattoo has reversed direction. Did it do an awkward little crawl while we weren't looking?

Interesting Trivia A number of Classic Series stories have had CGI effects added to their DVD releases. Purists may enjoy watching the stories with the original effects, such as the liquid detergent bottles creating *Nerva* station in "The Ark in Space." However, we suspect that the vast majority of viewers are quite happy to enjoy the tastefully updated special effects that don't take them out of the story. For "Kinda," this is especially noteworthy, because of the giant snake. (If you're new to the story, hopefully you watched it with the CGI effects and thus don't know what we're talking about. If so, enjoy your ignorant bliss!) Trying to create a spaceship is one thing; you kind of expect the effort to be middling at best. However, attempting to create a giant snake that has to interact with characters was a whole other level of ambition. And it failed miserably; the snake looked plastic and fake. Worse, it undercut the dramatic finale to a rich and layered story. (Although New Series writer Paul Cornell did once suggest that, just as bringing evil into the light robs it of its power, the very fakeness of the snake may be a way of diffusing the Mara as a force to be reckoned with.) The original snake almost has to be seen to be believed, except that we'd prefer if the new CGI version Stalinized the original from history altogether . . .

With the advent of Peter Davison's Doctor, the show underwent something of a sea change in its timeslot. Until now, *Doctor Who* had been a fixture of Saturday nights. In 1980, ITV started to win against the BBC's previously unassailable Saturday evening programming by having all its regional networks screen the same shows at the same time; *Doctor Who* consequently found itself losing to ITV's new American import, *Buck Rogers in the 25th Century.* The impact was brutal: after a decade with solid — often spectacular — ratings, *Doctor Who* was now in trouble. Tom Baker's final season had seen disastrous ratings, and there was a sense among the BBC management that the Saturday timeslot wasn't working. Starting with Season 19, the show was screened twice weekly, on Mondays and Tuesdays. The BBC were keen to see if the twice-weekly format worked, as they were then thinking of adding a twice-weekly soap to compete with *Coronation Street* (*EastEnders* wouldn't come into being for another three years). Ratings went back up, so the experiment was judged successful. However, the practical upshot was that the length of a season was effectively halved: whereas Tom Baker's final season ran for a little more than 28 weeks, Peter Davison's first lasted just 13 (it was two episodes shorter as well, to accommodate *K9 and Company*).

One of Bailey's original ideas was that the Mara would bring out

Tegan's sexuality when possessed. Janet Fielding was excited by this opportunity to stretch her acting muscles and delivered a sexualized, Bette Davis–like performance. However, producer John Nathan-Turner had a strict "no hanky-panky in the TARDIS" policy, and the sexual aspect was almost entirely removed. It survives in the finished program only when Tegan stretches languorously after awakening as the Mara and through the predatory sashay she does as she approaches Aris.

Shortly after "Kinda" was completed, Bailey was invited to pen a sequel, which became 1983's "Snakedance." That story picked up on the idea that the Mara remains in Tegan's mind following this story. It was set on the Mara's home planet and further explored the nature of the creature, with similar Buddhist-related themes.

The TARDIS Chronometer The planet Deva Loka, sometime in the future.

Brave Heart? (RS?) This being a review of "Kinda," you're probably waiting for me to tell you what the story is about.

Well.

"Kinda" is about colonialism, who's in charge, questions about missing people that are never answered, the entirely alien culture of a native species, dreams, an obsession with acronyms, chess, parallels between dream characters and the TARDIS crew, telepathy, apples, the imagined superiority of conquest, mental breakdown, Buddhist names, voice as a mark of wisdom, rejecting the science-fiction idea of hostile trees, duality, choice, possession, boxes, instruction manuals, the academic role of a jester figure, evil, clocks, reincarnation, the cycle of history, restoration, reflection and paradise.

It's not possible to nail down what "Kinda" is about. And I'd argue that this is part of the point. "Kinda" is an incredibly rich text, one you can go back to again and again. Symbolism mixes with metaphor, which is overlaid with allegory. Almost any one of the elements I note above could have sustained an entire story — and yet, "Kinda" doesn't feel overburdened either.

Doctor Who of this era was starting to flag, ever so slightly. Scripts were approved on the basis that they were good enough, rather than because they were great. (See the previous story, "Four to Doomsday," for an example of this. Or rather, don't.) But then, smack-bang in the middle of Davison's workmanlike first season comes this lyrical and thoughtful story that forces you to think, instead of giving you all the answers.

It's also a story that feels custom-made for its actors: Peter Davison's Doctor is very far from Tom Baker's overbearing performance, while Janet Fielding is clearly relishing the greater acting range she's able to explore. Even Matthew Waterhouse's Adric has a lot to do, trapped in the dome with a madman. Simon Rouse is incredible here, portraying madness in a way that feels real, rather than as an excuse for megalomania.

The direction is also inspired. The imagery is great and the fakeness of it doesn't hurt it at all. Small touches like the whispering of the trees that only Hindle can hear are excellent. And the scenes set inside Tegan's mind are genuinely unsettling; this was the only *Doctor Who* story to actually terrify me as a child.

However, what makes "Kinda" really sing is its story. Whether it's a blind woman calling the Doctor an idiot or a madman claiming that you can't mend people, this is a story with a huge amount to offer, both as entertainment and also as something more. It's television pushing itself right out of its comfort zone because it genuinely wants you to engage with it.

At the end of the day, "Kinda" is an academic text. It's dense and layered, but it's also something you could use to instruct people in the subject of *Doctor Who*. It defies analysis, but also welcomes it. It's the ultimate primary source. And, like all good academic studies, it was created out of a fight between the author and the people who funded him.

Entire textbooks have been written on the subject of "Kinda." But don't take their word for it. Or mine. Go watch it. If you just saw it, watch it again. And decide for yourself what "Kinda" is really about.

Second Opinion (GB) There are some stories that, when experienced multiple times, you react to differently depending on your age at the time. No *Doctor Who* story better illustrates this for me than "Kinda." When I watched "Kinda" for the first time as a 14-year-old, I was bored by it completely and utterly. When I watched "Kinda" in my midtwenties while in university, I was mesmerized.

Now, in my early forties, I'm somewhere between those two experiences.

What amazed me in my twenties was precisely the thing that bored me as a teenager: "Kinda" is a highly cerebral story full of symbol and mystery. It's a drama of ideas. In my teens, I hated this. I had little clue what was going on and little desire to understand it. I wanted *Doctor*

Who to consist of pacey science-fiction adventures. In my twenties, though, this was cutting-edge stuff. I was in university and studying the works of Beckett, Camus and T.S. Eliot, learning about Buddhism and reading graphic novels like *The Sandman*, and I had found a *Doctor Who* story that had layers of meaning and ambiguity . . . and wasn't just a pacey science-fiction adventure.

Coming back to "Kinda" as I enter (I can't believe I'm saying this) middle age, I find myself still drawn to the depth of it and the mystery of it. But I also understand again what bothered me so much as a teenager. It's full of layers of meaning, but it also has dialogue that lectures the audience like "the clown/jester figure" where the actor actually has to say "clown-stroke-jester." It is a story that requires a certain frame of mind while watching and demands careful attention. While that should be applauded on television, it can also be an excuse to not be accessible.

Don't get me wrong. I love it, and middle-aged me still mostly goes with twentysomething me. It's a story that revels in mystery. As my co-author says, counterintuitively for *Doctor Who*, it's not about solving those mysteries. What is the Mara? What is the box of Jhana? What happened to the missing dome members? In any other story, those would be the mysteries that are explored and solved over four episodes. Here, nothing is really solved, only obliquely explained by Christopher Bailey.

"Kinda" would be a lot more frustrating were it not for the standout performances, particularly by Simon Rouse, who is electrifying as Hindle. He never lets Hindle's madness rise over the top or descend to a series of actorly tics. It's one of the finest guest performances in *Doctor Who* from an actor who takes seriously what's on the page and just goes for it to make it seem real. It's chilling. Just about everything in "Kinda" that I really cared about has something to with Hindle: Rouse's performance drives the action. And, as we see again and again throughout the fifth Doctor's era, Peter Davison has a better rapport with a weekly guest star — in this case Nerys Hughes as Todd — than with the regular cast.

The CGI replacement for the snake in the climax is rather good, though honestly I don't think that will change your opinion of the story overall. "Kinda" is a fascinating experiment that works on the strength of the performances, making the mysteries behind them so compelling. I'm curious to know what I'll think of it when I'm 65.

Peter Davison

Born in Streatham in South London in 1951, Peter Moffett was a bit of an underachiever at school, but developed an interest in acting in his teens. He graduated from the Central School of Speech and Drama in the early 1970s and one of his first parts on television was playing what could charitably be called a space cowboy in his underpants named Elmer in a 1975 episode of the ITV children's science-fiction series *The Tomorrow People*. By this point, he had adopted the stage name Peter Davison.

Acting work was at first scarce for Davison, and he had worked at a tax office for 18 months when he was cast in a major role in the 1977 drama *Love for Lydia* opposite Jeremy Irons. This led to his breakout part as Tristan Farnon in the 1978–80 series *All Creatures Great and Small*, adapted from the books by veterinarian James Herriot. His portrayal of the young, affable and disaster-prone trainee vet rocketed Davison to stardom on British television and he followed up *All Creatures Great and Small* with two further sitcoms. (One of which, *Sink or Swim*, he did concurrently with his time on *Doctor Who*.)

Doctor Who producer John Nathan-Turner was a production unit manager on *All Creatures Great and Small*. When Tom Baker gave up the role of the Doctor, Nathan-Turner looked to his bulletin board, which had photos of various stars the producer worked with, and came across a photo of Davison at a charity cricket match. Davison had the qualities Nathan-Turner was looking for in the Doctor, which contrasted with Tom Baker: youth, seriousness and straight hair! Davison was dubious, feeling that, at 29 years old, he was too young to play the role of the Doctor. Nonetheless, he felt he couldn't turn it down: Davison had fond memories of watching William Hartnell and Patrick Troughton as a youth, and he didn't want someone else to play the part.

Davison used elements of earlier incarnations in his portrayal. Nathan-Turner was keen to keep cricket whites as part of the costume, echoing the photo of Davison that had inspired Nathan-Turner to cast him.

Patrick Troughton advised Davison not to play the role longer than three years, advice that Davison followed. When he left the role of the Doctor, he continued to be in demand as an actor, appearing in *A Very Peculiar Practice* (1986–1988), *Campion* (1989–1990), *At Home With the Braithwaites* (2000–2003) and *The Last Detective* (2003–2007), as well as various roles on the musical stage. In 2011, he joined the cast of *Law & Order: UK* alongside Freema Agyeman, who played Martha Jones in the New Series.

Davison reprised his role as Tristan Farnon in various revivals of *All Creatures Great and Small* and has come back to play the Doctor on TV in 1993's Children in Need skit "Dimensions in Time" and in the 2007 Children in Need mini-episode "Time Crash" (with David Tennant's tenth Doctor). Since 1999, Davison has continued to play the Doctor in audio adventures produced by Big Finish.

Davison has been married twice, the first time to actress Sandra Dickinson. (He appeared alongside her as the Dish of the Day in the BBC version of *The Hitchhiker's Guide to the Galaxy*.) Their daughter, Georgia Moffett, appeared opposite David Tennant as Jenny in the 2008 *Doctor Who* episode "The Doctor's Daughter." Georgia and David were married in 2012, meaning the man who played the fifth Doctor is the father-in-law of the tenth!

. . . .

Earthshock (1982)

Written by Eric Saward **Directed by** Peter Grimwade

Featuring Peter Davison (The Doctor), Matthew Waterhouse (Adric), Janet Fielding (Tegan), Sarah Sutton (Nyssa)

Supporting cast James Warwick (Scott), Clare Clifford (Kyle), Steve Morley (Walters), Suzi Arden (Snyder), Ann Holloway (Mitchell), Beryl Reid (Briggs), June Bland (Berger), Alec Sabin (Ringway), David Banks (Cyber leader), Mark Hardy (Cyber lieutenant)

Original airdates March 8, 9, 15, 16, 1982

The Big Idea An archaeological dig turns up a bomb that could blow up Earth. The Cybermen are behind it all, but this time the Doctor may be too late to save everyone.

Roots and References The 1980 Alvarez hypothesis that the dinosaurs were killed by an asteroid colliding with the Earth (the freighter crashing into prehistoric Earth; this may be the first TV program to dramatize this theory); IRA terrorism (the bomb); *Alien* (wiping out the rescue party). The silent end credits to episode four were derived from a longstanding tradition on *Coronation Street* when a character is killed off.

Time And Relative Dimensions In Space While preparing *Doctor Who*'s nineteenth season, it was decided that Adric had to die.

The character, originally intended as an artful dodger who was a genius, hadn't really connected with viewers, and Matthew Waterhouse was reportedly awkward to deal with on set. Producer John Nathan-Turner thought that killing off the character would shake up the series and give the show some added publicity. A script called "The Enemy Within" by science-fiction author Christopher Priest about a creature that lived in the heart of the TARDIS was underway. Priest dutifully incorporated Adric's death in rewrites. When Priest was asked by Nathan-Turner for further rewrites without any additional fee, the writer and producer had a huge fight and the script was withdrawn. Nathan-Turner turned to script editor Eric Saward to jump into the breach. Saward, along with Peter Davison, was keen to bring back the Cybermen, and so they were added to the mix.

Adventures in Time and Space The Doctor tries to get Adric to read George Cranleigh's book from the previous serial, 1982's "Black Orchid." Adric's room contains props from past stories, most notably the Android's death mask from 1982's "The Visitation." Adric wants to go back to E-Space and, during his argument with the Doctor, references are made to 1980's "Full Circle" (Alzarius and Terradon, the CVE), "Warriors' Gate" (Romana and K9) and "Logopolis" (Monitor). The Cybermen show clips of the first Doctor (1966's "The Tenth Planet"), the second Doctor (1968's "The Wheel in Space," though the Cyberleader sets it up as though it were from "Tomb of the Cybermen") and the fourth Doctor (1975's "Revenge of the Cybermen"). The Cybermen's weakness to gold was established in "Revenge of the Cybermen." The Doctor also mentions the Cybermen's origins from "The Tenth Planet." As we get closer to Adric's death, there are more and more elements lifted from Adric's first story, "Full Circle": the Doctor destroys Adric's badge of mathematical excellence; composer Malcolm Clarke uses Paddy Kingsland's "Adric's Theme" from that story at key junctures (a rare instance where a composer uses someone else's incidental music in *Doctor Who*); as the freighter crashes into Earth, Adric holds up the belt his brother, Varsh, gave Adric when he died.

Who is the Doctor? The Doctor claims he has emotions "of sorts." When asked if he has affection for Tegan he quickly adds, "She's a friend." He believes that small beautiful events are what make up life (though he stresses this is "for some people"). While he holds that having friends is a strength, the Cyberleader exposes this as a weakness because he complies with the Cybermen when his companions are threatened.

Companion Chronicles Adric's relationship with the Doctor is fraying. Adric feels like an outsider with Tegan and Nyssa on board the TARDIS and wants to leave. The Doctor cares enough not to want to jeopardize him and the two have a blazing row, though they later reconcile. Adric's mathematical skill is still staggering: he instantaneously gives a near approximate calculation of a complicated square root and cracks the logic codes to stop the freighter from destroying the Earth in the story's present day. But it's too late: Adric was the first long-term companion to die in *Doctor Who*. (Two other TARDIS crewmembers, Katarina and Sara Kingdom, were previously killed off, but primarily appeared during the single 12-episode serial, 1965's "The Daleks' Master Plan.")

Monster of the Week The Cybermen are back after a seven-year absence from the series. Their design is sleeker, more closely resembling a flight suit. They now carry energy weapons. They have a weakness to gold: it "clogs up" their chest units, making it impossible for them to function.

Stand Up and Cheer The Doctor defusing the bomb is one of the most genuinely tense sequences in *Doctor Who*, ever. It works through the music, some fast-paced editing but mostly Peter Davison's performance and the panic, desperation and yet eerie calm he brings to the scene. It's stunning.

Roll Your Eyes Adric tentatively handles the keyboard when he's about to enter the third logic code, as though with the foreknowledge that it will blow up momentarily — which Matthew Waterhouse certainly does know.

You're Not Making Any Sense Earth is about to join with other planets to stop the Cybermen . . . and no one on the freighter or Scott's party know who the Cybermen are. Either the government of Earth is keeping its citizens massively ignorant or this is a glaring inconsistency.

Interesting Trivia If we make an effort, we can understand why the Cybermen would send androids and a bomb to Earth rather than something bolder and riskier like using the freighter or an invasion. It would be simpler to penetrate Earth's defences with two androids and a device (if the TARDIS is too small to be detected, then inorganic creatures shot from space, possibly without a craft, would be even smaller). We can also understand why they would hide out in the freighter to monitor progress and, if necessary, invade by stealth having been given passage to Earth on the freighter. (This would also presume Ringway has managed to deceive or bribe anyone inspecting the cargo.) However, we do concede it is hugely, and needlessly, complicated.

With the Cyberleader's catchphrase, "Excellent!" (and he was using it long before Bill and Ted), the Cyber Lieutenant constantly questioning his leader's choices, the need to show clips of past episodes to explain who the Doctor is and bragging, "So, we meet again . . . Doctor," there is a pervasive sense that no one has received the memo stating that the Cybermen are emotionless creatures who share exactly the same goals. That said, we may just be facing the latest in cyber-evolution: their previous story, "Revenge of the Cybermen," features Cybermen using slightly synthesized treatments of the actors' voices rather than stylized mechanical speech. This indicates that they may be using more of the original human hosts, something confirmed by the plexiglas chin, which shows the human chin underneath. Perhaps more of the human body and brain is utilized by these Cybermen, which has the "side effect," if you will, of idiomatic speech, individual thought and spurious emotions. Or maybe it was just bad characterization.

The clip from "Revenge of the Cybermen" is somewhat odd. That story is supposed to be set in the future from the events of "Earthshock," presumably around the thirtieth century when the *Nerva* station was built originally, according to "The Ark in Space." Either the Cybermen are time travelling or this is yet another inconsistency.

Given the twin revelations of the Cybermen and Matthew Waterhouse's departure from the series as Adric, you would think viewers might have known about them in advance. But they didn't. John Nathan-Turner worked the publicity machine in different ways to ensure both details stayed secret. The BBC's listing magazine, *Radio Times*, offered *Doctor Who* a cover for the return of the Cybermen (the first time the series had been offered a cover since 1973). In spite of the prestige that came with a *Radio Times* cover, Nathan-Turner turned them down. He also closed the studio gallery, which often had visiting fans wandering in and out, in order to prevent unwanted visitors from seeing the Cybermen. With Adric's death, Nathan-Turner did almost the opposite: an illusion of Adric (played by Matthew Waterhouse) was seen in the next serial, "Time-Flight," which meant anyone looking at the following week's TV listings would see Waterhouse's name in the cast and assume nothing would happen to him in this week's episodes.

The TARDIS Chronometer In a cave system on Earth and a space freighter in sector 16, deep space, 2526. At the end, the freighter and the TARDIS travel back in time 65 million years.

Brave Heart? (GB) *Doctor Who* is often about eccentric people travelling to dark places in the universe and winning through cleverness, wit and innovation. Or, as Craig Ferguson put it so eloquently, "The triumph of intellect and romance over brute force and cynicism."

And yet, there are times when this utterly fails. When the darkness overwhelms. When brute force and cynicism wins. "Earthshock" is one of those times.

It ends in tragedy: a companion dead; the Cybermen slowed down, not defeated; dozens of people slaughtered indiscriminately — both betrayers (Ringway) and beloved (Kyle). The Doctor loses. Badly.

And yet, the loss is keenly felt because "Earthshock" plays for the most part by the rules. Every episode is a textbook example of *Doctor Who* as adventure thriller. It has a sense of ambition in its pacing and direction that is light years ahead of anything else: Peter Grimwade apparently directed twice as many shots as the average *Doctor Who* episode and it shows. The first episode is a mini-movie: *Alien* made before the 8 p.m. watershed and condensed into 24-and-a-half minutes. It has violent, gory deaths; building dread (poor Walters helplessly watching the blips on the screen representing his team getting picked off one by one); and a surprising cliffhanger that reveals the Cybermen are behind it all. The bomb-defusal sequence of episode two is a high watermark for Peter Davison's Doctor and there are some moody sequences on the freighter for good measure.

All along, we're getting an interesting array of characters. The four-square hero Scott (James Warwick, bless him, is just a little too stiff), meek little Kyle and then onto the freighter where we meet the concerned Ringway, the extremely competent Briggs (June Bland is superb) and the boldly cast Beryl Reid as Briggs. Reid was a huge star, known for light entertainment roles (though she had real dramatic pedigree: one of her biggest roles was in *The Killing of Sister George*), and some view her role as stuntcasting on John Nathan-Turner's part. It isn't. She's great, and the unlikely sight of a five-foot-three middle-aged woman playing the part of the captain adds unexpected colour and eccentricity to something that could have been rather grim.

The production values are superb. Having been stuck with an ersatz jungle in "Kinda," here we have a cave system that looks like an actual cave system, even though it was shot in studio. The lighting both here and on the freighter is moody and atmospheric. The plywood in the exploding door lets down the side a little, but it's otherwise great.

And then episodes three and four ratchet up the horror and the tension to even higher levels: Scott and company desperately trying to elude the Cybermen, the Doctor's briefly repelling the Cybermen by redirecting the anti-matter flow and melding the Cyberman with the door. They're super tense set pieces. The usual cat-and-mouse adventure is at the heart of this type of *Doctor Who* story, only here it's done 20 times faster and 20 times better. Which is a good thing because, between the all-too-human Cybermen and their plan so overcomplicated it might as well have been concocted by a team of management consultants, you don't want to linger too much on anything.

And then everything goes to hell.

No sooner does the one Cyberman get merged with the door than the other door to the bridge gets blown off and the Cybermen succeed anyway. And that's the beginning of the end. Ringway's concern for the other crewmen was a cynical act. The Doctor has his compassion thrown in his face before he's taken to the TARDIS and forced to watch his friends tortured and another one die.

In short, it looks and feels like a *Doctor Who* story, possibly even a great one, before the bottom drops out.

Which is why the ending is so bleak. This could have been any *Doctor Who* story: fast-paced set pieces, tense standoffs, the Doctor being immensely clever, eccentric supporting characters. Only this time everyone's luck has run out.

But the end of "Earthshock" is even bigger than that. The tragedy is about an awkward young man (played by an awkward young actor) who never quite fit in and acted out badly (both the character and the actor). And while the Doctor was outside explaining to Nyssa and Tegan about how the dinosaurs died — knowledge that might have changed Adric's mind about trying to save prehistoric Earth — Adric was inside the TARDIS, sulking.

The tragedy is that Adric has no clue that, by staying to solve the third logic problem, he's staying behind to fight against the inevitability of history. And he will lose. The sad, sick, pathetic thing about it is it was destined to happen because he could never connect with the Doctor and his friends.

"Earthshock" ends with romance and intellect being badly battered by brute force and cynicism. It won't be the only time that happens this decade. And yet, the Doctor still soldiers on. The fact that he can still

The 1980s

231

do so in the face of these things shows a beautiful heroism. Intellect and romance will triumph, yet.

Second Opinion (RS?) The cliffhanger is a mighty weapon. Used poorly, it can be a way to stall the action for a week, providing a momentary pause in the action before events continue much as they were before. But used well, especially when it coincides with a pivot around which the story hinges, it can be very powerful indeed. We sometimes forget how strong one can be, but viewers at the time, watching episodes separated by a day or a week, would have felt the full force of a good cliffhanger.

"Earthshock" is a story largely written around its cliffhangers. The entire first episode is a delaying tactic until the Cybermen can be revealed. The androids shouldn't even be there. (Why would Cybermen need robots instead of, say, other Cybermen?) And yet it doesn't matter one whit, because the result is one hell of a cliffhanger.

This is especially true if you were watching it at the time, when the last appearance of the Cybermen was seven years earlier. Even better, the lack of publicity would have played into this: instead of buying ad space or enjoying a *Radio Times* cover, the show benefitted from word of mouth on the playground about the return of the Cybermen. At the end of the day, you can't beat that for sheer power.

From this point on, the story fundamentally changes. We're now facing old and dangerous enemies, rather than sleek androids. The Doctor has an advantage because he knows the Cybermen's weaknesses, but it also gives them an advantage because they know his. The stakes have been upped considerably.

The second cliffhanger (Ringway discovering the Doctor and Adric with dead bodies and telling them that traitors are executed on this ship) is a good example of the weaker kind. It provides a momentary dramatic pause, but is immediately undercut by the reprise (when they aren't executed, but are instead given free run of the bridge). And since the Doctor was trying to get to the bridge anyway, the cliffhanger has no fundamental impact on the story. Worse, thanks to the twice-weekly schedule, at-the-time viewers only had a day to wait to see the first cliffhanger resolved, but they had almost a week to process this one.

The third is quite impressive indeed. After the Cybertroops have taken the bridge, the Cyberleader unleashes his army. Thanks to some clever photographic trickery, it appears as though the ship is being overrun with hundreds of Cybermen. This is a great "oh crap!" moment, because we've seen just how hard it is to kill individual Cybermen, so what are our heroes to do against an entire army? Sadly, this cliffhanger is also undercut, largely because the army doesn't do anything. They wander around the ship briefly, before departing.

It's the fourth cliffhanger that really ups the ante. Okay, so it's not technically a cliffhanger, more of a powerful emotional wallop, but it has the same function: it makes you want to come back next week and find out what happens. And it's incredible: trying to save the day, when we know he doesn't even need to, the Doctor's companion Adric is killed in action.

This packs an even greater punch than the return of the Cybermen. For essentially the first time (certainly the first in living memory for most viewers), one of the Doctor's companions is killed. What makes this such a powerful cliffhanger isn't just the silent credits (although that's an astonishing move), but it's the fact that there's no undoing this. Like all the best cliffhangers, the story is forced to pivot as a result — and *Doctor Who* will never be the same again.

The Five Doctors (1983)

Written by Terrance Dicks **Directed by** Peter Moffatt

Featuring Peter Davison, Patrick Troughton, Jon Pertwee, Richard Hurndall, William Hartnell, Tom Baker (The Doctor); Janet Fielding (Tegan); Mark Strickson (Turlough); Nicholas Courtney (Brigadier Lethbridge-Stewart); Elisabeth Sladen (Sarah Jane Smith); Carole Ann Ford (Susan); Caroline John (Liz Shaw); Richard Franklin (Mike Yates); Frazer Hines (Jamie); Wendy Padbury (Zoe); John Leeson (voice of K9); Lalla Ward (Romana)

Supporting cast Anthony Ainley (The Master); Philip Latham (Lord President Borusa); Dinah Sheridan (Chancellor Flavia); Paul Jerricho (The Castellan); David Banks (Cyber leader); Mark Hardy (Cyber lieutenant); Richard Mathews (Rassilon); Roy Skelton (Dalek voice); John Scott Martin (Dalek operator); Ray Float (Sergeant); Keith Hodiak (Raston Robot)

Original airdates November 23, 1983 (U.S.); November 25, 1983 (U.K.)

The Big Idea The Doctor's past incarnations, companions and enemies are being stolen out of time and brought to the Death Zone on Gallifrey, where they must play the Game of Rassilon.

Roots and References *The Wizard of Oz* (the timescoop, the quest to seek Rassilon); Robert Browning's poem "Childe Roland to the Dark Tower Came" (the Dark Tower); *Lord of the Rings* (the Ring of Rassilon gives immortality).

Time And Relative Dimensions In Space Terrance Dicks was woken by a phone call in the middle of the night. The former script editor and sometime writer for the series, now making a good living adapting past *Doctor Who* stories in the Target novel range, was in a hotel in New Orleans, where he had been attending a *Doctor Who* convention — and drinking into the wee small hours. The voice on the other end said, "Hello, this is Eric." To which a bleary-eyed Dicks said, "Eric who!? I don't know any bloody Eric!" It was Eric Saward, script editor on *Doctor Who*. He was calling to ask if Dicks would write the twentieth-anniversary special.

The BBC gave its blessing to produce a special featuring all five Doctors in July 1982. (ABC in Australia also provided some funding, the first time *Doctor Who* was made as a co-production.) The surviving Doctors, including Tom Baker, were amenable to returning. The brief was made — a story featuring not only past Doctors but past companions, the Master and Cybermen — and Eric Saward thought one writer could do it: Robert Holmes. Saward became impressed by Holmes's attitude to the series after reading his quotes in the 1983 academic book, *Doctor Who: The Unfolding Text*. Holmes hadn't written for *Doctor Who* since 1978, but Saward respected his work greatly. Holmes took the meeting and laughed his head off when given the brief. But he quickly put together a storyline called "The Six Doctors." (It was called that because one of the Doctors — the first, who would be played by a different actor, Richard Hurndall, since William Hartnell had died in 1975 — would turn out to be a robot imposter created by the Cybermen.) But Holmes found it difficult to develop the storyline into a script, so Saward called Terrance Dicks in the middle of the night in New Orleans to become plan B in case Holmes's script fell through (a practice that Dicks found loathsome) — which, eventually, it did.

Dicks quickly created a storyline from Saward's brief (adding K9, alongside a Dalek and other monsters he felt should be included), slotting in companions to Doctors as they were available. He had finished the script only to get another phone call from Eric Saward, telling him Tom Baker (who didn't want to be in a project where he was "one of the five") had decided to drop out. This necessitated even more rewriting. Fortunately, footage was available of Baker's Doctor from an abandoned story that would have been broadcast in 1980 called "Shada," so Dicks was able to nominally include the fourth Doctor.

As compensation for having his script rejected, Robert Holmes was asked to pen an original four-part *Doctor Who* story instead. We'll return to that shortly . . .

Adventures in Time and Space The story opens with a clip from William Hartnell bidding farewell to Susan from 1964's "The Dalek Invasion of Earth." The fifth Doctor is visiting the Eye of Orion with Tegan and Turlough, as they had discussed in the serial prior to this, 1983's "The King's Demons." A new version of K9 left to Sarah by the Doctor in the 1981 spinoff *K9 and Company* briefly appears. UNIT headquarters has the exact same location used in 1972's "The Three Doctors" and the Brigadier is still retired, as seen in 1983's "Mawdryn Undead." Borusa appears for the fourth time in the series (after "The Deadly Assassin," 1978's "The Invasion of Time" and 1983's "Arc of Infinity" — the latter as Time Lord president), while this particular Castellan makes his second appearance (after appearing in "Arc of Infinity"). The Doctors are on a quest to visit the Tomb of Rassilon, the founder of Time Lord society in "The Deadly Assassin" (the Eye of Harmony from that story is also mentioned). Sarah's vertigo is mentioned ("Genesis of the Daleks"). The first three Doctors remember meeting each other ("The Three Doctors"). The Doctor is asked to become president again (after serving in the role briefly in "The Invasion of Time"). When told that he's on the run once again in a rackety old TARDIS, the Doctor says, "Why not? After all, that's how it all started." This restates his origins as heard in "The War Games."

Who is the Doctor? The Doctor says, "A man is the sum of his memories; a Time Lord even more so." He means it too: when past incarnations are pulled out of time, he can feel it; when his fourth incarnation is lost in a time eddy, he almost disappears completely. The Doctor speaks old high Gallifreyan. Even the Master concedes that a cosmos without the Doctor is scarcely worth thinking about and is willing to rescue him.

Companion Chronicles Tegan and the first Doctor clash at every opportunity, while Turlough mostly stays behind in the TARDIS to deliver grim commentary. Each timescooped companion is brought back after their time with the Doctor: while viewers in 1983 are up to date on the

Brigadier (who retired from UNIT to become a maths teacher at an English public school in "Mawdryn Undead") and Sarah (who was still working as a journalist with K9 Mark III in *K9 and Company*), nothing is known about what happened to Susan after she left the Doctor to get married in 1964's "The Dalek Invasion of Earth." In fact, Susan is the only companion to participate in the Game of Rassilon that we don't see being timescooped, presumably to avoid having to show 22nd-century Earth onscreen!

Monster of the Week A Dalek returns (we have a rare glimpse of the creature inside), as do the Cybermen (much the same as their last appearance in "Earthshock") and a Yeti (from 1967's "The Abominable Snowmen" and 1968's "The Web of Fear"). The only original monster is the Raston Warrior Robot, a being that moves so fast it seems to disappear and reappear elsewhere. It can fire javelins and knives with deadly accuracy.

Stand Up and Cheer It really shouldn't work with its Georges Méliès–esque in-camera disappearance effects, but the Raston Robot's annihilation of a troop of Cybermen is visceral, gory, violent — and undoubtedly the coolest sequence in the special. The sequence was directed by John Nathan-Turner and shows that *Doctor Who*'s producer had real creative ambitions. It was a shame he wasn't allowed to realize them further.

Roll Your Eyes Paul Jerricho is, we're sure, a lovely man, but he's going to have "Nooo! Not the MIND probe!!!" written on his tombstone.

You're Not Making Any Sense These must be the universe's most myopic Cybermen. Seriously. They never notice anything at all: people directly ahead of them, the Master grabbing a Cyberweapon . . . the Raston Robot might as well have been working at half speed.

Interesting Trivia There is a remarkable conceit at the heart of this story, and every story featuring Time Lords for that matter: the Doctor only encounters his people in a strict chronological sequence. You would think that the Doctor would encounter Time Lords in a less linear fashion: meeting the soon-to-be-villainous Borusa before he meets the schoolmaster version from "The Deadly Assassin" before encountering the benign incarnation from "Arc of Infinity" and so on. Or that the fifth Doctor would stumble across earlier versions of the Master. But he doesn't. Naturally, the realities of TV production trump the fictional universe of *Doctor Who*: not only is there the difficulty of finding the same actors (particularly when several of them have passed on), but also there is an expectation on the part of viewers that they witness things in linear order; recurring settings and characters would be among them. Still, this conceit plays out in terms of there only being five Doctors and that this story is set in the fifth Doctor's "present." Again, TV realities trump fiction: Colin Baker wouldn't be cast as the sixth Doctor until three months after this story was made (and Matt Smith was only 13 months old when this story was broadcast!).

The Time Lords offer the Master a complete life cycle of regenerations. So next time you hear someone ask, "How can the Doctor survive after 12 regenerations?" you can give an answer. Apparently, the Time Lords have the ability to bestow further lives on their people. Or do they? Strictly speaking, this version of the Master isn't a Time Lord: he's a Time Lord who has taken over the body of someone from the planet Traken (1981's "The Keeper of Traken"). So perhaps the offer is simply to give a non-Gallifreyan a regenerative life cycle. Or is it? Presumably if they can do it for aliens, they can do it for Time Lords. Certainly, 2007's "Utopia" suggests that the Master is once again a Time Lord capable of regenerating.

If you've watched "The War Games," then you'll have spotted the continuity error in the second Doctor's encounter with the phantom Jamie and Zoe. The second Doctor wouldn't have known about Jamie and Zoe's memory erasure as it happened mere moments before his exile and regeneration. So how does he know? One option is that the Brigadier told him. Another option is that the Time Lords didn't regenerate the Doctor right away and instead he travelled on missions with the Time Lords. (The Doctor's claim to the Brigadier that he was "bending the rules" in visiting him in "The Five Doctors" lends credence to this idea.) Regardless of how you explain it away, the origins are far more mundane: the scene was originally written for Zoe and Victoria (who would have been spotted as a fake by calling Lethbridge-Stewart "Brigadier" instead of "Colonel" as she knew him). When Deborah Watling became unavailable and Frazer Hines became available, Saward hastily rewrote the scene and inadvertently introduced the error.

Originally, the first Doctor's involvement was to be quite minor and limited to staying in the TARDIS with Turlough and Susan. The largest part, the Doctor who transmatted to the capitol and exposed Borusa as the villain, was given to Tom Baker's fourth Doctor while the fifth

Doctor and Tegan went to the Tower via the main entrance. It was thought by Dicks that Baker's Doctor had the dark quality that would make it seem like he might be the villain. (Indeed, Tom Baker found this idea very attractive.) When Baker pulled out of filming, the first Doctor now went to the tower (still accompanied by Tegan) while the fifth Doctor was the one who transmatted back to Gallifrey. This gave the current Doctor's part greater weight. One of the nice things Dicks did was leave the script mostly intact, giving Davison the opportunity to deliver the sort of flippant dialogue reserved for his predecessor.

For a long time, the selection of companions was a game of musical chairs based on actors' availability: it was originally intended for Jamie to team with the second Doctor, while the Brigadier was going to travel with the third Doctor and Sarah would be with the fourth. However, Frazer Hines was busy on *Emmerdale Farm* (in the event, he was given enough time to perform a cameo). It was hoped to have Deborah Watling reprise her role as Victoria, but she too was already booked. When Tom Baker dropped out, Sarah was paired with the third Doctor and the Brigadier with the second Doctor.

Tom Baker's and Lalla Ward's appearances were taken from "Shada," a story written by Douglas Adams and directed by Pennant Roberts that was to have been broadcast in 1980 at the end of the program's seventeenth season. The story featured the Doctor and Romana visiting a retired Time Lord, Professor Chronotis, now living incognito as a Cambridge professor before encountering the evil Skagra who is searching for a book called *The Worshipful and Ancient Law of Gallifrey* that holds the location of the Time Lord prison, Shada. All of the location sequences in Cambridge were filmed in October and November 1979, along with one of the three studio sequences before a technicians' strike suspended shooting. By the time the strike was over, Christmas programs were given priority and "Shada" never had an opportunity to be completed. The story is the only one ever abandoned in *Doctor Who* history, though it has had an afterlife in many different versions. The first is the use of two clips (intended for episode one and episode three) for "The Five Doctors"; the second is a 1992 VHS release that had the unfilmed segments bridged with narration by Tom Baker (this was put out on DVD in 2013); the third is a 2003 webcast featuring Paul McGann's eighth Doctor and Lalla Ward (with the other parts all recast); and the fourth was a novelization written by Gareth Roberts in 2012. Lastly, Douglas Adams himself reused Chronotis, his time machine and the Cambridge setting for his book *Dirk Gently's Holistic Detective Agency.*

In 1995, this story was one of the first to be made into a "special edition," which updated special effects and used scene trims and alternate takes to make it longer. We're not fans of it — it opens with a lengthy series of menacing yet empty corridors in the Dark Tower and goes downhill from there — but it is available on the DVD as a special feature should you wish to give it a try.

The TARDIS Chronometer The second Doctor, the Brigadier and Sarah are picked up from contemporary Earth. The third Doctor is scooped from the near-to-present day his stories were set in. The fifth Doctor, Tegan and Nyssa are picked up from the Eye of Orion (though when is unclear). The first Doctor's initial location is unknown. The fourth Doctor and Romana are in Cambridge in October 1979. All of them except the fourth Doctor and Romana wind up in the Death Zone on Gallifrey. The time for that is unknown, though the TARDIS instruments read "zero"; presumably it is out of time.

Brave Heart? (GB) I love "The Five Doctors." I've loved it since I was a teenager when the twentieth-anniversary special was the sort of giant epic event a New Series episode such as "Journey's End" or "The Wedding of River Song" aspires to be. I liken it to *Star Wars* in that it's a story I've seen so many times I know the dialogue right from the start. ("Looks rather splendid, doesn't it?") I see no reason to hide my love for it, for I think it's one of the most exciting, entertaining, pure fun experiences the Classic Series ever produced.

That doesn't mean I'm blind to its flaws: Richard Hurndall's letter-*imperfect* portrayal of William Hartnell's Doctor; the ridiculous scene where Sarah falls down a mild incline; the singularly unimpressive Gallifrey scenes (how did we go from the impressiveness of "The Deadly Assassin" to a bland and floodlit place decorated by Ikea?); the character cameos for their own sakes; "Nooo! Not the MIND probe!!!" Yes, all that is true . . . but I think dwelling on such flaws misses the point. This is a celebration of *Doctor Who*: the story's remit is pure entertainment. It's all about the spectacle and the set pieces.

In fact, it's actually better than that. Terrance Dicks's plot is fiendishly clever: a mysterious figure is using the Doctors to play the Game of Rassilon in Gallifrey's Death Zone, so he can use their labours to his own end and win immortality. The result is a purpose-built funland designed to allow the spectacle and the set pieces to flourish. My only disappointment is that the scripted sequence with the Autons didn't make it into the final version.

Terrance Dicks has such a great grasp of the characters and the situations. It keeps the story going even though Peter Moffat sleepwalks through the direction. The scene where Anthony Ainley's Master is bribed by the High Council to rescue the Doctor may be Ainley's best scene as the Master, ever, because Dicks wrote him with wit and charm, like Roger Delgado once played the character, and Ainley relishes the opportunity to play him that way. He's conversational, not over the top, and he's very good.

Scene after scene is like this. The Yeti chasing the second Doctor and the Brigadier gets great laughs, and the Dalek chasing the Doctor and Susan gets nostalgic thrills (the throwback 1960s set helps), while the Raston Robot's slaughter of a troop of Cybermen is still shocking, even if the trick photography went out of style in 1902.

The story is deliberately structured to have a minimum number of scenes with the Doctors together (partially because Jon Pertwee and Patrick Troughton didn't get along during the making of "The Three Doctors"), which means that Richard Hurndall and Peter Davison turn out to be the only proper pairing of Doctors in the story, and one of them is a day player, so to speak. Hurndall is . . . okay. He was briefed to "suggest" Hartnell's performance, which I just don't see. While I applaud the desire not to descend into impersonation, Hurndall can't even "Hmm?" properly.

But Hurndall isn't the only one not really echoing the character he's playing. Jon Pertwee seems more like his convention persona than the character he played from 1970 to 1974: there's no karate, a minimal amount of action-man stuff, no brow-beating, barely even any rubbing of his neck. He's just . . . reacting to things, which is all very un–third Doctorish.

Patrick Troughton, on the other hand, is in his element. He steals every scene he's in. I adore the scene where the second Doctor and the Brigadier are hiding from the Yeti. It's absolutely appropriate for his Doctor and it's a great scene to boot. And the Brigadier is the perfect foil to Troughton's Doctor.

But when the Doctors do get together, it's like the gauntlet has been thrown down. The first Doctor has labels for his successors: "the little one" and "the young fellow." The second and third Doctor bicker like an old married couple. There's a moment where the old magic comes back with the third Doctor and the Brigadier, if only briefly, when we see Pertwee's Doctor treat him dismissively just once more for old times' sake. The climax is great, with the *deus ex machina* Rassilon showing up and despatching Borusa in a way that just seems totally appropriate.

What's odd is that it's the first Doctor who figures out Rassilon's riddle. There's something weird about how all the way through the Doctors defer to the first incarnation even though he should be the youngest of them. It's like deferring to yourself as a teenager. (Then again, perhaps there's a special deference given to the original incarnation.) Even so, it's worth it just to see the Doctors' response to being asked if they too want immortality. That's so very funny it makes you wish more had been done with them together. And it's hilarious watching the fifth Doctor's face once he's rid of his past incarnations: it's like watching someone who's had to put up with his beloved but overbearing relatives at Christmas.

There is so much more to love about this story. There's Peter Howell's superb score, which may be among the best from the series in any era. There's the footage from "Shada" to make up for the loss of Tom Baker that's so funny you don't care he isn't in the rest of the story. There are Carole Ann Ford's and Elisabeth Sladen's effortless comebacks to their old roles that made you wish they would return as regulars . . . I could go on and on. I love "The Five Doctors." It's quite possibly the most fun I've ever had while watching *Doctor Who*.

Second Opinion (RS?) When I watched "The Five Doctors" in 1983, I thought it was just about the most perfect thing I'd ever seen. This was *Doctor Who* at its most exciting ever! It had it all: old Doctors, old companions, old enemies, Time Lords, the Master, an exciting new monster in the Raston Warrior Robot . . .

When I watched it in 1993, as one of the first stories on VHS, I found it flat and dull. The acting was stilted and the plot seemed threadbare. *Doctor Who* had moved on in the decade since and "The Five Doctors" hadn't aged well. It looked old and creaky. The biggest flaw was the direction, being of the point-and-shoot variety. And it seemed as

The 1980s

241

though everyone was just going through the motions, recreating their greatest hits like a has-been band doing one last concert.

When I watched in 2003, as one of the first stories I saw on DVD, released in its special edition form, I was entranced by the new scenes and intrigued by different takes on scenes I knew so well. But I found the story itself desperately out of date: the new effects only served to make the original footage look cheap, and the pace was slow. I still found the direction flawed, but I did notice some very nice framing scenes, such as the Doctor driving Bessie through the woods, as seen through the curling branches, or the TARDIS half glimpsed through an archway. It again seemed as though everyone was going through the motions, with the exception of Patrick Troughton, who was bringing a witty and subtle performance to the proceedings. But I was mostly angry about the "ice cream swirl" effect that replaced the obelisk in the updated special effects.

Watching it in 2013, after having watched some of the very best *Doctor Who* stories, in order . . . I think it's just about the most perfect thing I've ever seen. This is *Doctor Who* at its most exciting ever! It has it all: old Doctors, old companions, old enemies, Time Lords, the Master, an exciting new monster in the Raston Warrior Robot . . .

Frontios (1984)

Written by Christopher H. Bidmead **Directed by** Ron Jones

Featuring Peter Davison (The Doctor), Janet Fielding (Tegan), Mark Strickson (Turlough)

Supporting cast Jeff Rawle (Plantagenet); Peter Gilmore (Brazen); Lesley Dunlop (Norna); William Lucas (Range); Maurice O'Connell (Cockerill); John Gillet (The Gravis); William Bowen, George Campbell, Hedi Khursandi, Michael Malcolm, Stephen Speed (Tractators)

Original airdates January 26, 27, February 2, 3, 1984

The Big Idea In the far future, the last surviving colony of humans on the planet Frontios is under attack from an unknown enemy.

Roots and References The 1982 Lebanon war (the bombardments); *M*A*S*H* (tending to the war-wounded in a makeshift hospital, the dark military comedy).

Time And Relative Dimensions In Space Script editor Eric Saward contacted his predecessor, Christopher Bidmead, with a request to write a monster-based story. Bidmead was happy to return to *Doctor Who* as a writer, but less than thrilled with the monster brief. An infestation of woodlice in his house provided inspiration for the Tractators, which he envisioned as being able to curl up into a ball. To make their movement as graceful as possible, dancers were hired to play the creatures, but in the end the costumes were so restrictive that not only could they barely move, but oxygen had to be pumped in from below so they could breathe!

As filming began, the production was struck by not one, but two tragedies. The original designer, Barrie Dobbins, committed suicide. Even more shockingly, the actor originally hired to play Mr. Range, noted character actor Peter Arne, was violently murdered. Arne had attended a costume fitting for the part and returned home, where he was beaten to death. The murder, and its connection to *Doctor Who*, made the news. The role of Range was hurriedly assigned to veteran actor William Lucas.

Who is the Doctor? He displays clear medical training here, something that the series has always skirted around. His cricketing skills are employed several times, including using a boulder like a cricket ball to knock over some Tractators. Since this adventure occurs in the very far future, there's a Time Lord limit on his visiting Frontios. As a result, he's careful not to leave any evidence that he was here.

Companion Chronicles Turlough dresses like a schoolboy because he was masquerading as one when he met the Doctor. However, he's actually an alien, although at this point his origins remain murky. Here we learn that he has a race memory of Tractators destroying his home planet from the inside.

Monster of the Week The Tractators are insect-like creatures that infest planets and burrow tunnels through them, in order to steer the planets around the galaxy. They can blend in with their surroundings and have the ability to move objects using gravitational beams. They've been marooned on Frontios for 500 years and need human parts to make their machines work. They're an intelligent but symbiotic species; without the Gravis, they're harmless, while the Gravis has no power when cut off from the rest of his species.

Stand Up and Cheer The excavation machine has been built up for some time, both in dialogue and through sound effects. It finally arrives at the cliffhanger to episode three — and, in a well-executed twist, we discover that it's powered by the barely alive body of original colony leader, Captain Revere.

Roll Your Eyes Why does the Gravis have a nose, when the other Tractators don't? No, really, why?

You're Not Making Any Sense Cockerill's revolution threatens to destroy the entire society of Frontios . . . until the final scene, when everything seems to be fine again, no questions asked.

Interesting Trivia The Time Lords have an upper limit on the TARDIS, meaning it isn't supposed to travel too far into the future. This seems like a strange thing for a time-active race to have. What's even more interesting is that the Gravis is very familiar with the Time Lords, treating the Doctor as a contemporary once he discovers who he is — and the Gravis isn't at all surprised to discover a Time Lord with a TARDIS in this era. So it's clear that the Time Lords are active in this time, despite their upper limit. One possibility might be that the Time Lords are actually from this time period and thus forbid interference in the recent past or contemporary times of their own planet, which also explains how the Gravis would know of them. Another possibility, hinted at in 2007's "Utopia," is that the TARDIS has a physical limitation in how far it can go and the Gravis — a being who has apparently lived for millennia — simply isn't aware that the Time Lords won't be interfering in his life from this point onwards.

The Tractators were originally going to be far more visceral, with a floating human head as the Gravis's translator and an excavation machine made up of disembodied hands. This was deemed either too gruesome for transmission or impractical to film, so the machine was scaled back and the translator idea dropped altogether. An external company built the excavating machine, but director Ron Jones was unhappy with the result, so he chose to film around it as much as possible. Bidmead's novelization of the story restored the horrific elements of both the Tractators' translation method and the excavating machine's human origins.

Oh, and if you're feeling especially brave, watch this story in black and white; it improves the experience no end.

The TARDIS Chronometer The planet Frontios, in the very far future.

Brave Heart? (RS?) "Frontios" may be the greatest one-episode *Doctor Who* story of all time. It involves the fifth Doctor being uncharacteristically eccentric ("Not hat people, are you?"), landing on a forbidden planet, helping with a minor medical problem and departing at the end of the episode.

Only one thing stops this from happening: the TARDIS gets destroyed.

It's hard to convey just how shocking this was at the time, when it seemed as though this might have genuinely happened. However, the larger mystery of the bombardments aside, everything is in place for the first episode to be the entire story.

Left with three more episodes to fill, "Frontios" cleverly inverts its central mystery. The bombardments come from the sky, so everyone expects the attacks to be from above, but the answer is instead beneath them. What makes this mystery so strong is the weight of history that's given to it. These attacks haven't just been going on for weeks or even months, they've been killing the population for 30 years. And that's following a decade of establishment for the colony before the bombardments began. Even worse, this is the last surviving colony of humans in existence. The situation couldn't be more perilous.

Furthermore, the crash of the ship isn't just something that happened, it's the most significant event in the colony's lifespan. ("Failure-proof technology." "What happened?" "It failed.") Nicknamed the Day of Catastrophe, what we see through this kind of language is exactly the type of thing real people would do when faced with an almost insurmountable disaster: they'd give it a name. This not only gives the story depth, it also provides a resolution when we discover that the Gravis was responsible for the crash.

But the background and plot mechanics are there because "Frontios" is particularly interested in one subject: accidental leadership.

The very first thing we witness is the loss of the colony's leader, Captain Revere. His son, Plantagenet, subsequently assumes the role, but he's too young and inexperienced for the job, having to be reminded that the people look to him to lead. But his very presence is holding the colony together; when people think he's dead, the result is anarchy. Yet, despite his ineffectual leadership role above ground, he's calm and confident when locked in the Tractators' cage, refusing to be cowed.

Brazen appears to be the power behind the throne, but he isn't a Machiavellian manipulator. He genuinely believes Plantagenet will grow into the role, just as his father did. He represents the hidden underbelly of the state: refusing to broadcast sensitive information without being in control of the facts and explicitly making the point that while living within the system isn't easy, living outside it is even more difficult. However, when the "deaths unaccountable" subplot is brought into the light, Brazen doesn't continue the state's secrecy — he acts.

This issue of unplanned leadership permeates the entirety of "Frontios." By picking up the hatstand, Turlough inadvertently gains authority for a short time, using what the colonists think is a weapon to instigate action. Plantagenet's leadership is an accident of birth. And then there's Cockerill.

Saved from being sucked into the Earth by pure chance, he's immediately proclaimed leader (even calling himself the new Plantagenet). The Retrogrades are those who've fled society, yet they organize themselves into a new one, with Cockerill as their head. The contrast is made clear when these organized Retrogrades subdue a wild Retrograde who was attacking Norna: instead of more violence, they tie her up, showing that order is part of society.

The entire plot is resolved when the Tractators are deprived of their leader and thus rendered harmless. And without them, the Gravis is also harmless. We thus see the mutually beneficial relationship between leader and subject: each needs the other and is functionally useless otherwise.

The only exception is the Doctor, who has leader-like qualities but no society to lead, nor any desire to form one. He stands at a skewed angle from the society he encounters, helping it out but rejecting any recognition. Even when accidentally thrust into a position of authority — when the Gravis mistakes him for a contemporary — the Doctor doesn't grab power, he simply plays along while searching for information until he can disrupt a society gone wrong.

Essentially, he's Br'er Rabbit, the trickster figure who stands apart from society and uses wit to mock authority. The resolution is almost exactly that of the Briar Patch: the Doctor pleads with the Gravis not to reassemble his TARDIS when, of course, that's precisely what he wants him to do. However, the trickster is an important figure in any society: a society that can survive being challenged and mocked is fit to survive, as the colony does, while those that cannot, such as the Tractators, do not deserve to.

"Frontios" thus posits that what makes a society is having a leader.

Not the quality of said leader, but simply the presence of one at all. With someone — anyone! — in charge, order can be maintained and a society created that can achieve goals that individuals can't. But it's not enough to simply go along with what the state demands. Secrets need to be brought out into the light, and the symbiotic relationship between a society and its leader strengthened, not weakened, by the truth.

Only then are we worthy of having a future.

Second Opinion (GB) My problem with Christopher H. Bidmead's prior efforts (which I mention in my review of "Logopolis") is that that they are two episodes of prologue and two episodes of story — and the actual stories don't have much room for niceties like characterization and drama as they're too concerned with high-minded science. But "Frontios" is gloriously different.

Here, Bidmead writes a proper four-act *Doctor Who* story and it's brilliant. The setting — a beleaguered colony with the last humans under siege from an unknown force — is really well-developed and the characters are vivid and fascinating. The Doctor gets to be properly Doctorish: he's fiery and flippant, and Davison grabs hold of the opportunity with both hands. The menace is well thought out and, even if the Tractators aren't 100% there as a monster, they certainly deserve a passing grade (there are far worse designed monsters in practically every other story this season). Even the usually ignored Turlough gets a great character arc.

Even more than that, what puts "Frontios" among Peter Davison's best is that it's so damn funny. It's as though the normally po-faced Bidmead consumed mescaline and just wrote the whole thing giggling. The Doctor passing off Tegan as an android is one of the silliest things ever and it's magnificently done, as is the deliberately pantomime means of convincing the Gravis to put the TARDIS back together. And that's not mentioning Turlough fending off attackers with the TARDIS hatstand, the Retrograde messiah or the Doctor's statement that the TARDIS has the offensive capabilities of a chicken *vol-au-vent*.

Okay, so Mark Strickson goes a bit over the top with the race memory stuff, the excavation machine could have been scarier and seeing the TARDIS blow up would have been cool (and the Doctor seems oddly unbothered about it, which adds insult to injury). But, honestly, every other performance is pitched perfectly, William Lucas as Range especially; even Peter Gilmore, in spite of the fact he seems to think he's playing Mr. Rochester in a BBC version of *Jane Eyre* — or perhaps because of that. And David Buckingham's design is, in every other respect, superb.

"Frontios" is often ignored and underrated by fans, and I think that's a great shame. Suddenly, after three sober years, everyone has decided it's okay to do comedy again in *Doctor Who*. And everyone is great at it. I think it's the best story of Peter Davison's final season not set on Androzani Minor (that might be damning with faint praise, but really it's not intended to do so). I'm constantly flabbergasted that this story *isn't* remembered, much less fondly so. It's a delight from start to finish.

The Caves of Androzani (1984)

Written by Robert Holmes **Directed by** Graeme Harper

Featuring Peter Davison (The Doctor), Nicola Bryant (Peri)

Introducing Colin Baker (The Doctor)

Supporting cast Christopher Gable (Sharaz Jek), John Normington (Morgus), Barbara Kinghorn (Timmin), David Neal (The President), Maurice Roëves (Stotz), Roy Holder (Krelper), Martin Cochrane (Chellak), Robert Glenister (Salateen), Janet Fielding (Tegan), Mark Strickson (Turlough), Sarah Sutton (Nyssa), Matthew Waterhouse (Adric), Gerald Flood (voice of Kamelion), Anthony Ainley (The Master)

Original airdates March 8, 9, 15, 16, 1984

The Big Idea On the planet Androzani Minor, the Doctor and Peri get caught up in a conflict between gunrunners and the army over spectrox, the most valuable substance in the universe.

Roots and References *The Phantom of the Opera* (Sharaz Jek and his kidnapping of Peri); Philip K. Dick's *Do Androids Dream of Electric Sheep?* and its film version *Blade Runner* (the androids); *Dune* (a life-extending drug found on a sand-blown planet); Jacobean drama (Morgus's asides).

Time And Relative Dimensions In Space Eric Saward watched a number of old *Doctor Who* stories when preparing for his role as script editor. He was particularly impressed by stories written by Robert Holmes and invited him back to pen "The Five Doctors." When that didn't work out, Saward offered him Davison's final story. Holmes was given carte blanche with the script, the one requirement being that the fifth Doctor had to be killed off.

Holmes wasn't very familiar with Peter Davison's portrayal and wrote with Tom Baker in mind, giving the Doctor his fourth incarnation's flippant dialogue. Holmes drew on elements he'd used previously, such as the masked figure lurking underground ("The Talons of Weng-Chiang") and gunrunners (1978's "The Power of Kroll"). Producer John Nathan-Turner was largely sidelined from the scripting process; he just asked that the new Doctor, played by Colin Baker, be given a line at the end of the story.

Adventures in Time and Space Peri mentions lava, an allusion to the previous adventure, 1984's "Planet of Fire." The Doctor says he once kept a diary, something we saw in 1966's "The Power of the Daleks." The Doctor's line "Is this death?" echoes the last words of Mawdryn in 1983's "Mawdryn Undead." When the Doctor is regenerating, we see visions of his former companions Tegan, Turlough, Kamelion, Nyssa and Adric, as well as the Master.

Who is the Doctor? We finally find out why the Doctor wears a stick of celery: he's allergic to certain gases in the Praxis spectrum. If the gases are present, the celery turns purple. (After that, he eats the celery; if nothing else, it will keep his teeth clean.) Celery is later said to be a powerful restorative on Gallifrey but the human olfactory system is too weak for it to be useful. This suggests that Time Lords have a superior sense of smell.

Companion Chronicles Perpugilliam Brown, known as Peri, joined the Doctor in the previous adventure. She's an American botany student who was visiting Lanzarote when she got caught up in the TARDIS. Here the Doctor goes to enormous lengths to save her, despite the fact that they barely know each other.

Monster of the Week The Magma Beast lives in the magma inside the caves. It comes to the surface to hunt, eating people, although it never ascends beyond blue level.

Stand Up and Cheer We could describe the intricacies of the plot and the way it unfolds beautifully, the all-male bloodbath, Morgus speaking into the camera, Christopher Gable's performance, the heartbreak of the regeneration . . . but instead we're just going to say: "So you see, I'm not going to let you stop me now!" Cue credits — and exhale that breath you've been holding. This is the fifth Doctor — and *Doctor Who* itself — at its most impressive.

Roll Your Eyes The Magma Beast. Oh dear. In a story full of gritty action that's plotted to perfection and acted like a dream, we're treated to a perfunctory monster that looks like a man in a cape with a hood ornament on his head. That's probably because it is a man in a cape with a hood ornament on his head.

You're Not Making Any Sense Why does the Magma Beast die at the end of the story? It lives in magma, so the mudburst can't kill it. And bullets clearly don't do the trick either. Did it have a coronary or something?

Interesting Trivia Spectrox has the ability to retard the ageing process. As a result, it's (rightly) described as the most valuable substance in the universe. And it's true that the story deals a lot with supply and demand in relation to a rare product. But what happens to spectrox afterwards? We never hear of anyone living unnaturally long lifespans in other stories, especially not any set in roughly the same era. It's possible that all the spectrox was destroyed in the fire in Jek's lab — and we're explicitly told the bats that are responsible for it have gone down into the lower levels to die — so perhaps this is the end of it. Even so, it's odd that the Doctor never heard about or investigated a generation of very long-lived humans before this.

John Nathan-Turner had long suspected that someone from the production office was leaking information to the fan press. As a result, he listed this story on his planning board as "The Doctor's Wife." The fan press duly reported it as such. You might recognize this title: it was used for the 2011 story by Neil Gaiman, in an homage to this ruse.

This is the first story directed by Graeme Harper, although by no means the last. Harper had worked as an assistant on the show in various capacities. After directing some sequences of "Warriors' Gate," John Nathan-Turner encouraged him to take the BBC's director's course. After doing so and adding some credits to his name, Harper then pleaded with Nathan-Turner to allow him to direct a *Doctor Who* story. Although he only directed two stories in the Classic Series, Harper's work is so notable that he was asked to direct for the New Series, starting with 2006's "Rise of the Cybermen."

The production ran short of time in the studio on this story, meaning two scenes had to be cut. The first was the opening TARDIS scene, where the Doctor's reason for visiting Androzani Major to find some sand for glass blowing was established. (Peri alludes to this later in a scene shot on location.) Instead, this was replaced with dialogue superimposed over scenes of the planet. The second cut scene was of the Doctor luring the Magma Beast to its death, which was deemed too costly and time-consuming. Instead, the Doctor simply stumbles over its corpse, adding to the tragic feel of the story.

The TARDIS Chronometer The planets Androzani Major and Minor, some time in the future.

Brave Heart? (RS?) The glue that holds this story together is surveillance. Jek has a tap on the interplanetary vid, allowing him to pick up transmissions between planets. Hidden cameras watch the army's every move. Most of Morgus's plotting is done via video link and it's the sight of the Doctor in the background of Stotz's video transmission that provides the key turning point in Morgus's actions. The androids can literally see through walls (and people), while the ersatz Salateen can communicate to Jek within seconds. Morgus even breaks the fourth wall, speaking directly into the camera on several occasions (an oddity for television of the time), making the viewer complicit in the surveillance.

With everybody either watching or being watched, the situation is a precarious one. It only takes a small disturbance to the status quo for it all to come crashing down. That disturbance? The arrival of the Doctor and Peri.

Our leads do very little other than look out for each other, but it's enough to set the incredibly tight sequence of events in motion, with everything reaching a crisis at the same time. What's more, for once the Doctor isn't interested in the political situation or saving people, he simply wants to rescue Peri and leave. They're two innocents, caught up in someone else's petty war. The result is a bloodbath, with every male character dead, including the show's lead. Even the nonspeaking flunky that Morgus sends to the Northcawl copper mine gets killed. Timmin's coup against Morgus is delicious, even though it's unlikely to end the mistreatment of workers or the Sirius Corporation's hold on the government. Robert Holmes's original title for this story was "Chain Reaction." And you can see why.

However, the script shares equal billing with the direction. Graeme Harper puts his stamp on the show with considerable style. He frames shots in unusual ways (such as the view of Stotz between Krelper's legs), using the camera to add resonance (Chellak saying he'll have Morgus dragged through every city in chains cuts to a shot of the Doctor in chains) and provide the punchline to jokes (such as the Doctor's face appearing suddenly when Jek says he must have beauty). The fade between Jek and Morgus when Jek mentions wanting Morgus's head is very well done, giving us a flash sideways to events at Sirius from Jek's imagination, capped by a dissolve from Morgus's face to Jek's.

The acting is also top notch. Peter Davison revels in the chance to be flippant, while Nicola Bryant never lets you forget that Peri is terrified and deathly ill. Davison also sells the Doctor's desperation: crashing the ship onto the planet, running until he drops and then rolling out of the way of a mudburst precisely when he's at the point of sheer exhaustion. Having the Doctor actually get dirty was an inspired touch.

And then the fifth Doctor dies. Not in some universe-saving act of heroism like his predecessor, but in a small, selfless act of saving one person he barely knows. It's senseless and unnecessary, but that's exactly what death is like. Even a minor dispute on a backwater can be deadly if you happen to get caught up in it. It's the perfect ending for the fifth Doctor, allowing him to be out-and-out heroic in a way that he hasn't always been.

Morgus's asides to the camera really shouldn't have worked — they were the result of the actor misunderstanding a stage direction — but John Normington is strong enough to pull them off, giving us a sense of unreality, as though the entire story was really the final entry in a TV series centred around Morgus. Indeed, Morgus's right-wing ethos and corporate practices, intended to be a caricature of big business, look positively tame these days.

But it's Christopher Gable as Sharaz Jek who steals the entire show. Gable is acting the part with every fibre of his being: he moves silkily, like a panther, which only makes his moments of psychosis more intense. Conveying menace through creepy touches and a perfectly pitched laugh, he oozes all-consuming madness. Only the burn makeup doesn't really work; how much better would it have been to leave the viewer pondering just how hideous he was, without actually showing us?

"The Caves of Androzani" stands at the pinnacle of Classic *Doctor Who*. Rightly voted as one of the all-time greats, its power hasn't diminished over the years. It's one of the rare times that script, direction and acting aren't just firing on all cylinders, they're actively adding to the production, each working to build on what the others are doing. The result is once-in-a-lifetime television. Now go watch it again.

Second Opinion (GB) What he said. Excuse me, I have something in my eye . . .

Vengeance on Varos (1985)

Written by Philip Martin **Directed by** Ron Jones

Featuring Colin Baker (The Doctor), Nicola Bryant (Peri)

Supporting cast Nabil Shaban (Sil), Martin Jarvis (The Governor), Forbes Collins (Chief Officer), Nicolas Chagrin (Quillam), Stephen Yardley (Arak), Sheila Reid (Etta), Jason Connery (Jondar), Geraldine Alexander (Areta), Graham Cull (Bax), Owen Teale (Maldak), Keith Skinner (Rondel)

Original airdates January 19, 26, 1985

The Big Idea The TARDIS needs Zeiton-7 in order to function, so the Doctor takes Peri to the only source, the planet Varos. Unfortunately for them, Varos is a former prison planet where the populace is governed through violent television.

Roots and References Nigel Kneale's 1968 BBC play *The Year of the Sex Olympics* and the 1983 film *Videodrome* (violent television as a means to titillate and pacify a populace); the 1980 film version of *Flash Gordon* (the very camp Quillam); *Nineteen Eighty-Four* (the fascist government, the viewscreens, the newspeak contractions like PollCorp); the U.K. miners' strikes of 1974 and 1984 (the Varosians' bargaining position with Sil's conglomerate); ancient Greek theatre (Etta and Arak as chorus figures).

Time And Relative Dimensions In Space Writer Philip Martin's 1976–1978 BBC series *Gangsters* was an acclaimed crime drama. Martin had followed that up with several more TV dramas, as well as plays at the National Theatre. In the early 1980s, Martin had taken to watching *Doctor Who* with his young daughter. He soon found himself with an idea for a story centred on what the media might become in 300 years' time and pitched it to the *Doctor Who* office. Script editor Eric Saward was delighted. Producer John Nathan-Turner was more hostile, insisting that Martin provide a storyline for his proposed serial like any other new writer. But Martin rose to the challenge and soon had

The 1980s

253

a commission for a story in the series' 22nd season. While writing it, Martin pondered seomething Isaac Asimov had said, that amphibious aliens were rarely portrayed on film and television, as water was difficult to manage in a studio. He decided to make one of his characters an amphibian with a water tank: Sil.

Adventures in Time and Space Peri mentions their recent adventure on Telos in 1985's "Attack of the Cybermen." When the TARDIS isn't working, Peri asks if it's the comparator, a rather important part of the TARDIS in her debut story, 1984's "Planet of Fire." The TARDIS manual made its first appearance in 1978's "The Pirate Planet."

Who is the Doctor? The Doctor's sixth incarnation is somewhat unstable, going though a series of manic activities in the TARDIS that culminates in burning Peri's cold supper! He's somewhat harsh and depressed in his outlook: confronted with the TARDIS's inability to travel, he's immediately resigned to his fate for all eternity. Fortunately, he snaps out of it when he sees there's residual power in the TARDIS. The Doctor seems indifferent to death, making a quip when the guards wind up in the acid bath and deliberately engineering the death of Quillam and the Chief Officer.

Companion Chronicles The Doctor and Peri have taken to arguing like a married couple: Peri has a long list of complaints about the Doctor, while he takes potshots at her American accent. She's desperate to engage him when the TARDIS stops working, going to the trouble to find the TARDIS manual. (Is it any wonder that, when put under Quillam's machine, she transforms into a bird, desperate to escape?) The Doctor refuses to tell the governor what he needs to know to save Varos unless she is safely returned.

Monster of the Week Sil is the representative of the Galatron Mining Corporation. He's a Mentor from the planet Thoros Beta, though this isn't revealed until 1986's "The Trial of a Time Lord." He is an amphibious reptilian slug who is carted above a water tank. Devoid of any morality, he will do anything to progress his business aims. His translator unit is faulty, causing him to use odd words ("Goveneur") and expressions ("Dead as death!"), though no one tells Sil about this as it amuses the Governor.

Stand Up and Cheer The end of episode one is tense, as the Doctor struggles through an illusion of a desert (something that looks fabulous visually, combining stock footage with the corridors of the punishment dome). However, when the Doctor collapses, the story unexpectedly breaks the fourth wall as the Governor gets the camera to have a closeup on the Doctor (in an era when many of the cliffhangers ended on a reaction shot from the Time Lord) and then says, "And cut it . . . now!" The screen goes blank. Cue end credits. Wow.

Roll Your Eyes Faced with the TARDIS effectively running out of gas, the Doctor doesn't try to figure out the problem, send out a distress signal or indeed do anything, well, useful. Instead, he pulls up a chair and takes part in the mother of all sulks, telling Peri she's lucky because she'll die sooner than him. Why Peri doesn't simply cudgel the Doctor until he regenerates into someone less miserable is beyond comprehension.

You're Not Making Any Sense When Galatron finds another source of Zeiton-7, they decide to stop haggling with the Varosians and pay any price. Huh? This flies in the face of economic sense. When supply increases, the price should go down, not up.

Interesting Trivia The task of finding a diminutive actor to play Sil was difficult for director Ron Jones. He had auditioned a number of little people, but wasn't happy. Producer John Nathan-Turner had been told about a theatre company, Graeae, which was entirely comprised of people with disabilities. Jones met with Graeae's founder, Nabil Shaban, and subsequently auditioned Shaban and other actors from the company, ultimately choosing Shaban himself for the role of Sil. Shaban had unsuccessfully tried to put his name forward to *Doctor Who* before, even submitting a story idea at one point. Some within the BBC were aghast at the casting, fearing it would misrepresent people with disabilities. Shaban was delighted and put his all into it, devising the way Sil rolls his tongue after watching a snake. John Nathan-Turner was impressed and assured Shaban that Sil would return.

And Sil would indeed return. Originally, it was supposed to be in a story commissioned for the 23rd season by Philip Martin called "Mission to Magnus," which was to bring back the Ice Warriors as well. However, the 18-month hiatus imposed on the series meant a rethink, and that story was consigned to oblivion (it would be novelized in 1990 and adapted for audio in 2009). Season 23 was redesigned to be a season-long story called "The Trial of a Time Lord" and Martin was asked to write episodes five through eight. This four-part segment of the story (known as "Mindwarp") was set on Sil's home planet,

Thoros Beta, and saw Sil involved in experiments involving transferring the consciousness of Sil's CEO, Kiv, into another body. It was Nicola Bryant's final story as Peri.

For the 1985 season, *Doctor Who* returned to Saturday nights after three years on weeknights, but BBC management decided to experiment with the format by running 45-minute episodes instead of the then-traditional 24-and-a-half minute episodes. The format change lasted only one season. It was not a wholly successful experiment from a storytelling perspective: rather than simply stitching together two episodes of the old format, the first 45-minute episode was often just a beefed-up version of the old first episode. The Doctor and Peri's arrival into the story would be delayed and more scenes with the supporting cast were included. This is quite noticeable when the stories were re-cut for foreign syndication at the old length. Part one of the 24-minute version of "Vengeance on Varos" ends with the Doctor and Peri still talking in the TARDIS during Jondar's execution!

The TARDIS Chronometer The planet Varos in the constellation of Cetes. While no exact date is given, Peri says it's three centuries in the future, so sometime during the 23rd century.

Unstable? Unstable? UNSTABLE? (GB) It's not often that a *Doctor Who* story improves because of its prescience, but that's precisely the case with "Vengeance on Varos." It was a story that many viewers found (and still find) uncomfortable to watch because it's so grim and violent. And yet it clearly anticipated so much: reality television, the instant news cycle, even *The Hunger Games*. It's Orwellian satire of the finest kind, the sort that sees what's coming and brings it to you with uncomfortable focus.

And what it shows us is uneasily familiar: torture and death being repackaged as entertainment to keep the populace docile while their welfare goes to hell in a proverbial handbasket. Take out the death part (so far) and you're not so far off from a world with *Big Brother*, *Celebrity Apprentice* and *Storage Wars*. "Vengeance on Varos" is reality television gone wild: *Survivor* where you don't get voted off the island, you just die horribly. But it's not just that. It's the notion of how TV, and TV with real people in staged but "real" circumstances — what we now call "unscripted drama" — can be used as a distraction from ineffective and inhumane governance.

When the New Series tried this with "Bad Wolf" in 2005, it veiled it in futuristic versions of current reality shows, which made the savagery more shocking when eviction from the *Big Brother* house meant actual disintegration. But Russell T Davies missed a trick that Philip Martin didn't: "Bad Wolf" doesn't show the viewers; "Vengeance on Varos" does. Using Etta and Arak as chorus figures is a stroke of genius. They respond exactly like television viewers would: Arak's comment that they always put a covered corpse in the acid to show how it works isn't a million miles away from the viewer grumbling that *Storage Wars* must have its interesting treasures planted in the storage locker. I love the contrast between the characters. Etta is a loyal party member who fills out her viewing surveys, stands at attention and threatens to report Arak, where Arak is a prole who thinks the politics and the entertainment are indistinguishable. And he's right.

It's the political satire that adds an extra layer to "Vengeance on Varos." Everyone, except for the Chief Officer and Quillam (who have learned how to profit from their situation thanks to colluding with Sil), is ultimately trapped within the system. Even the Governor is trapped, noting that his role is a sham: a bunch of hapless guards are forced to put their name in a hat and the loser gets to be Governor. "The theory being that a man scared for his life will find solutions to this planet's problems," says the Governor, "except the poor unfortunate will discover there are no popular solutions to the difficulties he will find waiting for him here." So all he can do is keep the crowd happy with executions and video sales until he faces the ultimate losing vote. It's unbelievably cynical, but it also points to the problem of the celebrity of a modern politician.

Is it any wonder that the Governor is an utter chameleon of a character, moving between opportunism, outright cynicism and benign concern, sometimes in the same conversation? No one other than Martin Jarvis could have made the Governor so sympathetic and yet so cold. And yet his speech to Maldak is stirring. Jarvis delivers it with such quiet passion, desperate to sway his captor into realizing how terrible the system is. It's delivered without histrionics, just the compelling idea that a well-stated argument can change minds. (And then he begs that Peri be killed if he loses the vote, which is cold and shocking.)

On the other side of the spectrum we have Sil, who represents the worst excesses of capitalism: rapacious desire reduced to a talking, slimy fish. Nabil Shaban is incredible. Every gesture, every bit of stage business he engages in (such as eating his green slimy marshminnows) is not only vile, but un-selfconsciously so. His two modes are outrage or utter pleasure. He's Mr. Creosote from Monty Python's *The Meaning of Life*, but in miniature. The wonky translator is a lovely comic touch.

Don't get me wrong. It's violent and nasty. It features a man about to be killed by what amounts to a staffer's production meeting pitch. The acid bath — poorly played for comedy I would concede — and vines are deeply uncomfortable to watch. I can understand people's position that a satire of violent television that is violent television may cancel out all satirical intent. I would suggest that that sort of a dark undercurrent is entirely necessary — that the underlying sadism requires the complicit participation of the voyeur, er, viewer at home. In many ways, works like *The Hunger Games* now mine that seam of dark violence for satire's sake.

It's amazing that all this is achieved, because "Vengeance on Varos" is hobbled out of the starting gate by its star and the new format. I wrote in my notes while watching, "15 minutes into episode one, and the Doctor and Peri have done nothing but argue." The 45-minute format should be giving us episodes like those in the New Series, but no one knows how to write for this format yet. It should be faster paced, bigger, more exciting and engaging with the Doctor in the thick of it, but instead it relies on the anthology part of the series, building the world and then having the Doctor and Peri make a mad dash through it. It works here because the world is so compelling and because the Doctor integrates himself seamlessly into that world when he gets there. The problem is that we get scene after deeply unpleasant scene of the Doctor and Peri bickering instead of being involved in the actual story.

Unpleasant doesn't begin to cover the problems with the sixth Doctor. His response to the TARDIS not working is mind-blowing: who on earth thought it was a good idea to make the hero of the program such a miserable person? To give Colin Baker his due, he's great when challenging the punishment dome and its terrors. But that's precisely the problem: he's as good — and as bad — as the material he's given.

"Vengeance on Varos" has some cringeworthy moments to be sure, and some dark ones too, but it also has some of the best qualities of *Doctor Who*: perceptive satire, cunning writing, great character and social commentary. And it's so very much ahead of its time in its view of television and the culture that watches it. And the ending is staggering, as our chorus figures, Etta and Arak, ask the question we've all wondered after the Doctor has overturned regimes: "Everything's changed. We're free." "Are we?" "Yes." "What shall we do?" "Dunno."

Second Opinion (RS?) My co-author is right: this story is ahead of its time. But who cares? So a 1985 story predicted that television in the future would be awful. And to do so, it made its point by becoming . . . awful television. This isn't actually something to be proud of. If Pink Floyd had decided to make a biting commentary on the future of pop music by making the blandest sellout pop record imaginable, it wouldn't be a work of genius ahead of its time, it would be a bad record.

There are so many things to dislike about this story. The violence is almost the least of it. Jondar has no dialogue aside from clichéd speeches, all Peri can do is whine and the Governor ordering people's executions to boost his own popularity isn't shown to be nearly as evil as it should be.

But the real problem is the sixth Doctor. Like the story, he's intentionally been designed to be unlikeable. And, like the story, the result is hard to watch. When Tom Baker portrayed an alien so divorced from ordinary concerns that you never knew what he'd say next, the whole world fell in love with him. When Colin Baker makes quips about not joining guards in an acid bath, but pays loving attention to a fly, the show got cancelled.

And, as unlikeable as the character is, it's the complete absence of his moral core that really kills the story. In a world where violence is commonplace, the Doctor should be the shining beacon of peace, a man who proves that violence is wrong through his very presence. Instead, he solves Varos's problems by murdering the Chief Officer and Quillam.

Make no mistake: it's murder. He ties back poisonous vines and gives the order to release them as soon as his victims are in range. If you or I did that, we'd be arrested (or worse), not given a parting gift of the rarest mineral in existence. Even if you argue that his action is the result of desperate circumstances (though if I assassinated the second and third in command of a foreign country, I'm not sure any judge would listen to such an excuse), he still sets up the laser weapon as a trap. Seconds later, it disintegrates a guard, making the Doctor guilty of manslaughter, at the very least.

The result is *Doctor Who* that's gone off the rails. An unlikeable Doctor and his unlikeable companion star in an unlikeable story where unlikeable characters do unlikeable things. Yes, the cliffhanger is brilliant and the viewers are a sublime touch. Sure, it predicted the future of television with surprising prescience. But the price it paid was too high. This isn't the triumph of intelligence and romance over brute force and cynicism. Not by a long shot.

· — · · —

Colin Baker

Born in 1943 in London, Colin Baker originally studied law and was on his way to becoming a solicitor when he decided to become an actor instead. Baker at first worked on stage and had a small but significant role in the 1972 BBC adaptation of *War and Peace*. In 1974, he was cast as Paul Merroney, the villain in the BBC serial *The Brothers*. Merroney was a "man you love to hate" and Baker achieved great popularity in the role.

Guest appearances in a number of series followed after *The Brothers* ended in 1976, including one in a 1983 *Doctor Who* story, "Arc of Infinity," where he played Maxil, the commander of the guard on Gallifrey. (Ironically, one of Baker's first scenes has Maxil shooting Peter Davison's Doctor!) Baker was disappointed at the time: having appeared in the series, he felt that he would never be able to play the Doctor.

Shortly after "Arc of Infinity" was made, Baker was at a wedding reception for a member of the *Doctor Who* production team. Producer John Nathan-Turner, who was in attendance, was impressed with Baker's ability to entertain everyone present. When Peter Davison announced his intention to leave at the end of the 1984 season of *Doctor Who*, Nathan-Turner was satisfied he had found a successor.

Baker was keen to have the Doctor be difficult and abrasive at first, with the idea that these unpleasant aspects would be gradually toned down over time (following a similar character arc to that of Mr. Darcy from *Pride and Prejudice*). John Nathan-Turner gave costume designer Pat Godfrey the brief to make his costume "totally tasteless" (in many ways mirroring the producer's own persona: Nathan-Turner favoured loud Hawaiian shirts at conventions) and Baker wound up with a garish costume full of clashing colours and patterns. Baker hoped that this too might be toned down in future.

However, Baker's long-term plans — early on, he publically stated he hoped to beat Tom Baker's record for longest tenure in the role — were cut short by BBC1 controller Michael Grade and head of drama Jonathan Powell. After the show came back from its 18-month hiatus in 1986, Grade, who disliked Baker's performance, laid the blame for the show's shrinking fortunes on the lead actor and felt a change of Doctor might boost the series. Powell agreed with his superior and ordered Nathan-Turner fire Baker from the part after only two seasons. Baker was asked to film the Doctor's regeneration, but he refused.

After *Doctor Who*, Baker concentrated his acting career on the stage and continued to make guest appearances on television, ranging from *Jonathan Creek* to *Hustle*. He gained public notice in 2012 by appearing in the British reality series *I'm a Celebrity, Get Me Out of Here!* He returned to the role of the Doctor in the 1993 charity skit "Dimensions in Time" and continued the role on audio from 1999 onward in stories produced by Big Finish Productions.

Revelation of the Daleks (1985)

Written by Eric Saward **Directed by** Graeme Harper

Featuring Colin Baker (The Doctor), Nicola Bryant (Peri)

Supporting cast Terry Molloy (Davros); Eleanor Bron (Kara); Hugh Walters (Vogel); Clive Swift (Jobel); Jenny Tomasin (Tasambeker); Trevor Cooper (Takis); Colin Spaull (Lilt); Alexei Sayle (DJ); William Gaunt (Orcini); John Ogwen (Bostock); Stephen Flynn (Grigory); Bridget Lynch-Blosse (Natasha); Alec Linstead (Stengos); John Scott Martin, Cy Town, Tony Starr, Toby Byrne (Dalek operators); Royce Mills, Roy Skelton (Dalek voices)

Original airdates March 23, 30, 1985

The Big Idea On the planet Necros, Davros has taken over a funeral home and solved the galaxy's food problem.

Roots and References Evelyn Waugh's *The Loved One* (the black comedy in a funeral home; several character names are derived from Waugh's novel); the 1968 film *They Saved Hitler's Brain* (Davros as just a head); *Star Trek* ("I'm a doctor, not a magician"); *Upstairs Downstairs* (Jenny Tomasin's casting was because the production team wanted someone "like Ruby" from that series, so they cast the actress who played her!); *Soylent Green* (food is people); *Othello* (Davros manipulating Tasambeker); *Don Quixote* (Orcini and Bostok's quest). Among the DJ's songs are "Hound Dog," "Whiter Shade of Pale," "Moonlight Serenade" and Jimi Hendrix's "Fire" (the latter was removed from the DVD release for copyright reasons). The glass Dalek is a reference to

The 1980s

261

one that was included in David Whitaker's 1964 novelization of "The Daleks," *Doctor Who in an Exciting Adventure With the Daleks*.

Time And Relative Dimensions In Space The BBC frowned on script editors writing for their own programs. However, Eric Saward found an ingenious way around this dictum: he wrote "Revelation of the Daleks" during the six-week gap between the end of his existing contract and the beginning of the next one. He vacationed in Rhodes and wrote the first draft there, taking several character names (such as Lilt and Orcini) from places and people he encountered. The bulk of the script was based on Evelyn Waugh's *The Loved One*, a black comedy set in a funeral home. Characters such as Jobel and Tasambeker were based on the mortician Joyboy and his secret admirer.

Adventures in Time and Space The Doctor and Davros discuss Davros's ship blowing up (1984's "Resurrection of the Daleks"). A Dalek says, "My vision is impaired," something they've been saying since 1964's "The Dalek Invasion of Earth." The Doctor cooks nut roast rolls for Peri in the opening scene, which is an indication that the Doctor is still a vegetarian, following events of 1985's "The Two Doctors." (Peri seems to be vacillating, moaning, "What I would give for a burger.")

Who is the Doctor? The Doctor states that he's 900 years old, significantly older than when we last heard his age. He comes to Necros deliberately, in order to investigate rumours of Stengos's death. He's callous in response to Davros losing his arm, making a bad pun and attempting to shake his hand.

Companion Chronicles Peri's grades "aren't up to much" (so she's not the most diligent student). She's collecting plants to bring back to Earth to impress her college. She and the Doctor argue like an old married couple, each complaining about how much the other weighs ("Watch it, porky"). Hearing the DJ's American accent makes her homesick.

Monster of the Week Davros is continuing his genetic experiments on Necros and has become known as "The Great Healer," due to his breakthrough in solving the galaxy's famine problem — although he's done so by harvesting the bodies of those sent to Tranquil Repose. The bodies of the particularly prestigious are being turned into Daleks that are capable of reproducing. These Daleks are cream and gold coloured, as opposed to the traditional grey.

Stand Up and Cheer On Davros's orders, Tasambeker stabs Jobel with a needle. He collapses to the floor, his wig falling off as he dies. This is black comedy that's grotesque, ridiculous and vicious all at once, and it definitely delivers the shocks.

Roll Your Eyes Almost every scene Jenny Tomasin as Tasambeker is in. She's awful. If we had to chose the worst moment, her attempt at getting angry at Takis and Lilt is horrendous. Why it impresses Davros, we'll never know.

You're Not Making Any Sense Why does Davros pretend to crush the Doctor with a massive tombstone when he could, you know, actually crush the Doctor with a massive tombstone?

Interesting Trivia When the crew arrived on location to film the opening scene, they discovered the ground had been carpeted in snow. Director Graeme Harper was quite enamoured of how it looked, especially as it gave the production an extra half hour of filming time because of the way snow reflects light. On the other hand, the snow prevented a planned scene where a Dalek prop would be catapulted, suggesting that Daleks could fly.

Both Davros and a Dalek are seen hovering above the ground. This was something the series had often tried to hint at (having Daleks appear on higher levels in the '60s, for instance) and it was felt to be important to counter popular jokes about the Daleks not being able to climb stairs. The special effects stumbled a little: Orcini's real leg is visible when Davros is hovering. This is fixed in the DVD release, with a CGI effect that mostly covers up the slip.

The story ends on a freezeframe as the Doctor is about to announce where they'll go next. The destination was Blackpool, a British seaside town famous for its amusement park (and it had hosted a *Doctor Who* celebratory event attended by Colin Baker and John Nathan-Turner). The next story, "The Nightmare Fair," was to be set in Blackpool and feature the return of the Celestial Toymaker, a villain from the 1960s. However, when the series was put on hiatus in February (a few weeks before this story was screened), these plans were scuttled, so the destination was left unsaid.

Producer John Nathan-Turner requested that, at some point in this story, the Doctor discover his own tombstone. (Saward later stated in interviews he presumed this was because Nathan-Turner wanted to use the piece in exhibitions). The tombstone was supposed to spurt blood out of the eyes of the bas-relief portrait of the Doctor (hence why the Doctor has blood on his jacket), but it was not used because it was deemed too graphic.

This was the last *Doctor Who* story to use a mixture of film and videotape. (Indeed, the entirety of the first episode shows the Doctor and Peri in scenes shot on film and they never even interact with any of the videotaped castmembers.) Location footage was filmed on Outside Broadcast tape for the remainder of the Classic Series. The 1996 TV Movie was made entirely on film. And the New Series is shot on video, but "filmized": i.e., given a treatment to make it look as though it were filmed and given more depth.

The TARDIS Chronometer Necros, the future.

Unstable? Unstable? UNSTABLE? (RS?) Usually in Dalek stories, the appearance of a Dalek is a shocking moment, sometimes reserved for the first cliffhanger (which typically fails to have a dramatic impact, given that the word "Daleks" is invariably in the title). With "Revelation of the Daleks," the first Dalek is seen about ten minutes into the first episode — and its appearance is so nonchalant you hardly even notice.

This is just one of many wry jokes that pepper "Revelation of the Daleks," a story full of black comedy and postmodern nods, long before such things were fashionable.

What's more, despite being a dramatic season finale and what would turn out to be Colin Baker's one and only encounter with the malevolent pepperpots, the Daleks are hardly in it. They're mostly used for guard duty, although one runs behind the Doctor and Peri, only noticed by her, who doesn't know what it is. The direction also gets in on the joke: the Daleks are framed in unusual ways, such as just in the edge of shot or nothing but an eyestalk.

Another in-joke is the title: there isn't really a revelation as such, but rather it's the biblical bookend to "Genesis of the Daleks." Instead of Davros being a mad geneticist, here he's the saviour of the entire galaxy. And he's done so by becoming a capitalist. (On not telling the galaxy that they've been eating their dead relatives, Davros says, "That would have created what I believe is termed 'consumer resistance.'")

It's also a story that consists almost entirely of double acts: Takis and Lilt, Jobel and Tasambeker, the DJ and Peri, Orcini and Bostok . . . Bostok even says that Kara and Vogel are "like a double act," a line that's a decade ahead of its time. The double act was a tool favoured by Robert Holmes (think Jago and Litefoot in "The Talons of Weng-Chiang"), but he usually restricted himself to just one. Here, Saward doesn't do anything else.

Like Holmes's "The Caves of Androzani," this is also an episode that's interested in surveillance. But where that story saw plots and counterplots based on who was watching whom, in "Revelation of the Daleks" everyone is watching everyone else, yet nobody pays attention. Davros watches everybody on his monitor; the DJ has multiple screens that see everything; Natasha and Grigory run behind funeral staff, but are seen on every camera. And yet, none of it makes any difference.

It's here that Graeme Harper's direction shines. We see what appears to be a standard shot of funeral staff going about their business, but then the image shifts vertically to a lower level showing Jobel at work — and then does so again to record Natasha and Grigory in the catacombs. This is a clever way of indicating that everyone is being watched, making the viewer complicit in the flaccid surveillance.

As a result, people frequently look into the camera: Jobel does so whenever he makes asides to Davros's camera, while the Doctor notices the camera as soon as he enters Tranquil Repose. Meanwhile, Davros observes everyone ("Suddenly, everyone sees and knows too much") and uses his observations of Tasambeker's infatuation to his own ends. Thus, the BBC camera becomes a stand-in for someone else's camera.

Then there's the DJ. He exists solely to relay messages to the dead, which is a great touch. It also adds a level of open comedy that the story desperately needs, and Alexei Sayle is brilliant. The DJ as observer isn't dissimilar to Arak and Etta from "Vengeance on Varos": his entire role in the first episode is simply to comment on the plot. However, in the second episode, things change dramatically. Not only does he interact with the main cast (unlike Arak and Etta), he actively gets involved. He helps Peri contact the Doctor, sends the signal to the president's ship, and then fights and destroys Daleks. This is a notable change for an observer character and — also unlike Arak and Etta — he's killed for his trouble.

The cliffhanger also plays with the conventions of television. The Doctor's gravestone looks like it's made of polystyrene, with an obvious crack in it, but that turns out to be precisely the point. It's even described as being part of an elaborate theatrical effect.

The downside, of course, is that to get to such an awesome cliffhanger requires the Doctor and Peri being withheld from the main plot for the entire first episode. It's here that the limitations of the 45-minute episodes become most apparent: as with "Earthshock," Saward clearly writes around the cliffhangers, but there's only the one this time, which is a huge structural problem. Consequently, the Doctor and Peri have very little to do, other than argue.

Even when he does get involved in the plot, the Doctor is oddly deferential to Orcini. Orcini is given a huge amount of respect, his abilities constantly being paraded, but his dialogue keeps him humble. The Doctor calls himself an idiot for trying to attack Orcini and his primary contribution to the resolution is to kick a gun in Orcini's direction. As a result, the only real role for the Doctor is to be overbearingly verbose when enquiring about the funeral services. Even after Orcini's death, the Doctor has to stress just how much of a contribution Orcini made, in destroying the reproducing Daleks.

"Revelation of the Daleks" is witty and clever, with a number of divine touches. Its script is helped enormously by the direction and the result is a story that's both ahead of its time and also a product of it. It's exactly the kind of story that could have excised the Doctor and Peri without much fuss, being far more interested in its own characters and Davros than the ostensible leads. But that's perhaps no bad thing: by sidelining the difficult sixth Doctor, it gets on with telling the story it wants to tell. More art-house television than *Doctor Who*, it transcends its roots to be something that's quietly impressive. You wouldn't want every story to be like this one, but once in a while it's a revelation.

Second Opinion (GB) If there ever was an example of a *Doctor Who* story that shouldn't work but succeeds brilliantly nonetheless, "Revelation of the Daleks" has to be it. In *Doctor Who Magazine*'s poll of readers in 2008, it was the top-ranked Colin Baker story . . . and yet, the Doctor and Peri barely clock in 10 minutes of the first 45-minute episode. Even stranger, the Daleks are in it even less. In the absence of Doctor, companion and Daleks, we have a drama in an intergalactic funeral home featuring the usual bitter and twisted toughs you'd find in an Eric Saward story along with some delightfully camp executives, a brilliant parody of Don Quixote, and Alexei Sayle as a DJ who talks directly to the camera.

With all that going on, who needs the Doctor and Peri bickering endlessly? That's the genius of Eric Saward's script and Graeme Harper's direction, which seems to take all the deficiencies of circa-1985 *Doctor*

Who and turn them into strengths. It's grim and nasty, so make it into a beautiful dark comedy. The 45-minute episodes were usually poorly expanded 24-minute episodes, so don't write for the old format (it works; part two is better paced than many New Series stories). The Doctor is too loud and colourful, so add even more colourful chracters to the mix, but get the actors (most of them, anyway) to underplay their roles.

The result, somehow, works. It shouldn't, but it does.

The Colin Baker era is at its best when it does acidic satire, and "Revelation of the Daleks" is the epitome of this approach. However, while "Vengeance on Varos" was quite precise in its approach, here Eric Saward takes on all comers: attitudes towards death, vanity, soap opera romance and even Colin Baker's performance all receive Saward's lampooning scorn. There's not a lot of plot, but the story doesn't need it. It's about the characters in what must be one of the best gothic soap operas ever made.

If there's one piece that really irritates me though, it's the Doctor and Peri, who bicker like an old married couple . . . or at least the one in *Who's Afraid of Virginia Woolf?* There is something borderline abusive about their relationship. The Doctor opens the episode making cheap shots about her ("You eat too much"), being jerkish (the weed plant is harmless but he'd rather leave doubt in her mind for kicks, apparently) and passive aggressive when she accidentally breaks his pocket watch. I often wonder if the cancelled 1986 season was going to include the revelation that Peri's father was actually a mean-spirited, pedantic, circus clown: it's the only reason I can see why Peri stays in this miserable relationship.

That out of the way, Colin Baker is very good at making the Doctor a foil to everyone else (as my co-author says, he does little else). But it's Terry Molloy who gets centre stage as Davros — mostly as a disembodied head at that — and he's superb as he plays people off against each other, like a sci-fi Richard III crossed with Iago. All of the other characters are eclectic and compelling, particularly Clive Swift's grotesque performance as Jobel and Alexei Sayle's off-kilter DJ (he's fabulous when he's awkward around Peri). However, it's William Gaunt, by imbuing Orcini with pathos and genuine nobility, who easily walks away with one of the best guest performances in *Doctor Who*.

"Revelation of the Daleks" is the sort of oddity that affirms the strength of the series' format in that it's so elastic it can even be *Doctor*

Who when the Doctor's not around. Now if someone could explain the title . . .

The Psychic Papers: The Cancellation Crisis

"DR WHO AXED IN BBC PLOT" read the headline of the *Sun* newspaper on February 28, 1985. In breathless prose, the article outlined how "TV bosses say they cannot afford to make any new shows about the famous time-traveller for 18 months" and quoted "furious fans" who claimed it "was a plot to back up demands for a higher license fee."

The BBC is a public broadcaster, and its funding comes from a license fee for each TV set owned by a household. By the early 1980s, the BBC was facing stiff competition in the ratings from private broadcaster ITV. The Thatcher government was making pronouncements that the BBC needed to demonstrate value for money like any other television network. At the same time, the license fee also needed to increase. What to do?

The BBC decided to go to Michael Grade, a wunderkind who had, as controller of one of ITV's networks, come up with the idea of making sure all the ITV networks showed the same programming on Saturdays and, in so doing, knocked the BBC off its ratings perch and sent *Doctor Who* to weekdays. Grade, now working in the American film industry, was actively courted to come to BBC1 to be its new controller. Though his salary would be only a sixth of what he made as an executive, he was given sweeping powers to create new programming, and to develop and schedule material as he saw fit.

Grade hit the ground running. He moved the flagship current affairs series *Panorama* — even more of an institution than *Doctor Who* — out of prime time. He advanced plans for several new shows that, alongside the new twice-weekly soap *EastEnders*, would revive the evening schedule. Grade was also determined to start daytime programming on BBC1. (Up until 1986, British television closed down service for several hours during the day after showing some news and children's programming in the morning.) All this — daytime TV particularly — cost money; they needed to either cancel several shows or defer them in the budget for 18 months.

There was one other very important detail: Michael Grade hated *Doctor Who*. He wanted it gone, feeling it was cheap, nasty and dated compared to other programs. Jonathan Powell, who had taken over as BBC head of drama, loathed *Doctor Who* as well. (Powell also had a personal animus against John Nathan-Turner, whom he felt was incompetent.) Powell and Grade intended to cancel the show outright.

When John Nathan-Turner was informed that the show would not return (all the stories currently in pre-production and the principal cast were paid off), he responded decisively. Through an intermediary, he stage-managed leaking the story to the press. Fortunately, February 28, 1985, was a slow news day so there was an immediate and large amount of negative publicity towards this decision. Soon there was a public campaign from *Doctor Who* fans.

The BBC was caught on the back foot by this. Grade and Powell were called to an emergency meeting with the BBC's head of publicity, who was concerned that the story was gaining global attention. (A plan by fans to bring Daleks to Parliament to protest particularly worried them.) Grade and Powell decided to step back from cancellation and decided that *Doctor Who* should return in 18 months (adding the spin that this had always been intended). In an unprecedented move, the managing director of the BBC board called the head of the Doctor Who Appreciation Society to tell him the series would return to BBC1 in 18 months.

In many ways, though, the public campaign to "save" *Doctor Who* (which included, no joke, an actual charity single called "Doctor in Distress") ultimately backfired even though it brought back the series. If anything, fans added fuel to the fire (British *Doctor Who* fans were openly criticizing aspects of the current production) and suddenly there were talking points in the media — discussions of the soft ratings, the overall quality of the show and the increased violence were cited by the BBC — that weren't there before the fans started speaking out.

When the show came back, it had its number of episodes halved and its budget substantially cut. Grade and Powell weren't interested in changing the direction of the show or putting new blood in it either.

In employment law, there is something known as constructive dismissal: a process wherein an employee isn't fired from a job but the employer makes the conditions so bad that eventually the employee resigns. In 1985, *Doctor Who* effectively began a form of constructive dismissal. It returned 18 months later with fewer episodes, increasingly worse timeslots, fewer resources and a BBC hierarchy hostile towards it. But *Doctor Who* wasn't axed yet. It still had some surprises.

Delta and the Bannermen (1987)

Written by Malcolm Kohll **Directed by** Chris Clough

Featuring Sylvester McCoy (The Doctor), Bonnie Langford (Mel)

Supporting cast Don Henderson (Gavrok), Belinda Mayne (Delta), Richard Davies (Burton), Stubby Kaye (Weismuller), Morgan Deare (Hawk), David Kinder (Billy), Martyn Geraint (Vinny), Sara Griffiths (Ray), Hugh Lloyd (Goronwy), Ken Dodd (Tollmaster), Brian Hibbard (Keillor), Johnny Dennis (Murray), Leslie Meadows (Adlon)

Original airdates November 2, 9, 16, 1987

The Big Idea The Doctor and Mel win seats on a time-travelling bus tour to 1959, but are pursued by Gavrok and his Bannermen who are after the Chimeron Queen Delta and her precious cargo.

Roots and References The 1980–1988 BBC comedy series *Hi-De-Hi!* (the holiday camp); *The Wild One* (Billy's look is patterned after Brando); *Grease* (rock and roll musical romance). Murray is reading the '50s British comic book *The Eagle*. The instrumental "Puffin' Billy" plays when the bus arrives at Shangri-La; the soundtrack riffs off the theme to *Peter Gunn* when Keillor dies. The songs "Rock Around the Clock," "Singing the Blues," "Why Do Fools Fall in Love," "Mr. Sandman," "Goodnite, Sweetheart, Goodnite," "That'll Be the Day," "Only You," "Lollipop," "Who's Sorry Now?" and "Happy Days Are Here Again" play throughout. (Licensing was expensive, so they're all covers played by the group the Lorells, led by musician Keff McCulloch, who are seen onscreen performing as Billy's band.)

Time And Relative Dimensions In Space John Nathan-Turner had to start all over again.

After the 18-month hiatus and the difficulties of the subsequent truncated season — punctuated by alternating indifference and interference on the part of the BBC hierarchy and a deteriorating relationship with script editor Eric Saward that ended acrimoniously with Saward quitting and airing out all his laundry in a lengthy interview with *Starburst* magazine — Nathan-Turner wanted out of *Doctor Who*. BBC controller Michael Grade ordered Nathan-Turner to fire Colin Baker — the only time an incumbent to the role of the Doctor was publicly dismissed — with the assurances that was the last thing he would have to do for the series before being reassigned to another.

Nathan-Turner returned from a holiday to discover the BBC reneged on that promise. He would still be producing *Doctor Who* and he would have to find a new Doctor and a new script editor (and start commissioning stories right away). Nathan-Turner decided to change the title sequence and theme music arrangement, effectively re-doing what he did in 1980.

One of the first things Nathan-Turner did was hire a new writer named Andrew Cartmel as script editor. The second thing he did was hire Sylvester McCoy to play the Doctor. McCoy's hiring wasn't easy: the actor had a career in theatre and children's television, with only a few dramatic credits, so he had to screen test with several other actors — a first for the series. McCoy handily won the part.

Andrew Cartmel began commissioning scripts, turning to writers who were new to television. One of these was Malcolm Kohll, whom Cartmel knew from the BBC script unit. With limited resources and only 14 episodes for the series' 24th season, Nathan-Turner was keen to have the final six episodes be two three-parters made by the same director and crew, one completely studio-bound, the other location-based. Kohll's script was the location story, with Wales suggested by Nathan-Turner as a possible setting. Kohll came up with a story set in the 1950s called "Flight of the Chimeron."

Adventures in Time and Space The seventh Doctor spouts malapropisms ("All haste and no speed makes Jill a dull girl"): the mangled aphorisms were introduced as part of his character in 1987's "Time and the Rani," though this is the only story that continues with that.

Who is the Doctor? The seventh Doctor is quieter and more comical than his predecessor. And the Doctor winds up in emotional terrain he's never experienced on television thus far: he's somewhat awkward when it comes to comforting a heartbroken Ray, like someone who hasn't had to do that sort of thing in quite a while. (Certainly, he never has onscreen!)

Companion Chronicles Melanie "Mel" Bush is a computer programmer from 1980s England (the first British companion in over a decade). Though she's initially rebuffed by Delta, Mel's friendliness ultimately wins Delta over.

Monster of the Week Gavrok and his Bannermen are warlords seeking to destroy the Chimeron race. They're humanoid, but nasty. They have red tongues and mottled hands, and eat raw meat.

Stand Up and Cheer At the end of this comic romp is a beautiful scene where the Doctor hugs a Stratocaster guitar while talking to Billy about the decision he's making and all the things that may go wrong. And then the Doctor says wistfully, "Then again, love has never been known for its rationality," like someone who knew this long, long ago. Sylvester McCoy's seventh Doctor has come into his own.

Roll Your Eyes As the kids from the future say, that hatchling is just plain fugly.

You're Not Making Any Sense We all know the story. Boy meets girl. Boy falls in love with girl. Boy ingests alien jelly to turn into girl's species, never knowing the consequences. All within a 36-hour period.

Interesting Trivia One of the downright revolutionary things this story does is take place on Earth less than 30 years before its broadcast date. It sounds strange, but until "Delta and the Bannermen" the TARDIS's visits to the past tended to stop around the 1920s or 1930s; generally, *Doctor Who* didn't make it out of the Victorian/Edwardian era. There are some anachronisms, most notably Weismuller's New York Yankees cap, which is a modern-day nylon mesh hat; a genuine 1950s one would have been made of cloth.

Holiday camps were somewhat like modern-day resorts, only within the British Isles, often near the seaside. They were cheap tourist accommodation, providing lodging, meals and entertainment on site, giving Britons somewhere to go on vacation in the days when air travel was prohibitively expensive. They flourished after World War II, though by the 1980s they were in decline as package holidays abroad became more affordable. But for a couple of generations, holidays at Butlins' and Warners' camps were a staple of vacation seasons. As the Doctor says, "This is the real '50s."

Some of the elements of this story would be all too familiar to British viewers in 1987. The holiday camp setting was used in the 1980s BBC sitcom *Hi-De-Hi!*, which was still in production at the time. (It would sort of be like setting a Matt Smith episode in the offices of a Scranton, Pennsylvania, paper company.) Ken Dodd, who plays the tollmaster, was something of a comedy legend in Britain. (His standup act, which borrowed from the Music Hall tradition, was a staple of British variety television since the '50s). Fans familiar with these elements found "Delta and the Bannermen" hard to accept at the time.

Bonnie Langford, who had joined *Doctor Who* the previous year, was leaving the show at the end of its 24th season. (Langford's part was stuntcasting on a similar scale to Catherine Tate as Donna; she was a huge star in light entertainment in Britain and was better known than either Colin Baker or Sylvester McCoy.) Two candidates in the final stories of the season were mooted at various points to be the next companion: this story's Ray, and a character called Alf (later called Ace) that script editor Andrew Cartmel was creating with writer Ian Briggs for "Dragonfire," the studio-bound story made in the same production block as this one.

The TARDIS Chronometer The Chimeron home planet and Intergalactic Tollport G7 (presumably sometime in the future). The Shangri-La holiday camp, Wales (not "in England" as Weismuller says), summer 1959.

Wicked? (GB) Appropriately for a decade that was three minutes to midnight on the nuclear doomsday clock, *Doctor Who* became an increasingly dark program during the 1980s, full of miserable people who only had surnames, nasty violence and grim deaths. And that's only the first 20 minutes of "Vengeance on Varos." But then the most marvellous thing happened.

"Delta and the Bannermen" came along.

"Delta and the Bannermen" may be the most stunning course correction *Doctor Who* has ever made. In just three episodes, it does half a dozen things *Doctor Who* hasn't tried before and another half a dozen things it hadn't done for a long time. It's set in the late 1950s; *Doctor Who* finally leaves Victorian and Edwardian drawing rooms for actual recent history. It has a love story as its B-plot. It uses period music to great effect (and has a great score by Keff McCulloch). It has comedy that's neither dark (as in previous seasons) nor over the top. It values whimsy. And optimism. And imagination. And charm. And for that, I'll forgive Ken Dodd (who's actually pretty good).

It's totally different to anything that had been *Doctor Who* for the previous ten years.

I love the first episode in particular. It shows a sense of grand imagination missing since Douglas Adams left. A galactic tollport awards the Doctor a prize on a space- and time-travelling tour bus going to Disneyland in 1959. Which then crashes into a satellite and winds up at a Welsh holiday camp. Only also travelling on the bus is the last Chimeron and she's pursued by a warlord. And there are bumbling FBI agents trying to find the satellite . . . There's more boldness and bravado on display here than was seen in television in 1987, never mind *Doctor Who* in the past. Heck, rustle through the DVD special features and you can see a 30-minute cut of the first episode that includes a TARDIS scene that's actually charming. In the 1980s. *I know.* I can't believe it either.

"Delta and the Bannermen" changes the game in every way. There are supporting characters with first names. People like Murray, the bus driver. Let me say here that Murray is probably my favourite supporting character in '80s *Who.* He's so enthusiastic and loveable. Johnny Dennis plays him as a guy who loves life even if he doesn't work for the best people. You feel for him when he breaks the crystal that operates the bus, just as you love his infectious enthusiasm when attending the dance. The scene where he tries to explain to the passengers that a Bannerman war party is on the way is priceless. There's also Sara Griffiths as Ray, the sweet Welsh mechanic with a crush on Billy, who embodies unrequited love and naïveté. And there's Billy, who tries to play Brando in *The Wild Bunch*, but is just too smooth.

Even the last-name-only bunch are charmers: Mr. Burton, the officious camp director who becomes a hero; Weismuller and Hawk, who should absolutely not work as stock American bumblers and yet bring a smile to my face every time they bicker; and Goronwy, played honey-sweet by Hugh Lloyd, who enables the plot exposition to happen laterally for the first time in recent memory.

The great thing about "Delta and the Bannermen" is that it's no candy confection either. It's a story that starts with genocide, features the wholesale murder of beloved characters (including Murray!) and finds the Doctor consoling a broken-hearted girl and later counselling the guy who jilted her, saying, "Love is not known for its rationality." It's surprisingly confident and mature. If anything, I'd argue that Chris Clough's leaden direction does Malcolm Kohll's script an extreme disservice by not letting those aspects breathe a little more.

But then Clough is probably the main problem with the story. He's inept at chase sequences, which is a disadvantage when the second episode is pretty much just that. (Worse, you can see Sylvester McCoy wearing his glasses when he rides the Vincent!) More damnably, Clough gets the actors to pitch their scenes just a bit too broadly and overall blows the substantial lead he had with the great cast, script and location.

On the other hand, Sylvester McCoy is fantastic, and you can really see him settling in the role here. His speech to Gavrok — and just because I haven't mentioned Don Henderson up until now doesn't mean I don't think he's brilliant, because he is — shows us the pathos and comedy of a little guy pushed a shade too far. He also fits comfortably in the quieter scenes with Ray (who would have made a great companion) and the scenes where he seems wryly amused by everything going on around him.

"Delta and the Bannermen" isn't a perfect *Doctor Who* story (Stubby Kaye is lovely but a bit too old; Belinda Mayne is wooden as Delta), but overall it does far more right than wrong. It's definitely one worth watching; taken in context, it's a stunning leap forward. It has all the 1980s tropes — a mercenary, a one-named villain, grim deaths — but it's oriented toward optimism.

No wonder Goronwy has a smile on his face at the end. Here's to the future, indeed.

Second Opinion (RS?) Chiefly remembered for being a piece of fluff, "Delta and the Bannermen" is nevertheless a story full of war, deaths of lovable characters and a vicious warlord. And yet the comedy is actually funny ("We're calling from Wales — in England!"), and the balance between the grim (Gavrok eating raw meat as he plots an act of genocide) and the light-hearted (I don't care what anyone says, the Tollmaster rocks) is just right.

What's amazing is the Doctor's confrontation with Gavrok on the stairs. Up until this point (both in this story and the previous two), Sylvester McCoy's Doctor has been a likeable clown. Suddenly and shockingly however, both McCoy and his Doctor come into their own when he marches up the stairs — ignoring both the Bannermen guards and his friends! — and lays into Gavrok in a burst of righteous fury. Gavrok gives as good as he gets, but the Doctor's speech about life is a triumph. This is also the first glimpse we get that McCoy is capable of being quite astonishing as an actor: he doesn't always let it out, but when he does, he's incredible.

And then the second cliffhanger is a delight: it's not the Bannermen pointing guns at our heroes, it's the Doctor admitting that he may have gone a little too far. That's awesome.

From there, the story becomes a series of escalating plots and counterplots, with each twist escalating the tension until the story reaches its breaking point. It's like "Doctor Who and the Silurians" with motorcycles.

"Delta and the Bannermen" is an incredible breath of fresh air. It's the link between what the show was (grim and miserable) and what it will be (whimsical and hopeful), set off with musical numbers, romance and an incredibly adorable pseudo-companion in Ray. The very sight of the comical seventh Doctor straddling a motorcycle is enough to make you rethink what *Doctor Who* is capable of. It certainly was for Andrew Cartmel.

I love this story like a brother. If you've seen this before and didn't like it, give it another try. If you've never watched it, enjoy!

Remembrance of the Daleks (1988)

Written by Ben Aaronovitch **Directed by** Andrew Morgan

Featuring Sylvester McCoy (The Doctor), Sophie Aldred (Ace)

Supporting cast Simon Williams (Group Captain Gilmore); Pamela Salem (Dr. Rachel Jensen); Karen Gledhill (Allison); Dursley McLinden (Sgt. Mike Smith); George Sewell (Ratcliffe); Harry Fowler (Harry); Jasmine Breaks (The Girl); Joseph Marcell (John); Peter Hamilton Dyer (Embery); Michael Sheard (headmaster); Peter Halliday (vicar); William Thomas (Martin); Derek Keller (Kaufman); Terry Molloy (Emperor Dalek); Hugh Spight, John Scott Martin, Tony Starr, Cy Town (Dalek operators); Roy Skelton, Royce Mills, Brian Miller, John Leeson (Dalek voices)

Original airdates October 5, 12, 19, 26, 1988

The Big Idea Two Dalek factions are in 1963 London seeking the Hand of Omega, a powerful Time Lord weapon. But the Doctor is one step ahead of them . . .

Roots and References Frank Miller's graphic novel *Batman: The Dark Knight Returns*, published two years before, in 1986 (reimagining a superhero as a complex individual); World War II (Daleks as Nazis, the Hand of Omega as a nuclear weapon); the 1950s BBC *Quatermass* serials (there's a direct reference to "Bernard" and the British Rocket Group). Speeches by John F. Kennedy, Martin Luther King and Charles de Gaulle from 1963 are heard during the pre-credits sequence. The Doctor reads Richard Gordon's *Doctor in the House* (as part of Sylvester

McCoy's running gag where the Doctor reads a new book every story with the word "Doctor" in the title). The Beatles songs "Do You Want to Know a Secret" and "A Taste of Honey" play along with the Mudlarks' "Lollipop" and "Puffin' Billy." A cover of Elvis Presley's "Return to Sender" plays on the jukebox in the first episode, while a cover of The Shadows' "Apache" is heard during the café in the third episode.

Time And Relative Dimensions In Space Between the first and second seasons of Sylvester McCoy's tenure on the show, script editor Andrew Cartmel had the idea of making the Doctor more mysterious, revealing a backstory that we knew nothing about. Sylvester McCoy himself was consulted (consulting the actor for the character's direction had rarely happened before) and the actor was enthusiastic, as he wanted to add more pathos to the Doctor. The seeds of this backstory would be sown over multiple stories, starting with the first story of the new season.

Ben Aaronovitch sent in a submission to the production office, and Cartmel, impressed with his writing, asked for a three-part story. When that proved too similar to another story planned for the season, it was held back a year (ultimately becoming 1989's four-part "Battlefield"). Given that it was the 25th season of the show, producer John Nathan-Turner wanted to feature the Daleks. As a result, Aaronovitch wrote a Dalek story that tied in to the show's roots in "An Unearthly Child." Aaronovitch was also inspired by the two Dalek factions seen at the conclusion of "Revelation of the Daleks." He decided to use this to explore the issue of racism, echoing Terry Nation's original conception of the Daleks as Nazis.

Adventures in Time and Space Much of this adventure ties directly into "An Unearthly Child." The action starts at Totter's Lane, in I.M. Foreman's Yard (misspelled as "Forman" here), the original junkyard. There's a book on the French revolution in the science lab, because that was the book that Susan borrowed from Barbara in the first story (it's now missing the dust jacket). The Doctor is known to the funeral director as an old man with white hair (the first Doctor), while the vicar notes that the Doctor's voice has changed, to which he replies, "Several times." The Doctor calls the group captain "Brigadier," a reference to Brigadier Lethbridge-Stewart. Rachel Jensen's look, dress and hairstyle echo Barbara Wright's.

The Daleks are described as the mutated remains of a species called Kaleds, which was established in "Genesis of the Daleks." The Doctor tells Ace they conquered Earth in the 22nd century, something we saw in 1964's "The Dalek Invasion of Earth." An Emperor Dalek previously appeared in 1967's "The Evil of the Daleks," although this one's design owes more to the one popularized in the 1960s *TV Century 21* comics. Daleks have time-corridor technology, as seen in 1984's "Resurrection of the Daleks." Davros asks the Doctor to have pity on him, echoing "Genesis of the Daleks."

The Doctor mentions the Zygon Gambit with the Loch Ness monster (1975's "Terror of the Zygons") — yes, this is the same Loch Ness monster Sarah refers to in 2006's "School Reunion" — and Yetis in the Underground (1968's "The Web of Fear"). He refers to a machine he rigged on Spiridon (1973's "Planet of the Daleks").

Reference is made to a Gallifreyan stellar engineer named Omega, seen in 1972's "The Three Doctors." Rassilon is also mentioned ("The Deadly Assassin," "The Five Doctors"). The Doctor introduces himself as president-elect of the Time Lords, something that occurred in "The Five Doctors," although his title was revoked in 1986's "The Trial of a Time Lord."

Who is the Doctor? The Doctor hints that he may been involved with the prototype Hand in the old times of Gallifrey, part of the new character backstory. He introduces himself as president-elect of the high council of Time Lords, keeper of the legacy of Rassilon and defender of the laws of time. He's much more proactive than he's ever been in the past, putting events into motion to destroy the Daleks, although he doesn't count on two Dalek factions turning up. He programs the Hand of Omega in advance and destroys Skaro, committing an act of genocide.

His calling card has a stylized question mark and Old High Gallifreyan symbols on it. After destroying the baseball bat, he declares, "Weapons: always useless in the end." He carries currency for 1963.

Companion Chronicles Ace flirts with Mike, who asks her out, but she's heartbroken when he turns out to be a traitor. As soon as the little girl collapses, Ace is immediately nurturing. She's ultimately unsure whether the Doctor acted correctly or not.

Monster of the Week Two opposing forces of Daleks, one traditional, the other mutated. Renegade Daleks are underdeveloped, with vestigial limbs, almost amoeboid. Imperial Daleks have functional appendages and a mechanical prosthesis grafted into their bodies. One of the

Imperial Daleks is a Special Weapons Dalek, which has a single enormous weapon that can blow multiple Daleks away in one shot.

Stand Up and Cheer There are so many contenders for this that it's honestly hard to choose. We could have chosen the scene of the Dalek rising up the stairs. Or the Doctor sitting in the café pondering his actions. Or Ace facing down three Daleks with nothing but a baseball bat. Or the reveal of the helmeted figure. Or the Doctor tricking Davros into destroying Skaro. But, despite how incredible those scenes, and many more, are, we're going to choose the scene of the Doctor walking into a confrontation with the Black Dalek alone . . . and talking it to death. Holy mother of Rassilon.

Roll Your Eyes The headmaster apparently knees Ace in the groin. Even more surprisingly, this seems to incapacitate her the same way it would a man. Is there something she's not telling the Doctor?

You're Not Making Any Sense Ratcliffe stands very close to the Dalek battle computer on multiple occasions yet singularly fails to notice that it's a small girl wearing a helmet.

Interesting Trivia "Remembrance of the Daleks" features the series' first deliberate retcon as it's revealed that the first Doctor was actually burying a Gallifreyan weapon of mass destruction when he was visiting 1963 London in "An Unearthly Child." The series had been full of "soft" retcons before this (such as changing the dates when UNIT stories were set, or changing the Daleks' origins), but this is the first time that a completely new motivation is imbued to the Doctor in a past story.

During our discussion of "Genesis of the Daleks," we described how Russell T Davies suggested the New Series' Time War had its starting point with the Time Lords sending the Doctor on a mission to stop the Daleks' creation and that 1984's "Resurrection of the Daleks" might be seen as an escalation of that war. Here, in "Remembrance of the Daleks," the Doctor himself engineers the destruction of Skaro, which could easily be seen as the tipping point for the Time War. In which case, the Doctor is responsible for the war's start, as well as its end.

At one point, Ace watches a BBC TV broadcast that announces the time as a quarter past five and promises "an adventure in the new science-fiction TV series, *Doc—*" before cutting to the next scene. It's a cute moment, suggesting that the date is November 23, 1963, and she's just missed the very first broadcast of *Doctor Who*. Except it can't be

5:15 p.m., the actual time of the first broadcast, because it's explicitly stated that it's still morning.

While filming the Dalek shootout, the special effects were so loud that local residents thought an IRA bomb had exploded. Car alarms were set off, and emergency services that had been called in response were bemused to find themselves confronted with Daleks.

When the head of drama, Mark Shivas, was screening the episode before production, he took a phone call during the "No Coloureds" scene. Script editor Andrew Cartmel was annoyed that Shivas had missed the scene and so requested that it be rewound, something that Simply Wasn't Done. Upon rewatching the scene, Shivas agreed that it was well done, but thought that Ace should have ripped up the sign.

There are a number of deleted scenes on the DVD, most of which are just trimmed for time, as the episodes overran. However, one is quite famous: during the Doctor's confrontation with Davros, Davros says, "In the end, you are just another Time Lord," to which the Doctor replies, "Oh, Davros. I am far more than just another Time Lord." It appears this scene was cut for artistic, rather than timing, reasons, presumably to keep the information about the Doctor's backstory to hints.

The TARDIS Chronometer Shoreditch, London, 1963, and a Dalek spaceship in geostationary orbit.

Wicked? (RS?) Throughout this journey of 50 *Doctor Who* stories to watch before we die, I've seen some absolutely stupendous television. I've gained new appreciation for stories I already loved, seen the joys of other episodes I'd only half-heartedly enjoyed previously and suffered through a few stinkers along the way (my co-author has eccentric taste). But what I haven't found is The One. The *Doctor Who* story that I can point to as easily my favourite, the one that surpasses all others, even among the legions of greats that this book offers up.

Until now.

Don't get me wrong, I've always loved "Remembrance." And Sylvester McCoy, that quirky clown with an edge of steel, is probably my favourite Doctor, all things being equal. He's the one who was on TV when I was a teenager, which is pretty much the same thing. But having watched the highlights of *Doctor Who* in rapid succession, "Remembrance" blew me away.

It's hard to pinpoint exactly what it is that makes "Remembrance" so good. It might be the rich characters: Group Captain "Chunky"

Gilmore, sardonic Rachel Jensen, love-interest and traitor Mike Smith, and Ratcliffe, with his five-pointed star badge that screams fascism, are all well developed with rich inner lives. You feel as though you know these people. Even the minor characters — Harry, John, Martin the undertaker, the blind reverend, the headmaster, the girl at the gate — feel meaty. Only Allison Williams isn't properly developed, but one failure among so many successes just shows how much better this story is at characterization than most.

It might be the shock moments. The story's full of them: a Dalek going up stairs; the discovery that it's the Doctor himself who set these events in motion; the Dalek battle computer turning out not to be Davros, as you might expect, but rather the girl; Davros actually appearing after all, but as the emperor; Skaro's destruction. Any one of these would be the "wow" moment of a lesser story, but here they're all packed in together. It's incredible.

It might be the regulars. Sophie Aldred hits the ground running, making Ace loud, flirty, secretive and compassionate, all at once. But it's Sylvester McCoy who's the real revelation, playing the Doctor darker than we've ever imagined and bringing a grim edge to the role. For once, the Doctor actually has character development and McCoy is superb in bringing it to the surface.

It might be the clever editing. The TV announcement of what appears to be *Doctor Who* cuts to a teletype machine, while a Dalek fires straight into the camera, making you flinch. Elements like these make the story move like greased lightning. Even better, the Doctor saying he may have miscalculated in the third cliffhanger isn't present in the reprise, suggesting that perhaps this didn't "really" happen and instead we're privy to his own thoughts (the elongated pause in the drama only accentuates this effect).

It might be the theme of racial purity. Ratcliffe believes England fought on the wrong side in World War II and was imprisoned when he spoke out. The (incredibly brave) "No Coloureds" sign in Mike's mother's boarding house speaks volumes about the offhand racism of the '60s without a single line of dialogue. Mike sells out his friends to Ratcliffe because he wants to keep the outsiders out, so his own people can have a fair chance. And all this is contrasted with two Dalek species at war over genetic differences. That's a brilliant analogy, the natural outgrowth of where the Daleks started. *Doctor Who* has never been better.

Or it might be the sugar scene. Late at night, alone in a café, two men have a discussion about sugar. Faced with a momentous decision to destroy Skaro — a mirror image of his aborted decision to wipe out the Daleks in "Genesis of the Daleks" — the Doctor pauses to consider the implications of his plan. What makes this brilliant is that John has absolutely no idea of the ramifications of what he's saying. Where the Doctor talks about decisions having ripples and agonizes about what he's about to do, John simply says, "Life's like that; best thing is to just get on with it." John thus plays a small but crucial part in the fate of billions, without any clue that the man he's talking to is far more powerful than he could possibly imagine. A powerful magician comes to Earth and asks an ordinary Joe to unwittingly help him decide the fate of gods? This is the stuff of fairytales.

However, I think I have an idea of what it might be that makes "Remembrance" so great, even among the greats of *Doctor Who*. It's a story that begins in a junkyard. It features a small, nondescript man fighting the ultimate embodiment of evil. He's aided by the military, even if he doesn't always agree with them. The military's scientific advisor proves open-minded to his proposals. His companion keeps him honest, fighting alongside him but displaying compassion for individuals that keeps him grounded. And he defeats evil, not by picking up a gun, but through words and trickery.

"Remembrance of the Daleks" deconstructs *Doctor Who* in its entirety. Not to poke fun at it or to act superior, but rather because it wants to take it apart to see what made it so great in the first place. And then it puts it back together and the result is even better than what came before. Oh, and the title is brilliant.

Choosing a favourite *Doctor Who* story is a bit like choosing a favourite sibling. You shouldn't really do it, but everyone has one anyway. "Remembrance" is mine. I'd apologize to all the other stories, but "Remembrance" is so good that somehow I think they'd understand . . .

Second Opinion (GB) Once upon a time, Daleks were outer-space foes from the future. *Doctor Who* adventures featuring the pepperpots took place in rock quarries or on sets in the BBC Television Centre with electric sliding doors. There were tantalizing hints of the fun that could happen if you put the Daleks in the world of the present, but it wasn't until *Doctor Who*'s 25th anniversary that someone had the stroke of genius of doing what every schoolkid had done since 1963: have the metal monsters exterminating humans on London city streets for 100 minutes. And, just for good measure, they climbed stairs as well.

If this sounds familiar, it's because pretty much all of the Daleks' appearances in the New Series have been in familiar, earthy surroundings. What "Remembrance of the Daleks" did, though, was a good deal cleverer: it had the Daleks come to near-contemporary London and then showed the uncomfortable parallels humans have with Daleks. Ben Aaronovitch had the "Aha!" moment of realizing that, since the Daleks are a metaphor for Naziism, you could make that the theme of the story by having the Daleks in the middle of an ethnic-cleansing civil war, and by setting it in the early '60s with its casual racism, where a Dalek faction is backed by a fascist organization. Making the metaphor behind the Daleks overt adds dramatic weight and poignance to the piece.

And then there's the radical reformatting of *Doctor Who* that's snuck into it, starting with the retcon of "An Unearthly Child." Referencing the first *Doctor Who* story actually works well: you don't have to have seen "An Unearthly Child" to get it and there are lots of lovely grace notes for those who have. But the Doctor's past involvement with the Hand of Omega, and the fact he knows the objectives of each Dalek faction — and will use that knowledge to destroy them — is a serious change to the status quo. Throw in the asides where the Doctor places himself as a contemporary of Rassilon and suddenly the Doctor has been made into a very different character.

When a main character knows the outcome of everything, the whole shape of the story could be thrown off dramatically, as effectively there are two episodes of stalling. Fortunately, the Dalek civil war and the intrigues of the Association hide this because it requires the Doctor and Ace to get intelligence and put themselves in jeopardy. Plus, it has lots of Daleks roaming Shoreditch and blowing things up. (And the Daleks are once again menacing, which is always a bonus.)

Sylvester McCoy is enjoying the chance to do something dramatically interesting with the Doctor, though at times he looks a little too amused with himself. The scene in the café, where he wrestles with the implications of his actions (in precisely the way — I'm sorry, dear co-author — the Doctor didn't really do in "Genesis of the Daleks") is beautifully played for its subtlety and world-weary sadness. And Sophie Aldred is wonderful as she takes Ace through her first proper adventure with wide-eyed wonder, plucky courage and heartfelt vulnerability. The supporting cast is fantastic: Simon Williams and Pamela Salem exceed expectations (the latter deserves an award for making observations so dry they practically turn to dust). The only disappointing performance is Dursley McLinden as Mike Smith who, bless him, is simply too sweet and cuddly to be convincing as either a butch military man or a racist dupe.

"Remembrance of the Daleks" is an incredible restatement of the series' ethos and the start of a fascinating experiment with the lead character that still echoes even today. But it's also unfailingly crowd-pleasing in that it gives us Daleks, and lots of action and excitement. It's the jewel in the crown of *Doctor Who* in the 1980s. Or any era, for that matter.

Sylvester McCoy

Sylvester McCoy was born Percy James Patrick Kent-Smith in 1943 to an Irish mother and an English father. He grew up in Dunoon, Scotland, and was training to become a priest until, as he now wryly states, he discovered girls.

By the mid-1960s, McCoy was working in the insurance industry while exploring the underground scene in London. McCoy wound up working in the box office of the Roundhouse, a venue for up-and-coming British music acts. (At one point, the diminutive McCoy was drafted into acting as bouncer for a gig with the Rolling Stones!)

It was during this time that comedian and experimental-theatre maven Ken Campbell discovered McCoy and recruited him to join his act, the Ken Campbell Roadshow. (Other compatriots in Campbell's show included a young Bob Hoskins.) McCoy's specialty in Campbell's roadshow was stunt acting. Playing a character called "Sylveste McCoy," he would hammer nails up his nose and, famously, stuff a ferret in his trousers (some of this act was captured in the 1979 film *The Secret Policeman's Ball*). It was this character that McCoy adopted for his stage name, adding the "r" to avoid a name with 13 letters.

From this experience, McCoy moved to more legitimate theatre and eventually television, appearing in the children's series *Tiswas* and *Vision On!* His theatrical work was acclaimed and even more versatile, appearing as Buster Keaton and Stan Laurel in separate one-man plays and then at a 1986 National Theatre production of *The Pied Piper* as the titular character — a part written specifically for McCoy. It was while he was in this play that

McCoy heard of Colin Baker's departure as the Doctor and immediately put his name forward.

Producer John Nathan-Turner liked the actor's eccentricity and lobbied for him to play the role. (Once cast, Nathan-Turner insisted McCoy's Doctor wear the hat he wore to his meetings with the producer.) The actor arguably had more influence on the role than any actor previously in the part and made suggestions ranging from carrying an umbrella (and then making the umbrella handle question-mark shaped) to playing the Doctor with a darkness that was based on the sadness he saw in his 100-year-old grandmother.

After *Doctor Who* went off the air, McCoy mostly kept busy in the theatre, playing in everything from Gilbert and Sullivan to Molière to Christmas pantomime — most notably playing the Fool in an acclaimed 2007 production of *King Lear* opposite Ian McKellan, which toured extensively and was filmed for television. In the early 2000s, McCoy auditioned for the role of Bilbo Baggins in Peter Jackson's adaptation of *The Lord of the Rings* trilogy but lost out to Ian Holm. Peter Jackson, a longtime *Doctor Who* fan, stayed in contact with McCoy over the years and eventually cast him as Radagast in the 2012–2014 trilogy of films based on *The Hobbit*.

McCoy has returned several times to play the Doctor, most notably in the 1996 TV Movie, which saw his Doctor killed off to regenerate into a new incarnation played by Paul McGann. (McCoy brought the same hat he wore as the Doctor to wear in the TV Movie.) Since 1999, he has been recording new adventures of the seventh Doctor in audios produced by Big Finish Productions.

The Happiness Patrol (1988)

Written by Graeme Curry **Directed by** Chris Clough

Featuring Sylvester McCoy (The Doctor), Sophie Aldred (Ace)

Supporting cast Sheila Hancock (Helen A); Ronald Fraser (Joseph C); Georgina Hale (Daisy K); Harold Innocent (Gilbert M); Lesley Dunlop (Susan Q); Rachel Bell (Priscilla P); Jonathan Burn (Silas P); Tim Barker (Harold V); John Normington (Trevor Sigma); Richard D. Sharp (Earl Sigma); David John Pope (Kandy Man); Philip Neve (Wences); Ryan Freedman (Wulfric); Steve Swinscoe, Marc Caroll (snipers)

Original airdates November 2, 9, 16, 1988

The Big Idea Ignorance is strength. War is peace. Happiness will prevail.

Roots and References The Thatcher government (Helen A and Joseph C); the Pinochet dictatorship (the disappearances); the British miners' strike of the mid-'80s (calling on the drones to down their tools and revolt); *Nineteen Eighty-Four* (running a dystopian future by altering language); *Charlie and the Chocolate Factory* (the Kandy Kitchen). The Doctor sings "As Time Goes By."

Time And Relative Dimensions In Space When incoming script editor Andrew Cartmel was being interviewed for his position in 1986, producer John Nathan-Turner asked him what he'd like to accomplish as script editor of *Doctor Who*. His response: "Overthrow the government."

Cartmel never quite got his wish — Margaret Thatcher's reign as Britain's prime minister outlasted *Doctor Who* by nearly a year — but he at least had the opportunity to take a shot at it, thanks to a writer named Graeme Curry, who came to Cartmel's attention after Curry had placed first in a scriptwriting competition. Cartmel invited Curry to pitch several stories, none of which were successful, until Curry suggested an adventure on a planet where unhappy people are persecuted. Curry was interested in satirizing what he saw as the Americanization of society: theme parks, fast-food outlets, being told to have a nice day. He was also a professional musician, who detested the preponderance of Muzak. He and Cartmel developed Terra Alpha as a society with a number of parallels to Thatcher's Britain. When actress Sheila Hancock read the script, she saw that Helen A was a parody of Margaret Thatcher and took the satire even further in her performance.

Adventures in Time and Space The Doctor mentions the Brigadier seeing a triceratops in the London Underground (1974's "Invasion of the Dinosaurs"). He also says that his nickname at college was Theta Sigma (1979's "The Armageddon Factor"). The Doctor plays the spoons, a talent he first demonstrated in 1987's "Time and the Rani."

Who is the Doctor? He continues his proactive involvement, here having deliberately travelled to Terra Alpha because he heard disturbing rumours of what was happening. He flexes his muscles here by bringing down the government in a single night. He loves the blues and can't resist singing "As Time Goes By" into an open mic. He also plays the spoons, something of a trademark for the seventh incarnation.

Companion Chronicles Ace is prone to angry outbursts, but the Doctor has a calming influence on her, telling her that she's no use to him like this. She claims Ace is her real name, even though we learned in 1987's "Dragonfire" that her real name is Dorothy. She loves dinosaurs and hates lift music. She can't play an instrument, can't dance and can't sing, although she briefly tries playing the spoons (badly).

Monster of the Week The Kandy Man is a robot made out of sweets — caramel, sherbet, toffee, marzipan, gelling agents — but perfectly adapted to his environment. He can't handle heat and gets stuck to the floor by lemonade but can be released by fire retardant. He was made by Gilbert M in the Kandy Kitchen, although the original robotic form hails from Vasilip.

Stand Up and Cheer Two snipers are on a balcony, one a reluctant jobsworth, the other a gun fanatic, eager to shoot demonstrators. And then the Doctor arrives, weaponless, and talks them out of it by inviting the fanatic to shoot him, because that's what guns are for. Life killing life. Every single moment of this scene, from the dialogue — "Look me in the eye, pull the trigger, end my life" — to the fact that the Doctor's in a hurry to get to the Kandy Kitchen and is mildly irritated at the delay, is a manifesto for *Doctor Who* itself.

Roll Your Eyes The Go-karts are slow. Embarrassingly slow. This might have been okay if the point was made that being in them somehow safeguarded the occupant from danger, following the bizarre logic of Terra Alpha. But it isn't.

You're Not Making Any Sense Trevor Sigma apparently conducts a planetary census every six months by going around the entire planet and asking everyone their names. And yet this method somehow produces an enormous list of the disappeared.

Interesting Trivia You might notice that the sets don't quite reflect the happiness that's supposedly mandatory on Terra Alpha. There are two reasons for this. One is that this story was made on a shoestring budget. It was planned as a story confined to the studio, but overspending on "Remembrance of the Daleks" ate into the budget and this was the result. The other reason is artistic: the production team felt that the obligatory happiness imposed by Helen A would be best contrasted by a society on the verge of falling apart. Notice in particular the '60s-style props, such as the flashing light bulb for communication and the old-style telephone in the Kandy Kitchen. These signify a society in transition, but have the advantage of being incredibly cheap for the production.

Richard D. Sharp (Earl Sigma) couldn't play the harmonica, so he just mimed what he thought was a good approximation. Subsequently, incidental music composer Dominic Glynn wrote a score based on what Sharp appeared to be doing. Glynn then worked this into the non-diegetic incidental music, so that the blues permeated the story.

The Kandy Man was originally intended to be a much more human-looking figure, wearing a lab coat, with the idea that he was made out of sweets kept fairly subtle. However, producer John Nathan-Turner and director Chris Clough decided to emphasize both his robotic nature and also his candy-coated body by designing a walking liquorice allsort. Unfortunately, the character as realized strongly resembled Bertie Bassett, the mascot for Bassett's Liquorice Allsorts. Bassett's was displeased that a character similar to theirs was a villain, so their CEO wrote a strongly worded letter to the BBC. After an internal investigation, the BBC concluded that no copyright violation had occurred but wrote back to assure them that the Kandy Man would not be returning to *Doctor Who*.

The TARDIS Chronometer Terra Alpha, the future.

Wicked? (RS?) OMG, this is, like . . . so gay. No, really: "The Happiness Patrol" is very, very gay.

Back in the '90s, the idea that there were gay undertones to this story was incredibly controversial. People were offended that *Doctor Who* might be pushing a gay agenda and thus went to enormous lengths to prove or disprove its orientation. It happened on both sides: advocates for its gayness swore that the first victim of the fondant surprise wore a pink triangle on his shirt (he doesn't, as DVD freezeframing makes clear; it's just the way his collar falls), while those against were convinced that there was nothing at all suggestive about Joseph C leaving his wife and running off with another man.

So what if Gilbert M and the Kandy Man squabble like lovers? ("And what time do you call this?" "He's terrible when he's roused. They don't know his moods.") Or if Joseph C is the very picture of an ageing queen? No, sirree, this is as straight a story as they come. Butch and macho, just like the rest of *Doctor Who*, its fans, its producers, you name it. Rawr. How about that local sports team, eh?

Part of the gayness is simply the story's campness. It's not exactly "The Seeds of Doom," is it? Very little seems realistic, from the sets and the staged acting to the drag-queen look of the Happiness Patrol. What we're seeing isn't *Doctor Who* that's normative, but a story that's different, quirky and determined to do its own thing, no matter what. And if it isn't to the mainstream's taste? Well, too bad because it's here, it's proud and it's not going to make things easy just because that's what people expect.

The big picture really comes with the society itself. Terra Alpha is a place where the rules are rigidly enforced. In this case, the rule is happiness. There are no prisons, just the waiting zone, because prisons are depressing places. Wearing dark clothes, listening to slow music, reading poems or walking in the rain without an umbrella are all verboten. And don't even think about protesting.

Susan Q, former member of the Happiness Patrol herself, outlines the theme: she woke up one morning and realized she was sick of trying to pretend she was something she wasn't. Her peers ostracize her for not fitting in: she never had the right attitude, never joined in, wasn't part of the team. For every kid who was picked last, gay or not, this cuts straight to the heart.

And "The Happiness Patrol" is extremely interested in society: what defines one, how one functions and whether its disparate elements can coexist. Yes, it's a strange society, where unhappy people are persecuted, but, once you accept it, the logic is impeccable. It also feels dangerous: Earl Sigma playing the blues on his harmonica and then switching to an upbeat melody when the patrol passes by is a clear indication of just how risky individual behaviour can be in this world. Say the wrong thing or think the wrong way and you'll disappear. For the greater good, of course.

It's no secret that this was based on Thatcherism ("Families are very important for people's happiness"), but where "The Happiness Patrol" succeeds is that its parody is broader than that. It's using the apparent charms of a modern democracy — entertainment, media, laws, the well-being of its citizens — to show how a dictatorship can form even when it doesn't outwardly resemble one. Things such as demonstrations or strikes are frowned upon or outlawed. Protestors wear masks to conceal their identities. Surely the stuff of wacky science fiction or an oppressive Third World regime, not something you can imagine in a modern civilized society. Right?

And, when confronted, Helen A insists that the disappearances and the punishments weren't there at first. This is a well-intentioned society whose road to hell is almost completely paved.

Faced with a society that's overwhelmingly oppressive, what do you do if you don't fit in? Why, you rebel, just a little. You don't quite conform. Even if it means talking to strange men on park benches, always knowing they could be the police, just waiting to entrap you. And yet, you do it anyway, because you can't hide who you are, no matter the risks.

Doctor Who isn't just a TV show that's trying to be good and sometimes failing. It's also a show that can be infinitely diverse. Can you imagine two more different stories shown back to back than "Remembrance of the Daleks" and "The Happiness Patrol"? We're often told that the only limit to *Doctor Who* is the imagination, but — for entirely sensible reasons — we so rarely see that in action. "The Happiness Patrol" is a story that's experimental, brave, fabulous and never quite able to fit in.

When we were assembling this book, we had a lot of discussions about which stories to include. We always knew that we wanted to push the envelope a bit, not just have a predictable list of 50 great stories. Along the way, we revised our list a few times. Every time we did, "The Happiness Patrol" almost fell off the list. But it never quite left it.

There are doubtless many people who are wondering why this story is here. It doesn't have sterling production values. The direction is flatter than it should be. The Pipe People are one element too many. It should have ended with Helen A crying rather than the final scene. But it's still a story you absolutely should watch. Because "The Happiness Patrol" represents something far more important than yet another high-quality adventure. It has something to say and it's determined to make you listen. If it has to put on a pink wig and white face paint to do so, then all the better that you pay it some attention. Once it was afraid, it was petrified. It kept thinking it could never live without you by its side —

Hang on, that's not right. But what the hell. Why do what everyone else does?

It all seems rather obvious now, in these more enlightened times. Yes, "The Happiness Patrol" is kinda gay . . . but so what?

Second Opinion (GB) I don't particularly care whether or not "The Happiness Patrol" is gay. With all due respect to my co-author, we might as well be proclaiming that "The Happiness Patrol" is mahogany. It's so pointless. The sorts of things that apparently make it gay — the subtextual relationships between characters, the camp production values — can be said of many, many other *Doctor Who* stories in the Classic Series.

What I care about is whether it's good or not. And I just don't think "The Happiness Patrol" is particularly good.

Don't get me wrong. I love the basic concept. I marvel at the deftness of the themes. The attempt at Swiftian satire with a world where it's a crime to be unhappy is sharp and incisive at times. But the execution is botched. Badly.

I don't place the blame on Graeme Curry here. (At least, not entirely. The "planet ruled by women" trope? Really?) Andrew Cartmel is welcome to attempt to bring down the government through a pre-watershed science-fiction show, and I think his vision for the series is incredible, but how about demonstrating the core competency of actually editing a script to length? The structure of the story is incompetently handled. There's too much going on for three 24-minute episodes of television: too many subplots (stopping the sniper is a cool moment, but it does nothing but take up time), too many characters (there was no need for Trevor Sigma), too many levels of society (the elites, the elite's enforcers, the underclass, the under-underclass . . . it's like a Russian novel). There's too much useless running around. There are way too many scenes with the Kandy Man getting caught in the same trap again and again. The result is a mish-mash. Ace and Susan Q are suddenly BFFs and I didn't even know who the hell she was talking to; the character hasn't even been established in any way. The DVD special features show us several deleted scenes that almost mitigate that, but they were cut because everything so badly overran. (Yes, it was even *more* needlessly complicated!) It's utterly inept.

As bad as the script is, the realization onscreen is worse. The math is clear on this: contrived premise + contrived setting = total lack of believability. It's crying to be taken outside the studio.

During pre-production, there was talk of shooting it in Portmeirion, where they made *The Prisoner*, but there are plenty of banal but soulless examples of modernism in and around London in 1988 that would have been perfect. It really needed more realism to sell the outlandish prospect. Instead, we get more artifice: the Kandy Man should be something horrific instead of an (admittedly brilliantly realized) cartoon.

Chris Clough's non-existent direction doesn't help, nor does the fact that the story has been edited to the point of being a non-sequitur. Never mind Ace and Susan Q suddenly being best pals, the Pipe People and the Griefs are no more than afterthoughts. The cast is sleepwalking, Sylvester McCoy overacts and badly. (I think "Pull the trigger, end my life" could have been a great scene. It's a shame McCoy chews the balcony scenery.) The only one making an actual effort is Sheila Hancock, who is thrilled to be doing a Thatcher impression and knocks it out of the park.

This story was Robert's choice and he's right that it nearly got voted out of the lineup. I really wish it had. There are much more effective political satires showing the Doctor toppling regimes in a matter of hours (check out 1977's "The Sun Makers" by Robert Holmes some time). This is cheap, ham-fisted and ineffective. No joy here.

Ghost Light (1989)

Written by Marc Platt **Directed by** Alan Wareing

Featuring Sylvester McCoy (The Doctor), Sophie Aldred (Ace)

Supporting cast Ian Hogg (Josiah), Michael Cochrane (Redvers Fenn-Cooper), Carl Forgione (Nimrod), Sharon Duce (Control), John Nettleton (Reverend Ernest Matthews), Katharine Schlesinger (Gwendoline), Frank Windsor (Inspector MacKenzie), Brenda Kempner (Mrs. Grose), Sylvia Sims (Mrs. Pritchard), John Hallam (Light)

Original airdates October 4, 11, 18, 1989

The Big Idea Something haunts a house in Perivale in the nineteenth century. But what does it have to do with Ace?

Roots and References *The Turn of the Screw* (Mrs. Grose); Stanley's search for Dr. Livingstone (Redvers's quest); William Blake's poem "The Tyger" ("Light burning bright"); Sir Arthur Conan Doyle (Redvers's tale of giant lizards in Africa references *The Lost World* and Sherlock Holmes is mentioned); *Pygmalion* (the Doctor calls Ace "Eliza," Control becoming ladylike); H. Rider Haggard's 1885 novel *King Solomon's Mines* (Redvers); the works of Lewis Carroll (bandersnatches and slithy toves, Gwendoline calls Ace "Alice," and there's a reference to going down the rabbit hole); *Heart of Darkness* (Redvers's story); the nursery rhyme "Oranges and Lemons" ("Here is a candle to light you to bed"); The Beatles ("He's had a hard day's night"); *The Hitchhiker's Guide to the Galaxy* ("Earthmen never invite their ancestors around to dinner");

the Bible ("Let there be light"); the 1967 BBC series *The Forsyte Saga* ("I'm a man of property"); *Blackadder* (a catalogue of missing imaginary items). Gwendoline sings the 1883 J.F. Mitchell song "That's the Way to the Zoo"; the Doctor hums "Rule Britannia."

Time And Relative Dimensions In Space Marc Platt was a *Doctor Who* fan who worked at the BBC in its music library. He'd submitted several script ideas to the production department over the years and had been deemed promising by Robert Holmes. In the late '80s, Platt submitted a story called "Cat's Cradle," involving the TARDIS splintering and creating a whole world, which script editor Andrew Cartmel liked, but he knew the production team couldn't afford to do it.

Platt then proposed a story called "Lungbarrow," about the Doctor facing his greatest fear. In it, the Doctor would have returned to his old house on Gallifrey and faced his family of cousins. (Both "Cat's Cradle" and "Lungbarrow" were later turned into novels as part of the New Adventures range in the '90s.) Producer John Nathan-Turner disliked "Lungbarrow," feeling it revealed too much about the Doctor's origins. Consequently, after discussions with Cartmel, Platt decided to retain the mansion but focus on Ace's greatest fear instead.

Adventures in Time and Space The Doctor recognizes a Chinese firing piece ("The Talons of Weng-Chiang"). Ace asks if there's a blacksmith on the village green, a reference to something the Doctor said at the end of 1987's "Dragonfire."

Who is the Doctor? The Doctor brings Ace to the house as a surprise, although it's really to force her to face her fears. He's a fellow of the Royal Geographic Society. He carries a Geiger counter and the fang of a cave bear. He can't stand burnt toast and loathes bus stations, unrequited love, tyranny and cruelty. He's not interested in money. As things get out of hand, he laments that even he can't play this many games at once.

Companion Chronicles Ace can't stand dead things. She has a thing about haunted houses. Traumatized by her best friend's flat being firebombed by racists when she was 13, she went to Gabriel Chase in 1983 and burned the place to the ground. When creatures come to life in the house, Ace re-experiences her fears viscerally, even hearing police sirens.

Monster of the Week A creature called Light takes human form when on Earth. He came to survey life on Earth, but his stone spaceship crashed. Light spent centuries cataloguing species, including taking Nimrod as the last specimen of Neanderthals. He can turn people to stone or reduce them to their constituent acids. Light can travel at the speed of thought but has little imagination.

Stand Up and Cheer The dinner scene starts with the Doctor aware that he's walking into a trap, reveals Ace's big secret, explains Josiah's plan, is the pivot between Josiah's dominance and Control's, has Inspector MacKenzie turned into primordial soup and ends with the Doctor outwitting Light via wordplay. In terms of things accomplished per minute, this might well be the most adroit scene in all of *Doctor Who*.

Roll Your Eyes Two episodes' worth of buildup for the most terrifying creature imaginable reveal . . . a butch bloke putting on a girly voice.

You're Not Making Any Sense The husks are supposed to represent earlier forms of Josiah's evolution, one a reptile and the other an insect, but evolution doesn't work like that. And why does Josiah keep them around anyway?

Interesting Trivia The relationship between Light, Josiah and Control needs a bit of unpacking. Essentially, Light is the scientist, investigating the concept of evolution. As with all scientific experiments, a concept is examined in two ways: by testing a hypothesis and comparing that to the situation when the test was not present. The former is the survey and the latter is the control. In this case, Josiah is the survey: he was sent out into the world to evolve, so that Light could understand how evolution works. Meanwhile, Control was kept behind, unchanging, so that Light would have something to compare the results to.

This was the last story made in the Classic Series. The last scene shot was the one of Mrs. Pritchard and Gwendoline turning to stone. However, the running order from the season was switched around and it was decided that the more thoughtful "Ghost Light" should be sandwiched by two four-part action stories, 1989's "Battlefield" and "The Curse of Fenric." After the running order of the previous season had changed at short notice, the stories from this season were designed to be thematically related, but so that they could be shown in any order.

Ratings for the season were unfortunately dismal. There was little promotion for the new season before it started. So little that John Nathan-Turner arranged a publicity event mid-season. This (and some positive notices in the press) helped get the series some notice and the ratings increased. However, the show was being screened opposite *Coronation Street*, a hugely popular soap opera. Furthermore, only the primary television set in a household was counted in the ratings; if a show was watched on a secondary television or videotaped and watched later, these viewings were not counted. It's not possible to know how well *Doctor Who* might have done if they had been, but it's exactly the sort of show that lent itself to this sort of thing.

The TARDIS Chronometer Gabriel Chase, Perivale, 1883.

Wicked? (RS?) *Episode 1: Hypnosis*

"Ghost Light" is a story of control. Everyone is exerting control over someone or having it exerted over them. From the very first scene, the silent, gliding maids and Mrs. Pritchard ignore the Doctor's presence entirely. Josiah imprisons Control, Redvers is controlled by his madness, Ace's fear dictates her actions and the Doctor uses the fang of the cave bear to gain power over Nimrod. Mrs. Pritchard and Gwendoline are explicitly said to be Josiah's toys, and the maids come out of the woodwork when the clock strikes six, even when the Doctor adjusts it. The entire affair is referred to as a puppet show.

And so much of this control is done through hypnosis. Light has clear telekinetic powers, controlling others through mental energy. He briefly controls Ace, then the Doctor resists. Control has power over the husks, even remotely, while the ending sees Josiah lose his self-control.

Despite this, the message is clear that morality still matters. Even though Gwendoline was hypnotized, as Redvers explicitly says, the fact that she enjoyed sending people to Java so much is what finally damns her.

Episode 2: Puns

"Ghost Light" is a story of puns. The dialogue is layered and witty, full of puns both clever and groan-worthy. Josiah sounds husky, Nimrod is out like a light and things get out of control. When Gwendoline changes her clothes, Josiah announces, "This is a metamorphosis!" The Reverend Ernest Matthews, upon seeing Josiah and Gwendoline cuddling, says, "You're no better than animals," despite the fact that he himself is at that moment becoming a monkey.

References to Victorian literature abound, as the dialogue mixes quotes with puns on light, change and control. ("It's now time to shed a little light on your plans.") When Nimrod is absent, he's "gone to see a man about a god." When offered a thousand pounds to assassinate Josiah's enemy, the Doctor says, "Now that's what I call Victorian value."

Josiah's role in Light's experiment is explained by the line "The survey got out of control." And when the spaceship is about to depart at the story's conclusion, the Doctor announces, "You're busy, must fly."

But the puns aren't just decorative. Sometimes they're nasty as well. When Inspector MacKenzie is turned into amino acids and served for dinner, the jokes about primordial soup are bad enough. However, the line "The cream of Scotland Yard!" is just devastating. It's not just verbal puns either: Control threatening to burn the invitation to Buckingham Palace provides the visual association that Ace makes with having burned down Gabriel Chase in the future.

And ultimately, the Doctor uses wordplay and puns to defeat Light. Faced with an abhorrence of evolution, Light learns that he himself evolves thanks to multiple puns on the word "change." The Doctor assails Light with these, from changing his position to changing his mind; when Light begs him to stop, the Doctor says it would make a change.

The net effect of this is that the story is fractal: the more you look, the more you see. "Ghost Light" is a story that doesn't just reward multiple viewings, it demands them. This is *Doctor Who* made for the video age, which is both its strength and its weakness.

Episode 3: Evolution

"Ghost Light" is a story of evolution. The theme of evolving permeates almost every aspect of the story. There's Josiah's study of moths adapting to survive industry's smoke, Control learning to speak and the evolutionary husks. This is a mixture of Darwinian and social evolution, survival of the fittest meeting serendipitous mutation in a Victorian setting.

Meanwhile, Josiah and Control are two aspects of an experiment that got out of hand. He was the survey, sent out to experience evolution, while she was kept behind, as the experiment's control element. Fast forward several millennia and evolution has produced Josiah Samuel Smith, a man of property.

Evolution also happens in reverse. The Reverend Ernest Matthews devolves into an ape, while Inspector MacKenzie is reduced to his constituent elements. Even Ace seeing things come to life in the house causes her to revert to a teenager. And Josiah eventually regresses to a base creature, becoming Control's pet.

Josiah believes that if he assassinates Queen Victoria (the crowned

Saxe-Coburg), he'll assume her place. This isn't how the royal line of inheritance works, but it is how survival of the fittest does. He's like the ape that challenges the alpha male of the pack: win that fight and you get to be the alpha male yourself.

Light, on the other hand, abhors evolution. He's a dry recorder of facts, but when those facts won't stay constant he wants to change them. This too is an evolution, because the cataloguer starts off as an observer but ends as a catalyst of change.

And one of the key facets of evolution is time. The spaceship crashed millennia ago, the house has been under Josiah's dominion for years and Redvers has been hunting his prey for ages. Even the episode itself has a weird jump in time. At 5:30 a.m., Josiah goes upstairs to change, and Doctor says we won't see them until nightfall. Ace falls asleep, not waking for almost 12 hours. During this period, all sorts of changes take place: the Doctor wakes Inspector MacKenzie, bargains with Control and frees Redvers. The story evolves.

So what is "Ghost Light" really about? Well, I'm sure it'll all be explained in episode four . . .

Second Opinion (GB)

Dear Robert?,

Thank you for agreeing to write another book with me, which I've been very much enjoying. As you know, I share your love of *Doctor Who*, in all its formats. And I adore the Sylvester McCoy era. It's one of the boldest experiments in the history of television. Take a show flagging in the ratings, in public esteem and in support from the BBC and try any damn thing with it — even if it's counterintuitive to how *Doctor Who* is done and how television is made. When it works, it's breathtaking; when it fails, it's epic.

I mention all this because I want to ask you a question: Why on earth are we including this story in this book?

Okay, okay, I know part of the answer. The McCoy era is a time of bold innovation, of trying different modes of storytelling, of telling stories obliquely in a way that has to be watched more than once. It could be said to be a precursor for shows like *Lost* or even Steven Moffat–era *Doctor Who*.

But seriously, "Ghost Light"?! I know our selections are the 50 *Doctor Who* stories people *should* watch, as opposed to the best. I know that we chose the stories in a way that allowed individual selections by each author. And I know there have already been stories that might not be your favourites. But really? "Ghost Light"?

It's not that I don't see the story's good points. Ian Hogg is a superb villain. That's great. It's also witty, I'll give you that. The confrontation between the Doctor and Light is a superb distillation of everything that makes *Doctor Who* alluring. But in spite of Alan Wareing's direction, it's nothing more than a series of creepy set pieces without any cohesion.

You can argue all you like about the layers and make a cute joke about the lack of explanation, but, at the end of the day, it's a mess. It prides itself on being oblique and not explaining itself, putting the viewer on the back foot to figure things out. That's like being proud of one's ignorance. Things like the husks needed better explanations, *multiple* explanations, in fact. The characters of Control and Smith should have been far better established. The characters of Inspector Mackenzie and Reverend Matthews are completely extraneous (though Matthews at least has a funny comeuppance). The most important moment in episode two — where the Doctor makes the deal with Control — happens *offscreen*!

If you wanted an intellectually compelling, genre-busting McCoy story, why not "The Greatest Show in the Galaxy"? That's a great story! And, crucially, far more accessible, with funnier jokes, a better production and — thankfully — a plot that can be discerned without making the viewer feel stupid. I wish I'd thought of it first time around, actually, but there were so many great *Doctor Who* stories to choose from that I overlooked it. And now I'm really regretting that.

So, um, great job for picking a story that shows the McCoy era at its most adult and mature. I appreciate that. But couldn't you have found a better one?

Your co-author,
Graeme Burk

The Curse of Fenric (1989)

Written by Ian Briggs **Directed by** Nicholas Mallett

Featuring Sylvester McCoy (The Doctor), Sophie Aldred (Ace)

Supporting cast Dinsdale Landen (Dr. Judson), Alfred Lynch (Commander Millington), Stevan Rimkus (Captain Bates), Marcus Hutton (Sgt. Leigh), Christien Anholt (Perkins), Tomek Bork (Captain Sorin), Peter Czajkowski (Sgt. Prozorov), Marek Anton (Vershinin), Mark Conrad (Petrossian), Nicholas Parsons (The Rev. Mr. Wainwright), Janet Henfrey (Miss Hardaker), Joann Kenny (Jean), Joanne Bell (Phyllis), Anne Reid (Nurse Crane), Cory Pulman (Kathleen Dudman), Aaron Hanley (baby Audrey), Raymond Trickett (Ancient Haemovore)

Original airdates October 25, November 1, 8, 15, 1989

The Big Idea The Doctor takes Ace to a secret naval base during World War II, only to find chemical weapons, a Russian black op, vampires from the sea . . . and evil since the dawn of time.

Roots and References *Dracula* (the Haemovores' vampiric nature, the Ancient One coming via Transylvania); Norse mythology (Fenric comes from Fenrir, the monstrous wolf foretold to kill Odin during Ragnarok, the end of the gods); Alan Turing's codebreaking efforts (Dr. Judson and the Ultima machine); the 1975 Jack Higgins novel *The Eagle Has Landed* (the Russians' mission on British soil); Alan Moore, Steve Bissette and John Totlbein's 1980s comic book series *Saga of the Swamp Thing* (the look of the Haemovores). Wainwright quotes from 1 Corinthians 13 (though anachronistically; in the 1940s he would have read from the King James version which used "charity" instead of "love"). The Doctor and Judson speak about the gaming theory known as the Prisoner's Dilemma (indeed, the Doctor's chess puzzle with Fenric employs some elements of it).

Time And Relative Dimensions In Space Ian Briggs had previously written for *Doctor Who* in 1987 when he penned Ace's introductory story, "Dragonfire." Script editor Andrew Cartmel was keen to use Briggs again and suggested an idea explored in Alan Moore's DC comics a few years earlier featuring an aquatic vampire. Briggs used this as a jumping-off point before alighting onto Viking legend, vampires and, eventually, a World War II setting. (Briggs's script was titled "The Wolves of Fenric" until John Nathan-Turner noted that the "wolves" concept wasn't employed until episode four, which would make the title difficult to grasp.) Cartmel and Briggs also wanted to continue to make the Doctor dark and manipulative, while bringing together various plot threads about Ace that had been dangling over the past two seasons, beginning in "Dragonfire."

Adventures in Time and Space The Doctor notes Fenric's hand in recent events, including the chess set he found in Lady Peinforte's study in 1988's "Silver Nemesis" (there, he noticed the arrangement of pieces and made a further move!). Ace's arrival by time storm on Iceworld in "Dragonfire" is mentioned as additional evidence (the same technique is used to bring the Ancient One back in time from his future). The Doctor demonstrates his faith by naming his companions (this is audible on the soundtrack of the special edition where he names Susan, Ian, Barbara and Steven before the scene cuts away). Ace talks about encountering the house in "Ghost Light" (originally, "The Curse of Fenric" was to have been broadcast before "Ghost Light" so the line was intended to be foreshadowing).

Who is the Doctor? When Kathleen asks the Doctor if his family is safe, he simply answers, "I don't know." The Doctor has fought Fenric before (in an unseen adventure). He knows what is happening on the base and is trying to stage-manage events in order to defeat Fenric. The idea that the Doctor is now long-lived enough to be playing this sort of a long game was, at the time of broadcast, a new and radical take on his character. (The Doctor tells Wainwright that "today's events haven't been written down," which either suggest the mutability of history or that he's had a peek ahead.) Ace accuses him of playing a game where he makes up the rules — a charge he doesn't deny. It's something that really comes into focus at the climax, when it's revealed the Doctor knew Ace was one of Fenric's "wolves" from the time they first met.

Companion Chronicles Ace develops an instant bond with Kathleen and Audrey, which confuses her when she finally learns that Audrey will grow up to become Ace's mother — the mother whom she hates. (From her first appearance in "Dragonfire," Ace wants nothing to do with her family.) She comes to terms with it, a little, by the story's end. The revelation that Ace has been one of Fenric's wolves shouldn't be surprising even within the context of this story: her actions move events towards Fenric's return and triumph. She finds the Russian pouch, figures out that the Viking runes are a logic diagram, finds the flask and solves the Doctor's chess puzzle. Even so, she has absolute faith in the Doctor, a faith he breaks in an ugly, brutal way.

Monster of the Week The Haemovores are what *Homo sapiens* evolve into thousands of years into the future when the earth is engulfed in chemical slime (chemical slime, it turns out, created by Fenric). Fenric brought a Haemovore known as the Ancient One back to ninth century Transylvania, where it tracked Fenric's flask, while creating more Haemovores and being responsible for humanity's vampire legends. The Haemovores work at the bidding of Fenric, an evil being from the dawn of time whom the Doctor trapped in a flask long ago. By killing Fenric and himself, the Ancient One averts this future.

Stand Up and Cheer The storm finally hits. Ace has seen how the events set in motion are going to hurt Kathleen and Audrey and she confronts the Doctor, who avoids her before he finally, angrily, tells her what's going on: "Evil since the dawn of time." An evil that should have shattered into fragments but never did and stayed incarnate is here, now. Sylvester McCoy works every single syllable of his dramatic monologue and yet it sounds appropriately anguished, like someone who has seen, and knows, too much.

Roll Your Eyes Ace goes to distract the soldier guarding Sorin with her womanly charms and . . . talks about time and quantum mechanics and stuff. By this point in its history, it's regularly joked that *Doctor Who* is only watched by adolescent males who never emerge from their basements. They apparently write it as well.

You're Not Making Any Sense Why do Sorin's men kill the British soldiers? For that matter, why threaten to kill the Doctor and Ace (and even Jean and Phyllis just for walking nearby)? Admittedly, Russian forces don't want to be caught stealing the ULTIMA machine, but wouldn't killing half a dozen or so soldiers and civilians draw attention?

Interesting Trivia This story has one of the most brilliant throwaway gags in the history of the series as the Doctor, needing to give himself a cover story (in the days before the psychic paper was invented), asks for official stationery, types a note, then asks for two pens and then forges the signatures of both the prime minister and the head of the secret service *using both pens at the same time.* And he does all this in front of Judson!

You would be forgiven, especially reading an anthology such as ours, if you thought Fenric was a returning villain. He's not. The Doctor's previous adventure with him — where he trapped him in the flask after defeating him with his chess game — never happened onscreen. In the novelization, it's suggested it happened while the Doctor was in his first incarnation, though we don't actually know.

We have something of a "grandmother paradox" at work. Ace sent Kathleen to her nan's in Streatham, but Ace doesn't recognize Kathleen as her grandmother, nor does her first name or surname tip her off. The implication is that Kathleen remarried, presumably to whomever is living at the address Ace sends her to!

John Nathan-Turner was hesitant about having vampires as the monsters, so Andrew Cartmel and Ian Briggs performed a global search and replace on the script, taking out all references to "vampires" and replacing them with "Haemovores." Haemovores or vampires, there was a more fundamental problem with using them: in spite of substantial savings thanks to the story being shot entirely on location, the budget couldn't extend to night shooting. Briggs and Cartmel came up with the idea that the Haemovores generated a black smoke that blotted out the sun. Problem solved. Except black smoke would have been toxic to the cast and crew, so it would have to be a white smoke, which now meant that the Haemovores generated a sort of fog. Except that didn't always look convincing, as the fog dissipated while filming on location, but the special edition patches this up somewhat.

How did we come to have a special edition of "The Curse of Fenric"? When this story was made, the script not only overran, there was an epic amount of extra material shot — almost 12 minutes worth, much of it from the final episode. At one point, it was hoped that there might be enough material to make a fifth episode (a move Ian Briggs strenuously objected to). Massive trims were made. When the story was released on VHS in 1991, about six minutes worth of material was added. Before director Nicholas Mallett died in 1997, he had discussed with Mark Ayres, who wrote the music for the story, the possibility of re-editing the story as a whole, making it into a feature-length movie. In 2003, Ayres took Mallett's notes and recut the story according to his wishes as a special edition for the DVD release. Other changes were made for this special edition, including regrading the colour (the scenes on the beach were meant to be set in hot weather but were shot in the freezing early spring of 1989, and it shows in the original) and adding new effects.

TARDIS Chronometer A secret naval base, presumably in Yorkshire (given what's written about the area in the Viking runes) in 1943.

Wicked? (GB) *Doctor Who* didn't do story arcs in the Classic Series. While there were stories linked by sequential plotline (the quest for the Key to Time, travelling in E-space, the Doctor being on trial), they're not story arcs in the manner we're used to seeing on television today, where elements from one episode are built upon in another episode months (or even years) down the road before finally coming to a head in a spectacular way.

"The Curse of Fenric" is the story where disparate plot and character elements from the past two seasons of *Doctor Who* come together powerfully: we find out that the improbable accident that brought Ace to another planet in the future in "Dragonfire" was part of a plot by Fenric; Fenric was behind the scenes during another (actually quite risible) story from the previous season ("Silver Nemesis"); and Ace's issues with her family, often unstated but at the heart of Ace's motivation as a character, find some resolution here. It's the sort of "arc episode" we're used to seeing in *Buffy* or *X-Files* or *Battlestar Galactica* or even post-2005 *Doctor Who*.

It's nice to see 1963–1989 *Doctor Who* finishing its run in trail-blazing glory. That alone would assure this story's inclusion in our list. But "The Curse of Fenric" is so much more than that. This isn't a simple story with monsters storming a naval base; this is a novel, with multiple subplots and character arcs: Judson's quest for knowledge; Millington's interest in Norse myth and Nazis, and consequent icy dispassion; Sorin's heroic leadership; Wainwright's lack of faith; Jean's and Phyllis' desires to be something other than maidens . . . all of these elements collide with each other, creating friction and increasing the momentum. It's gorgeously layered and so much of it pays off even when it doesn't contribute to the overall plot. Reverend Wainwright's only contribution to the storyline is in supplying the original Viking translations and the parish records, but his lack of faith and ultimate demise is heartbreaking.

It's bolstered by some wonderful performances, particularly Tomek Bork as Captain Sorin. Dinsdale Landen's double role as Judson and Fenric is Jack Nicholson–esque in a good way. (And kudos to Ian

Briggs for making Fenric so delightfully sarcastic.) But what steals the show is Nicholas Parsons's heartfelt portrayal of Wainwright.

And then there's Sylvester McCoy, who is clearly delighted to play the Doctor as someone far more dangerous than we initially suspect. It's a very different portrayal of the Doctor as a calculating chess player who knows how the game will unfold and works both sides to get things into place. (I love how the most crucial element of the climax, the Ancient Haemovore changing sides, happens as a result of a side conversation with the Doctor that is almost casual.) In many ways, only McCoy could make it work: his Doctor is always a study in contrasts, moving from the ranting and shouting and r-r-rolling his Rs to serene mystery to dark intent. When he breaks Ace's faith, you have a sense that, while he seems truly sorry afterwards, the Doctor was expressing some of his actual feelings about her nonetheless. We've had Doctors who are unlikable and Doctors who are eccentric. We've never had one where we don't know whether to cheer or be horrified by him. It is, as David Tennant's Doctor might say, textbook enigmatic.

So much of this story rests on Ace, and that's frustrating. Ace's tendency to instantly become best friends with the lead female character in any story has by this point become an irritating tic that borders on being creepy. When it's used as shorthand for bonding with her grandmother and mother, it's distracting in the extreme. (Ace's desperate cry that Kathleen tell her what's wrong when she receives the telegram is something that makes me wince every time I recall it.) And yet the relationship between Kathleen and Ace has some wonderful moments, particularly the one where Ace speaks from her vantage point in the future and assumes Kathleen is unmarried. Sophie Aldred is incredible in so many other moments; I always gasp to watch Ace scream her apology to her mum when she thinks she's dying.

It's a story with so many great character moments, so much going on — and little editorial control in the scripting. Television should work on first broadcast, not wait for a special edition DVD to be made 14 years later. There is no way this story should have run almost half an episode over without it being found out in the process of writing it. Which means that someone wilfully ignored that or was too inexperienced to do something about it. We're lucky that we have a special edition version to add all the missing material and provide an edit that makes sense of it. (It's not that the episodic version is bad; it's just that the climax in particular is very hastily put together.) "The Curse of Fenric" special edition is grander and more epic. Scenes flow together and have time to breathe. And what seems to be a frenzied hurrying up in the original story's episode four is nothing less than *Götterdämmerung* on a *Doctor Who* budget.

Which brings us to one of the biggest problems of "The Curse of Fenric": it had the misfortune of being made in 1989, when the budget was cut to the bone even by the standards of *Doctor Who*. While there are innovations like shooting interiors and exteriors on location (that would become standard procedure in making the New Series), a lot of material that would have been moody on film looks terrible on video. (The special edition doesn't do it favours: the colour regrading to improve the meteorologically challenged shoot pumps an awful lot of artefacts into the picture, which really look bad on 21st-century television screens.) The Haemovores are conceptually stunning but practically laughable. (Particularly the Ancient Haemovore, which cannot even move its mouth convincingly!) It looks cheap and nasty.

Which is a shame. As we come near the end of the Classic Series, we see all the ways *Doctor Who* is moving closer to its post-2005 form (story arcs, character-based storytelling, location shooting), but we see all the ways it's not working (lack of budget, lack of editing at script stage). And yet, despite this, "The Curse of Fenric" ensures the show goes out with a bang, not with a whimper.

Second Opinion (RS?) Where's the story of "The Curse of Fenric"? I don't mean its plot — my co-author rightly points out how fabulous this is — I mean the story itself.

Like the very first Dalek story, this tale exists in about four versions. There's the original broadcast, with episode one so sliced up that the Doctor and Ace appear to be teleporting around the base. There's Ian Briggs's novelization, which added crucial information about Ace's final fate (she ends up in the past with one of Sorin's ancestors). There's the VHS release, which is the broadcast version plus about six minutes of deleted scenes. And then there's the DVD special edition, all 102 glorious minutes of it, edited into feature-length format.

Purists will champion the broadcast version, and it's good that it's available on DVD, but I bet that very few people actually watch it. The special edition might look like the ultimate cut, but its structure is unlike any Classic *Doctor Who* story and the lack of cliffhangers is downright weird. (When the Doctor runs into the computer room and Millington says, "You're too late, Doctor!" there's a very awkward pause before the Doctor simply runs out again.) One might be tempted to split the difference and call the VHS version good enough, except that it's no longer widely available.

Which brings to mind another issue. "The Curse of Fenric," like "Ghost Light" before it, was a story made to be rewatched. In *Doctor Who*'s final year or two, the production team was cognizant that the show's fans were recording the episodes and rewatching them. As a result, the stories were structured to reward this. It's something we think of as commonplace now, when shows like *Lost* deliberately include clues that can only be seen by freezeframing, but at the time this was quite revolutionary. You can see the struggle they're having: on the one hand layering the story with subtlety, on the other not even being able to control the order in which the stories were broadcast. (Imagine trying to write for *Lost* if you had to account for the fact that the network might show the episodes in any old order, or leave some of them out.)

So what we get instead is a sort of fuzzy-logic version of "The Curse of Fenric." It doesn't have a definitive version, but two people who'd experienced different editions of it could still have a conversation about it. However, regardless of the mechanics of how they come to experience the story, at the very least that conversation would probably contain the word "awesome" somewhere in it. And, at the end of the day, that's what really matters.

The Psychic Papers: The Cartmel Masterplan

In 1987, incoming script editor Andrew Cartmel faced a problem: the Doctor was too well known. Stories throughout the fifth and sixth Doctors' tenures had turned increasingly inwards, with recurring enemies, regular trips to Gallifrey and a universe where it seemed everyone knew who the Time Lords were and that the Doctor was one. This not only undermined the Doctor's abilities, it resulted in a lack of mystery, something crucial to the show from its beginning. In short, the Doctor had lost his mojo.

With the help of a team of young and dynamic new writers, such as Ben Aaronovitch and Marc Platt, Cartmel conceived of a plan to re-inject the mystery into *Doctor Who*. His idea was to not simply ignore the preceding developments (although recurring enemies were drastically scaled back) but to gradually reveal that there was a hidden layer underneath what we knew. The idea was to use the fact that everyone seemed to know the Doctor and invert it, by giving him a whole new backstory, one that wouldn't contradict what we'd seen onscreen but that added a deeper level of mystery to the character. Much later, this scheme became known by fans as "The Cartmel Masterplan."

Hints of this new backstory for the Doctor first appeared in "Remembrance of the Daleks" when the Doctor talks about the old time of Gallifrey and suggests that he was involved with the prototype of the Hand of Omega, before quickly correcting himself. A deleted scene with Davros almost serves as a manifesto for the Cartmel Masterplan: Davros claims that, ultimately, the Doctor is just another Time Lord, to which he replies, "Oh, Davros. I am far more than just another Time Lord."

1988's "Silver Nemesis" contains several hints that the Doctor has a dark and terrible backstory that he'd go to enormous lengths to conceal. When Ace asks him who he really is at the story's conclusion, he merely puts a finger to his lips, shushing her. A planned scene in "Survival" would have had the Master questioning the Doctor's identity, only to be told that he'd evolved.

It was "Ghost Light" that was intended to bring many of these elements to the fore. The original storyline (called "Lungbarrow") involved the Doctor returning home to Gallifrey to face his greatest fear: his family. This would have revealed the Doctor to be something more than they were: he was a reincarnation of the Other, the third in the triumvirate of founders of Time Lord society (the others being Rassilon and Omega), whose name has been lost to history. The story also explained Susan's origins: she was the Other's granddaughter and when the first Doctor travelled back into Gallifrey's past, she recognized him as her grandfather.

However, producer John Nathan-Turner thought that this story would reveal too much of the Doctor's origins and so nixed it. As a result, the Cartmel Masterplan mostly plays out in the extreme background of the final two seasons of the Classic Series.

This wasn't the end of the Cartmel Masterplan though. Shortly after the show's cancellation, Cartmel, Platt and Aaronovitch sat down and wrote out their ideas about Gallifrey. They passed these on to the editor of the New Adventures, Virgin Publishing's range of books that continued the story of the seventh Doctor and Ace in print form. The books gradually revealed more and more details, including appearances by the Other in Gallifrey's distant past. This came to a head in the final story to feature the seventh Doctor, 1997's *Lungbarrow*, which revealed the remainder of the plan.

The Cartmel Masterplan was thus a sort of deep background source for the last few years of the Classic Series and the "Wilderness Years" between the Classic and New Series. Onscreen playing out only in hints, with most of its manifestations deleted from the series proper, its shadowy existence was nevertheless the most intriguing thing about it. And yet, it provided enough depth to sustain a character arc for the Doctor for almost a decade. By spreading the Cartmel Masterplan over several years and multiple media, its creators accomplished exactly what they set out to do: deepen the mystery of the Doctor.

Survival (1989)

Written by Rona Munro **Directed by** Alan Wareing

Featuring Sylvester McCoy (The Doctor), Sophie Aldred (Ace)

Supporting cast Anthony Ainley (The Master), Lisa Bowerman (Karra), Julian Holloway (Paterson), David John (Derek), Will Barton (Midge), Sean Oliver (Stuart), Sakuntala Ramanee (Shreela), Gareth Hale (Len), Norman Pace (Harvey), Kate Eaton (Ange), Adele Silva (Squeak)

Original airdates November 22, 29, December 6, 1989

The Big Idea Ace returns home to Perivale and finds it as boring as ever. Her gang of friends are gone — only it turns out they've been abducted by Cheetah People.

Roots and References *Cats* (the Cheetah People's look; a poster for it is noted in the youth club); the 1982 remake of *Cat People* (people transforming into cats). Ace looks through Midge's record collection and finds a copy of U2's album *War*. (Ace remarks, "Are they still on the go, then? They were practically drawing their pensions when I was clubbing it." It was a topical joke since at they were riding high on the success of *The Joshua Tree* and *Rattle and Hum*!)

Time And Relative Dimensions In Space November 23, 1989. Twenty-six years earlier, the very first episode of *Doctor Who* had been broadcast. It was the day after the broadcast of the first episode of the final story of the 26th season of *Doctor Who*, "Survival." And Sylvester McCoy was brought in to record a last-minute speech that was to be added to the end of the final episode in voiceover . . .

Two years earlier, script editor Andrew Cartmel was at a luncheon for a training session for promising writers at the BBC. One of them was a Scottish writer named Rona Munro, who would go on to great success as a writer for film (including the 1994 Ken Loach masterwork, *Ladybird Ladybird*) but at the time was a struggling playwright. Unlike many of the writers Cartmel encountered at that luncheon, Munro loved *Doctor Who* and was keen to pitch ideas to Cartmel. One of them was for a story called "Cat Flap" that featured Cheetah People who hunted humans. Working with Cartmel, Munro developed it into a workable storyline that John Nathan-Turner commissioned. (Munro was only the third female writer for the show; two other women had their names on scripts actually written by men.) Nathan-Turner asked that the story also include the Master, who hadn't been seen in *Doctor Who* for three years by this point. While it was filmed third in production order, it was going to be broadcast as the last story of the season.

But even while the story was made, there were concerns about what would happen next for *Doctor Who*. John Nathan-Turner, who had been keen to leave for the past four years, wanted to go once and for all, but there was no impetus to move him anywhere else in the BBC. Andrew Cartmel was getting offers from other programs. There were some loose notional ideas for stories for a 27th season, but nothing formally commissioned: Ben Aaronovitch wanted to do a space opera satire around food aid; Marc Platt was interested in a story set in the late 1960s featuring the Ice Warriors; there was talk about writing out Ace and possibly replacing her with an upper class thief; and talk of involving new writers such as Robin Mukherjee.

At the same time, there were also whispers from the higher echelons of the BBC. Peter Cregeen took over as BBC head of series and he felt that *Doctor Who*, along with several other venerable series, needed to be "rested" until such time as a producer could be found who had a significant vision for the series. The show had been up against ITV ratings behemoth *Coronation Street* for the entirety of Sylvester McCoy's tenure (and surprisingly held its own, even growing a little in spite of overwhelming odds) with a reduced episode count and a decreased budget. This was cited as evidence that it had its best days behind it, even in spite of the creative resurgence behind the scenes. (American science-fiction imports such as *Star Trek: The Next Generation* made *Doctor Who*'s production values seem even worse.) It was something of a self-fulfilling prophecy: the show was given little help in the way of budget, promotion or scheduling and then was pronounced a failure. Unlike the 1985 cancellation, the BBC never admitted to doing more than giving the series a hiatus, and so it was left to quietly fade into oblivion.

By the time the final story to go before the cameras was made ("Ghost Light"), it was clear to John Nathan-Turner and Andrew Cartmel that *Doctor Who* wasn't coming back in 1990. In September 1989, Nathan-Turner informed Sylvester McCoy and Sophie Aldred their contracts wouldn't be picked up for another season. The *Doctor Who* production office was wound down and closed for the first time since 1963. Nathan-Turner's and Cartmel's days with the series were numbered, but they still had a watching brief leading up to the transmission of the stories, and they decided to make a last-minute addition to the end of "Survival." The show originally ended with the Doctor and Ace walking off into the distance. Nathan-Turner urged Cartmel to add a voiceover to give it a more definitive conclusion.

Cartmel wrote a monologue that Sylvester McCoy recorded on the 23rd of November, 1989: "There are worlds out there where the sky is burning, where the sea's asleep and the rivers dream. People made of smoke and cities made of song. Somewhere there's danger, somewhere there's injustice and somewhere else the tea's getting cold. Come on Ace, we've got work to do!"

Doctor Who was over.

Adventures in Time and Space The Master is back, making his first appearance since 1986's "The Trial of a Time Lord." The Doctor's ability to stun with one finger harkens back to similar tricks performed by the third Doctor in stories like "Inferno." Patterson mentions that the police only let Ace off with a warning (presumably for setting Gabriel Chase on fire, as mentioned in "Ghost Light").

Who is the Doctor? The Doctor seems completely distracted by his hunt for the Kitling, to the exclusion of all else. He knows of the Cheetah People's planet and its properties.

Companion Chronicles Ace returns to Perivale and is filled with nostalgia for the place, even while she's reviled by its inherent boredom. (And yet she's apparently unfazed by her encounter with her mother in "The Curse of Fenric"; she expresses no interest in reconnecting with her mum, indicating she might be dead or still very estranged.) Ace is possessed by the Cheetah People's planet and is in the early stages of being converted into a Cheetah. She is saved though her sense of home: not Perivale, but the TARDIS.

Monster of the Week The Cheetah People are intelligent carnivores who use Kitlings (cats that can teleport from world to world) to hunt for carrion. Their home planet can infect and possess people, changing those who fight and hunt into Cheetah People themselves.

Stand Up and Cheer The Doctor's final confrontation with the Master is a thing of beauty. The initial conversation outside the TARDIS is beautifully directed by Alan Wareing, as the Doctor and the Master circle each other (and the camera, in turn, circles them). Then it jumps to the Cheetah People's planet and the Doctor is possessed by the planet and nearly kills the Master . . . until he realizes the only way to win is not to fight like an animal. It's the Doctor's last heroic gesture in the Classic Series. And it's magnificent.

Roll Your Eyes The animatronic Kitling. Oh dear. The fluffy toy trying to pass as a dead cat in Midge's house. Oh no.

You're Not Making Any Sense It's a cool visual (and an even more impressive special effect) seeing the two motorcycles collide into a fireball. Except . . . there shouldn't have been a fireball, two vehicles would just spectacularly crash. While we're at it, how the hell did the Doctor wind up on a conveniently placed sofa?

Interesting Trivia In the Doctor's final battle with the Master, he sees the Cheetah People disappear (noting, "They're gone," with the implication that he and the Master are the only ones left on the disintegrating world) and he later says to Ace that they've gone to the wilderness. So where do the Cheetah People go in the end? Given that Karra reverts to human form when dying, we can probably suppose that they eventually went back to wherever they came from before they were converted. But that does bring up the possibility of a variety of Cheetah People suddenly reappearing in the shops or something.

"Ghost Light," "The Curse of Fenric" and "Survival" form a loose trilogy of stories that explore Ace's troubled past, her relationships with friends and family, and her home. It was, at the time, an unprecedented look at a companion and her background. Sophie Aldred suggested that Andrew Cartmel's intention was that "Ghost Light" looked at Ace's past (the arson of Gabriel Chase as a result of the firebombing of her friend Manisha's flat), "The Curse of Fenric" at her present (her relationship with her mother) and "Survival" at her future (her choosing the TARDIS as her home and not Perivale).

The appearance of comic duo Hale and Pace in episode one was the last in a decade full of stuntcasting on the part of John Nathan-Turner, who was a great believer in getting any sort of publicity for the show. Nathan-Turner cast stars of British light entertainment, variety and comedy in order to get a few column inches and some attention. While many fans said such casting detracted from the program, often the casting was remarkably effective precisely because it was so counter-intuitive and gave the actors in question an opportunity to do something very different. In this instance, Hale and Pace add a nice scene that builds on the theme of survival of the fittest, then get out as soon as possible.

To this day, Ace remains the only companion never to be written out of *Doctor Who*. (Even Dodo and Liz Shaw received offscreen explanations!) There was talk (and little more) by Andrew Cartmel and various writers of having her depart the series by having the Doctor send her to Gallifrey to become a Time Lord in the 1990 season of *Doctor Who*. In the tie-in fiction of the '90s, Ace was written out in two different ways in two different media: in the *Doctor Who* New Adventures novels of the 1990s, Ace leaves the Doctor in revolutionary France where she travels through time, having adventures like the Doctor but on a smaller scale. In the comic strip in *Doctor Who Magazine*, Ace was killed off. The New Series spinoff *The Sarah Jane Adventures* sets up another version, one that presumably supersedes all the others. According to Sarah Jane Smith in the 2010 episode "Death of the Doctor," Ace (now using her given name, Dorothy) lives on contemporary Earth heading up the foundation A Charitable Earth, which has raised billions. Executive producer Russell T Davies admitted in an interview that had *The Sarah Jane Adventures* continued, it would have featured the return of Ace, in the same way it had brought back Jo Grant and the Brigadier in past seasons. Sadly, Elisabeth Sladen's death put an end to that before it could even grow past an idea.

TARDIS Chronometer Perivale, West London, and the planet of the Cheetah People, near to the present day.

Wicked? (GB) The final speech that ends *Doctor Who* is only 48 words long. Those 48 words are etched forever on my brain. I don't need a reference book to look them up; I know them by heart. For 15 years, those 48 words were the end of *Doctor Who* as a TV show. It's hard to review "Survival" without considering those final words for, in many respects, they completely overshadow the story itself.

It's a pity, because "Survival" itself is one of the finest *Doctor Who* stories of the 1980s. It's odd to watch "Survival" today because, like "The Curse of Fenric," it is in many ways almost like a prototype of the New Series: an adventure where the strange and alien meet the totally commonplace, with alien menaces stalking council estates and suburban high streets. It's also a story made entirely on location that's centred on the companion's uncomfortable homecoming. From this three-part story to "Rose" in 15 years time isn't a massive evolutionary stretch.

And yet, "Survival" is very much of its era; indeed, it exemplifies the best traits of the final years of the Classic Series. It's a story built around ideas and themes — specifically, how survival of the fittest plays out in humans, and how we're haunted by our animal nature even today — but Rona Munro is smart in that she never leaves the viewer bored, hoping that the ideas are enough. There's always some charming dialogue (Munro gives Ace the line we've all wanted to ask the Doctor when he explains to her who the Master is: "Do you know any nice people? You know, ordinary people?"), a fascinating conversation — at one point provided by Hale and Pace of all people! — or a tense set piece to keep things exciting and to keep the viewer engaged. Unlike so many other scripts during Andrew Cartmel's tenure as script editor, Munro's is tightly written and has a compelling throughline.

The script is a gift to director Alan Wareing who seems uncommonly attuned to its nuances — watch how the Doctor and the Master circle each other in conversation — and with a very limited budget makes Perivale and the planet of the Cheetah People feel vastly different. The story is let down a little by its design — the Cheetah People are a lovely piece of prosthetics but ultimately look too stiff and contrived to be effective, and the Kitling can't avoid looking like an animatronic cat — but both seem very much state of the art for their time and neither irreparably damages the story.

In his last TV appearance as the Master, Anthony Ainley finally gets to shine. If all you've seen of Anthony Ainley's Master are his appearances in stories from this book, then we've done you the public service of avoiding some really terrible performances. Not that it was entirely

Ainley's fault. Fans watching the taping of 1984's "Planet of Fire" witnessed Ainley getting the note from the director's gallery, "More OTT" (more over the top). But here, Ainley is doing all the quiet, conversational acting he was capable of but producer fiat made him avoid.

And the Master's involvement is perfect here. He's possessed by the Cheetah People's planet precisely because his instinct is to hunt and to fight. Before the Doctor arrives, he seems to have no ambition other than to rule the Cheetah People. In spite of his claims that he is not an animal, he has clearly lost his way, as we see once on he's on Earth (the image of the Master looking in a mirror in a council-estate maisonette trying to assert his dominance is beautifully pathetic). Only the Doctor has the wisdom to reject that. It's possibly the greatest distillation of their conflict ever seen.

Sylvester McCoy is also in good form, clearly loving every minute of Munro's oblique characterization of the Doctor. The guest cast is great, particularly Lisa Bowerman, who manages to do a lot in spite of the makeup and voice modulation, and Julian Holloway, who makes Paterson's tough guy illusions seem pathetic rather than oafish.

However, the story is really Sophie Aldred's. It again highlights a curious quirk I mentioned in my review of "The Curse of Fenric": Ace gets emotionally involved with someone (at least the planet's nature explains it this time) only for them to get killed off by the end of the story but not before Ace babbles about the feelings she's experiencing. The idea is that it's supposed to show how young Ace is, and to touch upon the emotional volatility of a teenager. But it often just feels like she has the maturity of a five-year-old. And yet, in spite of the obvious disaster, and in spite of it being done before (with Kathleen and Audrey), the fact that we care about Ace learning the thrill of the hunt with Karra is a sign of how much better Sophie Aldred is as an actress than she's given credit.

A 48-word soliloquy closes off the 26-year-long chapter of Classic Doctor Who. Typical of Doctor Who, it promises all sorts of things that it never could deliver — cities made of song, people made of smoke and rivers that can dream — but I love it all the same because it claims those possibilities could be true. Every time I hear "There are worlds out there," I get a little teary-eyed. It's a reaction from when this was the end of televised Doctor Who, when Doctor Who was killed by indifference and lack of imagination on the part of those who ran the BBC. Now we know different. Now we can see what takes place in seven years, in 15 years, with the pressing of a DVD remote, with the turning of a page. But, at the time, that strange, funny, sad eulogy was the end.

Come on, Ace, we've got work to do.

Second Opinion (RS?) The best thing about "Survival" is that they never saw it coming.

Had the production team known further in advance that this was the last Classic Series story, it's very likely more would have been done to wrap up the storyline. The seeds are all there: Ace is home; the Master is back, itching for a fight; and the Doctor is forced to take Ace's place in a final confrontation to the death. Had the Doctor been definitively killed in that explosion (perhaps vanquishing the Master as he did so), with Ace left behind to mourn, it would have been a fitting end to *Doctor Who*. And the show would never have returned.

What's more, the series has come full circle. When we started off, in "The Daleks," the point was made that pacifism was wrong, with Ian convincing the Thals to take up arms and fight. Here, the moral is the exact opposite: fighting is wrong and those who do so (exemplified in Patterson) are both ridiculed and come to no good. *Doctor Who* has finally grown up.

In the 1993 documentary, *Thirty Years in the TARDIS*, writer Ben Aaronovitch was asked what he'd do if he was given the very last episode of *Doctor Who* to write. His answer was "I'd have to kill him." It's an enormous temptation, of course, but it's the wrong instinct. Just as *Doctor Who* had no beginning, it should have no end.

"Survival" was the population bottleneck of *Doctor Who*. Just as the human race once dwindled to a mere 10,000 individuals, taking us within a hair's breadth of extinction, "Survival" almost saw the end of our favourite series. And yet, just as the human race rebounded into something larger and more magnificent than those 10,000 people could have possibly imagined, thanks to the rushed schedule or Andrew Cartmel's instincts or a simple lack of time, so too *Doctor Who* has now grown into a behemoth the likes of which Rona Munro, Ben Aaronovitch and John Nathan-Turner could never have dreamed. It just took a bit of time.

My co-author is right about those 48 words, but where he's wrong is the emphasis. It's not the cities made of song or people made of smoke that matter. It's the fact that the very last line is "We've got work to do." That's how a TV show ensures its own survival.

The 1990s

Starring
Paul McGann *as the Doctor*

Doctor Who in an Exciting Adventure in Development Hell

Doctor Who was over.

Except that it wasn't. Not yet.

On July 12, 1989, mere weeks before taping began on "Ghost Light," the final *Doctor Who* story to be produced in Britain in the 1980s, a fax came to Roger Laughton, director of co-productions at BBC Enterprises. It was from Philip Segal, head of development at Columbia Pictures in the U.S. Segal, a British ex-pat from Southend, was a long-time *Doctor Who* fan who had fond memories of watching the show in its early days with William Hartnell. He was now living in Hollywood where he worked as an executive (his past posting was at ABC, where he helped bring *thirtysomething* to air), developing television series for Columbia's television arm. Segal was enquiring if *Doctor Who* could be developed as a property for American television.

Segal's inquiry was followed up with a phone call and he was passed up the line to the BBC's head of series, Peter Cregeen, who explained the series was in the process of being taken off the air. Furthermore, the series had been optioned for a film produced by a company called Coast to Coast. Segal was excited about the prospect of a *Doctor Who* TV series co-produced by the BBC and Columbia. But talks stalled due to a combination of political factors, ranging from support for the possible movie and a belief the show needed to be "rested" further. Segal moved on from Columbia back to ABC and that avenue of exploration came to a close.

As the 1990s dawned, the BBC began to become slightly warmer to the idea of *Doctor Who* being made as a co-production with a third-party. (The climate of British television in the 1990s was moving towards the co-production model, with the BBC doing less and less in-house.) It even entertained some proposals, including one from Dalek creator Terry Nation and Cybermen co-creator Gerry Davis.

A production company called Black Light got a little bit further, even developing some concept art. But none of the proposals went anywhere.

After two years, Philip Segal left ABC to join Amblin Entertainment, Steven Spielberg's production company. At the time, Amblin had just moved into TV and was working with various studios (its biggest success was *ER*, which it produced with Warner Bros.). By 1993, it was producing several series with Universal Television, including *seaQuest DSV*, where Philip Segal was a production executive.

Segal kept in touch with the BBC even after his move to Amblin, and was able to use his connection to Steven Spielberg to his advantage in continuing to press for a U.S./U.K. co-production of *Doctor Who*. (For his part, Spielberg was happy for Amblin to acquire the property.) One day, the controller of BBC1, Alan Yentob, was among a junket of BBC personnel wanting a tour of the *seaQuest DSV* set. Segal seized the opportunity and briefed Yentob on his efforts to date. Yentob (who was a rare breed of BBC executive at the time in that he liked the series) was impressed, and the wheels were further greased when Segal started dealing with Tony Greenwood, who was responsible for the BBC's international co-productions and was amendable to the idea.

After much lawyering, a deal was struck between Amblin, the BBC and Universal Television. The BBC were so confident in the deal, they allowed the option to lapse on the film project (which had tried to employ Leonard Nimoy to direct, using a script by Denny Martin Flynn). Segal brought in Peter Wagg, who had worked on the 1980s series *Max Headroom*, to produce the series. Segal was anxious to use a writer from the original series, such as Terrance Dicks, or at least a British writer, but Universal's participation required Segal to use one of their writers. Thus John Leekley, a writer who had worked on a variety of American TV series and movies (more recently responsible for the *Knight Rider* sequel *Knight Rider 2010*), was brought onto the project to develop a bible for the series and write a pilot script.

What Leekley produced was effectively a rebooting of the *Doctor Who* concept along the lines of what would be done a decade later with *Battlestar Galactica*: it used concepts from the original series as part of a completely new continuity. The Doctor would be travelling through space and time, searching for his father, Ulysses, aided by his grandfather, Borusa, in non-corporeal form. The Master was the Doctor's brother (the Doctor himself was half-human) who betrayed Gallifrey to the Daleks (who were now spider-like in form). The series bible set out an elaborate backstory for Gallifrey and the Time Lords and the Doctor, suggesting possible adventures. (These were mostly rewritten versions of original BBC episodes ranging from "The Talons of Weng-Chiang," now set in 1990s New York, to "Earthshock," which featured the Cybermen recreated as "Cybs," cyborg space pirates!) Leekley provided an outline for one such episode, "Don't Shoot, I'm the Doctor," a rewriting of "The Gunfighters," and a script that saw the circumstances of the Doctor's departure from Gallifrey, his quest for Ulysses and a plot that wound up in World War II during the Blitz.

The script was written, so Segal and Wagg began to scout locations for the pilot TV movie (settling on Utah) and the BBC started working on casting. Segal initially wanted Michael Crawford for the role of the Doctor, but Crawford, coming off a long run of *The Phantom of the Opera* on stage, was too tired and felt he was too old. Dozens of people were auditioned. Segal was really interested in Liam Cunningham, but Jo Wright, the producer assigned by the BBC, lobbied for Paul McGann, whose star was rising in a number of British TV series and films. Peter O'Toole was looking likely to play the Doctor's grandfather, Borusa.

Segal shopped the project out to American broadcasters. ABC and NBC weren't even interested. CBS looked at it and turned it down. The only network to show interest was FOX, which had some recent success with science fiction with *The X-Files* and *Sliders*. But they weren't interested in it as a series. The head of their TV movie division, Trevor Walton, was interested in it as a TV movie, and side deals were made so that it might be considered by FOX as a "backdoor pilot": if the TV Movie was successful enough, it could go to series.

And then it came to a crashing halt.

While the BBC and Universal were happy, Steven Spielberg didn't like Leekley's script. He found it too similar to Indiana Jones (and presumably *The Young Indiana Jones Chronicles*, which Amblin was making it at the time) and withdrew Amblin's involvement from the project. Segal kept the partnership with the BBC and Universal (and now FOX) together, and Segal produced the TV Movie as an independent production. Other parties didn't think much of the Leekley script either. Segal was forced to employ another writer held under contract by Universal, Robert DeLaurentis, whose script followed Leekley's bible, only more outrageously: the Doctor and his overweight companion, Sherman, fight the Daleks (who resemble Terminator-styled androids; later drafts called them something else) only for Sherman to be killed. The Doctor then travels to Blitz-era London to meet Winston Churchill and a new companion, Lizzie.

The DeLaurentis script had even less traction than Leekley's — all the relevant parties hated it — so Trevor Walton at FOX suggested a new writer, a British ex-pat named Matthew Jacobs.

By this point, it was early 1995. A year later, *Doctor Who* would return. For one night only. We pick up the story from there.

Doctor Who (The TV Movie) (1996)

Written by Matthew Jacobs **Directed by** Geoffrey Sax

Featuring Paul McGann (The Doctor), Daphne Ashbrook (Grace)

Supporting cast Sylvester McCoy (The Old Doctor), Eric Roberts (The Master), Yee Jee Tso (Chang Lee), John Novak (Salinger), Michael David Simms (Dr. Swift), Eliza Roberts (Miranda), Dave Hurtubise (Professor Wagg), Delores Drake (Curtis), Catherine Lough (Wheeler), William Sasso (Pete), Joel Wirkkunen (Ted), Jeremy Radick (Gareth), Gordon Tipple (The Old Master)

Original airdates May 12, 1996 (Canada); May 14, 1996 (U.S.); May 27, 1996 (U.K.)

The Big Idea En route to Gallifrey to return the Master's ashes, the TARDIS crash lands in San Francisco in 1999. But the Doctor's troubles are just beginning . . .

Roots and References Jules Verne's speculative fiction (the TARDIS interior); *Jurassic Park* (tremors in a tea cup); *Terminator* (the Master's look); Arthurian legend and *Star Trek* (the Doctor being half human); the 1973 film *The Creeping Flesh* (the Doctor looking through the magnifying glass); *Ghostbusters* (the guards are slimed); *The Hitchhiker's Guide to the Galaxy* (the Master says, "Life is wasted on the living"); *Superman: The Movie* (time is unwound). The Doctor reads H.G. Wells's *The Time Machine*, while Puccini's *Madame Butterfly* is heard at both the opera and during the operation (and the Doctor hums it while wandering the hospital after his regeneration). The Doctor's regeneration cross-cuts with scenes from the 1931 film version of *Frankenstein*.

Time And Relative Dimensions In Space In May 1995, Matthew Jacobs began work on a TV movie version of *Doctor Who* for FOX (which would broadcast it in the U.S.), the BBC (which would broadcast it in the U.K.) and Universal (which was the bankrolling producing partner). Unlike past concepts for a U.S. series, which were effectively reboots of the Classic Series, Jacobs was given the option of building on the original show, even starting with a recently regenerated Doctor. There were strictures that not every party liked but went along with: Trevor Walton at FOX wanted it to be based on Earth in the present day without any history hopping (the BBC, represented by producer Jo Wright, objected). There was a suggestion of creating a new antagonist (executive producer Philip Segal kept pushing for "the new Daleks," something that would do for the '90s what the Daleks did in the '60s), though Jacobs elected to use the Master.

Jacobs's initial outline had the logline, "Only when Doctor Who knows who he is will he be able to save us all. Only if you know yourself can you save yourself." His initial outline had the Doctor (still played by Sylvester McCoy) fighting with an evil force and being mortally wounded and regenerating. It turns out the evil force is the Master, now in a snake form. The story, set at Halloween, would see the Master, who has taken over the body of a human, using the TARDIS to resurrect the dead and create an army to plunge the world into hell. The Doctor is aided by a surgeon named Kelly Grace, while the Master uses a boy named Jack and his father to further his ends. Segal, the BBC, FOX and Universal all had notes. As the months wore on, elements changed. Jack became Chang Lee, and there was a subplot with his grandfather that was later dropped. Kelly Grace became Grace Wilson (and finally Grace Holloway). The setting was moved to New Year's Eve, 1999. The threat from the TARDIS involved the Eye of Harmony in the Cloister Room (though Jacobs also toyed with an external threat called "The Millennium Star"). The latter half continued to be written by committee as Jacobs attempted to mollify the needs of Segal, FOX, Universal and the BBC.

Meanwhile, other bartering was taking place with the various parties. The casting of the Old Doctor (as the Doctor's past incarnation is credited) was contentious with the BBC and Jo Wright, who preferred using someone they deemed to be a more popular Doctor such as Tom Baker rather than Sylvester McCoy. Segal pressed for it to be a direct continuation and won the day. Universal and FOX meanwhile were concerned about the casting of Paul McGann as the Doctor, who remained Segal's first choice and was popular with the BBC. They wanted an actor they had under contract named Harry Van Gorkum. Universal, which put the majority of the money into the project, held the purse strings and was concerned about budgetary concerns that held up the casting of the Master (the first choice, Christopher Lloyd, was knocked out even though Eric Roberts's fee was ultimately higher). This caused the production to lose a number of shooting days, much to the dismay of director Geoffrey Sax. The fights over budget continued between the various parties with all sorts of issues contributing — including getting the rights to the original theme music, which proved to be expensive as the rights were not owned by the BBC — and the substantial overage of $170,000 was ultimately paid by Universal, which soured relations between the partners even before the project aired.

Production began in Vancouver in January 1996. Segal managed to win the fight to cast Paul McGann and his star arrived on set, his hair shorn from his most recent role as an SAS officer. Segal wanted the character with long hair and so wigs were fashioned. The TARDIS sets were constructed and Geoffrey Sax attempted to compress a complex shoot into fewer days.

The TV Movie premiered on FOX on May 14, 1996 (though it was initially shown two days earlier on a station in Edmonton, Canada, thanks to the vagaries of distribution), and May 27, 1996, in the U.K. Ratings were far better in the U.K., where the production was greeted with nine million viewers, though sales of the VHS, where BBC's merchandising arm hoped to recoup their money, vastly underperformed. Unfortunately, in the U.S., where the ratings really mattered, the TV Movie aired during sweeps, opposite a crucial episode of *Roseanne* where John Goodman's character suffers a heart attack. Consequently, ratings were disastrously low, with only 5.6 million viewers (and a 9% share of the audience). This was not high enough to convince FOX to turn *Doctor Who* into a series.

Doctor Who lay fallow again for another nine years . . .

Adventures in Time and Space The Master returns, as do the Daleks and Skaro (briefly). It's stated that Time Lords have 13 lives, a fact first established in "The Deadly Assassin." We see the TARDIS tool kit (1976's "The Hand of Fear"), complete with neutron ram and magnetic clamp ("Earthshock"). The sonic screwdriver returns, having been destroyed in

1982's "The Visitation." The Cloister Bell rings ("Logopolis") and we see Gallifrey on a scanner ("The War Games" *et al.*). We also see the Doctor's 900-year diary (1966's "The Power of the Daleks"), a yo-yo, jelly babies and a multicoloured scarf (all items the fourth Doctor used), and the seal of Rassilon ("The Deadly Assassin" *et al.*). The TARDIS carries gold dust (presumably to defeat Cybermen, as seen in 1975's "Revenge of the Cybermen"), contains the Eye of Harmony ("The Deadly Assassin") and the staffs contain a bust of Rassilon ("The Five Doctors"). The TARDIS key is ankh shaped (1974's "Planet of the Spiders").

Who is the Doctor? The new Doctor speaks in doubles — mixing his dialogue between the conversation he's having and random observations, as in the "These shoes fit perfectly!" scene — and only uses a gun when he threatens to shoot himself. He namedrops like he did in his third incarnation, mentioning Madame Curie, Puccini, Freud and da Vinci. He knows Grace's and Gareth's futures (though that's probably because of his time travelling rather than precognition). He speaks about his family explicitly for the first time, remembering lying on the grass with his father on a warm Gallifreyan night. He kisses a woman for the first time onscreen. He also claims he's half human, on his mother's side.

Companion Chronicles Grace Holloway is a San Francisco cardiologist. She initially lives with her boyfriend, but he leaves her because she's too devoted to her job — a job she quits when the Doctor's death is covered up. She thinks the Doctor is the "right guy" but decides not to travel with him or learn her own future, because she knows who she is.

Monster of the Week Having been exterminated on Skaro, the Master's ashes transform into a jelly-like snake, which then takes over the body of Bruce, an ambulance driver. This causes his eyes to glow green and he can spit a slimy substance that can incapacitate people or bend them to his will. He's finally sucked into the Eye of Harmony and destroyed. (Upon his return in the New Series, the Master was reconstituted for the Time War, so this appears to be the final end for the original character.)

Stand Up and Cheer The seventh Doctor's last stand on the operating table is incredibly harrowing. He pleads with the surgeons, he grabs instruments and tries in sheer desperation to stop them from accidentally killing him. His final scream is so powerful, it's haunting.

Roll Your Eyes The Master likes to "drezzz for the occasion." Not only does he take the time to change into Gallifreyan robes for no explicable reason, he then camps it up (you almost expect him to slide down the banister and do a dance, complete with a little clap). It's also about this point that credibility flies into the Eye of Harmony, never to return.

You're Not Making Any Sense So we're expected to believe that the Doctor just waltzed onto Skaro, while his mortal enemies, the Daleks, handed him the Master's ashes, so that his final request could be granted, and then allowed the Doctor to go merrily on his way? Because we all know that the Daleks are the kind of ethical creatures who like to honour an enemy's dying wishes.

Interesting Trivia You might notice above that this story doesn't really have a title. That's because it was credited simply as "Doctor Who" onscreen. That, however, is clearly the name of the show, so what do we call this episode? (It's not the first time a story didn't have its title onscreen; this was the practice in the '60s, although individual episodes had their own titles then.) Producer Philip Segal, when asked at a convention, suggested "Enemy Within," which is probably as good a title as any, although it doesn't appear in any official documentation. The BBC's DVD range calls it "*Doctor Who* The Movie." Fans usually refer to it using a descriptor, such as "the TV Movie," rather than picking a title. We've gone with this practice, although we do worry about what will happen when someone decides to make a series of *Doctor Who* TV movies in 2030 . . .

The opening voiceover states that a Time Lord has 13 lives, something the Doctor also mentions to Grace. But if you watch his lips when he does, you'll notice that he actually says, "12." Both the Doctor's dialogue and the opening voiceover originally specified that Time Lords have 12 lives (a misunderstanding based on the fact that they have 12 regenerations but 13 incarnations). Shortly before transmission, an early edit was shown to Shaun Lyon, the director of the Gallifrey One convention in Los Angeles, who noticed the error. Consequently, Paul McGann was brought back to dub the correction.

The eighth Doctor shares three kisses with Grace here: the first when he regains his memory, the second when she immediately asks him to do that again and the third when they say farewell. This was very contentious at the time, especially among fans, but Philip Segal was adamant that he saw the Doctor as a romantic character. Paul McGann was familiar with the Classic Series and so ensured that the kisses were as chaste as possible. Today, we're familiar with the Doctor kissing all manner of people, from Rose and Captain Jack to River Song and Clara, so it doesn't seem nearly so strange.

What is a bit odder, however, is the Doctor being half human. This would have been part of an ongoing arc if the TV Movie had gone to series. (It's present in the bible that Segal produced for the show's backstory and in most of the earlier drafts.) Fans have debated this since the TV Movie's debut. On the side that claims it isn't true is the fact that the Doctor intends to tell Grace a secret but is interrupted by Professor Wagg. The mood becomes much more jovial and the Doctor tells Wagg that he's half human, but as a ruse to steal Wagg's ID card. However, on the other side is the Master discovering the evidence of the Doctor's ancestry when the Eye of Harmony opens and also him telling the Doctor outright that he's only half human. Some have attempted to claim that it's only the eighth Doctor who is half human (without really explaining how this is possible) or that everybody involved was lying or mistaken. Interestingly, there's no evidence in the Classic Series that outright contradicts this claim and it does make a certain kind of sense. Sensibly, however, the New Series has chosen to ignore the issue entirely.

One thing that fascinated fans ever since the TV Movie aired was the identity of the song played at the start. Well, the answer turned out to be that it's not really a song. It's a piece of library stock music called "In a Dream" sung by an artist named Pat Hodge. It's music written and produced to be used in the background in films and television when you need something that, say, sounds like Billie Holliday, but you can't afford to use an actual Billie Holliday song. And that was the case here: originally, the Bing Crosby song "Swinging on a Star" was used, but it was too expensive to license.

The TARDIS Chronometer San Francisco, 1999. (We also briefly glimpse events on Skaro.)

Yes, Yes, Yes? (RS?) The TV Movie is a classic example of a horse designed by a committee. Almost everything good about it flows from Matthew Jacobs's witty and engaging script in the first half, while everything bad occurs in the second half, where you can almost see the committee rewriting the whole thing into mush.

Frustratingly, some of it is extremely impressive. The TARDIS sets are incredible: they actually look lived in and the Victorian feel is a stroke of genius. The theme music is awesome. The CGI looks great. There are big, exciting set pieces, like the car chase. The scanner in the TARDIS dome makes it a place of wonder in a way not seen since the '60s. And the acting ranges from the perfectly acceptable (Daphne Ashbrook, Yee Jee Tso) to the very good (Eric Roberts, Sylvester McCoy) to the outstanding (Paul McGann). The fact that the TARDIS has multiple rooms is a trick the New Series has essentially never mastered.

Where the story really shines is the directing. The opening montage, with the eye motifs, is spectacular (especially the fish eye). Images such as the juxtaposition between *Frankenstein* and the regeneration or the Jesus-like emergence of the eighth Doctor are amazing. Small touches, like the TARDIS dematerialization creating actual wind (something retained in the New Series) or the "Visit London" poster, are very welcome. Shots like the Doctor's breath escaping as he revives, his bare feet walking over the "Get Well Soon" card or Grace's and Lee's bodies framed by autumn leaves add to the mood enormously. And the various collages are very nicely executed, from the Doctor and the Master waking at the same time to the Doctor looking through clothes just as Lee looks through his things. There's a visual power to the storytelling here that enhances the production enormously.

However, there are conceptual flaws that the production simply can't overcome. Starting the story inside the TARDIS was a colossal mistake (people at the time didn't see the connection between the blue box and the large cavern); filling the first 20 minutes with a leading man who's then killed off and replaced by another was a massive error of judgement; and having the resolution consist of time unwinding and resurrecting dead characters robs the story of any credibility it hoped to retain.

It's also founded on massively improbable coincidences: the Eye just happens to suck the Earth through at the stroke of midnight, there just happens to be a beryllium atomic clock in the same city where the TARDIS has landed and the entire day is saved only because Grace somehow learns how to rewire the circuitry of a fantastical space-time machine from an advanced civilization in a matter of seconds.

Sometime after it was released, there was a fan edit of the TV Movie that started with the seventh Doctor sipping tea. When the record jumps, the edit continues with the eighth Doctor sipping tea — and then the credits roll. It's witty, but it also speaks to a greater truth: that perhaps we didn't really miss very much in between. Indeed, we've only included this story in our list of 50 because we think everyone should watch Paul McGann as the Doctor. (Because the ladies demanded it . . .)

Reading the various drafts of what might have been, it's clear we dodged a bullet. Any of those other versions would have been indescribably worse. But that also suggests that the moment simply wasn't right: the '90s weren't the right time to resurrect the show and the U.S. wasn't the place to do it. What we ended up with is half decent and half ridiculous, best viewed today as a road not taken. Thankfully.

The TV Movie. It's half *Who*, on its mother's side.

Second Opinion (GB) It was, as the Doctor said of Puccini's death, so sad. In so many ways, you had to be there to get the full effect: the first new *Doctor Who* for seven years, the great hope of it coming back to television. And it failed.

There's so much that works. Paul McGann, in particular, is superb, instantly making the Doctor an intimate character, full of passion and mystery. (His smile is utterly electric.) The Doctor/Grace romance is quite charming. The Doctor is brilliantly quirky. The idea for the Master might have worked. Director Geoffrey Sax's work with editor Patrick Lussier and director of photography Glenn MacPherson is gorgeous and nearly flawless. It's probably the best-directed American television movie in the past 25 years. The first half hour is stunning. And, yes, there's the TARDIS set.

Where does it go wrong?

Eric Roberts as the Master for a start. He plays as a variety of ciphers — robot, dude, vamp — depending on the needs of the scene. Perhaps it might have helped had Roberts been able to wear the prosthetic makeup that showed his new body decaying (an allergic reaction prevented him), but I'm not convinced because we never get a sense of his character or what motivates him beyond the banal catch-all of survival. (Chang Lee has the same problem, only quadrupled: he goes from thug to decent guy to loveable rogue to dupe to . . . I can't be bothered.)

"Unmotivated" pretty much captures the central problem of this story. It's supposed to be a potential backdoor pilot for a series, but there's no real template of what can be done with the series or its format. Watch the pilot for the '90s series *Sliders* (its third season is what FOX effectively went with instead of *Doctor Who*) and you know it's about how Quinn Mallory has a device that can take him and his friends to any parallel Earth and he's trying to find a way home. What does the backdoor pilot for *Doctor Who* say it's about? It's about . . . a guy and another guy who are from the same planet. And stuff happens in the one guy's spaceship that could destroy the world. Where's the time and space travel? The monsters? Why start the story inside the TARDIS?

It's as though Philip Segal was seduced by that backstory invented for the project. I disagree with my co-author: I think the "Millennium Star" idea and the "TARDIS resurrecting the dead" idea have the basis for something interesting, but instead we got the Eye of Harmony as a MacGuffin. And the heavy continuity references do something designed to launch *Doctor Who* to the U.S. market no favours whatsoever.

Not that there was a chance of that happening. All the problems — the unmotivated plot, the convoluted backstory, Eric Roberts — come to roost as a committee of chimps arrives to write the final act where things occur because, well, stuff happens. The Earth being sucked into the Eye of Harmony? Stuff happens. The Master using it to suck the Doctor's life? Stuff happens. Grace restarting the TARDIS using the metaphor of setting an alarm clock but actually jumping two leads together? Stuff happens. The TARDIS somehow stopping disaster by going back in time? Stuff happens. A golden glow that brings the two dead characters back to life? At this point, the committee of chimps aren't even bothering.

It was, as the Doctor said, so sad.

. . . .

Paul McGann

John Paul McGann was born in 1959 in Liverpool to a large Catholic family. Paul, his older brother Joe, and his younger brothers Mark and Stephen all trained to become actors — at one point even releasing a single in the early 1980s as a boy band, the McGann Brothers! Paul had his first taste of success with the 1983 ITV series *Give Me a Break,* but his real breakout role was playing British criminal Percy Toplis in the 1985 BBC drama *The Monocled Mutineer.* From there, McGann moved on to his best-known role, playing the eponymous "I" opposite Richard E. Grant in Bruce Robinson's 1987 film *Withnail and I.*

McGann continued working in film and television and was all set to play the title role in the historical drama series *Sharpe* when a football injury early into filming meant he had to drop out and was replaced by Sean Bean. A role in *Alien³* was vastly reduced in editing. In 1995, he appeared in a drama about the Irish famine, *The Hanging Gale*, with his other brothers.

Once his work on *Doctor Who* stalled and didn't make it to a series, McGann moved on to a BBC adaptation of Dickens's *Our Mutual Friend*. In 2000, McGann was the lead in the series *Fish* and in 2003 co-starred in the *Hornblower* series of films. Throughout the 2000s, McGann made a series of guest appearances in various TV shows before appearing in the crime series *Luther* starting in 2010.

McGann only appeared as the Doctor onscreen in the TV Movie, but in 2001 he delighted fans by reprising the role in audios produced by Big Finish Productions and has appeared annually in a series of CDs produced by them since, many of which have been broadcast on the BBC digital station Radio 4 Extra.

· ·

The 2000s and 2010s

Starring
Christopher Eccleston (2005)
David Tennant (2005–2010)
Matt Smith (2010–2013)
as the Doctor

Tips for Newbies

- **Enjoy the special effects.** It might be shallow to say, but after decades of *Doctor Who* being mocked for its bad special effects, they're finally just about perfect.

- **Adjust to the pacing.** If you're used to the Classic Series, or have been watching these stories in order, the New Series pacing takes a bit of getting used to. Entire adventures are over and done with in 45 minutes, the space of only two Classic Series episodes. Information comes at you quicker, sometimes in infodumps by the Doctor, and there's less time to world-build. It's in line with modern TV pacing, so, unless you've been living in a cave, you probably won't have problems coping.

- **Learn to love the music.** Unlike in the Classic Series, the music is rather omnipresent here. It's sometimes all pervasive, telling you what to feel at every moment, but once again that's a facet of modern television, so just go with it.

- **Bear with the continuity.** You might be one of those people who loves continuity, like Graeme. Or you might find it intrusive, like Robert, and feel the constant referencing of *Doctor Who*'s past is annoying. Try not to let it get to you.

- **A note on this section of the book.** In the remaining entries, you might notice that we've dropped a few categories. Largely, this is because we'd already covered them in *Who Is The Doctor* and don't want to repeat ourselves.

The Rebirth of *Doctor Who*

In retrospect, it was inevitable that *Doctor Who* would come back. It just took the right people in British television to remember it fondly as a viewing institution.

However, in 2003, on the fortieth anniversary of show, the possibility of *Doctor Who* returning seemed like sheer fantasy. The series had been off the air for 13 years. The TV Movie had failed. For the diaspora of its hardcore fans who kept the torch going, *Doctor Who* had become a multimedia experience: fans followed the Doctor's adventures in books, as audio plays and, increasingly, as webcast adventures. At first, these webcasts were slideshows of drawings to audio adventures of Classic Series Doctors, but 2003 heralded an important innovation: an all-new, completely animated webcast featuring a new actor in the role of the Doctor, Richard E. Grant. This webcast, "Scream of the Shalka," and the team behind the official BBC *Doctor Who* website, would play a small role in bringing the show back to television. But we're getting ahead of ourselves.

By 2003, there were people in place at the BBC who wanted to bring back *Doctor Who*. One of them was Mal Young, the corporation's controller of drama series. Young had pressed for the series' return for a long time, arranging talks with Russell T Davies in 1999 (more on that in a moment) and even working out a budget for it (and adjusting it annually). Another was Jane Tranter, the controller of drama at the BBC. And the final of these executives was Lorraine Heggessy, the controller of BBC1.

Heggessy had made the most promising of pronouncements on the future of the series when she responded to a query by the coordinator of the Doctor Who Appreciation Society in May 2003.

> *Doctor Who* is a classic BBC format, beloved by millions, myself included! If there was a refreshing, affordable treatment for a new series available and we could navigate ourselves around some potentially troublesome rights issues, then I would

consider reviving the series. It's only a wish, there is nothing substantial to back things up, so I don't want to raise false hopes with die-hard fans! Suffice to say that *Doctor Who* has its fans among my commissioning team, most of whom spent the seventies behind the sofa on Saturday evenings too!

What were these "troublesome rights issues"? At the time, it was speculated that the issue concerned the complicated way the rights to the series were carved up for the 1996 TV Movie between the BBC and Universal. Furthermore, starting from the late 1990s, BBC Films was actively shopping the film rights to the series, leading to an inevitable story about the possibility of a *Doctor Who* film around the time of the Cannes International Film Festival each year. There were interested parties, but nothing came of it.

Which brings us back to the webcast "Scream of the Shalka" and the official BBC *Doctor Who* website team. They too heard Heggessy's comments and were concerned about the rights situation when it came to webcasting an animated series.

James Goss, who was in charge of the BBC *Doctor Who* site at the time, explains what happened.

> Daniel Judd . . . was working on the site, and we needed to make sure that we actually had the rights to make a "Scream of the Shalka" webcast. He very patiently rang round a lot of people, and did a lot of the groundwork to make sure we had the rights. Then Lorraine Heggessey started making speeches about how she'd love to bring back *Doctor Who*, but didn't have the rights. And so Daniel patiently pursued a long trail of paperwork and emails and people, and then put together a story on the site saying, "Well, the BBC *does* have the rights."

The BBC *Doctor Who* website's article documented that the rights to *Doctor Who* were still owned jointly by BBC and BBC Worldwide (the BBC's commercial arm, which held the key trademarks internationally) and noted that the rights acquired for the TV Movie by Universal had reverted back to the BBC. While BBC Films had plans to develop a film project, it was early days.

The article ended, somewhat cheekily, "So, the BBC could commission a new *Doctor Who* series for TV if it wanted to."

Fans noting this, and noting what the BBC controller had said, sent some pointed questions to Heggessey. James Goss tells what happens next.

> And then we got rung up by her office. "It's terribly embarrassing," they said, "She's saying one thing and you're saying the other." "But it's true [we have the rights]," we said. And Daniel sent off the paperwork [proving it,] to a thundering silence. And then, a fortnight later, our boss was called to a meeting. He came back grinning from ear to ear and told us. It was then, I think, that we realised that poor old "Shalka" was fucked. But we were all . . . I dunno. Just stunned. I mean — can you imagine *Doctor Who* back on BBC1? Not then. No.

Heggessey immediately worked to get BBC Films to cede its claim to a film and began the process of bringing back *Doctor Who*. Jane Tranter got the wheels in motion for BBC Wales to make the series; the BBC had plans to make BBC Wales a centre for drama in the corporation (effectively making Cardiff the U.K. equivalent to Vancouver). BBC Wales' head of drama, Julie Gardner, was brought in as an executive producer.

On the creative side, Heggessey and Tranter had one person in mind to make this new *Doctor Who*: Russell T Davies.

By 2003, Russell T Davies was a force to be reckoned with in British television. His series *Queer as Folk* had won huge acclaim (and an American remake). He followed it up with *Bob and Rose* and *The Second Coming*; the latter was a controversial telling of the Son of God (played by Christopher Eccleston) coming back to Earth. It was a big ratings winner for rival ITV. By that year, Davies was already on *Entertainment Weekly*'s list of the 100 most influential people in the entertainment industry.

And yet, all of Davies's work was on the commercial channels. Davies would only work with the BBC, he said, if he could bring back *Doctor Who*.

An avowed *Doctor Who* fan, he wrote *Damaged Goods*, one of the last novels in Virgin Publishing's New Adventures range in 1996. He made one of the lead characters in *Queer as Folk* a *Doctor Who* fan. (K9 even made a cameo appearance!) Even when he was working for Granada Television in the early '90s, he was suggesting Granada make *Doctor Who* as an independent producer. (Davies ruefully notes he was laughed out of the room.) The closest Davies had previously come was a preliminary idea meeting with Mal Young's development producer in 1999, but the BBC Films project had scuttled things. Now Heggessey and Tranter were giving Davies the opportunity he'd always wanted.

Together with Julie Gardner and Mal Young (who left the BBC after the first season of the new show), Russell T Davies set to creating the miracle that not only saw the Doctor return to TV screens, but become a unbelievably successful global phenomenon. We pick up the story from there . . .

Rose (2005)

Written by Russell T Davies **Directed by** Keith Boak

Featuring Christopher Eccleston (Doctor Who), Billie Piper (Rose Tyler)

Supporting cast Camille Coduri (Jackie Tyler); Noel Clarke (Mickey Smith); Mark Benton (Clive); Elli Garnett (Caroline); Alan Ruscoe, Paul Kasey, David Sant, Elizabeth Fost, Helen Otway (Autons); Nicholas Briggs (Nestene voice)

Original airdate March 26, 2005

The Big Idea Shop window dummies are coming to life. Legends of a mysterious man called the Doctor and his blue box are all over the internet. And Rose Tyler is about to get caught up in it all.

Time And Relative Dimensions In Space When Russell T Davies was given the greenlight to bring *Doctor Who* back to television, he hadn't written a single word for it. The series was commissioned purely on the desire to bring it back and on the strength of Davies's work. Knowing, however, that BBC executives and, eventually, other writers brought on board would need to see some sort of direction about the general approach and kinds of stories the series would tell, Davies put together what he termed a "pitch document," even though the BBC was already committed.

Written in the autumn of 2003, this outline began with a simple logline: "A girl meets an alien, and together they travel the universe.

Forging a friendship across time and space." The notes on the first episode and the stories to follow were an extrapolation on that, telling the story of Rose Tyler (a character whose name was announced as early as November 2003), a girl from the ordinary world, with a mother named Judy (eventually changed to Jackie) and a boyfriend named Mobbsy (later rechristened Mickey), who encounters the Doctor in an incident involving the Autons from "Spearhead From Space." From the outset, it was Davies's intention to tell the story from Rose's point of view, an instinctive decision that typified what Davies said in his pitch document: "Big ideas, great characters and real emotions. Simple as that."

Adventures in Time and Space The Autons and the Nestene Consciousness return after their appearances in "Spearhead From Space" and 1971's "Terror of the Autons." The scene of the shop window dummies breaking out is a recreation of the famous scene from episode four of "Spearhead From Space." The new Doctor has been at Krakatoa, where a past incarnation had also been, according to the Doctor in "Inferno." He's still using the sonic screwdriver after the events of the TV Movie, though it's been subsequently modified. The D in TARDIS now stands for "Dimension"; it was written in the script as "Dimensions" (as it's been since 1965's "The Time Meddler") but Christopher Eccleston wanted to go back to the original derivation.

Who is the Doctor? The Doctor has perhaps recently regenerated (he checks his reflection and says, "Could've been worse. Look at the ears!") and now speaks with a northern English accent. More than that though, he's angrier, calling humans "stupid apes" and grousing about how humans just sleep and eat and don't have a clue what's going on. In many ways, he's the same old Doctor: in spite of having the means to do so, he refuses to kill the Nestene Consciousness outright, wanting to give it a chance (that said, he carries the anti-plastic as insurance). He seems to suffer guilt as a result of a recent war, telling the Nestene Consciousness, "I couldn't save your world. I couldn't save any of them."

Companion Chronicles Rose Tyler works in a shop until fate intervenes and she meets the Doctor. She's clever enough to suggest the dummies are students, which impresses the Doctor (even though she's wrong). Rose doesn't dismiss the Doctor's story of alien invasion, even though she doesn't believe him, and is resourceful enough to try to track the Doctor down on the internet. She challenges the Doctor for his callousness towards Mickey. All of this, and her willingness to risk her life to save the Doctor, impresses the Time Lord enough to actually trust her — something it seems the Doctor hasn't done in a while.

Monster of the Week The Autons and the Nestene Consciousness return after their appearances in the Pertwee era. The Autons (never called this onscreen, though listed as such in the credits) still function in the same way as their counterparts in the 1970s, though the Consciousness itself is now molten plastic in a giant vat.

Interesting Trivia The New Series was initially co-produced by the Canadian Broadcasting Corporation. The CBC didn't actually have any say in the final program as an ordinary co-producer would. Instead, they put up the money to acquire the series during pre-production, giving the series a cash injection and the CBC a co-producer credit for its first three seasons. A month or so before broadcast, the BBC sent the CBC a viewing copy of "Rose" for internal use. The tape was in PAL format, so the CBC sent it to an outside dubbing facility in Toronto. An employee at said facility, realizing what he had, made a copy of it and put it on BitTorrent to share with perhaps hundreds of thousands of others. The leak of "Rose," which occurred on March 6, a mere 20 days before broadcast, made headline news in the U.K. and in Canada, highlighting the issue of digital piracy. (The employee in question was subsequently fired.) The main change from the viewing copy to the broadcast version is that a stereo mix of the original Delia Derbyshire theme music is used on the opening title sequence.

For long-time fans, the first glimpse of Christopher Eccleston in the new costume during filming in July 2004 was a shock, as received wisdom was that the Doctor always dressed with a sort of Edwardian/ Victorian look. A leather jacket and collarless shirt was quite radical. Right from Russell T Davies's pitch document, the Doctor's costume was going to be more basic: he wanted to move on from what he called "that neutered, posh, public-school, fancy-dress-frock-coat image." He took his inspiration primarily from the reaction in 1996 by his then-boss at Granada Television, David Liddiment, to Paul McGann's costume in the TV Movie, which he chided as being "fancy dress." An early draft of the script described his costume as "clothes once stylish, now battered, maybe a crumpled brown leather jacket." Davies described the look as Terence Stamp running a market stall.

One of the key tenets of the pitch document and indeed the whole approach to the first season was that *Doctor Who* had 40 years of backstory . . . that they would ignore except for "the good bits." Davies felt strongly that beyond the basics — the TARDIS, the sonic screwdriver, the two hearts and the Daleks — the mythology of the series needed to be discovered by a new audience and in the narrative by Rose. Which is why there's only a brief mention of his past incarnations (and why Clive only has photos of the ninth Doctor on his website), why "Time Lord" only gets uttered by the Nestene Consciousness at the very end and why the Autons are never called anything but "dummies." At the same time, Davies wasn't against continuity with past stories (he even mused about adding K9 to the mix in his pitch document!), noting that there was a certain joy in watching a new generation of fans discover the series' rich past — something that has since been realized.

TARDIS Chronometer Rose's home on the Powell Estate in South London and various locations in Central London including Henrik's department store and below the London Eye. "Aliens of London" (2005) and "The End of Time, Part Two" (2010) establish the date as 2005.

Fantastic? (GB) I have seen "Rose" probably more times than any story in the New Series (at least a dozen of those viewings took place in March 2005!). I showed it to my teenaged goddaughter and she loved it. I showed it to two of my best friends and got them interested in new *Doctor Who*. I showed it to their then-eight-year-old daughter a couple of years ago, and now she's a giant fan who had a faux-Lego Dalek construction set on her Christmas list. I showed it to my seven-year-old nephew and my five-year-old niece last year, and they've begged me to show them more *Doctor Who* ever since.

"Rose" is just that good. It's just that exciting. It's just that fun.

First episodes of any new series are curious beasts. The characters aren't quite right (the Doctor is garrulous and goofy, and Jackie and Mickey are played very broadly). Rose gets a backstory (she left school because of Jimmy Stone; maybe she could go back and do her A levels) that never comes up again. There are visual flourishes that never quite happen again, like the opening montage to the poptastic soundtrack by Murray Gold. And yet, even with all of this, "Rose" still immediately establishes what's so wonderful about *Doctor Who*.

For me, both "Rose" and this new *Doctor Who* are defined by three moments. The first is when the Doctor rescues Rose and trundles her out of the store, gruffly telling her off about her mundane life while he's about to face certain death. He then slams the door. Pause. The door

re-opens. "I'm the Doctor by the way. What's your name?" "Rose."
And suddenly the Doctor's all giddy and sweet. "Nice to meet you,
Rose. Run for your life!"

Ladies and gentlemen, the Doctor is back!

The second moment is the Doctor's exchange with Rose as she
walks with him back to the TARDIS. There's this beautiful scene where
the Doctor takes her hand and talks about feeling the turn of the Earth,
falling through space. It's an incredible scene. It's played brilliantly by
Christopher Eccleston, who establishes that this silly, odd Doctor is
actually a much richer character. It's really when Rose falls in love with
the Doctor. And when the audience does too.

The last moment is the climax. Who knows why three Autons
would suddenly, execution-style open up their guns at Jackie, and the
edit suffers from a few too many shots of the Doctor struggling, but
I love when it suddenly comes down to Rose to be a hero. She's got
nothing to show for her life except the bronze medal she got as a little
kid for swinging on a rope. And a willingness to risk her life. It's a
punch-the-air moment when she saves the day.

There are things about "Rose" I could do without, such as Keith
Boak's clunky direction, which emphasizes the comedic and juvenile
aspects a little too much (though part of that is probably the problem of
figuring out the tone). But there are things I think are absolute genius:
using Rose as the starting point and having everything shown through
her eyes is brilliant. Instead of the muddle of the TV Movie, which
tried to establish everything about the Doctor before he even arrives on
Earth, here we have discovery: piece by piece, Rose — and the viewer
— gets drawn into the Doctor's world. Using the Autons is another
stroke of brilliance. To sell what terrors lurk in the Doctor's world,
you don't need anything elaborate; drawing from the rich tapestry of
Doctor Who's past gives a convenient shorthand for it. Indeed, plun-
dering from "Spearhead From Space" wholesale shows a new audience
what makes *Doctor Who* so utterly different from anything else.

People forget this now, but, at the time, a new version of *Doctor
Who* was a huge gamble. Everything had to be absolutely right for it
to work. For it had to convince not only jaded fans like me, but people
indifferent to the show and kids who had never seen *Doctor Who*.

Did it succeed? Oh yes.

Second Opinion (RS?) It's the extended opening of "Rose" that gets me every time. And everything you need to know about the New Series is there.

The super-fast-paced opening titles tell us that this isn't the Classic Series. The rapid zoom down to London and to Rose's alarm tells us that this is a show with confidence and verve. Rose's day in fast-forward tells us everything we need to know about her life in seconds.

The elevator's descent to the basement ending in sudden silence tells us that the story knows precisely where to start. The creepy menace of the deserted storeroom and the Autons slowly coming to life tell us that this is a show that knows how to scare. And the Doctor taking Rose's hand and uttering a single word ("Run!") tells us that this isn't the TV Movie.

The Doctor wrenching the Auton's arm off and then waving it at her tells us that comedy hasn't been forgotten. Rose being brusquely sent on her way tells us that this is a traumatized Doctor, one afraid of company. The Doctor introducing himself and then ordering Rose to run for her life tells us that this series has a manifesto. Henrik's blowing up (in the age of terrorism) tells us that this isn't a comfortable show. And Rose running down the street past the TARDIS, with only the slightest lingering on the camera's behalf, tells us that this is a show we've already fallen in love with, without even noticing.

"Rose" is an excellent episode in its own right. It's funny, sweet, exciting and well paced. It's a perfect vehicle to introduce new fans to the show and it's so ridiculously confident that you can't help but laugh and go along with it. But it's the opening scene that tells us everything we need to know. *Doctor Who* is back — and it's about time.

· ·

Christopher Eccleston

Born in the Salford area of Manchester in 1964, Christopher Eccleston achieved critical acclaim for one of his first major roles, in 1991's *Let Him Have It*, but he became known by the British public for his portrayal of Robbie Coltrane's boss, DCI Bilborough, in *Cracker*. Eccleston continued building his name with edgy roles including David in *Shallow Grave* (1994) and Nicky Hutchinson in the acclaimed BBC series *Our Friends in the North* (1996). Other roles included *Jude* (1996), *Elizabeth* (1998), *eXistenZ* (1999), *Gone in 60 Seconds* (2000), *The Others* (2001) and *28 Days Later* (2002). In

2003, he played a modern-day incarnation of the Son of God in Russell T Davies's *The Second Coming*.

Eccleston emailed Davies when he heard about the new *Doctor Who* to express his interest in the role of the Doctor; he wanted to play a part that could be watched by children and he was interested in the approach Davies would take with the series.

He only played the Doctor for a season and has rarely spoken about his time in the role. Subsequently, Eccleston played Claude in *Heroes* (2007), Destro in *G.I. Joe: The Rise of Cobra* (2009), John Lennon in *Lennon Naked* (2010) and Malekith in *Thor: The Dark World* (2013). He returned to television with 2011's *Shadowline* and 2012's *Blackout*.

· ·

Dalek (2005)

Written by Robert Shearman **Directed by** Joe Ahearne

Featuring Christopher Eccleston (Doctor Who), Billie Piper (Rose)

Supporting cast Bruno Langley (Adam Mitchell), Corey Johnson (Henry van Statten), Anna-Louise Plowman (Diana Goddard), Steven Beckingham (Polkowski), Nigel Whitmey (Simmons), John Schwab (Bywater), Jana Carpenter (De Maggio), Nicholas Briggs (Dalek voice), Barnaby Edwards (Dalek operator)

Original airdate April 30, 2005

The Big Idea In a bunker in Utah, the Doctor encounters the last surviving member of a race he thought he'd destroyed.

Time And Relative Dimensions In Space During the 15-year gap between the Classic and New Series, Big Finish Productions had been releasing *Doctor Who* stories on CD. These audio adventures featured Peter Davison, Colin Baker, Sylvester McCoy and Paul McGann. One of the writers to achieve very positive notice was Robert Shearman, a playwright who, at the time, was writing for British theatre legend Alan Aykbourn. In 2003, Big Finish released "Jubilee" penned by Shearman, featuring the Daleks and the sixth Doctor. Set in a parallel timeline where the Dalek Invasion of Britain had been foiled by the Doctor 100 years earlier in 1903, "Jubilee" examined the effect this had on British culture. It was a dark satire on the commodification of history and the banalization of evil, with the Daleks seen as comedic figures of fun while British culture became more like the Daleks they had eradicated.

Russell T Davies listened to the Big Finish audios, partially as an (unsuccessful) attempt to stop smoking. He was particularly impressed with one sequence in "Jubilee" where the Doctor's companion, Evelyn, met the remaining Dalek who had been imprisoned and tortured in the Tower of London. Davies was keen to bring back the Daleks in the New Series as one of the parties in the war where the Time Lords were destroyed. In his "pitch document," he wrote a brief outline for a story set in 2010 where a Dalek was a captive of a Bill Gates–type figure (named "Will Fences" in the outline!). The concept was taken from "Jubilee" and Shearman was asked to write the episode.

Shearman proceeded to develop the story (initially under the title "Creature of Lies"). By the fifth draft, Shearman felt confident things had taken shape. However, negotiations between the BBC and Terry Nation's estate had stalled (executive producer Mal Young prematurely soured developments by saying "We've got the Daleks!" in an interview with *Broadcast* magazine before negotiations had finalized). Now, using the Daleks at all was up in the air. Davies had a solution at hand, which was to substitute psychotic, deadly spheres from the future. (The spheres became the Toclafane in 2007's "The Sound of Drums"/"The Last of the Time Lords.") Shearman wrote a draft with these — he wryly titled this draft "Absence of the Daleks" — before negotiations worked out with the Nation estate, and the Daleks returned to *Doctor Who*.

Adventures in Time and Space The contents of van Statten's museum include a Slitheen arm (2005's "Aliens of London"/"World War Three") and a Cyberman head (the version is from 1975's "Revenge of the Cybermen" though the plaque, admittedly unseen on TV, indicates it most likely came from 1968's "The Invasion"). When van Statten's helicopter descends, it uses the call sign "Bad Wolf," a reference to the ongoing motif in the 2005 season that culminates in "The Parting of the Ways." The Doctor is also described as "the coward" by the Dalek, something that has greater resonance at the end of the season when he's given the choice of killer or coward and happily chooses the latter.

We're told that the Daleks are genetically engineered, with all emotions removed except hate, harking back to "Genesis of the Daleks." The Dalek asking for pity also echoes that story. The Daleks' creator, Davros, is described (as "a man who was king of his own little world"), but not named.

Who is the Doctor? Upon seeing the Dalek, he immediately panics. Subsequently, he has no compulsion about committing genocide, either by pulling the lever himself or by ordering the Dalek to commit suicide. He goes so far as to point a gun at the Dalek, but Rose's compassion for it forces him to confront the fact that the Time Lords are truly gone.

Companion Chronicles Rose is attracted to Adam in part because he reminds her of the Doctor (when he says, "Fantastic!"). The Dalek says outright that Rose is the woman the Doctor loves, even though she insists they're still friends.

Monster of the Week A single Dalek. Initially in chains, with noticeable damage, it can't exterminate. It fell to Earth, landing in the Ascension Islands 50 years ago. It was sold at private auction, moving from one collection to another. It can calculate a thousand billion combinations in one second flat, absorbs bullets in a force field and can rotate its sections independently of the others. As a result of absorbing Rose's DNA, it begins to change, deciding it wants freedom.

Interesting Trivia The Time War had been hinted at in the past few stories, but this is where we learn that it was a war between the Time Lords and the Daleks, and the Doctor was responsible for its end. This involved 10 million Dalek ships on fire and the Doctor's ultimate survival, but not by choice. What's not revealed is how recently this was or whether it caused him to regenerate. It seems probable that it did; if so, given that the Doctor seems unfamiliar with his reflection in "Rose," it's likely that the Time War only ended a very short time before he met Rose. No wonder the Doctor's so traumatized.

It's 2012, so why doesn't van Statten know what a Dalek is? Later events, such as 2006's "Doomsday" and 2008's "The Stolen Earth" — both of which are set before this story — see Daleks invading Earth in a way that makes their presence obvious. As an alien connoisseur, van Statten should know about their presence in 1930s New York (2007's "Daleks in Manhattan"), to say nothing of their stealing the entire planet he was on. Adam also seems to know nothing of these events. Two explanations are possible. The first is that the timelines changed as a result of the Doctor's later interference; had he not been present, "The Stolen Earth" wouldn't have happened. The other possibility is that we're seeing a version of the universe where the crack in time had swallowed knowledge of the Daleks. So just as Amy Pond didn't know who the Daleks were when she should have, neither does van Statten.

The TARDIS Chronometer A bunker in Utah, near Salt Lake City, 2012.

Fantastic? (RS?) Yes, yes, the episode draws a parallel between the Doctor and the Dalek. Both the last surviving members of their species, both damaged and alone, both locking themselves inside a hardened shell that must be metaphorically (or literally) opened up at the story's end. And both have breakthroughs because of Rose: the Dalek because it absorbs her DNA and the Doctor because she cracks his emotional armour. When the Dalek asks Rose if she's frightened at the story's conclusion and then admits that it is as well, we see that the creature started as a parallel to the Doctor, but ends as a parallel to Rose.

What I'm more interested in is van Statten. Okay, sure, laugh it up. It's true, he's rubbish — but only in the acting. Put aside Corey Johnson's performance (if you can) and look at the character underneath it. He's a guy who hangs a huge picture of himself in his office and who spends his time boasting about how great he is but who's nevertheless obsessed by being recognized by the Dalek.

He looks like a villain, but he's not. Sure, he tortures both the Dalek and the Doctor, but he's also capable of being reasoned with. He releases the Doctor because he wants to live, although he's still trying to keep control of the situation, even as his personnel are being massacred. Interestingly, everyone's stopped listening to him by this point: the troops ignore his orders and Goddard has started deferring to the Doctor. And the Dalek simply choosing to stay silent in front of him is a stroke of genius: it shows just how arrogant the creature is by simply refusing to engage with its torturer.

The Doctor finally gets through to van Statten in the scene when he asks what the nearest city is. When told it's Salt Lake City, population one million, the Doctor's reply of "All dead" leaves van Statten visibly shaken. From this point on, van Statten stops behaving like Ricky Gervais in *The Office* and starts to help.

The Doctor's subsequent putdown of him is withering in its intensity. In a story replete with intense acting from Christopher Eccleston ("Why don't you just die?"), it's his demolition of van Statten's character that's actually painful to watch. When the Doctor and the Dalek go toe to toe, it's a contest of equals. When the Doctor accuses van

Statten of dragging the stars down and burying them, you actually feel sorry for the man.

And then, finally, the inevitable happens. The Dalek confronts van Statten, finally agrees to talk — and has just a single word to say to him: "Exterminate."

This should be van Statten's comeuppance, killed by the creature he tortured. In most *Doctor Who* stories, it probably would be. The best way to demonstrate the power of the primary villain is to watch it wreak vengeance on the secondary one (think Sutekh killing Namin in "Pyramids of Mars").

Only . . . van Statten is spared. Partly this is to demonstrate Rose's compassion: she's aghast at the idea of the Dalek killing even the unlikeable van Statten. It also demonstrates the Dalek's evolution: not just sparing the companion, it's now refusing to kill a one-off guest star. But it also saves van Statten for his final fate: he's rightly punished for his earlier actions, in allowing his people to be killed.

Having him mindwiped and left on the street isn't pleasant, but it isn't horrendous either. It seems like a fair punishment. Even better, Goddard doesn't just take over his role; the bunker is being cemented in, ending van Statten's legacy for good. Any other story would have killed him as penance, but those sorts of deaths rarely feel significant. What we see here is *Doctor Who* putting its money where its mouth is: the message is that killing is wrong, regardless of whether you're a Dalek or the Doctor. Sparing van Statten reinforces this stance.

In the end, van Statten is a misguided fool, but he isn't a murderer. His actions led to the deaths of hundreds and they could have led to the deaths of millions, but he was driven by greed, not evil.

And so in "Dalek" we see a high-octane action-adventure episode that's nevertheless layered with parallels and is also a fascinating character study. The story engages the brain as well as the adrenaline and gives us a villain who's truly human. Now if only he'd been played by Simon Pegg . . .

Second Opinion (GB) For me, "Dalek" will always be about the Doctor and the Dalek. Two sides of the same coin: battle-scarred creatures, one losing and the other gaining a sense of humanity, and the struggle both have to get back to where they were.

The Doctor loses his sense of humanity as he confronts his anger and guilt. The scene where the Doctor realizes he has power over the broken-down Dalek is chilling: the Doctor sets about a torture-ridden death for it without a second thought. Even his use of his catchphrase "fantastic" is sour and without humour. Christopher Eccleston brings incredible intensity to the role and here is its greatest expression.

The Dalek gains a sense of humanity and it's the worst possible thing that could happen to it: it cannot kill. Instead of escaping the bunker to exterminate Salt Lake City, it opens itself up and the creature inside stretches its tendril to the sunlight. And it views this as sickness. Nicholas Briggs's vocal performance is often lost in the fireworks Eccleston brings and that's a shame. It's amazing how he wrings so much emotion from what should be a ring-modulated monotone. And the final speech where the Dalek begs Rose for its life is chilling.

It's that climactic scene that shows how both sides regain what they lost. Rose makes the Doctor, carrying an obscene-sized gun, see past his anger and hatred. And the Dalek asserts the only thing left defining it as a Dalek. It begs her to order it to exterminate itself. This element of Rob Shearman's script is terrific: it identifies that the Daleks are bound by orders, by a hierarchy; forcing it to find another person to be its superior, and eventually landing on the person who infected it with humanity, is glorious in its cunning.

"Dalek" is probably the most essential story featuring the pepper-pots in their 50-year history, precisely because it defines what they are capable of and how they are motivated. And how their presence, in turn, motivates the Doctor.

. . . .

Making *Doctor Who* in the Modern Era

In the 2000s, BBC Wales became a centre for the production of several British dramas including *Doctor Who*, *Torchwood*, *Life on Mars*, *Casualty*, *Upstairs Downstairs* and *Sherlock*. All of them follow more or less the same model as *Doctor Who*: productions filmed extensively on location (usually within Wales, but also elsewhere in Britain), supplemented by studio work where needed (particularly with standing sets).

Doctor Who's interior and exterior locations have been dressed to look like the past, present or future (or anywhere else). While mostly shot in Cardiff, the series goes further afield for specific locations (like London in "Rose" or the Elizabethan-era surroundings of Warwick in 2007's "The Shakespeare Code").

Increasingly, more material is shot in studio. The standing set of the TARDIS is there alongside other sets built for specific episodes. At first, these sets were in a converted warehouse space in Newport outside Cardiff. In 2006, the series moved to Upper Boat Studios in Pontypridd, which housed not only *Doctor Who* but its spinoffs *Torchwood* and *The Sarah Jane Adventures*. (Often *Doctor Who* would take over the studio space of the other series; for example, 2008's "The Next Doctor" completely redressed the Torchwood hub standing set to be a Victorian workhouse.) In 2012, a new, state-of-the-art facility for BBC Wales productions was built in Cardiff Bay at Roath Lock and *Doctor Who* relocated there.

Doctor Who is made on digital video (and in 2008 moved to high-definition format), which is now customary in the British television industry. The finished program is "filmized" in post-production. (Watch the outtakes on several DVD box sets — which have not had the film effect added — and you'll see 21st-century *Doctor Who* looking very much like its twentieth-century counterpart!) While all aspects of *Doctor Who* were done in-house at the BBC in the Classic Series, in the New Series, it's largely just pre-production elements like design that are kept close. Practical special effects have been subcontracted to a variety of firms, while CGI effects have been created primarily by effects firm The Mill since 2005. Music for the entirety of the New Series has been provided by composer Murray Gold.

In 2013, BBC Television Centre, the home of *Doctor Who* for much of its original 26 years, was closed. *Doctor Who* had one last hurrah there when the 2013 docudrama about the creation of the series, *An Adventure in Space and Time*, used its offices and corridors for filming, making it the last drama made there. The Television Centre's closing set off a wave of nostalgia for a bygone era when making *Doctor Who* was determined by union rules (which meant that studio taping would cease at 10 p.m.) and made by a series of in-house departments within the BBC. While *Doctor Who* is produced in a vastly different way today, the same creativity, innovation and spirit of hard work continues into the second decade of the 21st century.

Love & Monsters (2006)

Written by Russell T Davies **Directed by** Dan Zeff

Featuring David Tennant (The Doctor), Billie Piper (Rose Tyler)

Supporting cast Camille Coduri (Jackie Tyler), Marc Warren (Elton Pope),

Peter Kay (Victor Kennedy/The Abzorbaloff), Shirley Henderson (Ursula Blake),

Simon Greenall (Mr. Skinner), Moya Brady (Bridget), Kathryn Drysdale (Bliss),

Paul Kasey (The Hoix), Bella Emberg (Mrs. Croot)

Original airdate June 17, 2006

The Big Idea Elton is an ordinary bloke, living an ordinary life. Well, except for his obsession with ELO . . . and the fact that he keeps encountering the Doctor.

Time And Relative Dimensions In Space Work had begun on devising and commissioning the second season of the New Series of *Doctor Who* before the first had even been broadcast. There was a great deal of confidence that the show would be a success. So much so that an extra episode, a Christmas special, was added to the 2006 lineup. However, this posed a problem for executive producer Russell T Davies. Fourteen episodes would have to be shot in the same amount of time it took to make 13 the previous season. The only solution was to "double-bank": make two episodes simultaneously with different directors and casts and crews, and have one of the episodes require minimal involvement from the actors portraying the Doctor and Rose. In the event, "Love & Monsters" overlapped with the making of 2006's "The Impossible Planet"/"The Satan Pit."

In creating this "Doctor-lite" episode, Davies went back to an idea he suggested for a 2004 *Doctor Who Magazine* comic strip, about an ordinary man who grew up in the backdrop of *Doctor Who*'s alien invasions of London: as a child, he was evacuated from Shoreditch (during "Remembrance of the Daleks"), he experienced the killer plastic daffodils used by the Autons in 1971's "Terror of the Autons" and encountered the Loch Ness monster in the Thames (1975's "Terror of the Zygons"). Davies had proposed a story about a female stalker of the Doctor under similar circumstances called "I Love the Doctor" (he changed his mind about the character's gender because of the number of strong female roles that season). Davies left the overall story loose, in order to build in other elements that came up; the most notable of which was a "Design a *Doctor Who* Monster" competition on the BBC children's series *Blue Peter* that promised to put the winner's entry into a *Doctor Who* story. Nine-year-old William Grantham won for his creation, the Abzorbaloff.

Adventures in Time and Space We see reenactments (with Elton) of the events of "Rose," 2005's "Aliens of London" and 2005's "The Christmas Invasion," complete with musical cues from those stories. Jackie laments the departure of Mickey, who left for a parallel world at the end of 2006's "The Age of Steel." Victor Kennedy mentions the Torchwood Insitute (as part of that season's story arc dealing with Torchwood) but talks about their data being corrupted by the "Bad Wolf virus," a shout-out to the previous season's recurring meme. The Abzorbaloff is related to the Slitheen, coming from Clom, the twin planet of Raxacoricofallapatorius.

Who is the Doctor? Brigid, Mr. Skinner, Bliss and even Kennedy all have their ideas about who the Doctor is, but ultimately, the Doctor gets the final word. While he concedes being passionate, even sweet, he refuses to be seen as nice — and demonstrates by showing he's happy to let Elton die . . . though he does give those absorbed the means to destroy Kennedy, even as it kills them too. When you think about it, it's contradictory and a little terrifying.

Companion Chronicles Rose is fiercely protective of her mother — enough to get the Doctor to pilot the TARDIS through time and space to give Elton a piece of her mind.

Monster of the Week The . . . Absorbatrix? Absorbaclon? Abzorbaloff? Yeah, that one. It's a creature from the planet Clom that can absorb people with one touch. Once absorbed, the Abzorbaloff's victims are kept alive and sentient inside its body, the outline of their face visible through its skin.

Interesting Trivia This won't be the last time *Doctor Who* double-banks. In 2007, we had "Blink" (you can read about that in a little bit); in 2008, the series had one story solely feature the Doctor ("Midnight") and another solely feature the companion, Donna Noble ("Turn Left"). A similar split was used in 2011 with the Doctor only in brief scenes in the TARDIS in "The Girl Who Waited," while Amy and Rory only show up briefly during "Closing Time."

The casting of popular comedian Peter Kay came about when Kay sent Davies a fan letter praising the revived series. Davies sent him a script for the story thinking he might play Elton. Kay was more interested in the dual role of Victor Kennedy and the Abzorbaloff, thinking the role might stretch him more. They both agreed that while Kennedy spoke with a posher accent, Kay could speak in his native Bolton accent once he was the Abzorbaloff.

TARDIS Chronometer In and around London in 2007 (present-day stories at the time were the current year plus one, ever since 2005's "Aliens of London"). There are also flashbacks to Elton's childhood (in the late '70s or early '80s; we hear the TARDIS materialize), as well as to the Nestene invasion of 2005, and the Slitheen and Sycorax invasions of 2006.

Brilliant? (GB) *A is for Abzorbaloff.* Created by a nine-year-old fan. In a story about fans. That's quite sweet.

B is for Bold. With the Doctor and Rose's presence minimal at best, Russell T Davies pulls the rip-cord and gives us a story with narration, talking (literally) to the camera, flashback, flashforward and melancholy, tough but gorgeous character pieces and funny gags all at a breakneck pace.

C is for Cold Open, or the pre-credits sequence, which is sublime. Elton running around, the Doctor and Rose nowhere in sight. The TARDIS! The Doctor's and Rose's voices! More running! A monster! Cut to: Elton, nerding out on video, telling us, "I put that at the beginning because it's a brilliant opening." And he's right.

D is for Double-Banked. Any other show doing an episode without its leads would be madness. But the genius here is making the story about people obsessed with the Doctor and where that obsession takes them.

E is for ELO. There is no better song to express the various moods of this story than "Mr. Blue Sky." It's like the soundtrack of every happy memory in your life and a few of the saddest ones too. Perfect.

F is for Fan. If you're reading this book, you probably are one. (If you're not, we hope you're having a good time anyway!) And if you're fan enough of something to read a book about it, you know what it's like to want to know more about something. To have that yearning to be with others who know what the hell you're talking about — and to sometimes find the whole scene just a little too freakish. This story is for you.

G is for God among Writers. Okay. That's what I call Russell T Davies most days. I have a little shrine with votive candles and everything. I've adored him long before *Doctor Who.* He grasps the modern television medium like no other. As much as I've loved all his *Doctor Who* work,

I've always wanted something that showcased the genius of Russell's non-*Who* writing in *Doctor Who*. "Love & Monsters" is that story.

H is for Howling Halls. Elton's realization that the Doctor was present at his mother's death is so perfectly sad.

I is for "I've had the most terrible things happen. And the most brilliant things. And sometimes, well, I can't tell the difference. They're all the same thing. They're just me." Which may be one of the truest things said in *Doctor Who*.

J is for Jackie Tyler. Camille Coduri is an absolute revelation here. Without Rose to dominate, we get to see Jackie at her best — she's confident, flirtatious, funny, dominant — and at her most vulnerable. Coduri makes the most of the opportunity.

K is for Kooks. You would think from the delightfully comedic tone of the episode that Russell T Davies would want to mock fans of *Doctor Who*. And yet, he doesn't. The fans on display here are eccentrics but the sort of eccentrics that everyone is, in their own way. They're people with rich inner lives with pain, hope and imagination. I know these people. You know these people. I'm one of them. You might be too.

L is for LINDA. LINDA offers this place where we see these beautiful relationships form: shy, nerdy Mr. Skinner with his pulp novel falling for the bereft Bridget who lost her child to drugs; Elton's budding friendship with Ursula that blossoms to love. All from a group talking about some weird conspiracy thing. That's kind of wonderful.

M is for Marc Warren. Without the Doctor, you need a central character played by an actor who's strong enough to ground it all, but not so much as to distract from the Doctor's absence. Marc Warren as Elton is perfect. Elton isn't an innocent; he's a bit incompetent, but he's always wonderfully honest and Warren nails that.

N is for Nice. I love the unselfconscious way Elton dances to ELO.

O is for Outside Looking In. The thing about LINDA is that none of them actually knows who the Doctor is. They have no idea he's a time traveller or about the TARDIS. But he's a figure that is enigmatic and compelling.

P is for Police Box. That wonderful moment when Elton hesitates outside the TARDIS in the opening. It's what we would do.

Q is for Questions. Why don't we ever see Ursula as a paving stone on Elton's video? How often does Elton change his clothes in the videos? Did the episode "really" happen or was it some Doctor-based fan fiction? What does Elton mean by "we even have a bit of a love life"? That's the great thing about this story: there are all sorts of levels of meaning and possibilities.

R is for Raxacoricofallapatorius. It's my favourite name for a planet, ever. And its twin planet is named . . . Clom.

S is for "Salvation and damnation are the same thing." A quote from Stephen King used by Elton to indicate that the things we love that give us sustenance in our lives will often destroy us. We need to remember that more often.

T is for the TARDIS Dematerialization Sound. I fetishize it the same way everyone here does. Ahem.

U is for Unhappy. This is a story about those who get left behind in the wake of the Doctor; in this case, we see inside Jackie's heart and soul, and how she copes without Rose — and how she'll defend her to the death.

V is for Victor Kennedy. My only real quibble with the episode is with Peter Kay, who is brilliant while he's Victor Kennedy but less so when his true villainy is revealed. The story is written in a slightly exaggerated way, with everyone just a touch off the ground. Kay, however, soars into the stratosphere.

W is for Workhouse. The moment where LINDA's gathering place changes to a strictly ordered workhouse is a moment every fan recognizes. When the hobby they engage in to make them happier suddenly becomes . . . drudgery, often thanks to the influence of others. It's remarkably observant.

X is for Xeroderma. Abnormal dryness of the skin. If Kennedy had said that word, we wouldn't have had the dispute over the pronunciation of "eczema."

Y is for Yakkity-Yak. I think the dialogue is unbelievably funny. "I had to invent this rudimentary pulley system, just to reach my boots." Or Elton to Jackie after sampling the wine: "Very nice. What's that, French?" "I suppose so."

Z is for . . . Whatever you want it to be. (It could be for the ampersand, the only time it's used in a *Doctor Who* title!) And that's what's great about "Love & Monsters." It's a story about people who love the Doctor that speaks in the language of people who have loved the Doctor for decades. It's what Elton says at the end, when he reflects on the normal life we're told about as kids, "The world is so much stranger than that. It's so much darker, and so much madder. And so much better."

Second Opinion (RS?) ♥ *is for Love.*

The Psychic Papers: A Brief History of *Doctor Who* Fandom

Ever since there has been popular entertainment, there have been fans. Jonathan Swift's *Gulliver's Travels* had cheap knock-off sequels (effectively fan fiction; the Master of the Land of Fiction in "The Mind Robber" would have been pleased). Twenty thousand fans of Sir Arthur Conan Doyle's Sherlock Holmes unsubscribed en masse from *Strand* magazine when Conan Doyle killed off Holmes. By the early 1930s, American fans of the nascent genre of science fiction had organized themselves into societies and were printing fanzines (fan magazines) chock-full of opinion and amateur (and sometimes even professional) fiction, and holding the very first conventions.

Doctor Who has almost always had some form of organized fandom. The first sign of it was the William (Doctor Who) Hartnell Fan Club, which was set up in 1965 by a fan in Stoke-on-Trent. It produced a newsletter and the BBC supported it by offering its members free publicity photos of the series' stars. The organization eventually changed its name to the Official Doctor Who Fan Club and produced mimeographed newsletters for its members throughout the 1960s. It cost its successive organizers a fortune in postage.

In 1971, a 14-year-old named Keith Miller wrote to the *Doctor Who* production office to inquire about the fan club. The club was about to be abandoned, so producer Barry Letts's production secretary, Sarah Newman, was happy to give it over to Miller. Perhaps because Miller was so young, Newman and Letts saw to it that the teenager had an unprecedented amount of support from the production office, supplying him with stencils to make the club fanzine, and reproducing and mailing it from the BBC. They even arranged for Miller to watch the production of several episodes. The relationship had a few bumps in the road: Jon Pertwee objected to Miller's heavy emphasis on discussing the show's history and its early stories, which led to Pertwee attempting to unseat the fan club; Miller was supported but instructed to stop the 1960s worship. Miller also had competition from other fans who felt they should have been allowed to run the fan club; one of those fans was Peter Capaldi, now a respected British actor who, 40 years later, would become the twelfth Doctor!

One element that distinguishes *Doctor Who* fans was a tendency we call "open source fandom." Books like *The Making of Doctor Who* (1972) talk about how the program was made in great detail. Consequently, *Doctor Who* fans knew what a "script editor" was and became fascinated by every facet of the series' making, from costumes to camera work.

By the mid-1970s, the active assistance from the BBC began to cool. Incoming producer Philip Hinchcliffe felt the club should be doing more to expand its member base. (Tom Baker was more sympathetic and even offered Miller money to get address labels for his membership printed!) Miller kept at it, though, and improved the quality of the 'zine. However, Miller was not impressed with producer Graham Williams's tenure on the program and that, coupled a crackdown from the corporation's legal department on the use of BBC copyrighted photos in the 'zine, drove Miller to give up the Doctor Who Fan Club in early 1978.

A replacement for Miller's club was already on the horizon. The Doctor Who Appreciation Society was formed in 1976 by Stephen Payne and Jan Vincent-Rudzki, two students at the University of London's Westfield College. The group went national shortly after and became the official British fan club. The DWAS, as it is known, was much more interested in social events than Miller's 'zine-based club. They organized the first *Doctor Who* convention in August 1977 and even bigger events followed in the next several years.

As DWAS took hold in Britain, *Doctor Who* was growing in popularity in North America, thanks to PBS running the series. The first *Doctor Who* conventions in the U.S. and Canada happened in the late '70s. (Australia and New Zealand have also had fan networks since the 1970s and 1980s respectively.) At first, DWAS served the North American fans but quickly realized how under-resourced the organization was and left that fandom to take care of itself. New clubs were formed, including the Doctor Who Fan Club of America (which folded in the 1990s) and the Doctor Who Information Network (which still exists today).

The 1980s were the first golden age of *Doctor Who* fandom. There were large conventions throughout Britain, North America and Australia. Fanzines were numerous, mostly disseminating news and pithy opinion in the way that internet forums do today. Producer John Nathan-Turner actively courted the fanbase, making sure favourite characters and monsters came back to the program, and regularly taking part in the convention circuit (and actively pressing actors from the show to join him).

This hit its zenith with the celebrations of the series' twentieth anniversary in 1983. A BBC Enterprises–sponsored weekend celebration of 20 years of *Doctor Who* at the Longleat Estate during Easter 1983 attracted 40,000 fans (and saw many more turned away). That same year came the largest American fan gathering, which saw 20,000 fans at the Spirit of Light convention in Chicago. These conventions were similar to the ones we know today, with cosplay (dressing up in costume) and fan creativity. They were just larger.

The popularity of the show among fans in America continued through Colin Baker's and Sylvester McCoy's tenures. In Britain, however, fans developed a more critical tone: when the series was put on hiatus in 1985, the very fans John Nathan-Turner had courted grew extremely critical of him in print.

As the series went off the air in 1989, the interest from fans cooled as they moved on to other series and fandoms like *Star Trek: The Next Generation* or *The X-Files*. But a core group stayed on. With the rise of the internet, this remnant flourished: thoughtful critique and dazzling fan fiction emerged in the fanzines. With Virgin Publishing producing the New Adventures range of books (which had an open call for submissions), as well as a line of non-fiction works, many of these fan writers became professional authors.

Thanks to the various making-of books (and a long-running monthly publication documenting the making of the series in *Doctor Who Magazine*), *Doctor Who*'s "open source fandom" only became more educated and fascinated by the process of TV production. Steven Moffat was one such fan, who began working in British television in the early '90s. Russell T Davies preceded him by a few years. *Torchwood* head writer (and *Doctor Who* writer) Chris Chibnall could be found slagging off 1980s *Doctor Who* on a BBC talk show in 1986. Many, many others have similar stories.

The New Series has seen the second golden age of fandom, with large conventions, new fan clubs, even a resurgence of the fanzine. There are new internet-era innovations such as podcasting, blogging and YouTube-ing, and the creativity, thoughtfulness and passion of fans remains. At first the focus was more on the New Series, but — rather like young Keith Miller in the early 1970s — a fascination towards *Doctor Who*'s rich past has grown. And the cycle continues.

During a 1997 radio interview, a reporter suggested to Tom Baker that *Doctor Who* fans were not "ordinary people." To which Tom replied, "*Doctor Who* fans aren't ordinary people. Ordinary people grow tired, they grow disenchanted with the things they love. *Doctor Who* fans are superior. They never stop loving."

Isn't that the truth?

· ·

Human Nature / The Family of Blood (2007)

Written by Paul Cornell **Directed by** Charles Palmer

Featuring David Tennant (The Doctor/Smith), Freema Agyeman (Martha Jones)

Supporting cast Jessica Hynes (Joan Redfern), Rebekah Stanton (Jenny), Thomas Sangster (Tim Latimer), Harry Lloyd (Baines), Tom Palmer (Hutchinson), Gerard Horan (Clark), Lauren Wilson (Lucy Cartwright), Pip Torrens (Rocastle), Matthew White (Philips), Sophie Turner (vicar)

Original airdates May 26, June 2, 2007

The Big Idea The Family of Blood want the Doctor's Time Lord essence in order to become immortal. There's only one way to defeat them: if he stops being a Time Lord altogether.

Time And Relative Dimensions In Space In 1991, Virgin Publishing began a new range of original *Doctor Who* novels known as the New Adventures. Many of the writers on the New Series — including Russell T Davies, Mark Gatiss, Paul Cornell and Gareth Roberts — wrote for the range, which lasted until 1997 when the BBC took the license for original fiction from Virgin.

In 1995, Paul Cornell wrote a novel for the New Adventures range called *Human Nature*, which features the seventh Doctor visiting alien bodysmiths to turn himself into a human in order to better empathize with the grief his companion, Bernice Summerfield, is experiencing. The now human "John Smith" works in a pre–World War I school and falls in love with the school nurse, Joan Redfern. However, the village comes under threat from the alien Aubertides, who wish to capture the pod that holds the Doctor's essence, only it has been stolen by student Timothy Dean. The novel was acclaimed in its day, hailed as one of the best in the New Adventures range.

One of the earliest stories executive producer Russell T Davies commissioned for the third season of the New Series was an adaptation of *Human Nature* by its author. (Indeed, Cornell was commissioned so early in the process, details of the new season hadn't been worked out. The character of Martha was originally to have been from 1913, and she would have been visiting home; this aspect was revised when Martha became a companion from contemporary Earth.) Paul Cornell was concerned that the romance angle might have been covered by 2006's "The Girl in the Fireplace" and originally started his storyline more radically, with Smith and Joan in bed and married. Davies encouraged Cornell to go back to ideas in the original novel of the school and the romance between Smith and Joan.

Adventures in Time and Space Smith's *Journal of Impossible Things* features illustrations of the TARDIS console, the sonic screwdriver, gas masks (2005's "The Empty Child"), a Dalek, the Moxx of Balhoon (2005's "The End of the World"), Autons ("Rose"), the werewolf (2006's "Tooth and Claw"), the pocket watch, clockwork droids ("The Girl in the Fireplace"), Cybermen, the police box, images of the first, fifth, sixth, seventh and eighth selves (among the others, though they can't be seen onscreen), a Slitheen and Rose.

When Timothy opens the watch, he sees flashes of the Doctor using the sonic screwdriver held out before him (2007's "The Lazarus Experiment"), a Dalek in chains ("Dalek"), marching Cybermen, an Ood, the werewolf ("Tooth and Claw"), the Sycorax (2005's "The Christmas Invasion"), the Racnoss (2006's "The Runaway Bride") and Professor Lazarus ("The Lazarus Experiment"). Later, we also get a flash of the Doctor amid the flames from "The Runaway Bride." Joan says, "A girl in every fireplace?" ("The Girl in the Fireplace"). When Joan asks if Gallifrey is in Ireland, the Doctor says he supposes it must be, following a running gag since 1976's "The Hand of Fear" where people naturally assume Gallifrey is Irish.

When Timothy runs away from the fighting, Hutchinson says, "Latimer, you filthy coward," to which Timothy responds, "Yes, sir, every time," echoing the ninth Doctor's line in 2005's "The Parting of the Ways." The Family stole a Time Agent's vortex manipulator similar to the one used by Captain Jack (in stories such as 2007's "Utopia") and, later, River Song.

Who is the Doctor? John Smith, the Doctor's human form, is appalled by Tim's assessment of the Doctor as an elemental being who "sees the turn of the universe." He's equally appalled by the idea that the Doctor would never countenance the idea he would fall in love as a human.

Smith dreams of the Doctor's heroism but falls short: he's cowardly and is even willing, initially, to use armed children as a defence against the Family. In the end, though, he sacrifices himself — and his future with Joan — in order to become the Doctor. The Doctor insists to Joan that Smith is part of him and tries to get her to travel with him to "start again." But Joan knows better.

Companion Chronicles The Doctor trusts Martha to take care of him during the three months he is human. However, Martha still suffers under the burden of her unrequited love for the Doctor and is brokenhearted to see the Doctor, now human, falling in love with another woman. She confesses her love for the Doctor to Smith and Joan, and tells Smith that the Doctor travels with her because "he's lonely."

Monster of the Week The Family of Blood are gaseous entities who reside in globes. They have limited lifespans, no more than a few months, so they want to steal the Doctor's existence. They possess the bodies of humans and can access their memories, although they can also die in their new bodies. They fly an invisible spaceship and have soldiers made of straw, dressed as scarecrows and brought to "life" with molecular fringe animation.

Interesting Trivia The hymn sung throughout is "To Be a Pilgrim," adapted from the works of John Bunyan; the first verse has an intriguing phrase, "He who would valiant be 'gainst all disaster, / Let him in constancy follow the Master." It's the sort of line that makes a *Doctor Who* fan's ears prick up, particularly in a season foreshadowing the arrival of the Master, and almost makes one think it was intentional. Except it was chosen because it was a staple in chapel services in most British schools since it appeared in the English Hymnal in 1906.

Among the many changes in adapting Paul Cornell's 1995 novel, one of the more intriguing is to Timothy Latimer. In the novel, Timothy (who has the surname Dean) adopts the Doctor's peace-loving stance and serves in World War I in the Red Cross. Hutchison, at the front, dies from the shell Timothy predicted would come. At the Remembrance Day ceremony at the end, Timothy wears a white poppy — a symbol used by pacifists in Britain who want to remember the war as an alternative to the usual red poppy. The televised version has Timothy as a soldier, saving the life of Hutchison from the shell he knew would come, and no white poppies appear at the very end. It's representative of a change that happened with Cornell himself, who viewed the Doctor as a pacifist hero when he wrote the novel. (Indeed, Cornell stated in an interview with one of the authors in 1996, "The Doctor is the last pacifist hero in popular culture.") By 2007, Cornell had moved away from that stance. It's an intriguing political shift; then again, it's not often that a writer revisits a work they've written 12 years previously.

The villains in Cornell's novel, the Aubertides, were shapeshifters that could become anything they consumed. That aspect was deemed too close to the Slitheen (who wore the skins of people they killed), so the Family of Blood, gaseous entities that possessed humans, came into being. One aspect that didn't make it was the idea that the Aubertides/Family not only were the human form but any object the human held on to as well: in the novel, Lucy Cartwright's balloon was a deadly extension of the Aubertide form. It was tried out in the script, with Martha discovering Jenny was possessed by accidentally spilling hot tea on Jenny's handbag, but it didn't work and was dropped.

TARDIS Chronometer A newspaper reveals that it's Monday, November 10, 1913, in the village near the Farringham School for Boys. The TARDIS has been there for two months (with one to go), hidden in a shed and on emergency power so it can't be detected. The Doctor and Martha later visit Latimer as an old man on Remembrance Sunday (probably sometime in the late 1990s, given Latimer's age and the female vicar).

Brilliant? (GB) "'I've discovered a lot in the last few weeks,' Smith began. 'I've found out that being the Doctor . . . it's not about having special knowledge or abilities. It's about not being cruel. It's about not being afraid.'" From *Doctor Who — The New Adventures: Human Nature* by Paul Cornell (1995).

I don't think either my co-author or myself realized it until now, but three out of the four David Tennant stories we've selected for this book have been about the absence of the Doctor. "Love & Monsters" is a story about the people who are intrigued by the Doctor from afar; "Blink" is a story about how the Doctor influences events in the future from the past in a wibbly-wobbly-timey-wimey way; and "Human Nature"/"The Family of Blood" is about what happens when the Doctor is not the Doctor. I won't apologize for this, because I think it's interesting that at this stage of the series' history we're recognizing the power and influence the character has and the dramatic weight that exists even when the Doctor technically isn't present.

What exists in the Doctor's absence in "Human Nature"/"The Family of Blood" is twofold: one is the threat of a character that is, as Tim says, "like fire and ice and rage." One of the clearest flashbacks we have of the Doctor through the watch is him at the end of 2006's "The Runaway Bride," destroying the Racnoss without pity. The Doctor's very mission to become human is one of mercy — so he doesn't have to unleash his wrath on the Family and let them die.

The other thing that exists in the Doctor's absence is John Smith. Martha totally called it: the Doctor is rubbish as a human. When things go to hell in a handbasket, Martha and Joan save the people at the dance, and the Headmaster takes the brave stance against the Family. John Smith is a man of his times, who allows Latimer to be beaten and thinks nothing of arming children against an unknown foe. But the remarkable thing about that is Joan remonstrating him for the latter, not because (as Martha notes) it's beneath the Doctor, but because she believes *John Smith* is capable of better.

And here we have the beautiful, tragic, haunting dilemma at the heart of "Human Nature"/"The Family of Blood": John Smith needs to become a better man. But for him to do that, he'll need to give up everything. I burst into tears watching Smith's response to Martha's remark that the Doctor takes her along because he's lonely: "And that's what you want me to become?!" This is a man experiencing real love for the first time, who later sees a long and beautiful life ahead of him, and he has to give it up to become some kind of fantastic lonely god incapable of understanding love. It's gut-wrenching.

This story would not have worked without David Tennant's incredible performance. Smith could have just been the Doctor by a more human name, but Tennant creates a totally different character with ramrod-straight posture, perfect Edwardian diction and virginal awkwardness. Everyone else — particularly Freema Agyeman, Jessica Hynes and Rebekah Stanton (Mother of Mine talking about consuming Jenny is terrifying) — is stunning as well. And Charles Palmer's too-short tenure directing New Series *Who* hits its peak here.

Ultimately though, "Human Nature"/"The Family of Blood" is about John Smith, in the absence of the Doctor, realizing he has to stop being cruel and stop being afraid. But that comes at a terrible, terrible price for him. Because nothing is easy, and everything is messy. There are no heroes. Just people working up the courage to do the right thing. Or as Smith himself put it, "Everyday life can provide honour and valour." How gloriously human.

Second Opinion (RS?) This is a story about the passage of time. When the story starts, Smith and Martha have been in England for months. Their entire plan is predicated on simply waiting out the Family's lifespan. Meanwhile, the 1913 setting adds poignancy, devised solely to illustrate its moment in history. Time is also measured by the progress of war, from imagined natives with spears to flashes of the trenches.

What's perhaps even more impressive is the way the passing of time is established via something both powerful and simple: the telling of stories. Smith has a fake past, he writes down his dreams not in a diary but as fiction, and when he confronts the truth of his existence he asks, "So who am I then? Nothing. I'm just a story."

The flashbacks and flashforwards also tell their own stories. The fast-paced opening scene of the Doctor and Martha in the TARDIS turns out to have taken place inside a dream, while the Doctor becoming human is told via flashbacks. For the bulk of the episode, the Doctor's existence is hidden inside the watch, only revealed in momentary glimpses or whispers from other episodes. Martha's instructions are given via pre-recorded video, Latimer sees flashforwards of the future and the war, and there's even a flash-sideways showing Smith and Joan's life together, the life the Doctor could never have.

It's through stories that we learn about character. The story of Smith's parents echoes the show's genesis, while Joan discovers that Smith isn't real by asking him to tell her stories of his childhood (and he can't). His own moment of realization happens when he sees the TARDIS: an item from his story come to life. And the ultimate illustration of the Doctor's character comes through the "fury of the Time Lord." The fate of the Family of Blood is told via voiceover, its purpose to illustrate precisely who the Doctor is: a man who is kind to his enemies.

The final progression, from a field in England to war in France to the memorial, with an aged Latimer seeing the Doctor and Martha unchanged, is so powerful you'll weep every time you watch it. These two episodes have done something incredible. They've taken the science-fiction premise behind *Doctor Who* and used it to show just how powerful time itself is. They haven't done this with fancy gadgets or causal paradoxes. Instead, they've done it with the most powerful thing humans have ever invented: stories.

David Tennant

Born in 1971, Scottish actor David John MacDonald had to adopt a stage name because there was another David MacDonald in Equity, the U.K. actors' union. He took the name Tennant from Neil Tennant of Pet Shop Boys fame. His first major role was in the BBC Scotland series *Takin' Over the Asylum* (1994). He developed his career in the British theatre, particularly the Royal Shakespeare Company. A *Doctor Who* fan since childhood, he had several small parts in Big Finish's range of *Doctor Who* audios, most notably Colonel Brimmicombe-Wood in *Doctor Who Unbound: Sympathy for the Devil*.

In 2004, Tennant played his breakout role as Detective Inspector Peter Carlisle in *Blackpool*. He followed this up with the lead role in Russell T Davies's 2005 adaptation of *Casanova*, which then led to his being cast as the tenth Doctor. He played the Doctor from "The Parting of the Ways" (2005) to "The End of Time, Part Two" (2010). Since leaving *Doctor Who*, Tennant has continued to act on stage (notably in an acclaimed Royal Shakespeare Company production of *Hamlet*), in film (including 2011's *Fright Night*) and on TV (including 2011's *Single Parent* and 2013's *Spies of Warsaw* and *Broadchurch*). In 2013, he agreed to reprise the role of the tenth Doctor and star with Matt Smith in *Doctor Who*'s 50th anniversary special.

Tennant is married to Georgia Moffet, who played the Doctor's "daughter" Jenny in 2008's "The Doctor's Daughter" (and is the real-life daughter of fifth Doctor actor Peter Davison).

Blink (2007)

Written by Steven Moffat **Directed by** Hettie MacDonald

Featuring David Tennant (The Doctor), Freema Agyeman (Martha)

Supporting cast Carey Mulligan (Sally Sparrow), Lucy Gaskell (Kathy Nightingale), Finlay Robertson (Larry Nightingale), Richard Cant (Malcolm Wainwright), Michael Obiora (Billy Shipton), Louis Mahoney (Old Billy), Thomas Nelstrop (Ben Wainwright), Ian Boldsworth (Banto)

Original airdate June 9, 2007

The Big Idea Trapped in 1969, the Doctor must create a web of causality to stop the weeping angels from accessing the TARDIS in 2007.

Time And Relative Dimensions In Space Steven Moffat was slated to write the 2007 season's two-parter but was so busy he asked to be reassigned to a single episode. He felt bad about letting the production team down, so he agreed to write the double-banked episode for the season. He reworked a short story he'd written for the 2006 *Doctor Who Annual* (which was published in 2005) about a 12-year-old girl named Sally Sparrow who is contacted by the Doctor from 20 years earlier. At the end, Sally wrote up her adventures as homework and gave it to the Doctor when she grew up to become a spy. This story didn't have the Weeping Angels, but it did include a video conversation that could only occur because the Doctor had the future transcript and a note behind wallpaper. Where most stories went through multiple rewrites by Russell T Davies, Moffat had a clause in his contract that limited this. So he produced this script in only two stages: a first draft and a polish.

Adventures in Time and Space The security protocol hologram of the Doctor is very similar to the one that the ninth Doctor used in 2005's "The Parting of the Ways."

Who is the Doctor? He's been married before, but weddings aren't good for him, due to his complex relationship with time.

Companion Chronicles In 1969, Martha is forced to work in a shop, something she finds particularly egregious — possibly because this was Rose's occupation before she met the Doctor.

Monster of the Week The Weeping Angels look like statues with their eyes covered as though weeping. But, in fact, they're assassins that turn to stone whenever they're observed — even by each other, which is why they need to hide their eyes. They're creatures of the abstract, living off the potential energy of their victims by displacing them in time. They're nearly as old as the universe.

Interesting Trivia Why can't the Angels move when Sally isn't looking? This happens early on when she's upstairs in the house and then again in the cellar. Indeed, although the Angels clearly move when they're rocking the TARDIS, we don't actually see movement, just the displacement whenever the lights are out. Sally and Lawrence are inside the TARDIS at the time, so there's nothing to stop the Angels dancing the Macarena if they wanted to. All this points to a very nice suggestion: the Angels can't move when anyone is looking at them — including the viewer. With this in mind, a lot of things about the Angels click into place.

An interesting detail about this story comes into focus when you've seen its sequels, particularly 2010's "The Time of Angels," which establishes that the very image of an Angel becomes an Angel. Since Sally hands the Doctor an image of an Angel at the conclusion of "Blink," it's possible that this image becomes an Angel . . . perhaps even creating this group of Angels in Wester Drumlins in the first place.

Who threw the rock at Sally in the teaser? It seems a bit odd that the Angels might have done it, as throwing large stones through windows isn't really their style. To figure this out, we need to unravel the causality. Originally, the Doctor arrived in 2007, whereupon the Angels sent him and Martha back in time to 1969. The Doctor met Billy, who eventually becomes a DVD producer, enabling the Doctor to record the easter eggs and make contact with Sally in the present. Billy's only caught by the Angels because they are following Sally, so his life is a causal loop. But why does Sally meet Billy in the first place? She's at the police station because Kathy disappeared and the reason why Kathy disappeared is because Sally brought her to the house. And the reason Sally brought Kathy to the house was because of the strange message behind the wallpaper, telling her to duck. Had that message not been there, none of this would have happened and the Doctor would still be trapped in the past. So in whose best interest is it that the rock was thrown in the first place? Clearly, it can only have been the Doctor, travelling back from his relative future, to ensure Sally gets involved. At least he had the decency to wait until she actually ducked to throw it.

The TARDIS Chronometer A spooky house called Wester Drumlins in London, 2007 (and the final scene is set a year later). Kathy is transported to Hull, December 1920, while Billy, the Doctor and Martha end up in 1969.

Brilliant? (RS?) "Blink" is truly awesome and that's all there is to it.

No really, that's all there is.

You see, the problem with "Blink" is that it's just too darn awesome. Watch it and you'll surely agree with me on the sheer unbridled awesomeness of it. Think back to the letter from Kathy's grandson, delivered while a young Kathy is *still in the house*. Or Sally giving Billy her phone number and a decades older Billy calling her moments later. Or the way that, at the end, causality becomes the key problem that Sally needs to solve, explaining why she collects everything — and then restarts the entire process. Awesome, right?

But the problem is, for all its awesomeness, there's just not that much to say about it. Oh sure, you can quote dialogue with double meanings like "Go to the police, you stupid woman" or any of the Doctor's easter egg dialogue that gets used twice. That's awesome. Absolutely. But quoting dialogue isn't reviewing the story.

Alternatively, you could point out little things around the fringes, the sort of things only fans care about, like the fact that Kathy's daughter is probably Billy's wife, on account of the fact that they're both named Sally and the ages match up. That's pretty awesome.

Maybe, just maybe, if you're particularly clever, you can point out that it's all built on a house of cards and that nothing actually holds together and so many questions are left unanswered. Like the fact that there are so many empty cars parked at Wester Drumlins, but we have no idea what drew any of their occupants there. Were the Angels sending out invitations to a particularly rocking party? Was there an entire chain of causality that devoured itself, the net result of which is a gang of teenage investigators now scattered throughout the 1920s? (Which would be pretty awesome in its own right.) And if you're especially good at this, you'll surely note also that none of this matters, because of just how stupidly awesome the whole story is. But then, my co-author already did that, in *Who Is The Doctor*, so that's too bad for me, really.

Instead, all I can do at this juncture is point out just how utterly awesome the episode is and implore you to agree with me on the merits of its awesomeness — because it is indeed awesomely awesome — and let's, just this once, agree to bypass the entire reviewing process because there's only one thing that's really left to be said about the episode, isn't there?

Awesome.

Second Opinion (GB) Nope. I've got nothing. It's awesome.

The Waters of Mars (2009)

Written by Russell T Davies and Phil Ford **Directed by** Graeme Harper

Featuring David Tennant (The Doctor)

Supporting cast Lindsay Duncan (Adelaide Brooke), Peter O'Brien (Ed Gold), Aleksander Mikic (Yuri Kerenski), Gemma Chan (Mia Bennett), Chook Sibtain (Tarak Ital), Alan Ruscoe (Andy Stone), Cosima Shaw (Steffi Ehrlich), Michael Goldsmith (Roman Groom), Lily Bevan (Emily), Max Bollinger (Mikhail), Rachel Fewell (young Adelaide), Anouska Strahnz (Ulrika Ehrlich), Zofie Strahnz (Lisette Ehrlich), Paul Kasey (Ood Sigma)

Original airdate November 15, 2009

The Big Idea Bowie Base One is the first human colony on Mars. And its destruction is a fixed point in time. But the Doctor has other ideas.

Time And Relative Dimensions In Space After four years of producing *Doctor Who*, during which time he not only brought the series back from oblivion but saw it become a genuine hit, executive producer Russell T Davies wanted to move on. David Tennant also wanted to leave after three years. Both were persuaded to stay on for a shortened series of specials that would air throughout 2009, providing a "gap year" before new executive producer Steven Moffat took over. The first special, "The Next Doctor," was made at the end of the 2008 season and was broadcast on Christmas Day, 2008; the second, third and fourth specials were made in early-to-mid 2009 for broadcast throughout the year.

The third of these specials — intended to air on Christmas 2009 — had a troubled genesis. Russell T Davies was initially interested in the idea of a grandmother staying at a hotel with her grandchildren and suddenly finding no one left in the hotel — or on Earth — except the Doctor. Davies recruited Phil Ford, head writer on the spinoff *The Sarah Jane Adventures*, to develop it into a workable script. After several drafts, it was abandoned. While Davies liked Ford's work overall, he was less enthused about the "sword and sorcery" elements the empty hotel idea was taking on. Davies suggested that Ford instead work on another idea Davies had: a futuristic story set on a Martian base. Ford came up with the title "Red Christmas" and set the tale closer to contemporary times, moving from an era of a fully colonized and terraformed Mars to one with its pioneers. (Scheduling eventually put this episode into November, and the Christmas aspect was all but eliminated.)

Even after all this, the existence of this special was threatened. Just before Russell T Davies was to begin rewrites on the scripts, funding for the specials was reduced by BBC Worldwide. Concerned that there wouldn't be enough money for both "The Waters of Mars" and the extra-length two-part finale, Davies and fellow executive producer Julie Gardner considered their options, and were leaning towards cutting the Mars story all together. At the eleventh hour, Gardner was able to secure additional funds. Davies added elements from the tenth Doctor's backstory; the events of the story force the Doctor to confront his grief over being the last Time Lord, with disastrous results.

Adventures in Time and Space The Doctor has been informed in the previous televised adventure (2009's "Planet of the Dead") that "his song is coming to an end" and that "he will knock four times." The Doctor wears the same orange spacesuit he wore in 2006's "The Impossible Planet"/"The Satan Pit." Ood Sigma from 2008's "Planet of the Ood" appears at the end; he was one of the first people to talk about the Doctor's song ending and is summoning the Doctor to his eventual end, which will take place in the next story, "The End of Time."

The Doctor discusses the Ice Warriors, Classic Series villains from Mars who first appeared in 1967's "The Ice Warriors." The destruction of Bowie Base One is a fixed point in time and cannot be changed, a piece of cosmology in the *Doctor Who* universe established in 2008's "The Fires of Pompeii" (the Doctor goes on to talk about some of the details from that episode). The Doctor tells Adelaide that there are laws of time and that once there were people in charge of those laws, but they died (2005's "Father's Day"). There is a flashback to an incident set during the events of 2008's "The Stolen Earth"/"Journey's End," when a Dalek flies to young Adelaide's window.

There are audio clips from past episodes of the Doctor saying he's the last of the Time Lords (including 2006's "Rise of the Cybermen"/"Doomsday," 2007's "Gridlock" and "Utopia"), that the Time Lords died (the Time War) and also that the walls of reality are closing ("The Stolen Earth"/"Journey's End"). The Doctor finds the idea of a domestic robot dressed a dog sweet, a reference to K9. The Cloister Bell rings twice at the end of the story; it first rang in "Logopolis." After all his issues with people saluting him in 2008's "The Sontaran Stratagem" and elsewhere, the tenth Doctor salutes Adelaide, the only person this incarnation ever formally salutes.

Who is the Doctor? Watching the doomed plight of everyone on Bowie Base One, the Doctor comes to believe that as the only surviving Time Lord he is capable of breaking the rules and interfering in a fixed point in history. It's an act of supreme hubris that turns the Doctor cold and inhuman. Adelaide Brooke's suicide makes the Doctor realize the folly of his actions — and realize that his end is near.

Monster of the Week The Flood (named in a scene that was cut from the episode, available as a deleted scene on the DVD) hides in water and infects people when as little as a single drop touches them. It can create water, sometimes in massive amounts. Infected humans have mottled faces, with cracked and grey jawlines. They can communicate telepathically, breathe water and don't need air. They can survive outside in the Martian atmosphere, thanks to internal fission, but can be immobilized by freezing.

Interesting Trivia The final scene was originally written very differently, with Adelaide surviving and the Doctor realizing his wrongdoing by the presence of Ood Sigma. He departs, leaving Adelaide crying outside her house. Davies reconsidered this and realized that the Doctor would only recognize the monstrousness of what he had done if Adelaide, whom he was desperate to save, died. This darker ending required a lot of careful rewriting, particularly since it was depicting a suicide during a family-viewing timeslot. Consequently, Adelaide was shown to be using a "futuristic" weapon and the death was not shown onscreen.

The original idea of the Flood was to show creatures made of water, along the lines of the aliens in the 1989 James Cameron film *The Abyss*. Budgetary concerns dictated a different visualization of the Flood, with the Bowie Base One crewmembers being possessed by the creature rather than consumed by it, an illusion achieved with makeup and prosthetics rather than expensive CGI. (This included having water pumped through the actor's mouths. Don't try this at home!) When watching the rushes, Russell T Davies worried that the makeup made the Flood's victims look terrifying, like movie zombies. It was decided a big part of this was to do with the eyes, and taking out the contact lenses would make them slightly less frightening. So the change was made and mentioned (though never explained). When Steffi and Roman transform, their eyes stay normal.

Brilliant? (GB) The great thing about watching "The Waters of Mars" on its own, divorced from the final mini-season of specials it was a part of, is rediscovering what a taut thriller it is. The horror starts just five minutes in and it never lets up. The Flood is a magnificent idea precisely for the reasons the Doctor says: water is patient, water always wins. And water so deadly that it kills with a single drop is the ultimate *Doctor Who* menace. How do you stop something that's unavoidable?

The result is incredible. "The Waters of Mars" is a creepy sci-fi horror story in the tradition of *Alien* that starts out with giant thrills and then everything gets even more intense. The futile struggle of Bowie Base One against the Flood and the torrents of water everywhere is unbelievably tense — Roman being lost to a single drop from the ceiling — and unbelievably dramatic — Steffi losing her humanity while listening to her daughter speak to her in a pre-recorded message.

It's beautifully directed by Graeme Harper, whose use of closeups really emphasizes every horrifying, tragic moment.

If the Doctor wasn't in "The Waters of Mars," you would have the setup for an incredible sci-fi horror film. But the Doctor is in it, and Russell T Davies and Phil Ford double down by putting the Doctor in a scenario that he is powerless to stop. The idea that the Doctor knows he can't change these events — brilliantly implemented here through the glimpses of a future news website documenting events — adds a whole layer of doom to the proceedings.

But the genius is that the Doctor's powerlessness is the lever for some incredible character moments. His whole relationship with Adelaide is based on him knowing how special she is and how important her sacrifice is. This manifests itself both warmly, as the Doctor tells Adelaide how her grandchildren will change the universe, and harshly, as the Doctor in the airlock has to coldly explain to her that, no matter how much he admires and loves her, he can't save her. David Tennant and Lindsay Duncan are haunting in all those scenes.

And then the unthinkable happens: it goes for broke. The Doctor snaps. All the angst and survivor guilt and pent-up anger that has been developed and intensified over four years of stories comes through as he watches Bowie Base One head towards destruction. Even the execution of that is smart: the Doctor has ferocious intensity but he's babbling and joking and being very Doctory. It's only in the aftermath that we see he's done something very, very wrong. The final scene on Earth is eerie: Mia is frightened to death by the TARDIS and the Doctor, and gets the hell away from him. The moment the Doctor says, "Tough," you know he's turned the wrong corner. He even opens the door to Adelaide's house as if to say, "The matter is closed." This isn't a happy end-of-Christmas-special ending. This is watching a nascent megalomaniac getting his kicks. I initially thought Adelaide was actually drawing her gun to use it on the Doctor.

Adelaide's death is the *coup de grâce*. She has railed against dying the whole episode, has struggled against the doom facing the crew, but she realizes the sin the Doctor is committing. It works in the visceral moment, though one wonders how her suicide would inspire her granddaughter. But perhaps that's the point: history wins regardless. The Doctor is reminded of his limits and how monstrous he's become.

In many ways, "The Waters of Mars" is the true finale of the David Tennant era. It's a thrilling, scary story overlaid with a powerful character drama and it takes the Doctor to a dark place his tenth incarnation can never fully recover from. It's beautiful. And frightening.

Second Opinion (RS?) Once upon a time, back when *Doctor Who* was very young, it used to do a funny thing called the historical story. Nowadays, you'd recognize that as the "celebrity historical," characterized by a famous personage — Charles Dickens, Agatha Christie, Shakespeare *et al.* — but with a sci-fi twist: blue elementals, giant wasps, Carrionites, etc. But that's not what I'm talking about.

Long, long ago, the Classic Series used to do proper historicals. Stories with no science fiction whatsoever. It was even in the original remit of the show: they wanted to educate youngsters like yourself about history, so the best way to do that was to have the TARDIS visit ye olden times and see what it was like to live back then or to witness an important event in history.

Which brings me to "The Waters of Mars." No, don't laugh, I'm serious. Yes, I know, it's set in the future — and on another planet to boot. But everything else about it has all the aspects of a pure historical.

Bowie Base One is obviously a hugely important event in future history, so the Doctor getting the chance to witness its operations and bump into the people involved meets the criteria of a historical. Where most other science-fiction stories — the kind you like so much — would have had him immediately helping the humans stave off an alien threat, here he refuses to get involved for the majority of the story.

What's more, one of the key tenets of historical stories was that the TARDIS crew absolutely, positively could not get involved. When they occasionally did, as in "The Aztecs," it was an unmitigated disaster. Worse, for all the meddling that might have taken place, the end result was always the same: nothing fundamentally changed and the only effect they could have on events was minor. Sound familiar?

Oh sure, you can cover this by talking about fixed points and the like, but the basic outcome is the same: the Doctor can't change anything and it's wrong to try, because this isn't some pliable future that's yet to be set in stone. It's history. It just hasn't happened yet.

Now look at the story again. And then tell me how boring you think historicals are.

Vincent and the Doctor (2010)

Written by Richard Curtis **Directed by** Jonny Campbell

Featuring Matt Smith (The Doctor), Karen Gillan (Amy Pond)

Supporting cast Tony Curran (Vincent), Bill Nighy (Dr. Black, uncredited), Nik Howden (Maurice)

Original airdate June 5, 2010

The Big Idea After finding a monster painted into one of van Gogh's pictures, the Doctor travels back to meet the man himself.

Time And Relative Dimensions In Space In 1999, Steven Moffat had written a *Doctor Who* comedy spoof for Comic Relief, called "The Curse of Fatal Death." The story was commissioned by Comic Relief's founder, Richard Curtis, of *Blackadder* and *Four Weddings and a Funeral* fame. Curtis knew Moffat through Moffat's new wife (and Curtis's producer) Sue Vertue and offered "The Curse of Fatal Death" as a sort of wedding present. When Moffat became executive producer of *Doctor Who* for the New Series' fifth season, he reached out to well-known writers (in television and elsewhere) including Simon Nye, Toby Whithouse and Neil Gaiman (whose episode was deferred to the following season). Moffat also took this opportunity to return the favour to Richard Curtis.

For his part, Curtis was comfortable with historical episodes and had an idea about van Gogh floating around: namely, that van Gogh never knew how famous he was in his lifetime. Curtis decided that time travel was a great way to examine that and was pleased to work within *Doctor Who*'s boundaries, rather than having to invent everything himself, as he usually did. Despite being quite familiar with van Gogh's life, Curtis nevertheless read a 200-page biography of van Gogh — far beyond the level of research he usually performed — in part because he felt writing for *Doctor Who* made him seem like a legitimate writer to his kids!

Adventures in Time and Space The Doctor's being especially nice to Amy, taking her to Arcadia, the Trojan Gardens and the Musée D'Orsay, because Rory has recently been erased from existence (2010's "Cold Blood"). Interestingly, Arcadia was said to have fallen in the Time War (2006's "Doomsday"). The fact that it now exists is likely due to the effect of the crack in the universe (2010's "The Eleventh Hour"). The Doctor says, "Here's the plan: Amy, Rory . . ." much to Amy's confusion, but immediately moves on.

Images of the first and second Doctors pop up on the Doctor's machine. Amy says that time can be rewritten, a reference to 2010's "The Time of Angels"/"Flesh and Stone."

Who is the Doctor? He thinks van Gogh is the greatest artist who ever lived but also describes Gainsborough as a proper painter. Not realizing the Krafayis is blind makes him face the fact that he's getting old. He doesn't know how to deal with Vincent when his depression is at its worst — which may be why he takes Vincent to see his future. He is profoundly bored when forced to wait while Vincent paints.

Companion Chronicles Amy Pond met the eleventh Doctor shortly after he regenerated, when she was still a child, then again as an adult before joining him in his travels. Although she grew up and got engaged to Rory Williams (who joined the TARDIS for a few stories, but was erased from time in the previous episode), her life has been touched by the Doctor in fundamental ways.

Amy is unaware that she's just lost Rory, but Vincent hears the song of her sadness and notices that she's crying. She says she's not really the marrying kind, despite the fact that she and Rory had been engaged. She notably doesn't flirt with the Doctor (as she had a few episodes back) and isn't interested in Vincent, despite being single (as far as she's aware). Perhaps compensating for all this, she is anxious to see that history changes as a result of taking Vincent to the future, and is crushed to learn her efforts fail. Even so, Vincent dedicates his painting *Still Life: Vase with Twelve Sunflowers* to her.

Monster of the Week The Krafayis are invisible to most people, but look like a four-legged reptile with a head like a parrot. They travel in space as a pack, scavenging across the universe. Sometimes one gets left behind, as here.

Interesting Trivia Did the Doctor and Amy actually make Vincent's suicide happen sooner? We meet Vincent in early June 1890, which is said to be months before his suicide and part of the final year of his life. However, in the scene at the end, when Amy notes that time can be rewritten, we see that one of his last paintings was of sunflowers and is dedicated to Amy. In reality, he committed suicide in late July 1890, a mere seven weeks after this story is set. We know that the prospect of the Doctor and Amy leaving Vincent was enough to trigger an episode, so it's possible that the Doctor's interference may in fact have shaved several months off Vincent's life.

The crew (on location in Croatia) had some trouble finding a café that looked suitably like the one in *Café Terrace at Night*. Eventually, they found one vaguely similar but still had to install an awning, change the windows and add an outside platform.

The TARDIS Chronometer The Musée d'Orsay, Paris 2010, and Provence, June 1890.

Cool? (RS?) *Pile 1: The bad things.*

Vincent's impending suicide looms over the story. We're told about it in the opening scene, we witness his depression and Amy hopes that taking him to the future will change history, resulting in him surviving and hundreds more paintings coming into existence. But, tragically, it doesn't.

When Vincent has an episode, the Doctor is completely unable to comfort him. The Doctor's forced jollity only makes things worse. Later, the Doctor tries to talk to Vincent about depression, but Vincent silences him, as he's working. This shows just how out of his depth the Doctor is when faced with something as complex — and as human — as mental illness.

Vincent notes that he and the Doctor have fought monsters together and that they won. On his own, however, he fears he may not do as well — and, indeed, as the final scene shows, he commits suicide when just 37 years old. All the wonders and mystery that the Doctor and Amy showed him were unable to change the final result.

Pile 2: The good things.

This is a story about — and powered by — visuals. One of the most interesting things this episode does is lovingly recreate van Gogh's paintings. The opening scene shows just Vincent's eyes between the painting and his hat, echoing the poster of his eyes seen in the museum. Later, he stands in front of the same poster in the same pose. Other aspects from Vincent's paintings include Amy's gathering of sunflowers, Vincent consistently wearing his straw hat and the Doctor noting that it's a starry night. The café and Vincent's room are recreated almost exactly, while *The Starry Night* is brought to life from the night sky while the Doctor, Amy and Vincent stare up at it.

The plot is initiated by a visual, seeing a monster in a painting, while Vincent believes there's more to life than the eye can see and hears colours shouting at him. The Krafayis is invisible and blind, whereas Vincent sees too much. The Doctor can only see the monster via reflection and when looking backwards, showing that the secret is to look at the world from a different angle, much as seeing the night sky through Vincent's eyes gives the Doctor (and us) a renewed sense of wonder.

The visual power of sunflowers is used three times: first by Amy to cheer up Vincent, second on top of a coffin in the funeral procession to indicate loss and then finally to provide a bittersweet coda by way of the painting.

The location filming in Croatia makes this a visual feast and comes complete with touches such as the TARDIS covered with posters (including when viewed from inside as the door opens). Vincent's wonder at his paintings in the museum is expressed wordlessly, as he takes in the scene around him.

Piles 1 and 2: The command of colour.

Dr. Black's assessment is that Vincent transformed his pain into beauty, that pain is easy to capture, but to use your passion and pain to portray the ecstasy and joy and magnificence of our world is what makes Vincent not only the greatest artist of all time, but perhaps one of the greatest men.

However, as the Doctor says, life is a pile of good things and bad things, and while the good may not soften the bad, the bad doesn't spoil the good. So just because the end result is unchanged doesn't mean that their actions — or life itself — aren't worth it. Vincent took the pain of his tormented life and transformed it into ecstatic beauty.

Now, if you'll excuse me, I have something in my eye . . .

Second Opinion (GB) In 2010, 11 days after "Vincent and the Doctor" aired, I was let go from my job. It was a job in which I had hoped to have a long future. It was a devastating experience: losing that job was one of the first times in my life when I felt as though I and my skills had been deemed not good enough. I spent much of the summer of 2010 in a daze, utterly depressed by how the bottom had dropped out of my life.

I spent the week afterward listening to two songs on my iPod: Jeff Buckley's cover of Leonard Cohen's "Hallelujah" and Athlete's "Chances," which accompanies the incredible climax to this episode and has me in tears every time.

"Take all your chances while you can . . ."

During that summer, I watched "Vincent and the Doctor" a lot. Not just because I thought it was the best story of Matt Smith's first season.

Not just because I love the way Richard Curtis puts Silly Putty over the *Doctor Who* historical and bends and stretches it in delightful ways. Not because Tony Curran is so damn incredible or the scene where they lie in a field and recreate *The Starry Night* is so beautiful. But because it said something to me that was utterly true: that in life there are experiences you're incapable of seeing past. That depression isn't simple or easy. At the end of the day, as my co-author explained, all you have is the good pile and the bad pile. In the words of the Doctor, "The good things don't always soften the bad things, but, vice versa, the bad things don't necessarily spoil the good things and make them unimportant."

That, for me, is one of the most achingly real things ever said in *Doctor Who*.

Life got better for me in incremental ways (that summer, Robert and I put together the proposal for *Who Is The Doctor* for a start) but, like Vincent, I realize how fragile things can be. And I've never forgotten the lesson "Vincent and the Doctor" offered me.

Matt Smith

Only 26 years old when he was cast as the eleventh Doctor in late 2008, Matthew Robert Smith is the youngest actor ever to play the role. Among the first candidates who auditioned for the role, Smith blew away executive producers Steven Moffat and Piers Wegner with his refreshingly different performance. Moffat had been planning to cast someone in his forties, and he was completely taken by surprise by the young actor.

As a teenager, Smith trained to become a professional footballer, but an injury caused him to put that aside and take up acting. By his early twenties, Smith was performing in West End plays such as *Swimming With Sharks* with Christian Slater and his future *Doctor Who* co-star Arthur Darvill. In 2008, his performance in the BBC series *Party Animals* received acclaim. He also appeared in *Moses Jones* (2009) and opposite Billie Piper in *The Ruby in the Smoke* (2006) and a 2008 episode of *The Secret Diary of a Call Girl*.

In between seasons of *Doctor Who*, Smith played Christopher Isherwood in the 2011 BBC drama *Christopher and His Kind* and Olympic rower Bert Bushnell in 2012's *Bert and Dickie*. He departed the role of the eleventh Doctor in the 2013 Christmas special. His first starring role in a feature film is in *How to Catch a Monster* (2014).

Asylum of the Daleks (2012)

Written by Steven Moffat **Directed by** Nick Hurran

Featuring Matt Smith (The Doctor), Karen Gillan (Amy Pond), Arthur Darvill (Rory Williams)

Introducing Jenna-Louise Coleman (Oswin Oswald)

Supporting cast Anamaria Marinca (Darla von Karlsen); David Gyasi (Harvey); Naomi Ryan (Cassandra); Nicholas Briggs (Dalek voices); Barnaby Edwards, Nicholas Pegg (Dalek operators)

Original airdate September 1, 2012

The Big Idea The Daleks beg the Doctor, Amy and Rory to save them by journeying to their asylum: a planet full of insane Daleks — and one junior entertainment manager from the starliner *Alaska*.

Time And Relative Dimensions In Space With the exception of the 2009 specials, the Russell T Davies era had featured a Dalek story every year, from 2005's "Dalek" to 2008's "Journey's End." Executive producer Steven Moffat felt that the Daleks were in danger of becoming the most easily defeatable race in the universe and so had given them a rest since 2010's "Victory of the Daleks," with only brief cameo appearances thereafter. Fearing they were becoming too cuddly, he decided to reintroduce the fear factor by making them madder than usual with the asylum planet.

Moffat also decided to feature a range of Daleks from the New Series and the Classic Series. The production team gathered props from various locations, including one owned by Russell T Davies. In all, 25 different kinds of Daleks are featured, although most only appear in the background. Moffat was concerned about how the different Daleks would look together, but was ultimately pleased, feeling they seemed like a species of individual beings rather than a series of identical robots.

Adventures in Time and Space The opening tells of the legend of the Doctor's death from 2011's "The Impossible Astronaut" and "The Wedding of River Song." Amy's continuing her modelling career, as seen in 2011's "Closing Time." Amy and Rory's marital problems were glimpsed in the 2012 webisodes, "Pond Life."

Just about every kind of Dalek is seen. Examples include the New Paradigm Daleks first seen in 2010's "Victory of the Daleks," the Special Weapons Dalek from "Remembrance of the Daleks" and the original 1960s Classic Series Daleks with blue and white casings. Oswin mentions Spiridon (1973's "Planet of the Daleks"), Kembel (1965's "The

Daleks' Master Plan"), Aridius (1965's "The Chase"), Vulcan (1966's "Power of the Daleks") and Exxilon (1974's "Death to the Daleks").

Rory mentions waiting for Amy for 2,000 years, which he did in 2010's "The Pandorica Opens"/"The Big Bang." Amy mentions giving birth at Demon's Run (2011's "A Good Man Goes to War"). The Doctor refers to himself as the Oncoming Storm (2005's "The Parting of the Ways"). His dancing and asking "Doc-tor who?" three times echoes that of Dorian asking the same question three times at the end of "The Wedding of River Song."

Who is the Doctor? He's known to the Daleks as their predator. He's not affected by the nanocloud that turns humans into Dalek servants. He has pinpoint aim with teleports. Oswin deletes all information related to the Doctor from the Daleks' collective telepathic field, meaning they now have no idea who he is.

Companion Chronicles Rory was resurrected in the past and subsequently married Amy. Amy and Rory have gone from being happily married to being on the edge of divorce. She kicked him out because he's always wanted kids, but she is no longer able to have them (she did have a daughter who grew up to be the Doctor's wife — long story — but they didn't raise the child). Rory has always believed that he loves her more than she loves him, but she denies this and they reconcile.

Companion-to-be Oswin Oswald was converted into a Dalek, but has resisted its programming. She makes soufflés (in her dreamscape, anyway) and can hack Dalek technology. She's killed here, beginning a mystery that is explored in 2012's "The Snowmen" and the 2013 episodes.

Monster of the Week Daleks, Daleks and more Daleks. We see all kinds, from the New Series Daleks in the Parliament of the Daleks to a mixture of Classic and New Series Daleks on the planet. They refuse to exterminate the most scarred of their race, believing such murderous creatures to be beautiful. Curiously, the Daleks exterminate no one in this story!

Interesting Trivia This story kicked off the first half of a season that was broadcast in two parts, over two years, the first time this had happened. (Previous seasons in the New Series had been contained within a single calendar year; the Classic Series sometimes had seasons that crossed over two years, but always more or less contiguously.) The title sequence was slightly redesigned for this half-season, where the *Doctor Who* logo reflected an element of the story; in this case, it's decorated with Dalek bumps.

Jenna-Louise Coleman had been announced as the new companion, intended to debut in the 2012 Christmas special. However, executive producer Steven Moffat had the brainwave of casting her as Oswin, months before she was due to appear. Select fans in the London, New York and Toronto got to see a sneak preview of this story, some weeks before its broadcast. (The New York screening featured Matt Smith and executive producer Caroline Skinner answering questions afterwards.) These screenings were carefully monitored and a specially filmed segment with Steven Moffat was recorded, where he pleaded with the lucky fans in attendance not to post spoilers online. It worked: the secret of Coleman's appearance was kept, and Moffat issued a thanks to both fans and the media.

A brief recipe for a soufflé: eggs; stir; min: eight.

The TARDIS Chronometer Inside a giant Dalek-like structure on the planet Skaro; on present-day Earth; inside a Dalek spaceship; and on the asylum planet.

Cool? (RS?) "Asylum of the Daleks" might just be the most exciting *Doctor Who* episode I've ever seen.

Spoilers are a funny thing. There's a part of my brain that really craves them, because the merest hint of what's to come is intoxicating. But I also know that even the smallest clues can get my brain working overtime to put the pieces together. If you can figure out which ones are likely there for misdirection and which are hints of a larger whole, then — without even meaning to — you've already figured out most of the episode in advance.

My co-author and I were lucky enough to nab tickets to the Toronto advance screening of this story at FanExpo Canada. We lined up for hours in order to get the first tickets, sat through an unrelated panel to get the second tickets, exchanged them some time later for the third tickets and then had to sign all manner of non-disclosure agreements in order to get into the screening itself. And then they had security guards with night vision goggles — yes, really! — patrolling the theatre so that nobody recorded it or, worse, tweeted about it.

What's worse are the spoilery hints that actually imply something that isn't in the episode. Sometimes they imply something so awful that you're relieved it isn't there. (I'm still grateful that "Bad Wolf" didn't reveal the entire 2005 season was a reality TV game for the Doctor and Rose.)

Amusingly, I'm such a spoilerphobe that I didn't actually realize that Jenna-Louise Coleman wasn't supposed to be in this episode; I just assumed this was her debut and it was only when Graeme whispered to me in disbelief about her appearance that I took in the magnitude of what they'd accomplished here. So at least I knew what not to spoil!

But the hints can also imply things much more impressive than the show can actually pull off. (The trailer for "Boom Town" makes it look like the most action-packed story ever.) So I don't even watch the "Next Time . . ." previews at the end of the story.

You might think that the circumstances of that first viewing were so exciting that they coloured the feel of the episode. And, in truth, I was a bit worried about that. I deliberately didn't watch the story again until reviewing it for this book, in case the magic disappeared when watching it more prosaically in my living room. (Or, rather, due to my travel schedule, on a laptop in the Australian bush. As you do.)

Not spoiling "Asylum" for friends afterwards was a delicious thrill. But it's a thrill I was only able to enjoy thanks to the fact that I knew nothing about it beforehand.

Fortunately, I'm pleased to report that "Asylum of the Daleks" remains just as exhilarating as when I first saw it. The Daleks asking the Doctor to save them is brilliant. The battered and insane Daleks slowly coming to life is terrifying. Oswin is both immediately loveable and incredibly intriguing. Amy and Rory's marital difficulties give them an actual emotional arc, something that was long overdue. And Matt Smith is spectacular, showing emotions in the Doctor that range from incredible fear at being exterminated by the intensive-care Daleks to smugness when he fixes his companions' relationship to joy when the Daleks forget who he is. Not to mention all the lovely small things he does along the way.

Of course, the downside to seeing the episode this way was that I couldn't switch off the "Coming Soon . . ." trailer they showed at the end. So my spoilerphobic brain was suddenly given all manner of information about the half-season to follow, including the episode titles. (Watching my discomfort made Graeme laugh out loud.) But it was a small price to pay.

My adrenaline rush from watching "Asylum of the Daleks" on the big screen proved to be an illusion. It wasn't the big screen that made it exciting, it was what was in the episode itself. It has fun set pieces, emotional resonance, an intriguing mystery and an unmissable Doctor. What more could you want?

Second Opinion (GB) Five things that make this story great:

- **Fun.** Oh my God. This story is one of the best thrill rides ever built for *Doctor Who*, with the best high-concept idea: the Doctor, Amy and Rory are sent to an asylum where the Daleks keep their insane. Then even more jeopardy is added, with a nanocloud that can turn you into a Dalek zombie if you stay long enough. With those two elements you have enough suspense and high-octane excitement to thrill over repeated viewings (and, unlike my co-author, I have watched it many, many times!).

- **Jenna-Louise Coleman.** The new companion's stealth appearance here almost belies the fact that she's wonderful. Charming, witty, flirtatious and sweet. Every moment Oswin shows up, there's a smile on my face. It made me a believer in whatever it is Steven Moffat is planning for that character.

- **Emotion.** Readers of *Who Is The Doctor* will know that I have often castigated Steven Moffat for being more interested in clever plot delivery than actual emotional storytelling. But here, he manages to do both. Bringing Rory and Amy's marital problems to the fore could have been disastrous, but the payoff is beautiful as both get to articulate some of their deeper fears brought about by travelling with the Doctor. And the punchline that the Doctor actually engineers the solution is just icing on the cake.

- **Innovation of the Daleks.** There are so many kooky ideas on display here: the Daleks' definition of beauty; the idea they would have a parliament, a prime minister or an asylum; the idea that the Doctor is considered their predator. I'm quite taken with the idea of the human Daleks. There are some who would say these are goofy and silly. I would say that's true of the Daleks generally. So, in short: hell yes!

- **Surprise.** The great thing about this story is that something surprising happens every five to ten minutes. The Daleks all chanting to the Doctor, "Save us!" Oswin's first appearance. Amy's and Rory's real reasons for breaking up. And all of it pales in comparison to the revelation of what has happened to Oswin. All the clues are there — the milk, the sudden use of English in the Daleks' heads-up displays — but the moment you realize what's happened is genuinely heartbreaking (kudos to Nick Briggs for making the Dalek component really touching).

More like this, please!

The Name of the Doctor (2013)

Written by Steven Moffat **Directed by** Saul Metzstein

Featuring Matt Smith (The Doctor), Jenna-Louise Coleman (Clara)

Introducing John Hurt (The Doctor)

Supporting cast Alex Kingston (River Song), Richard E. Grant (The Great Intelligence), Neve McIntosh (Madame Vastra), Catrin Stewart (Jenny Flint), Dan Starkey (Strax), Eve de Leon Allen (Angie), Kassius Carey Johnson (Artie), Nasi Voustsas (Andro), David Avery (Fabian), Michael Jenn (Clarence), Paul Kasey (Whisper Man)

Original airdate May 18, 2013

The Big Idea The Doctor must face his greatest secret in his tomb on the fields of Trenzalore. And Clara Oswald discovers why she is the impossible girl . . .

Time And Relative Dimensions In Space Over the years, the executive producers of *Doctor Who* have had to play elaborate games in order to keep key details from leaking to the public. With past season openers and season finales, crucial footage had been cut from press screenings (such as Rose's reappearance in 2006's "Partners in Crime") and Steven Moffat has asked fans at advance screenings to keep certain details quiet (such as Jenna-Louise Coleman's appearance in "Asylum of the Daleks").

In this tradition, "The Name of the Doctor" was released to the press with its final scene excised. However, there was another, more maddening, development. A week before the story was broadcast, word came that 210 copies of the boxset of the second half of Series Seven, which included this story, were sent out to select purchasers in North America three weeks early. (Steven Moffat remarked wryly that it was only the Blu-ray release: "Listen, we don't just leak any old rubbish, we leak in high-def — 1080p or nothing, that's us. Every last pixel in beautifully rendered detail. It's like getting caught extra naked.") That meant 210 people had the finale before everyone else. The BBC went into overdrive, begging and pleading those people not to spoil anything. Astonishingly, it worked.

Adventures in Time and Space The leaf that blew in the face of Clara's father, causing him to meet her mother, is recounted in 2013's "The Rings of Akhaten," which we see in flashback here. There's also a flashback to 2013's "Journey to the Centre of the TARDIS" as Clara remembers the Doctor's conversation about her impossible nature from a now-rewritten timeline. We first met Madame Vastra, a Silurian turned Victorian detective; her maid, bodyguard and lover Jenny; and Strax, a disgraced Sontaran turned nurse turned Victorian footman in 2011's "A Good Man Goes to War." By the time of 2012's "The Snowmen," this group, called "The Paternoster Gang," are all good friends of the Doctor. Clara has been caring for Artie and Angie since 2013's "The Bells of Saint John." Her love of making soufflés (seen with Oswin in "Asylum of the Daleks") is mentioned.

The Great Intelligence was a villain from the second Doctor's era, where it was the force behind the Yeti in 1967's "The Abominable Snowmen" and 1968's "The Web of Fear" (the latter is used in a brief clip of the Great Intelligence defeating the second Doctor). It was given an origin story in "The Snowmen" where it took the body of Dr. Walter Simeon.

The Fields of Trenzalore were mentioned by Dorium in 2011's "The Wedding of River Song." The version of River Song seen here is the copy placed in the Library from the first time the Doctor met her (and the last time River saw the Doctor before her death) in 2008's "Silence in the Library"/"Forest of the Dead."

The domed city of the Time Lords on Gallifrey was first seen on TV in 2007's "The Sound of Drums" (it had appeared years earlier in the *Doctor Who Magazine* comic strip). This is, however, the very first time we've seen the Doctor steal the TARDIS with Susan.

Clips from a variety of episodes are repurposed or used outright as part of Clara's journey through the Doctor's timeline. The first Doctor's sequence on Gallifrey is footage from "The Aztecs" (though his dialogue is taken from 1965's "The Web Planet"). The second Doctor running is from "The Five Doctors" (with the Doctor now running in what looks like California), as is the third Doctor's drive in Bessie. The fourth Doctor is encountered in a scene from 1978's "The Invasion of Time," while the fifth Doctor is found trapped in the Matrix in a scene from 1983's "Arc of Infinity." Clara sees the seventh Doctor hanging from his umbrella in the "literal cliffhanger" at the end of the first episode of 1987's "Dragonfire." The remaining Doctors are seen at various points at a distance or out of focus, using new footage with stand-ins wearing the respective Doctors' costumes. It's possible that she also bumped into the eighth Doctor just before seeing the second Doctor, though he's so close to the foreground it's impossible to tell. There are also audio clips of a variety of episodes including "An Unearthly Child," 1967's "The Moonbase," 1972's "The Time Monster," "The Genesis of the Daleks," "The Caves of Androzani," 1986's "The Trial of a Time Lord," 2005's "The Parting of the Ways" and 2007's "Voyage of the Damned."

The Great Intelligence calls the Doctor on his murder of the Sycorax leader in 2005's "The Christmas Invasion" and his leaving Solomon to die in 2012's "Dinosaurs on a Spaceship." His litany of names the Doctor will come to be known by includes the Storm (or the Oncoming Storm, as he's been called by the Daleks ever since 2005's "The Parting of the Ways") and the Valeyard (the amalgamation of the Doctor's darker side from "The Trial of a Time Lord").

The Doctor says, "The dimensional forces this deep in the TARDIS tend to make one giddy," a verbatim quote from 1982's "Castrovalva." Vastra notes that when the Great Intelligence ravages the Doctor's timeline, he kills the Doctor on Androzani ("The Caves of Androzani") and at the Dalek asylum ("Asylum of the Daleks").

Who is the Doctor? Why, that's an excellent question . . .

Companion Chronicles The Doctor has already encountered Clara Oswald twice in different times as different people. He has spent most of the episodes shown in 2013 trying to figure out the riddle of her existence. And yet, in spite of this, the Doctor is tremendously fond of Clara: the normally awkward eleventh Doctor is very affectionate towards her. In the end, it turns out the mystery around Clara's existence lies in her sacrificing herself to save the Doctor, entering the scar tissue in time left by his death and saving him from the Great Intelligence.

While she isn't technically a companion, River Song is nonetheless very special to the Time Lord. This is the first time after several "are they or aren't they" moments where the Doctor outright admits that River is, in fact, his wife and that he loves her. On top of that, the Doctor actually kisses River (or the echo of River only he can see, much to the puzzlement of Vastra and her friends). Outside of the TV Movie's fleeting kisses with Grace, this is the first time in 50 years that the Doctor has ever initiated a full-on snog.

Monster of the Week The Whisper Men are this week's monster race. They have fanged mouths amid a blank white face.

They belong to the Great Intelligence
and speak in couplets rhyming only, hence.

Interesting Trivia Just how does Clara save the Doctor? Apparently, the Great Intelligence disperses itself throughout the Doctor's timeline, destroying it at multiple points, but Clara doesn't seem to do anything to actually battle the Great Intelligence in any of these instances. The best guess is to go to simple physics: two objects cannot co-exist in the same space. By converging at the same points as the Great Intelligence, she simply "overwrites" him, erasing his attempt to corrupt the Doctor's timeline. (Given Steven Moffat's tendency to come up with analogies from the world of technology, we're surprised he didn't just call Clara anti-virus software!)

Taking that one step further . . . Clara manifests herself in beings born throughout time and space to fulfil their destiny of encountering the Doctor at whatever convergence point the Great Intelligence originally manifested himself. As we see Victorian Clara from 2012's "The Snowmen" born and then growing up, presumably this means that, in some timey-wimey, spacey-wacey way, Clara's DNA (with echoes of her personality and memories) keeps replicating in people that were supposed to have been born. Surely this alteration to the timeline will cause some consequences? Why do Oswin Oswald from "Asylum of the Daleks" and Clara Oswin Oswald in "The Snowmen" share names with the original Clara Oswald? (Even more confusing is that "Oswin" is an invented username created by Clara in 2013's "The Bells of Saint John.") If they're separate people born in disparate times and spaces, why would they have the same family name? Our heads hurt from thinking about all this . . .

While we're at it, Clara's appearances on Gallifrey — in the old days just before the Doctor left, following the fourth Doctor in the Gallifreyan capitol during 1978's "The Invasion of Time" and seeing the Doctor in the Matrix in 1983's "Arc of Infinity" — suggest that at least three of the Claras are Gallifreyans, or even Time Lords. Or perhaps all three are the same Time Lord at different points in time . . .

In "The Wedding of River Song," Dorium stated that silence will fall on the fields of Trenzalore, at the fall of the eleventh; "when no living creature can speak falsely or fail to answer," the question will finally be asked and answered, a question the Doctor has been running away from all these years: Doctor who? This is a question the Silence (as seen throughout Series Six of the New Series) are desperate to prevent being asked. So are the events of "The Name of the Doctor" the fulfilment of that prophecy? There are surface similarities: the stars and time being undone by the Great Intelligence's invasion of the Doctor's timeline would be the universe-shaking calamity that brings about silence. Also, the Doctor's real name gives the Great Intelligence access to the Doctor's tomb to cause that to happen. However, it's just as possible that the events on Trenzalore that lead to the Doctor's death and burial are the circumstances that concern the Silence (the Doctor is said to have died in battle and the Silence have an army) and form Dorium's prophecy. Time will tell, as they say.

The fact that the Doctor's secret name is the one word that unlocks his tomb — his TARDIS — opens up some interesting speculation about the Time Lords. Perhaps upon choosing a TARDIS, a Time Lord's true name is how the ship becomes bonded to its operator. Maybe the Time Lord's name then becomes secret to everyone including fellow Gallifreyans. (If anyone knew it at all in the first place: we know from 1979's "The Armageddon Factor" that the Doctor was referred to by a designation, "Theta Sigma," at the Gallifreyan Academy. Perhaps they never knew his proper name.) It would explain why so many of the Time Lords we saw in the Classic Series had adopted titles as well — the Master, the Monk, the Rani — and why in "The Deadly Assassin" (and subsequent Gallifrey stories) they talk of "the Doctor" and "the Master" rather than calling them by their actual names.

And of course there are many unanswered questions, some of which might be answered later: How did the Great Intelligence bring the Paternoster Gang to Trenzalore? How is River still able to communicate with the Doctor if Clara is dead? Who constructed a secret entrance to the Doctor's tomb via a gravestone with River's name?

And who is the Doctor played by John Hurt? The mystery continues . . .

TARDIS Chronometer Madame Vastra and her friends are in London, 1893; Clara is summoned on April 10, 2013 (according to the address on Vastra's note, Clara lives in Chiswick in London); there is no date for when the Doctor and Clara arrive on Trenzalore. When Clara splinters into echoes, she goes all across space and time, especially Gallifrey "a very long time ago."

Cool? (GB and RS?) In many ways "The Name of the Doctor" wraps up 50 years of *Doctor Who*. It opens with the one thing we never saw in 1963: the Doctor leaving his home planet in the first place (already having chosen to wear Edwardian clothing no less!). It follows this up with two more things never contemplated on the series before: the Doctor initiating a romantic kiss with someone he loves and the Doctor visiting his own grave.

It's bizarre to compare the very first *Doctor Who* story with the story that concludes its 50th anniversary season: the crotchety scientist who was mostly a supporting character to Ian Chesterton and Barbara Wright is now a full-fledged hero that the universe cannot live without. If he dies, the stars go out.

Some might suggest this now overstates the central character's role in the show that bears his name. We don't think so. Take out the Doctor's role in "Logopolis" alone and you lose most of the universe to entropy. Over the past 50 years, we've seen the Doctor evolve from someone who fled Gallifrey in favour of exploring the universe to someone who now sustains it. Perhaps this is what *Doctor Who* was always destined to become: is there any other fate for a time-travelling hero who saves worlds?

The Doctor as we knew him for most of the past 50 years has been asexual. With the TV Movie and the New Series, we've seen a gradual embracing of the Doctor as a (hetero)sexual being. From chaste kisses to unwilling snogs, he's now a married man who kisses his wife as a matter of course. It's a shocking development for the character . . .

. . . or is it? The footage of William Hartnell ushering Carole Ann Ford into the TARDIS on Gallifrey is repurposed from "The Aztecs," a story where the Doctor was engaged to a human woman. (Indeed, the moment he turns back to look in the original story is him being overcome by feelings for Cameca.) And Susan herself was his granddaughter, suggesting a past sexual history for the character. The asexual Doctor isn't where he started and it's not where he is now. Everything old is new again.

We can also see from "The Name of the Doctor" how television has evolved in 50 years. We've gone from a weekly serial with adventure, suspense and monsters to a series with ongoing character and story arcs, and recurring roles: River Song and the Paternoster Gang make appearances in a story that offers the solution to this year's mystery of

Clara the impossible girl. But it's not as though that transformation happened recently in *Doctor Who*. In the early 1960s, the only recurring characters were the Daleks. By the 1970s, we had a recurring cast in UNIT. By the latter part of that decade, *Doctor Who* was experimenting with season-long story arcs. By the 1980s, it began to look at the central characters in new ways. *Doctor Who* has always been a grand adventure, full of change. Even now, it continues to surprise. In the 2000s, recurring cast members meant the companion's family and friends like Jackie and Mickey; now it means Vastra, Jenny and Strax.

"The Name of the Doctor" is a testament to the elasticity of the *Doctor Who* format. In this one story alone, we see a fusion of genres: horror, romance, comedy and mystery. This speaks to the DNA of the show; as Steven Moffat once told us at a convention, the genius of *Doctor Who* is that, each week, you have no idea what sort of story you're going to get. "The Name of the Doctor" takes that idea and puts everything into the mix, stirring it like a soufflé.

Because this story isn't just an homage to the past. While the pre-credits sequence hits any number of continuity tickle spots, it's doing so from a mash-up perspective, mixing old footage with new, colourizing black-and-white episodes while cross-mixing dialogue from different stories, and employing stand-ins. Like a techno remix of a classic song, the old and the new coalesce, forming something that echoes the hits of the past, adds an up-to-the-minute beat from the present and creates a combination that's richer than either could manage. We defy you not to watch the pre-credits sequence over and over again.

As for "The Name of the Doctor" itself, it's not perfect; Clara becomes the impossible girl we knew her to be . . . but we never see how that's done. This robs her of some autonomy; she should be the heroic figure of the story, but by denying us the chance to witness her saving the Doctor, the end result is that the major heroic action we see is that of the Doctor rescuing her. There are all sorts of hand-waving gestures in lieu of plot, like the sudden appearance of the Great Intelligence and the Paternoster Gang on Trenzalore without explanation (given Jenny's death, they must do so in a matter of minutes — but how?) or the nature of the Whisper Men or how Clara's replication works. We won't deny any of this. And yet, the pacing is relentless, with a radical change of direction every 15 minutes (Earth/Trenzalore/the TARDIS), making this a textbook three-act story.

Then there's the moment where Clara meets the pre–"Unearthly Child" first Doctor, bringing *Doctor Who* full circle. The implication is that he was originally going to take a functioning TARDIS, which would have led to an entirely different sort of show, one that was more linear, more homogenized and more straightforward. Clara's entire contribution to saving the Doctor might well be in that one scene: by switching TARDISes, the premise of the program — and the Doctor himself — fundamentally changes.

But isn't that what makes *Doctor Who* great? For 50 years, it never quite goes to the places you think it will go. Is it a tea-time series to teach history and science? Is it a show set in the future with monsters? Is it a program set on Earth with a paramilitary organization fighting the unknown? Is it a gothic-horror pastiche of cult films? A spoofy comedy? An adventure series? A dark tapestry of itself? A spacey soap opera? A paradoxy puzzle? It's been all of these things and much, much more.

One thing's for sure: it's never safe, and it's never ordinary.

Doctor Who is exactly like the Type 40 TARDIS that Clara suggests the Doctor should steal. The navigation's knackered and we'll never know where it's going — but it's a whole lot of fun. Look at where the series has been for its first 50 years. See where it is now. What will it be in the future? Who knows?

That's why we love *Doctor Who*.

Who is the Doctor? After 50 years of adventures, we still don't know the Doctor's name. The name he was given in "An Unearthly Child" — the Doctor — is the name he's chosen. That name is a promise of the person he is. He saves lives. He battles monsters. He saves worlds. He stops nightmares.

Doctor Who? We don't need to know that. All we need to know is that he's out there, travelling in his blue box, keeping the promise of his name.

The adventures in time and space continue . . .
with Peter Capaldi as the twelfth Doctor

Recommended Resources

"You want weapons? We're in a library. Books are the best weapon in the world."
— The Doctor, "Tooth and Claw"

One of the most brilliant things about *Doctor Who* is that it is probably the most documented program in the history of television. If you want to find out more about *Doctor Who*, there is so much to read, watch and experience. A simple bibliography won't do it justice, so here are our annotated musings on what we think would help anyone in learning more about the wonderful world of *Doctor Who*.

The Classic Series

The gold standard for books about the making of the Classic Series is David J. Howe, Mark Stammers and Stephen James Walker's *Doctor Who: The Sixties* (Virgin Publishing, 1992), *Doctor Who: The Seventies* (Virgin Publishing, 1994) and *Doctor Who: The Eighties* (Virgin Publishing, 1996). The research involved in these books is still staggering almost 20 years later, as the authors meticulously sifted through BBC records and interviewed anyone and almost everyone associated with the series behind the scenes. Sadly, these books are out of print but are still available on eBay.

Another volume that is out of print but utterly invaluable is Philip Segal and Gary Russell's book about the making of the 1996 TV Movie, *Doctor Who: Regeneration* (HarperCollins, 2000). Russell documents the tortuous history that led to the TV Movie while Segal adds his own reminiscences as executive producer. It also reprints the bible for the would-be American reboot among other fascinating treasures. Again, it's very easy to find on eBay.

If you're looking for something in one volume, then *Doctor Who: The Legend* (BBC Books, 2003) or its reprint *Doctor Who: The Legend Continues* (BBC Books, 2005) by Justin Richards might be for you. It's not as detailed, but it is lavishly illustrated and the reprint brings the reader into the first season of the New Series.

The *Doctor Who* DVD range is unparalleled in the extra content they add to their Classic Series DVDs. Just about every disc has some sort of a making-of featurette, along with commentaries (text and audio) and a wealth of information. Four are utterly essential: "Origins," a documentary on the creation of the series (which includes archival materials and an otherwise-sealed interview with Sydney Newman) on the "An Unearthly Child" DVD; "Trials and Tribulations," a documentary on *Doctor Who* in the mid-1980s and the 1985 "cancellation crisis," found on *The Trial of a Time Lord* DVD boxset; "End Game," about the end of the Classic Series, found on the *Survival* DVD; and "The Seven Year Hitch," about the making of the 1996 TV Movie, found on that DVD.

The BBC Archives website has available a fascinating series of documents, including the reports and memos that led to the creation of *Doctor Who* and audience reports and information throughout the run of the Classic Series. These can be found at bbc.co.uk/archive /doctorwho/.

The New Series

The best book on how *Doctor Who* came back to television is Shaun Lyon's *Back to the Vortex* (2005, Telos Publishing). Lyon, the director of the Gallifrey One convention and at the time the editor of the *Doctor Who News Page* website, sifted through an unenviable amount of news to create a cohesive narrative about what led to *Doctor Who*'s return and its first season. (It also includes an episode guide to Series One.) Lyon's follow-up on the making of Series Two, *Second Flight*, is also recommended.

If you want an intensive look at what goes on behind the scenes making New *Who*, then you need to get *Doctor Who: The Writer's Tale* (BBC Books, 2008) by Russell T Davies and *Doctor Who Magazine* contributor Benjamin Cook. It's a collection of detailed emails between Davies and Cook that tracks the making of Series Four from its earliest concepts through to production. Included are scripts-in-progress for several episodes; the discussion about them is a master class in TV script writing. The 2010 follow-up, *Doctor Who: The Writer's Tale — The Final Chapter*, chronicles writing the final specials in the David Tennant era.

Every season or so, *Doctor Who Magazine* produces excellent companion volumes that examine in detail how each story went from script to screen, courtesy of *Doctor Who*'s premier historian, Andrew Pixley. Earlier volumes include material from Russell T Davies — such as his original pitch document for the New Series — and annotated outlines for the first couple of seasons.

Every episode of the first six seasons of the New Series was the subject of a making-of series, *Doctor Who Confidential*, which is included in abbreviated form on the various DVD boxsets for each season. They're a bit too much of an electronic press kit, with canned answers by producers and stars, but they do get behind the scenes and show how the magic was made.

The Worlds of *Doctor Who*

If the fictional universe is more your thing, then there's plenty out there. Chief among them is *Doctor Who: The Encyclopedia* by Gary Russell (BBC Books, 2011), which captures just about everything ever mentioned in *Doctor Who*. It keeps being revised and updated, most recently for the iPad. More kid-friendly but useful is *The Ultimate Monster Guide* by Justin Richards (BBC Books, 2009), which is a compilation of various books about *Doctor Who* monsters and aliens that Richards wrote from 2005 to 2008.

General Resources

Doctor Who Magazine is the longest-running magazine devoted to a television series, continuously publishing since 1979! There's a reason for this: 14 times a year, it delivers brilliantly written behind-the-scenes features and interviews, lively and intensively researched forays in *Doctor Who*'s rich history, and thoughtful analysis and reviews. Plus it features a regular column by the executive producer, which is always entertaining.

In terms of episode guides, the Classic Series is well covered by *Doctor Who: The Programme Guide* by Jean-Marc Lofficier (the first version was published by W.H. Allen in 1981; the last by Virgin Publishing in 1990). It's out of print (though Lofficier did publish it himself in the early 2000s) but worth seeking out on eBay. Paul Cornell, Martin Day and Keith Topping's *Doctor Who: The Discontinuity Guide* (Virgin Publishing, 1994; reprinted by Monkeybrain, 2004) includes thoughtful and irreverent analysis and reviews, and was the inspiration for your humble authors' work here and elsewhere. And, of course, for the new series, there's *Who Is The Doctor: A Guide to Doctor Who — The New Series* (ECW Press, 2012), which provides reviews for the first six seasons of New *Who,* written by some guys named Burk and Smith? (What? You thought we were going to suggest something else . . . ?)

Shannon Patrick Sullivan's site *A Brief History of Time (Travel)* (shannonsullivan.com/drwho) continues to be the best compendium online of information on the making of the more than 200 episodes of the Classic and New Series. The *Doctor Who News Page* (doctor whonews.com) is essential for up-to-date news of what's happening in the world of *Who.*

Analysis

Another hunt on eBay that will reward you is for *Doctor Who: From A to Z* by Gary Gillat (BBC Books, 1998), a stirring series of essays on various elements of the Classic Series that are still provocative a decade and a half after publication. We edited and recommend *Time Unincorporated: The Doctor Who Fanzine Archive, Volumes 2 and 3* (Mad Norwegian Press, 2010 and 2011) as they contain brilliant fan essays on the Classic Series and New Series. If you want to ponder gender politics in *Who,* look no further than *Chicks Unravel Time: Women Journey Through Every Season of Doctor Who* (ATB Publishing, 2012), edited by Deborah Stanish and L.M. Myles (Mad Norwegian Press, 2012), which features essays by women about every single season of the Classic Series and the New Series to date.

If you want to read reviews of every single Classic Series story, all 160 of them, written by 160 different fans, we would direct your attention to *Outside In: 160 New Perspectives on 160 Classic Doctor Who Stories by 160 Writers* (ATB Publishing, 2012), which is edited by some guy with a question mark at the end of his name.

Fandom

Meeting up with *Doctor Who* fans either online, in print or in person is a great way to continue the conversation that this book might have started for you. Online, we recommend gallifreybase.com for discussion forums and *The Doctor Who Ratings Guide* (pagefillers.com/dwrg, edited by that question-mark guy) for reviews. In terms of conventions, we love Gallifrey One in Los Angeles in February (gallifreyone.com) and Chicago TARDIS in November (chicagotardis.com).

Podcasting is an increasingly popular medium among fans to discuss and build community around *Doctor Who*. There are so many *Who* podcasts to choose from that we couldn't name them all, but we highly recommend *Radio Free Skaro* (radiofreeskaro.com) and the *Verity!* podcast (veritypodcast.wordpress.com).

If you're looking for a fan community in Canada, there's the Doctor Who Society of Canada (doctorwhosociety.com), which has fantastic social events and a great community. The Doctor Who Information Network (dwin.org), also based in Canada, is North America's oldest and largest *Doctor Who* fan club. They too have social events and publish a bimonthly fanzine, *Enlightenment*, full of lively commentary on the world of *Doctor Who*, which both of your authors have been contributing to for more than a decade!

Appendix:
The Producers of *Doctor Who*

Classic Series

In the Classic Series, the production of *Doctor Who* was supervised by a producer (the equivalent of a showrunner/executive producer today) and a script editor (the equivalent of a writer/executive producer).

Producers

Verity Lambert (1963–1965)
Mervyn Pinfield (associate producer 1963–1964)
John Wiles (1965–1966)
Innes Lloyd (1966–1968)
Peter Bryant (associate producer 1967, 1968–1969)
Derrick Sherwin (1969–1970)
Barry Letts (1970–1974, also executive producer, 1980–1981)
Philip Hinchcliffe (1974–1977)
Graham Williams (1977–1980)
John Nathan-Turner (1980–1989)

Script Editors

(Note: until 1968 the role was called "story editor")
David Whitaker (1963–1964)
Dennis Spooner (1965)
Donald Tosh (1965–1966)
Gerry Davis (1966–1967)
Victor Pemberton (1967)
Peter Bryant (1967–1968)
Derrick Sherwin (1968–1969)
Terrance Dicks (1968–1974)
Robert Holmes (1974–1977)
Anthony Read (1978–1979)
Douglas Adams (1979–1980)

Christopher H. Bidmead (1980–1981)
Antony Root (1982)
Eric Saward (1982–1986)
Andrew Cartmel (1987–1989)

TV Movie Executive Producers (1996)

Philip Segal
Jo Wright
Alex Beaton

New Series

In the New Series, the production of *Doctor Who* is supervised by an executive producer (made up of production executives and showrunners) and a producer (who does the day-to-day line producing activities).

Executive Producers

Russell T Davies (2005–2010)
Julie Gardner (2005–2010)
Mal Young (2005)
Phil Collinson (2007–2008)
Steven Moffat (2010–present)
Piers Wenger (2010–2011)
Beth Willis (2010–2011)
Caroline Skinner (2011–2013)
Brian Minchin (2013–present)

Producers

Phil Collinson (2005–2008)
Susie Ligatt (2007–2008)
Tracie Simpson (2009–2010)
Nikki Wilson (2009)
Peter Bennett (2010)
Patrick Schweitzer (2010)
Sanne Wohlenberg (2010–2011)
Denise Paul (2011–present)
Marcus Wilson (2011–present)

Acknowledgements

They said it couldn't be done. Fifty *Doctor Who* stories from *Doctor Who*'s 50 years. A looming deadline. Co-authors increasingly separated by geography . . .

And it wouldn't have been done. Not without some very important people.

The first is our editor at ECW Press, Jen Hale, who saw the potential in this project, championed it and made many incredible, thoughtful suggestions that always made the book better. It's been worth it just to get the emails hearing her squee about how much she loves Jon Pertwee and Sylvester McCoy. Thanks also to ECW Press's publishers, David Caron and Jack David, our incredible copy editor, Crissy Calhoun, and Carolyn McNeillie, who came up with the wonderful cover.

We're especially grateful to a group of people who gave very incisive responses to our work in progress, told us when we were wrong and gave us a great deal of encouraging and critical feedback. Chief among these were Shannon Patrick Sullivan, Jon Arnold, Jon Preddle and Jim Sangster, whose knowledge and thoughtful critiques were essential to the success of our venture. We're also grateful for the help Deborah Stanish, Scott Clarke and Paul Scoones gave at several key junctures and for Matthew Kilburn's last-minute read-through. Mistakes and missteps will inevitably occur in a work like this. But there are far fewer, thanks to these people.

No book is developed inside a bubble, particularly in the world of *Doctor Who*. This book was shaped through conversations with many friends and fans including Erika Ensign, Shaun Lyon, Mark Askwith, Erik Stadnik, Dennis and Christine Turner, Cadence Gillard, Hindy Bradley, Mike and Nina Doran, Steven Schapansky, Christopher Burgess, Warren Frey, Chip Suddeth, Sean Homrig, Cameron Dixon, John Anderson, Laura Riccomi, Arnold T. Blumberg, Steve Roberts, Phil Ford, Richard Dinnick, Tony Lee, Gary Russell, Philip Hinchcliffe, Lars Pearson, Christa Dickson, Barnaby Edwards, Daniel Changer, Anthony Wilson, Paul Condon, Alexander Kennard, Steve Traylen, Jason A.

Miller, Felicity Kuzinitz, Greg McElhatton, Kathleen Schowalter, Laura Collishaw, Sarah Hogenbirk, Catherine Beauchemin, Quiana Howard, Taylor Deatherage, Bill Evenson, Eva Monaghan, Laura Gerald, Katie Moon, Dallas Jones, Tony Cooke, Paul Deuis, Dave King, Henry Yau, Lauren Davis, David Patterson, Rob Jones, Robin Careless, the guy who gave us the awesome theory about Sally Sparrow's photographs in "Blink" at the 2013 Ottawa ComicCon, Gian-Luca Di Rocco, Rod Mammitzsch, Mike Deed, Cindy Peters, Ari Lipsey, Andrew Flint, Kenyon Wallace, Heather Murray, Ryan Piekenbrock and pretty much the entirety of the Toronto Doctor Who Tavern (first Thursday of the month at Pauper's at Bloor and Bathurst!).

As ever, we're profoundly grateful to Julie Hopkins and Shoshana Magnet, to whom we owe many, many favours now. As well as our continued, undying love.

This work was greatly helped by a grant from the Ontario Arts Council Writers' Reserve and we are appreciative for their support.

This book was put together in Austria, Australia, the Dominican Republic, Haiti and, in Canada and the United States, in Ottawa, Toronto, Montreal, Oakville, Chicago, Lombard, Fort Myers, Los Angeles, Boston, Phoenix, Tempe, Vancouver, Ladner, New York, Quebec City, Lunenberg, Kingston and a cottage on Christie Lake. Once again, we're thankful for modern technology, especially laptops and wi-fi, as we're quite certain we would have never have been able to have written this book in 1963.

And thank you, the reader, for going on this journey with us. If you want to ask us questions, give feedback or just query what we were thinking when we chose certain stories, feel free to email us at whoisthedoctor@gemgeekorrarebug.com.

We hope that, by watching these 50 stories from *Doctor Who*'s 50 year history, you realize that, more than just being a television series, *Doctor Who* is an idea. The best, most exciting, most thrilling idea that has ignited all our imaginations for over five decades.

Quite simply, it's fantastic. We hope you agree.

GRAEME BURK is a writer, communications professional and *Doctor Who* fan. He is the co-author (with Robert Smith?) of the award-winning *Who Is The Doctor: The Unofficial Guide to Doctor Who — The New Series* (ECW Press, 2012). He also co-edited (with Smith?) two anthologies of fan writing on the Classic and New Series, *Time, Unincorporated* (Mad Norwegian Press, 2010 and 2011). He has had his work published by magazines, websites and small presses throughout North America; three of his stories were included in the *Doctor Who* short fiction anthology series *Short Trips*. For ten years, he was the editor of *Enlightenment,* the fanzine of Doctor Who Information Network, North America's oldest and largest *Doctor Who* fan club where he still contributes DVD reviews. A finalist for a Writers Guild of Canada screenwriting prize he currently has a screenplay in development. He still loves Toronto but still lives in Ottawa. His website can be found at gemgeekorrarebug.com; follow him on Twitter @graemeburk.

ROBERT SMITH? has the dubious distinction of being the world's foremost expert on the spread and transmission of Bieber Fever. Don't hate him for it. Oh yeah, and he accidentally invented the academic sub-discipline of mathematical modelling of zombies. In addition to the co-authored work with Mr. Burk mentioned above, he single-handedly edited *Outside In: 160 New Perspectives on 160 Classic Doctor Who Stories by 160 Writers* for ATB Publishing (with contributions by his co-author, ECW's Nikki Stafford and 158 other *Doctor Who* fans he could name if he had the book about his person); *Braaaiiinnnsss!: From Academics to Zombies* for the University of Ottawa Press (the definitive showcase of what academics actually do, as viewed through the lens of a zombie invasion); and also wrote *Modelling Disease Ecology with Mathematics* for the American Institute of Mathematical Sciences. The last one's probably the scariest reading for most of you. He lives on a plane, somewhere.

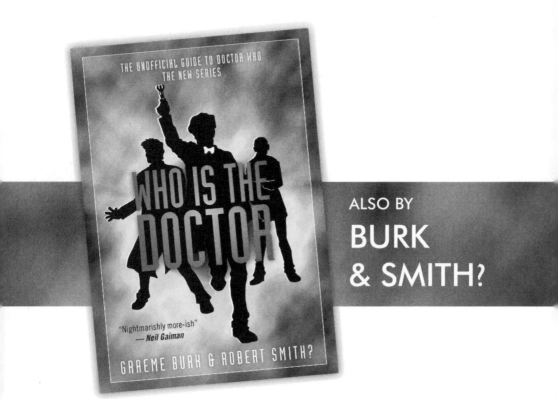

THE UNOFFICIAL GUIDE TO DOCTOR WHO
THE NEW SERIES

WHO IS THE DOCTOR

"Nightmarishly more-ish"
— *Neil Gaiman*

GRAEME BURK & ROBERT SMITH?

ALSO BY
BURK
& SMITH?

At ECW Press, we want you to enjoy *Who's 50* in whatever format you like, whenever you like. Leave your print book at home and take the eBook to go! Purchase the print edition and receive the eBook free. Just send an email to ebook@ecwpress.com and include:

- the book title
- the name of the store where you purchased it
- your receipt number
- your preference of file type: PDF or ePub?

A real person will respond to your email with your eBook attached. And thanks for supporting an independently owned Canadian publisher with your purchase!